池田晃久
AKIHISA IKEDA

I just realized that with this volume, this manga is in its second year! To all you readers—thank you! Creating literature is the result of "passion." As for myself, thanks to the inner fire of "I want to draw!" I've kept going all this time! All right, it's only been two years, but still... Maybe it's because I have energy to spare, but this volume's story might have gotten a little intense... Once in a while, please humor me when I do stuff like this, okay? *[laugh]*

Akihisa Ikeda was born in 1977 in Miyazaki. He debuted as a mangaka with the four-volume magical warrior fantasy series *Kiruto* in 1999, which was serialized in *Monthly Shonen Jump*. *Rosario+Vampire* debuted in *Monthly Shonen Jump* in March of 2002, and is continuing in the new magazine *Jump Square* (Jump SQ). In Japan, *Rosario+Vampire* is also available as a drama CD. In 2008, the story was released as an anime.

Ikeda has been a huge fan of vampires and monsters since he was a little kid.

He says one of the perks of being a manga artist is being able to go for walks during the day when everybody else is stuck in the office.

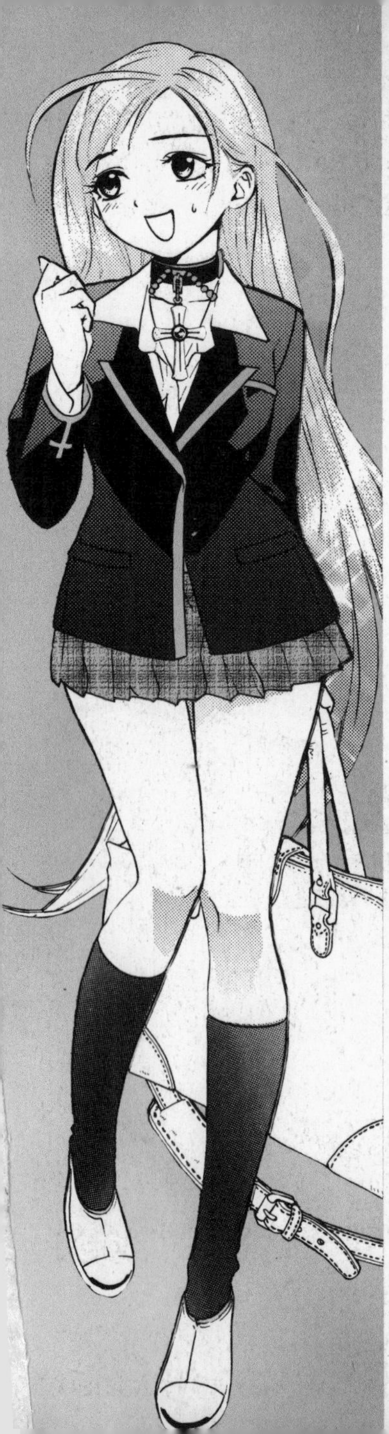

ROSARIO+VAMPIRE 6

The SHONEN JUMP ADVANCED Manga Edition

STORY & ART BY AKIHISA IKEDA

Translation/Kaori Inoue
English Adaptation/Gerard Jones
Touch-up Art & Lettering/Stephen Dutro
Cover Design/Ronnie Casson
Interior Design/ Ronnie Casson
Editor/Annette Roman

Editor in Chief, Books/Alvin Lu
Editor in Chief, Magazines/Marc Weidenbaum
VP, Publishing Licensing/Rika Inouye
VP, Sales & Product Marketing/Gonzalo Ferreyra
VP, Creative/Linda Espinosa
Publisher/Hyoe Narita

Printed in the U.S.A.

Published by VIZ Media, LLC
P.O. Box 77010
San Francisco, CA 94107

10 9 8 7 6 5 4 3 2 1
First printing, April 2009

www.viz.com

www.shonenjump.com

RATED T+ FOR OLDER TEEN

PARENTAL ADVISORY
ROSARIO+VAMPIRE is rated T+ for Older Teen and is recommended for ages 16 and up. It contains suggestive situations.

ratings.viz.com

Rosario+Vampire

Ghouls

6

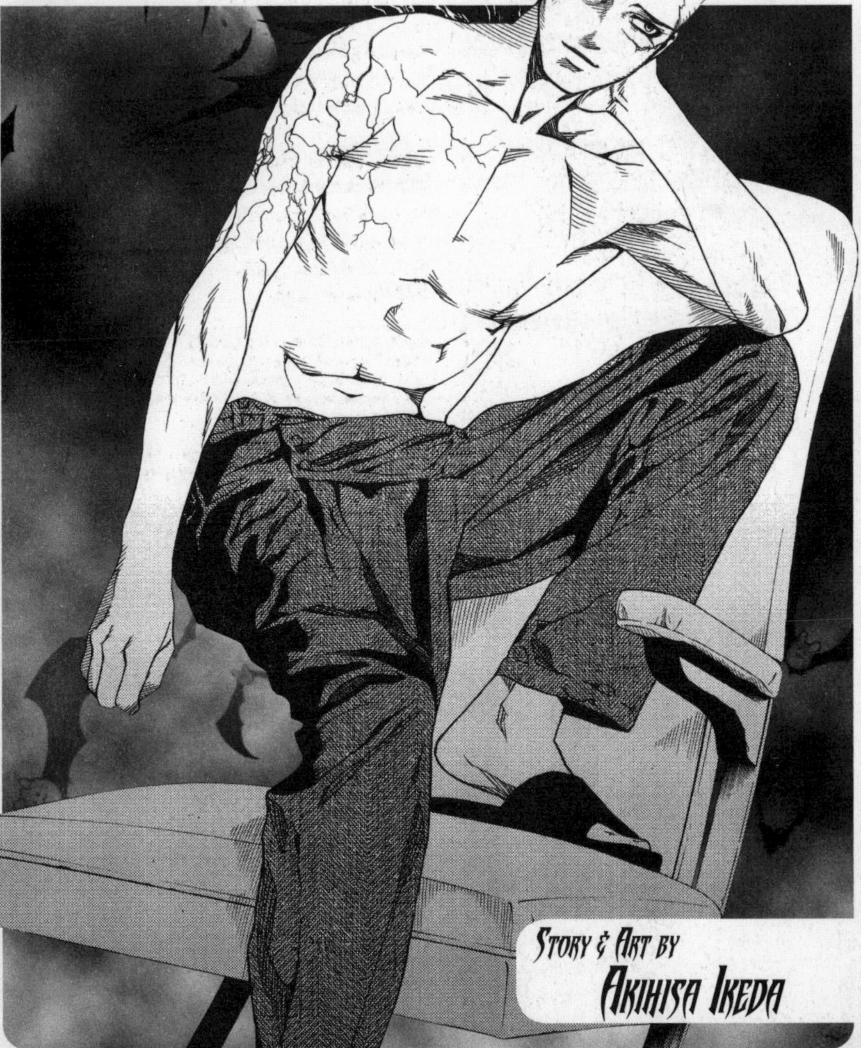

Story & Art by

Akihisa Ikeda

The Horror Story Thus Far...

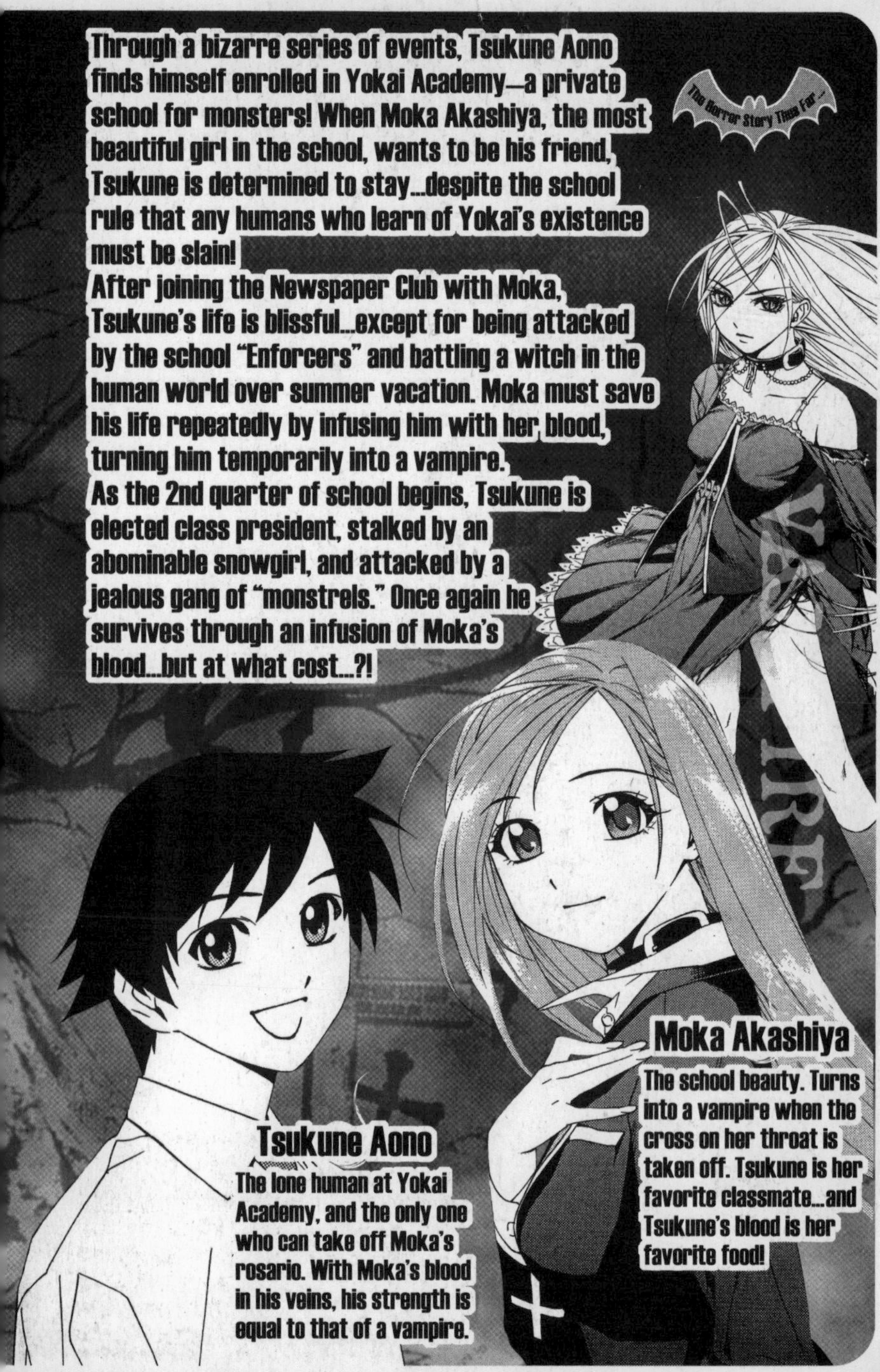

Through a bizarre series of events, Tsukune Aono finds himself enrolled in Yokai Academy—a private school for monsters! When Moka Akashiya, the most beautiful girl in the school, wants to be his friend, Tsukune is determined to stay...despite the school rule that any humans who learn of Yokai's existence must be slain!

After joining the Newspaper Club with Moka, Tsukune's life is blissful...except for being attacked by the school "Enforcers" and battling a witch in the human world over summer vacation. Moka must save his life repeatedly by infusing him with her blood, turning him temporarily into a vampire.

As the 2nd quarter of school begins, Tsukune is elected class president, stalked by an abominable snowgirl, and attacked by a jealous gang of "monstrels." Once again he survives through an infusion of Moka's blood...but at what cost...?!

Moka Akashiya

The school beauty. Turns into a vampire when the cross on her throat is taken off. Tsukune is her favorite classmate...and Tsukune's blood is her favorite food!

Tsukune Aono

The lone human at Yokai Academy, and the only one who can take off Moka's rosario. With Moka's blood in his veins, his strength is equal to that of a vampire.

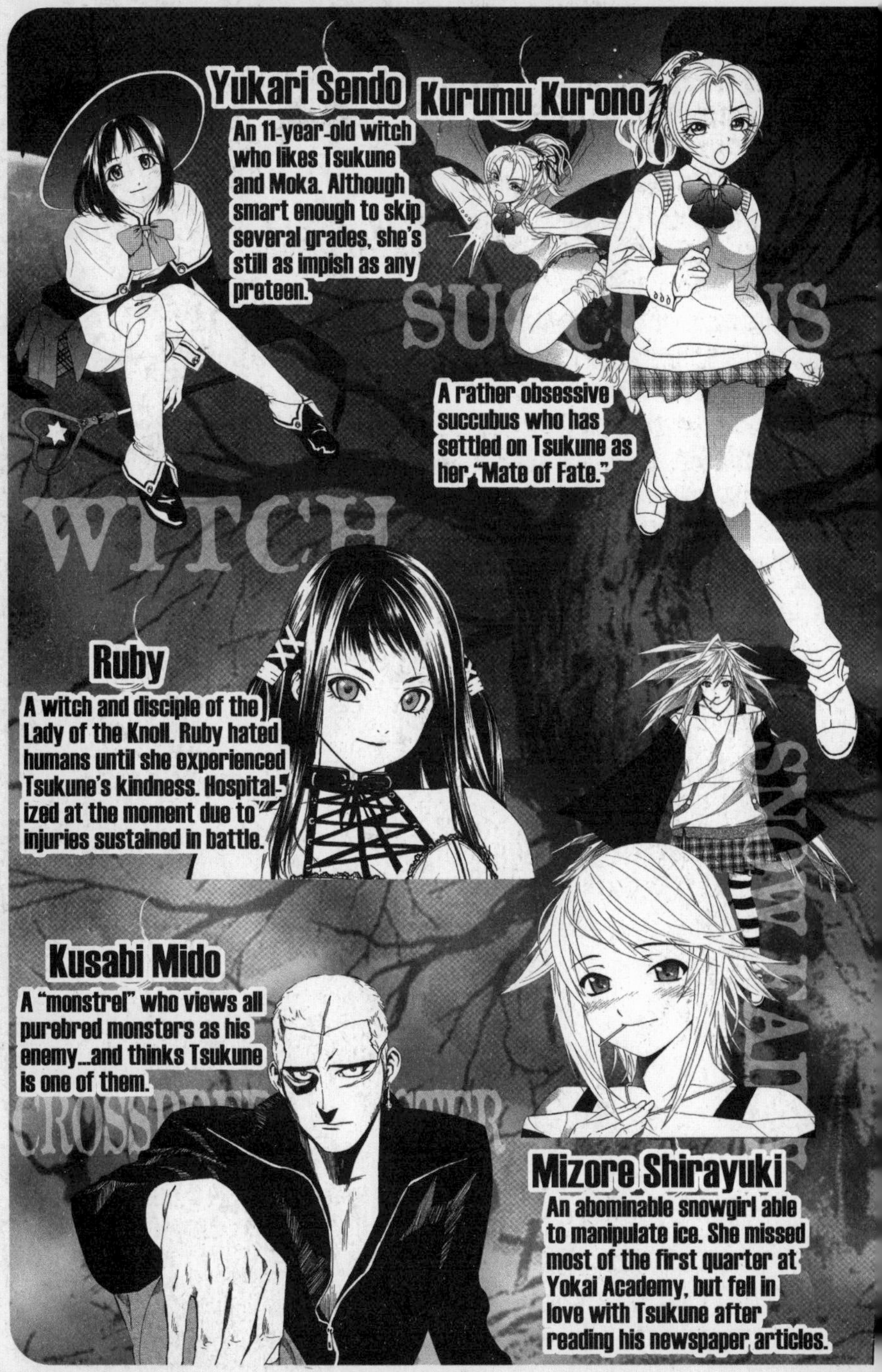
Yukari Sendo
An 11-year-old witch who likes Tsukune and Moka. Although smart enough to skip several grades, she's still as impish as any preteen.
Kurumu Kurono
A rather obsessive succubus who has settled on Tsukune as her "Mate of Fate."
WITCH
Ruby
A witch and disciple of the Lady of the Knoll. Ruby hated humans until she experienced Tsukune's kindness. Hospital-ized at the moment due to injuries sustained in battle.
Kusabi Mido
A "monstrel" who views all purebred monsters as his enemy...and thinks Tsukune is one of them.
Mizore Shirayuki
An abominable snowgirl able to manipulate ice. She missed most of the first quarter at Yokai Academy, but fell in love with Tsukune after reading his newspaper articles.

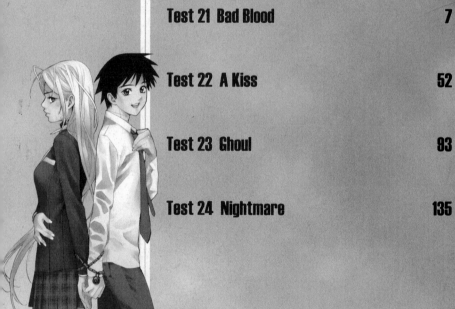

CONTENTS

Volume 6: Ghouls

21: Bad Blood

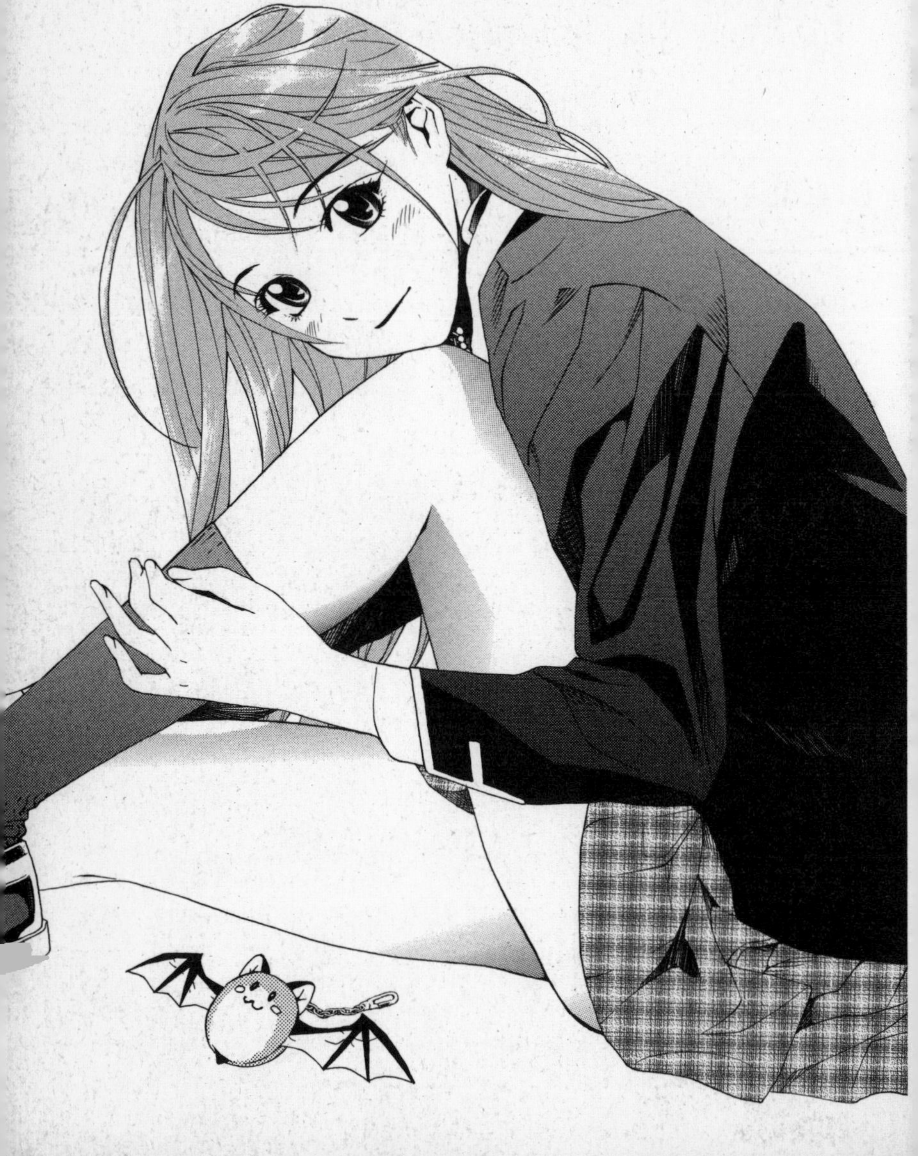

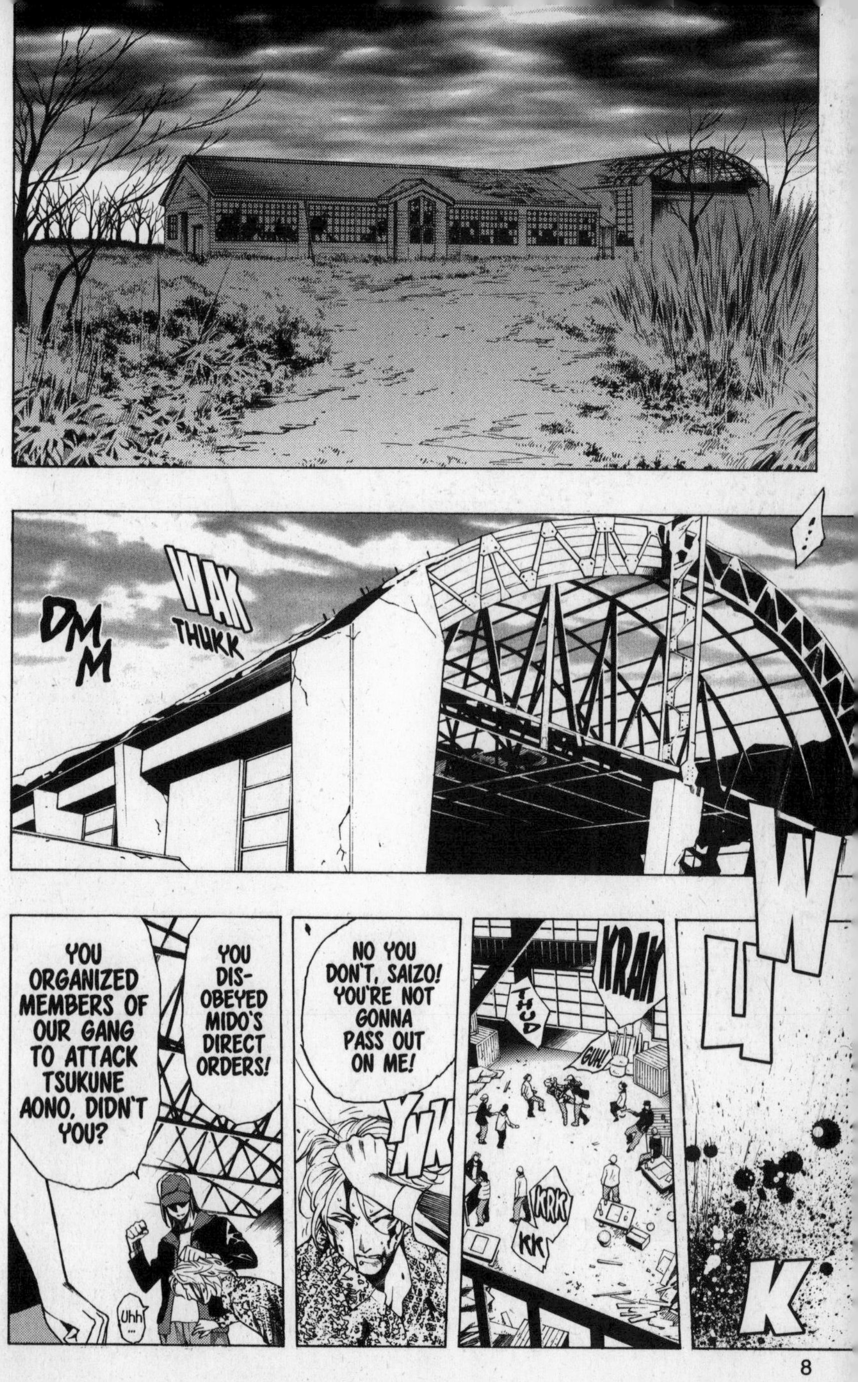
WAK
THUKK
DMM
WHUMK
KRAK
THUD
GUH
KRK
KK
NO YOU DON'T, SAIZO! YOU'RE NOT GONNA PASS OUT ON ME!
YNK
YOU DIS-OBEYED MIDO'S DIRECT ORDERS!
YOU ORGANIZED MEMBERS OF OUR GANG TO ATTACK TSUKUNE AONO, DIDN'T YOU?
Uhh...

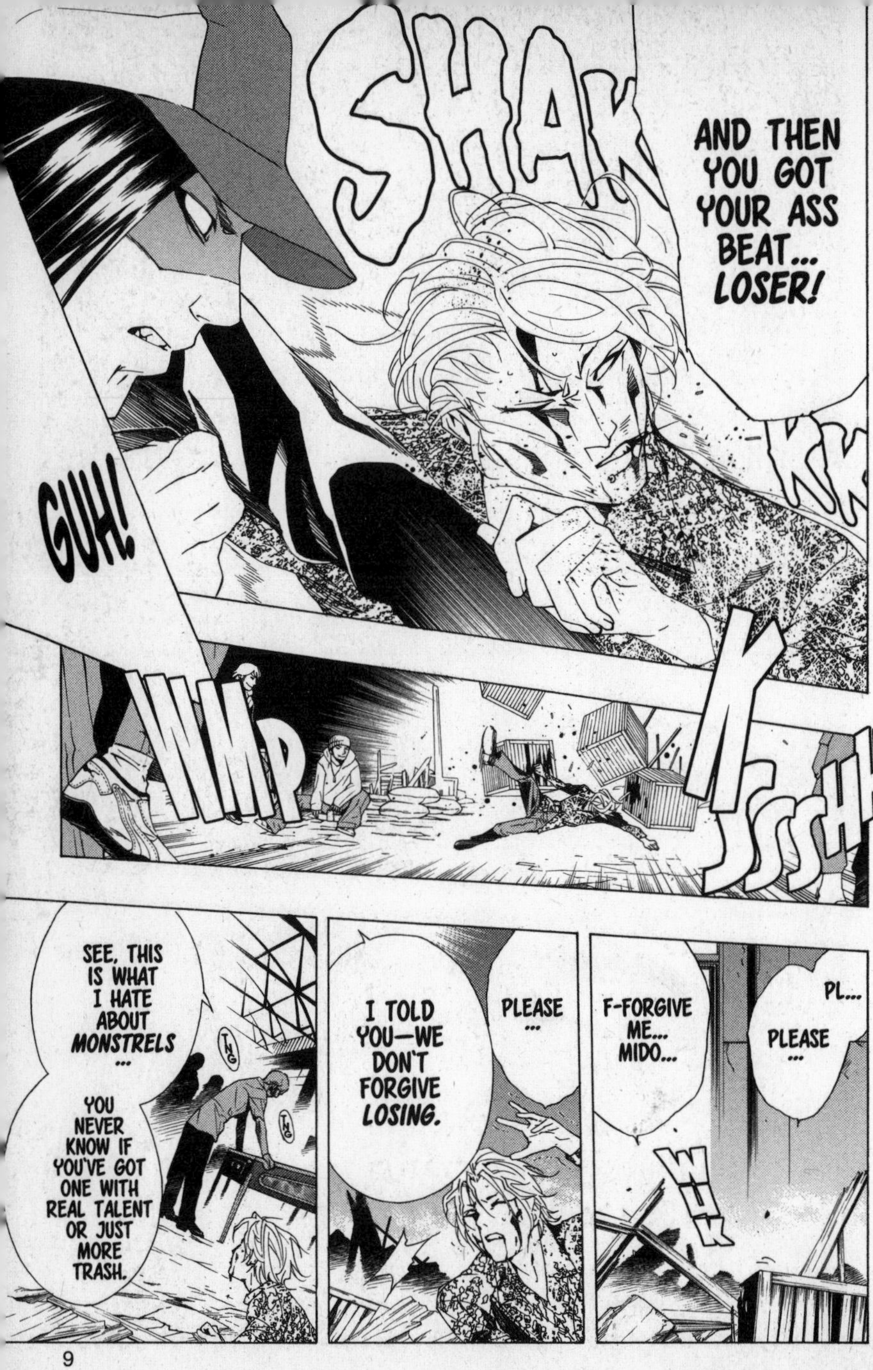
SHAK
AND THEN YOU GOT YOUR ASS BEAT... LOSER!
KKK
GUH!
WMP
KSSSHH
PL...
PLEASE ...
F-FORGIVE ME... MIDO...
WUK
PLEASE ...
I TOLD YOU—WE DON'T FORGIVE LOSING.
SEE, THIS IS WHAT I HATE ABOUT MONSTRELS ...
YOU NEVER KNOW IF YOU'VE GOT ONE WITH REAL TALENT OR JUST MORE TRASH.
TNG
TNG

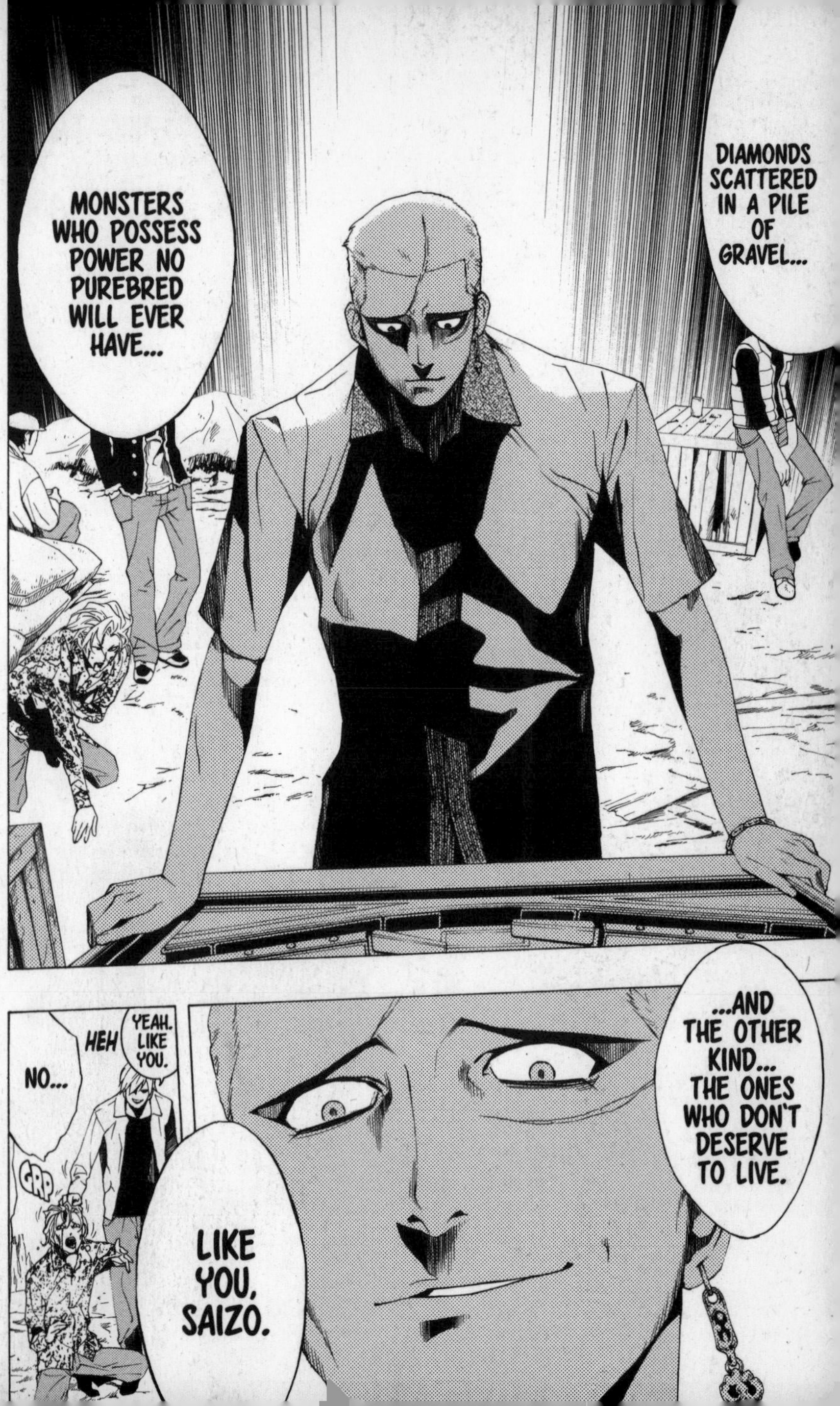
DIAMONDS SCATTERED IN A PILE OF GRAVEL...
MONSTERS WHO POSSESS POWER NO PUREBRED WILL EVER HAVE...
...AND THE OTHER KIND... THE ONES WHO DON'T DESERVE TO LIVE.
LIKE YOU, SAIZO.
YEAH. LIKE YOU.
HEH
NO...
GRP

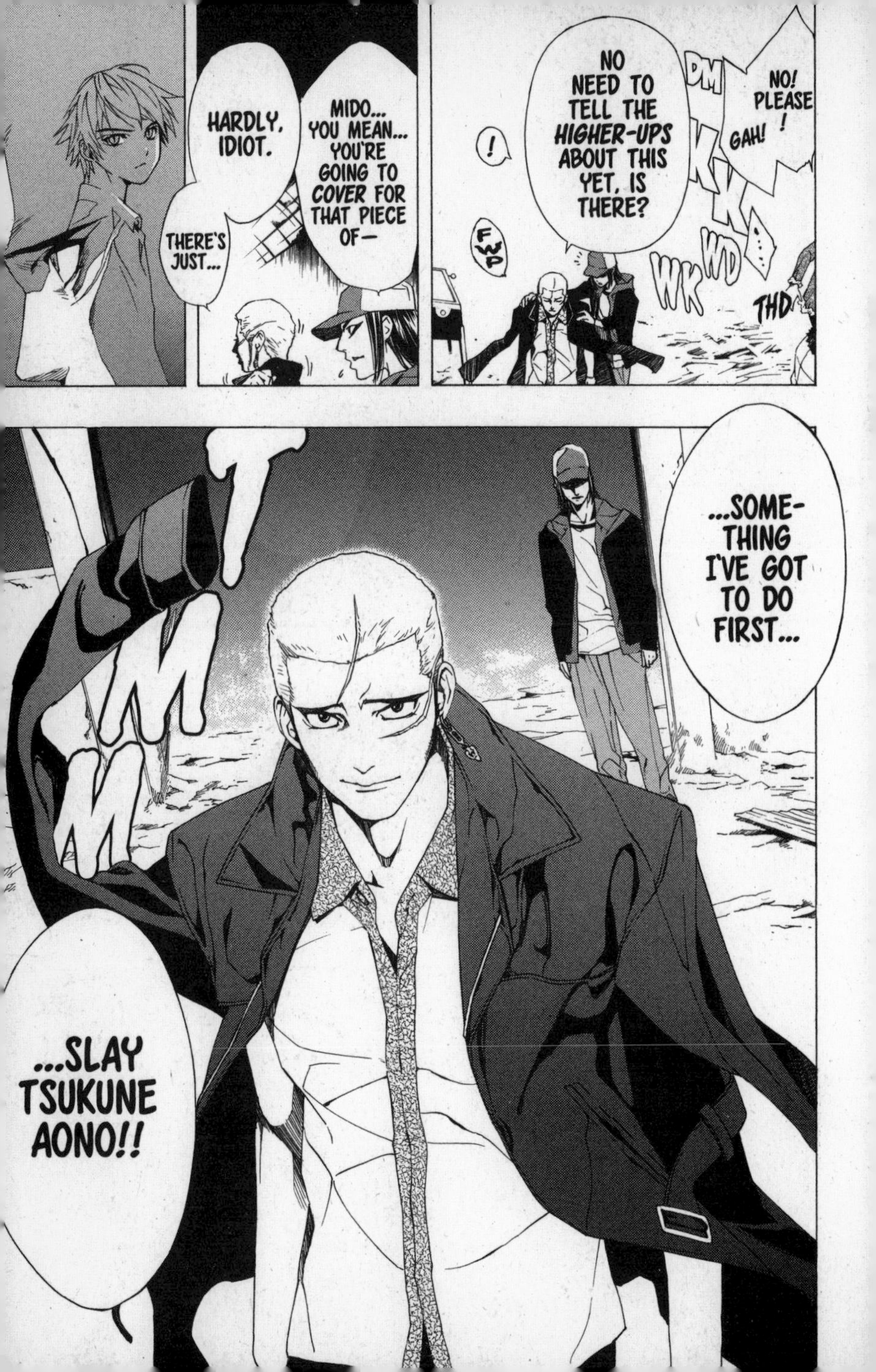
NO! PLEASE!
GAH!
DM
K
K
WD
WK
THD
NO NEED TO TELL THE HIGHER-UPS ABOUT THIS YET, IS THERE?
!
FWP
MIDO... YOU MEAN... YOU'RE GOING TO COVER FOR THAT PIECE OF—
HARDLY, IDIOT.
THERE'S JUST...
...SOMETHING I'VE GOT TO DO FIRST...
...SLAY TSUKUNE AONO!!

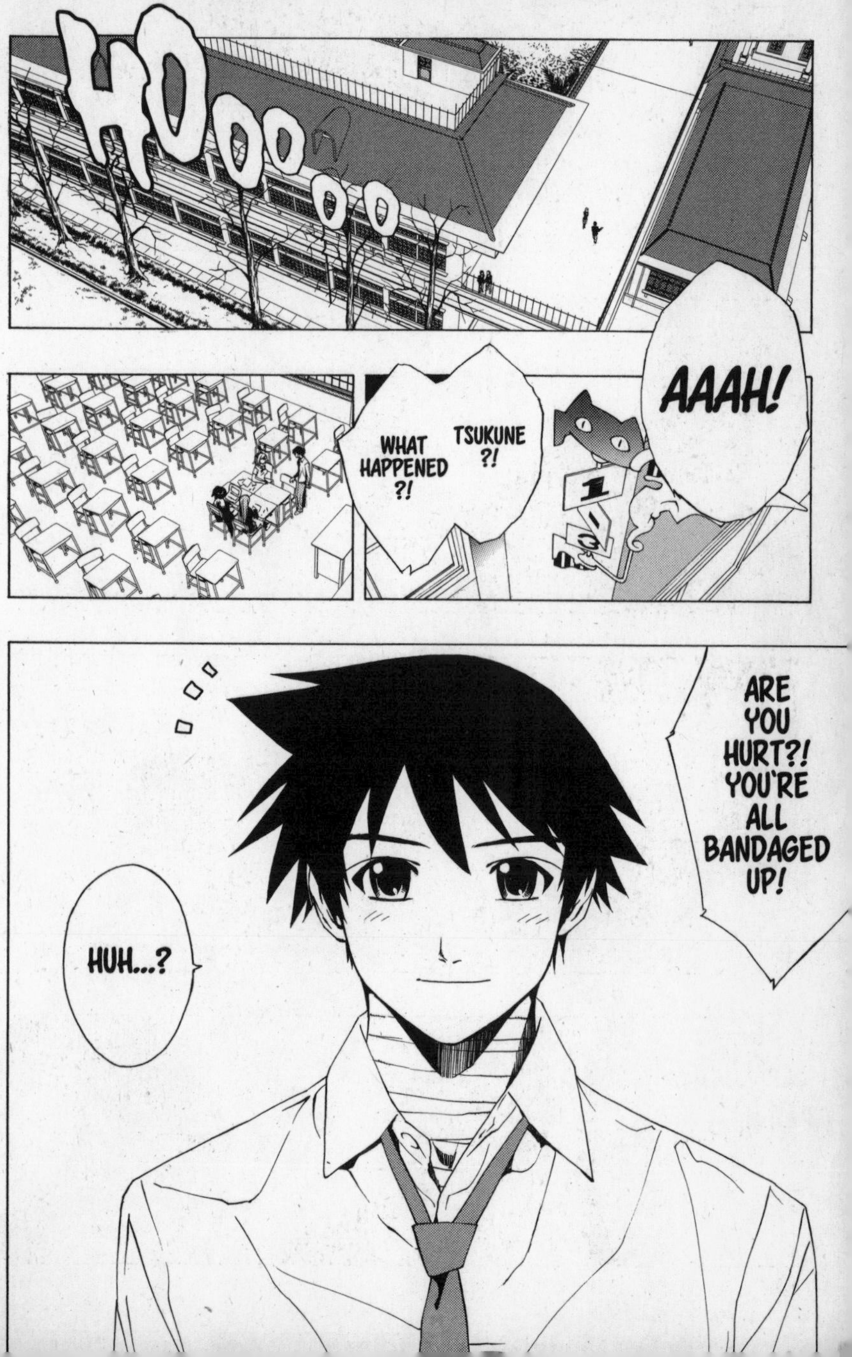
HOOOOOO
AAAH!
TSUKUNE ?!
WHAT HAPPENED ?!
ARE YOU HURT?! YOU'RE ALL BANDAGED UP!
HUH...?

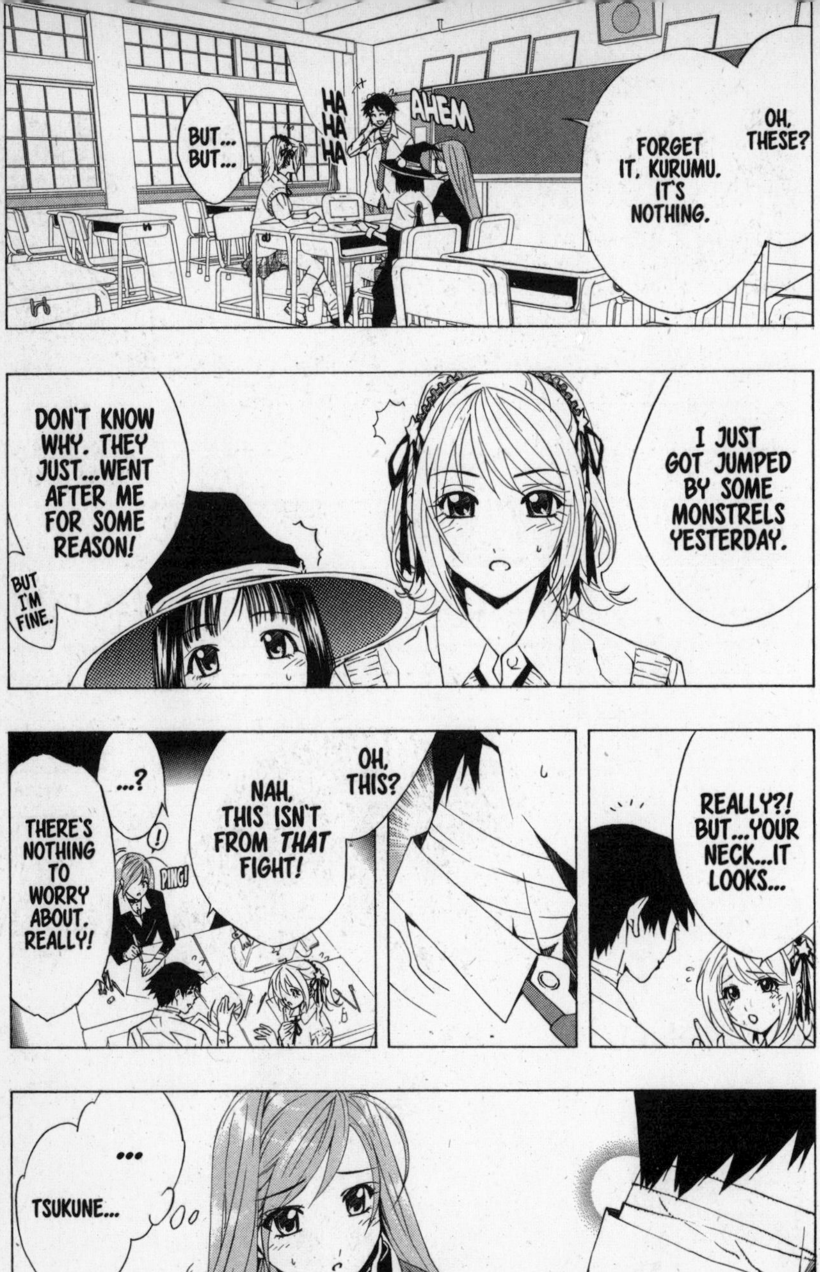
OH, THESE?
FORGET IT, KURUMU. IT'S NOTHING.
AHEM
HA HA HA
BUT... BUT...
I JUST GOT JUMPED BY SOME MONSTRELS YESTERDAY.
DON'T KNOW WHY. THEY JUST...WENT AFTER ME FOR SOME REASON!
BUT I'M FINE.
REALLY?! BUT...YOUR NECK...IT LOOKS...
OH, THIS?
NAH, THIS ISN'T FROM *THAT* FIGHT!
...?
!
PING!
THERE'S NOTHING TO WORRY ABOUT. REALLY!
...
TSUKUNE...

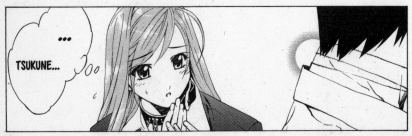

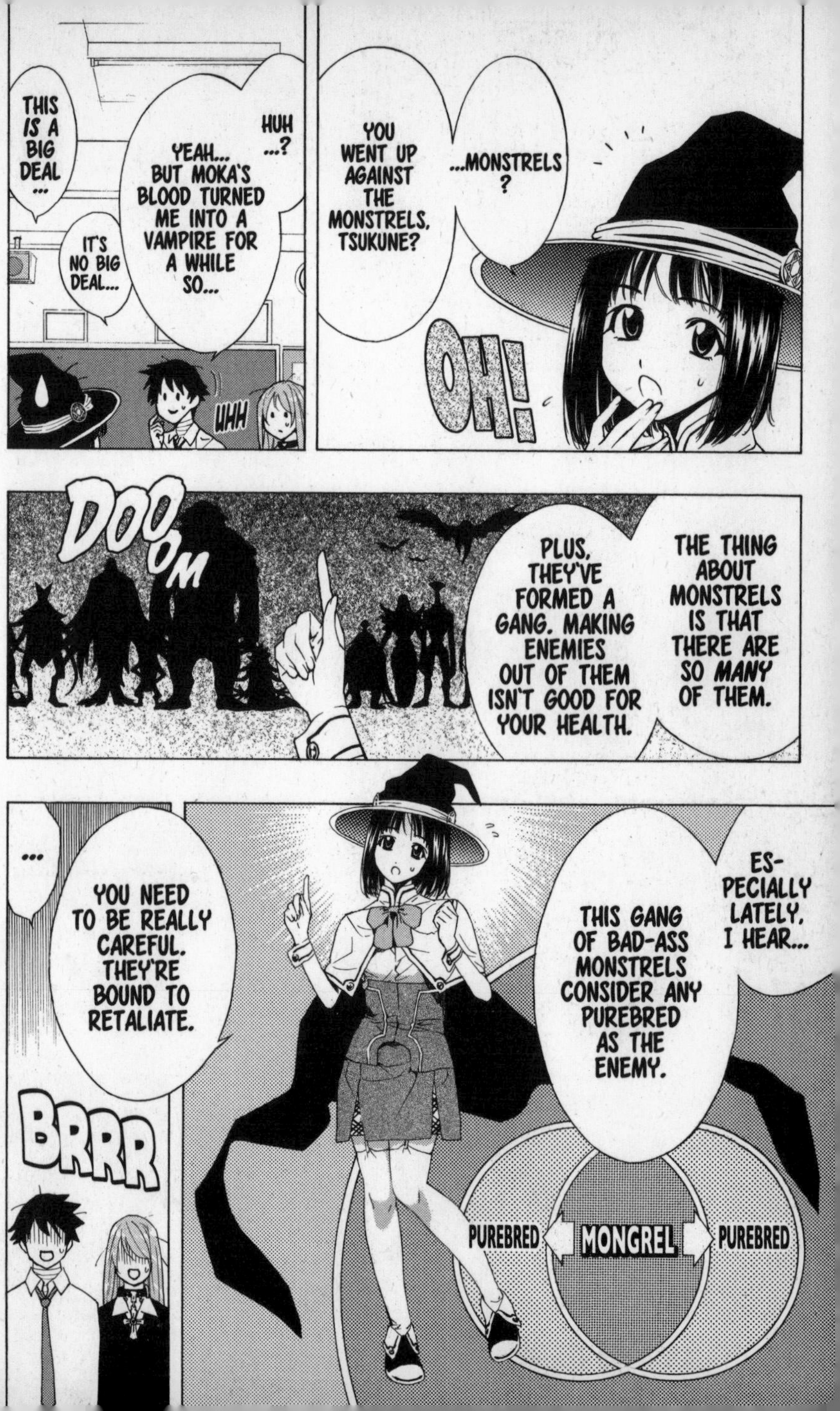
...MONSTRELS?
OH!
YOU WENT UP AGAINST THE MONSTRELS, TSUKUNE?
HUH...?
YEAH... BUT MOKA'S BLOOD TURNED ME INTO A VAMPIRE FOR A WHILE SO...
IT'S NO BIG DEAL...
THIS *IS* A BIG DEAL...
UHH
THE THING ABOUT MONSTRELS IS THAT THERE ARE SO *MANY* OF THEM.
PLUS, THEY'VE FORMED A GANG. MAKING ENEMIES OUT OF THEM ISN'T GOOD FOR YOUR HEALTH.
DOOOM
ES-PECIALLY LATELY, I HEAR...
THIS GANG OF BAD-ASS MONSTRELS CONSIDER ANY PUREBRED AS THE ENEMY.
PUREBRED
MONGREL
PUREBRED
YOU NEED TO BE REALLY CAREFUL. THEY'RE BOUND TO RETALIATE.
...
BRRR

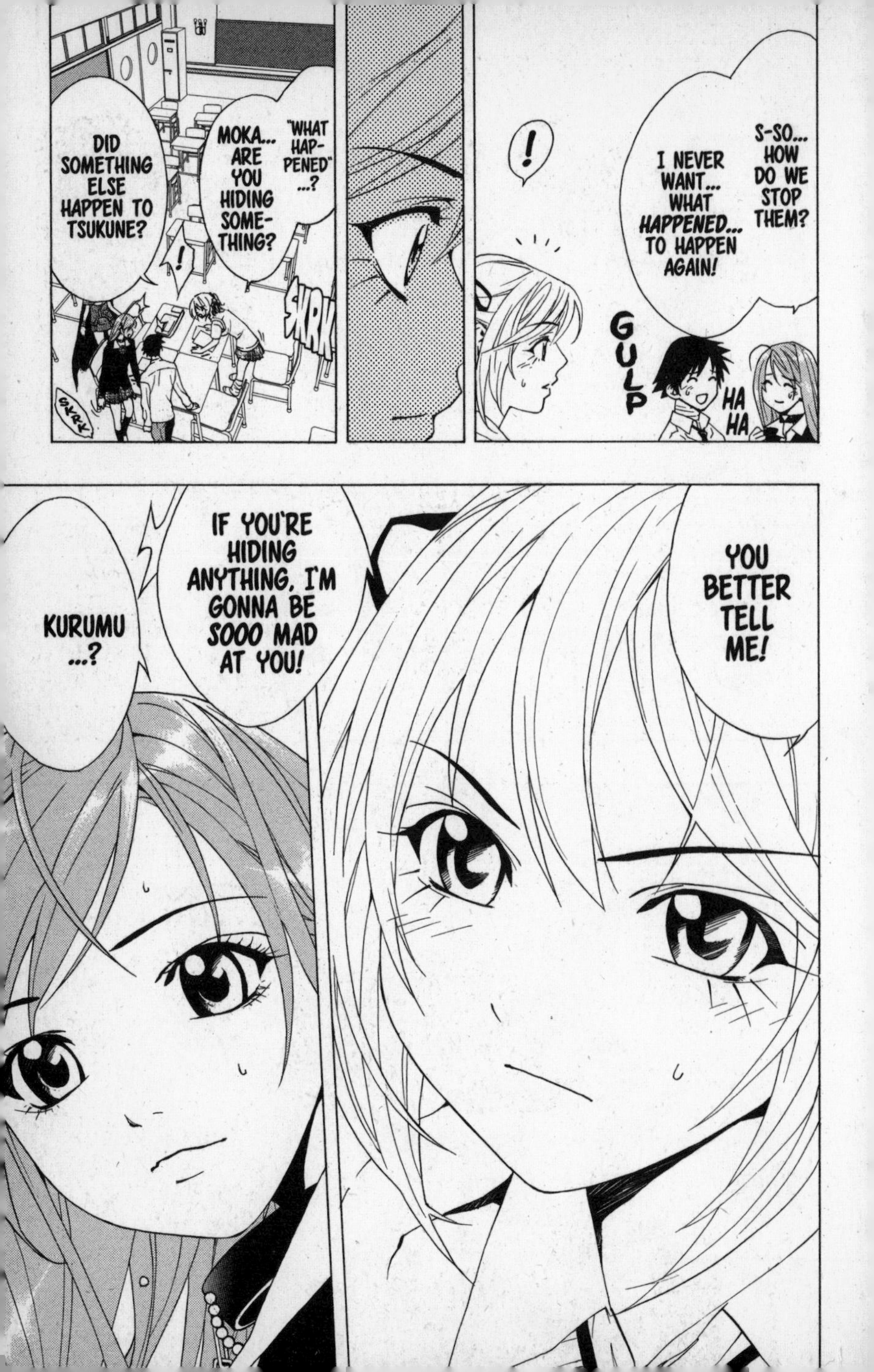
!
S-SO... HOW DO WE STOP THEM?
I NEVER WANT... WHAT HAPPENED... TO HAPPEN AGAIN!
GULP
HA HA
"WHAT HAPPENED" ...?
MOKA... ARE YOU HIDING SOMETHING?
SKRK
DID SOMETHING ELSE HAPPEN TO TSUKUNE?
!
SKRK
YOU BETTER TELL ME!
IF YOU'RE HIDING ANYTHING, I'M GONNA BE *SOOO* MAD AT YOU!
KURUMU ...?

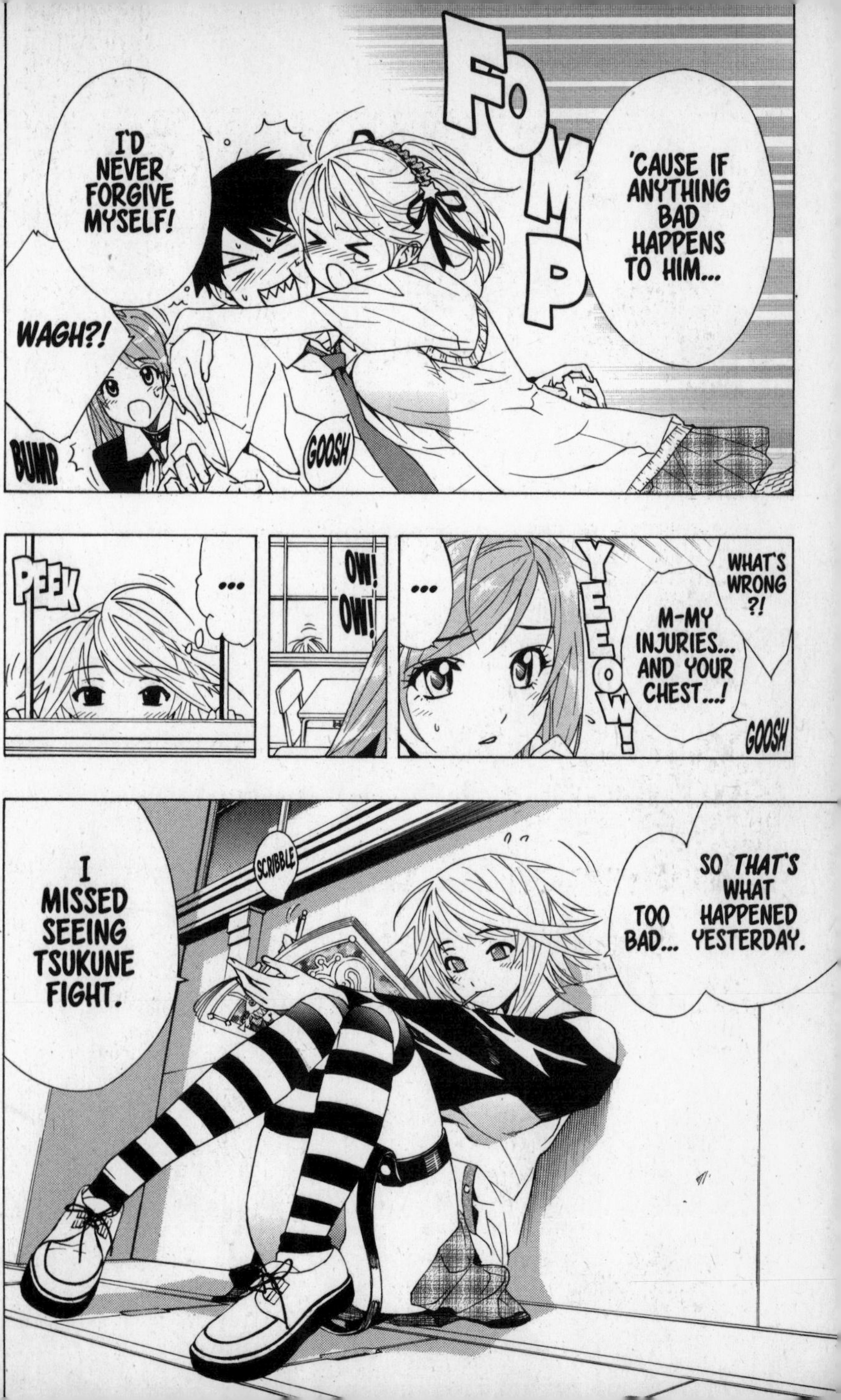
FOMP
'CAUSE IF ANYTHING BAD HAPPENS TO HIM...
I'D NEVER FORGIVE MYSELF!
WAGH?!
GOOSH
BUMP
YEEOW!
WHAT'S WRONG?!
M-MY INJURIES... AND YOUR CHEST...!
GOOSH
...
OW! OW!
...
PEEK
SO THAT'S WHAT HAPPENED YESTERDAY.
TOO BAD...
I MISSED SEEING TSUKUNE FIGHT.
SCRIBBLE

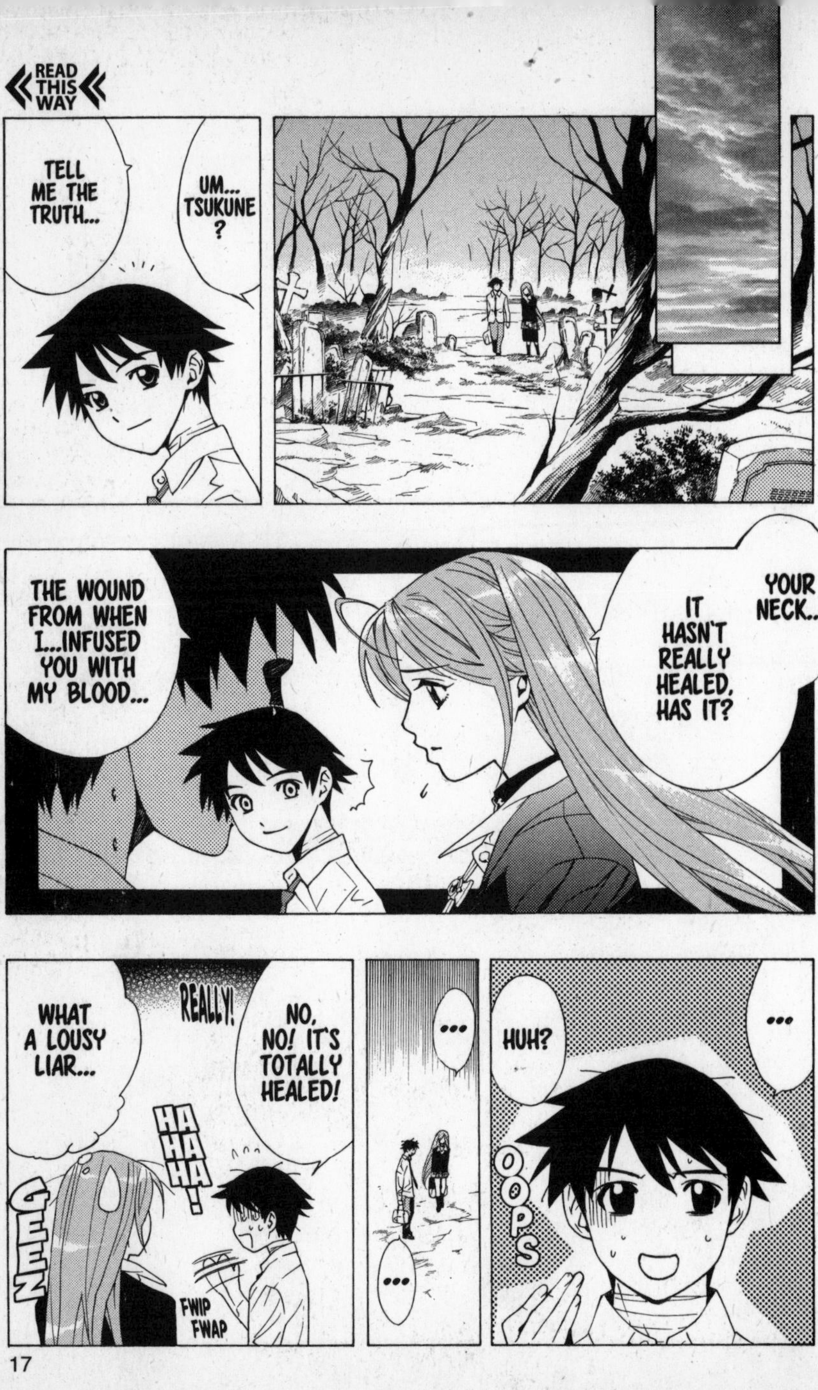
READ THIS WAY
UM... TSUKUNE?
TELL ME THE TRUTH...
YOUR NECK...
IT HASN'T REALLY HEALED, HAS IT?
THE WOUND FROM WHEN I...INFUSED YOU WITH MY BLOOD...
...
HUH?
OOPS
...
...
NO, NO! IT'S TOTALLY HEALED!
REALLY!
HA HA HA!
FWIP FWAP
WHAT A LOUSY LIAR...
GEEZ

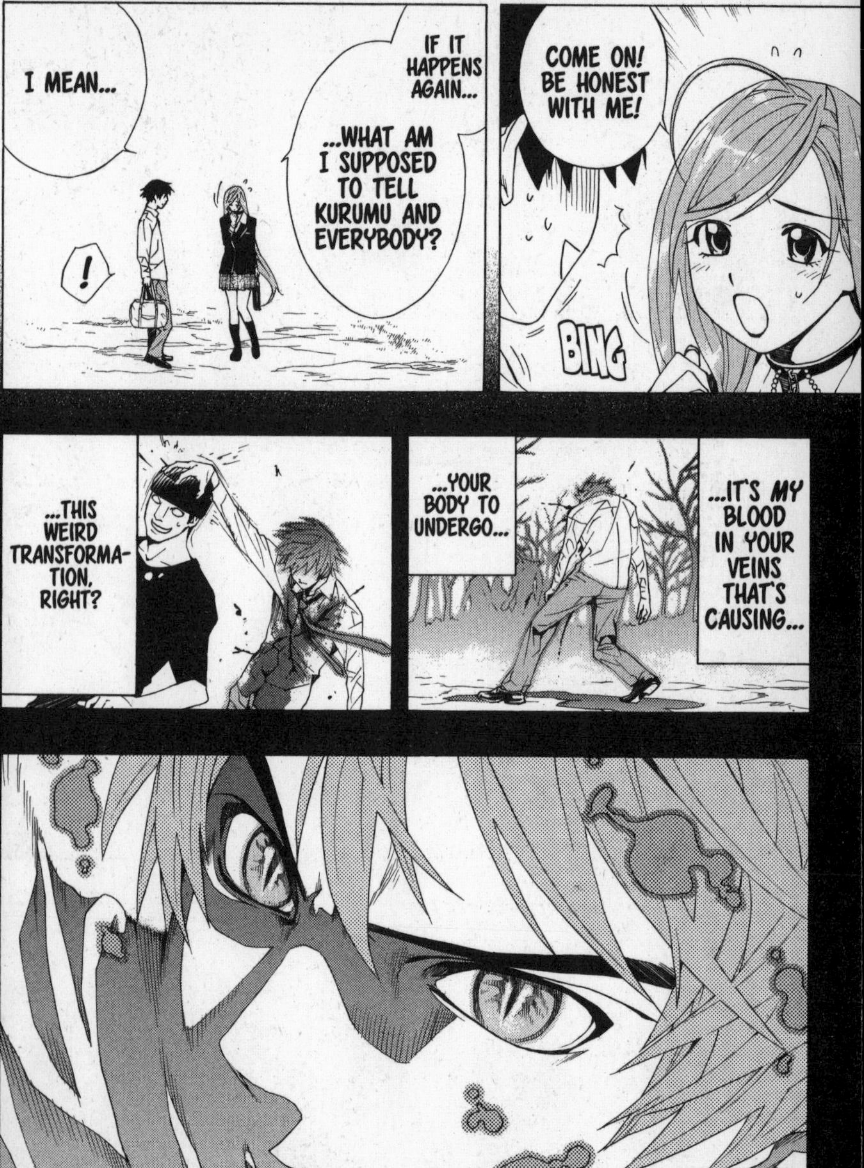
COME ON! BE HONEST WITH ME!
BING
IF IT HAPPENS AGAIN...
...WHAT AM I SUPPOSED TO TELL KURUMU AND EVERYBODY?
I MEAN...
!
...IT'S MY BLOOD IN YOUR VEINS THAT'S CAUSING...
...YOUR BODY TO UNDERGO...
...THIS WEIRD TRANSFORMA-TION, RIGHT?

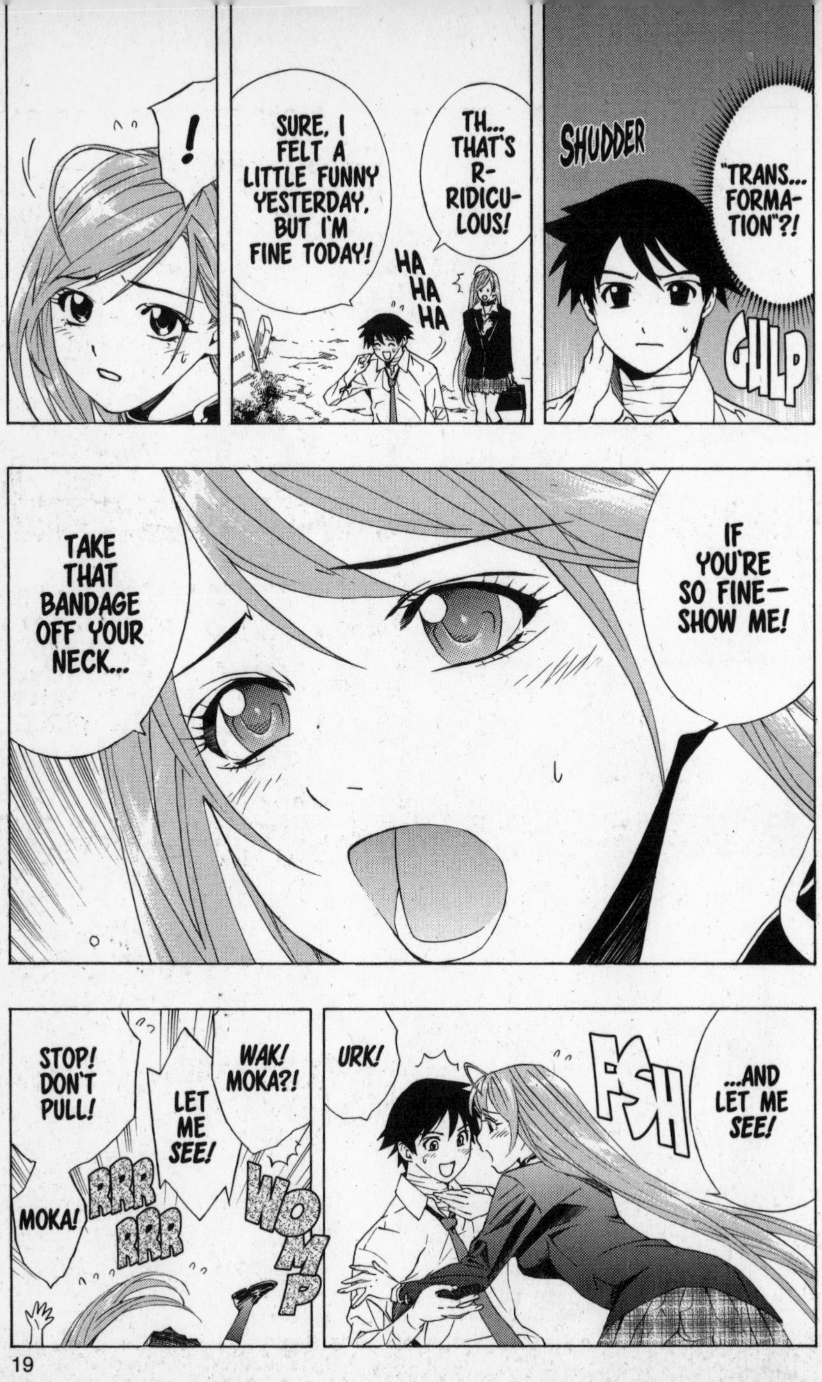
SHUDDER
"TRANS... FORMATION"?!
GULP
TH... THAT'S R-RIDICULOUS!
HA HA HA
SURE, I FELT A LITTLE FUNNY YESTERDAY, BUT I'M FINE TODAY!
!
IF YOU'RE SO FINE—SHOW ME!
TAKE THAT BANDAGE OFF YOUR NECK...
...AND LET ME SEE!
FSH
URK!
WAK! MOKA?!
WOMP
LET ME SEE!
STOP! DON'T PULL!
RRR RRR
MOKA!

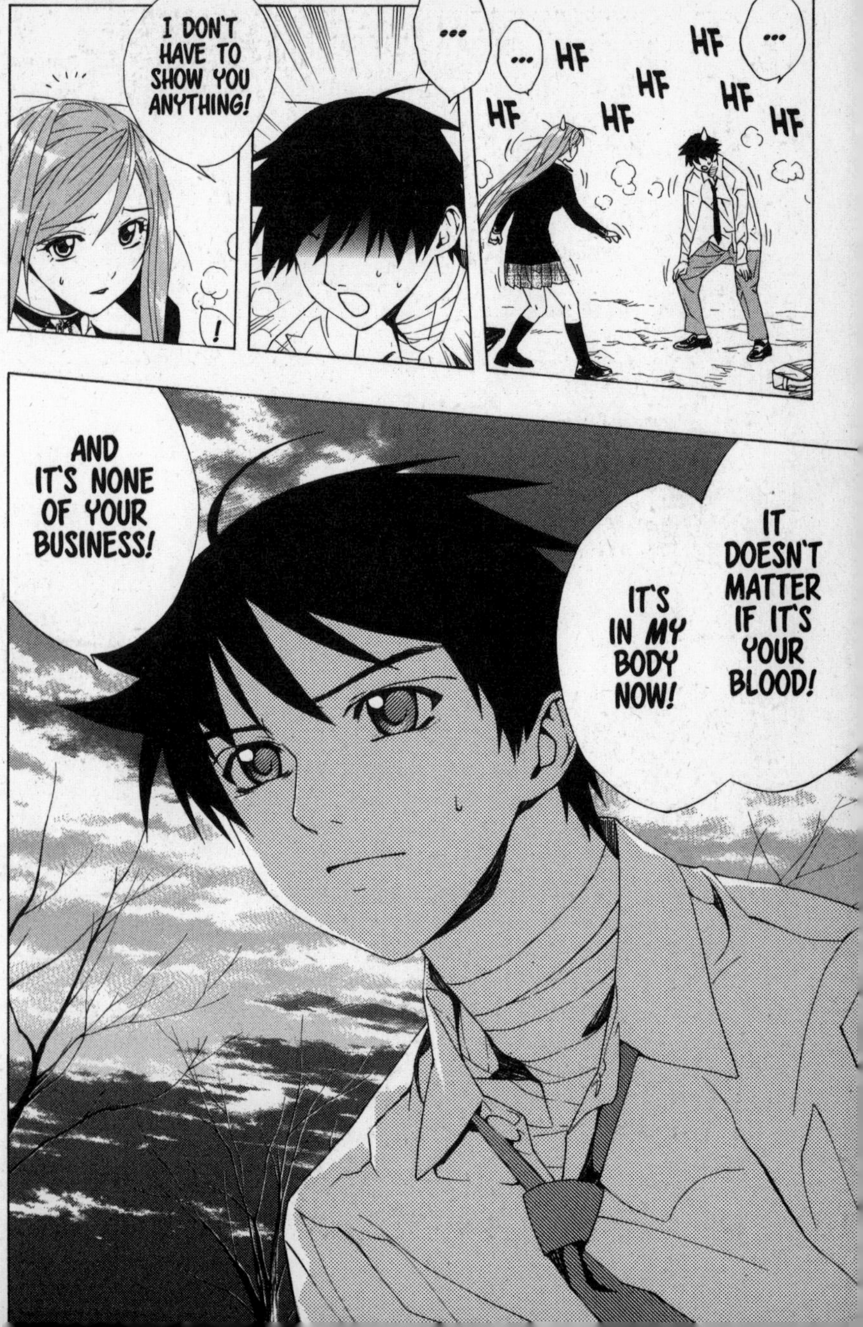
...
HF HF HF HF HF HF HF
...
...
I DON'T HAVE TO SHOW YOU ANYTHING!
!
IT DOESN'T MATTER IF IT'S YOUR BLOOD!
IT'S IN MY BODY NOW!
AND IT'S NONE OF YOUR BUSINESS!

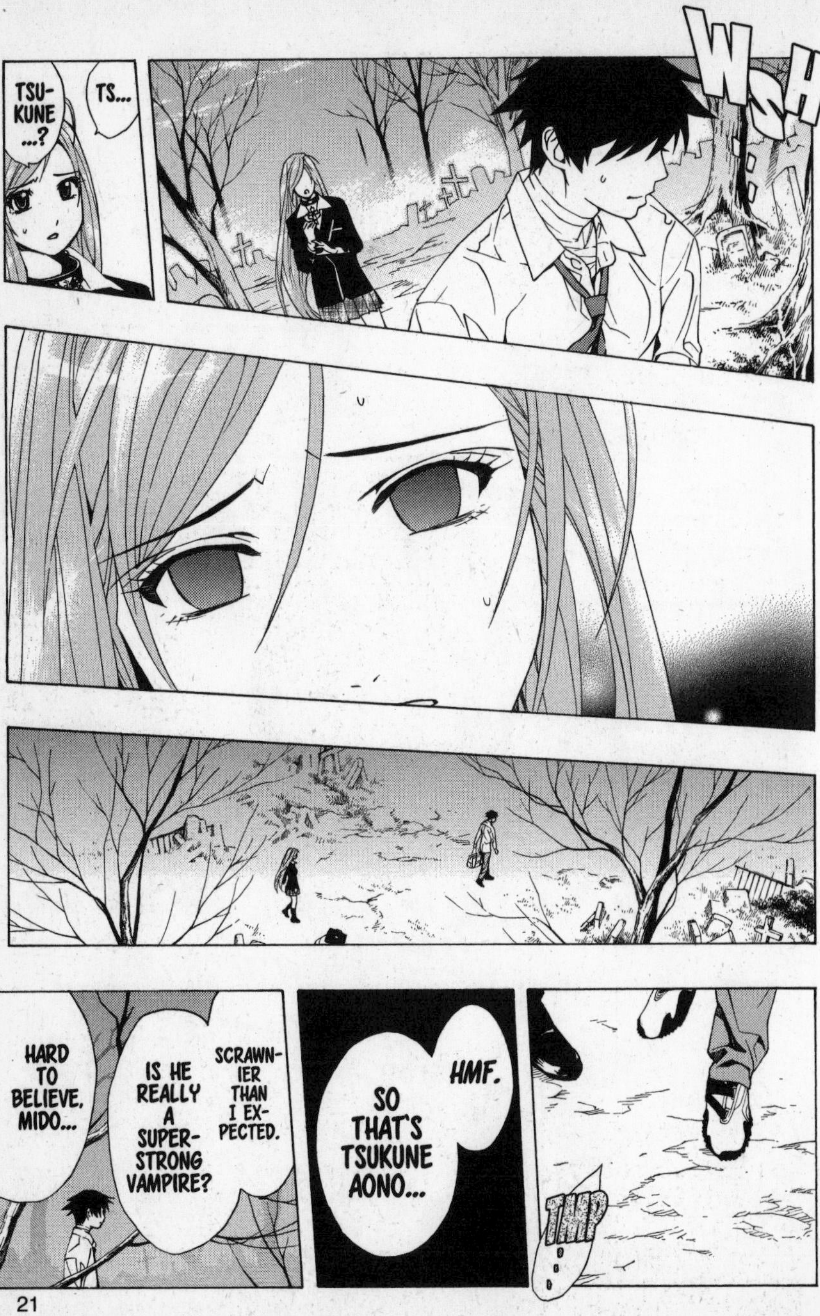
WSH
TS...
TSU-KUNE ...?
HMF.
SO THAT'S TSUKUNE AONO...
SCRAWN-IER THAN I EX-PECTED.
IS HE REALLY A SUPER-STRONG VAMPIRE?
HARD TO BELIEVE, MIDO...
THP

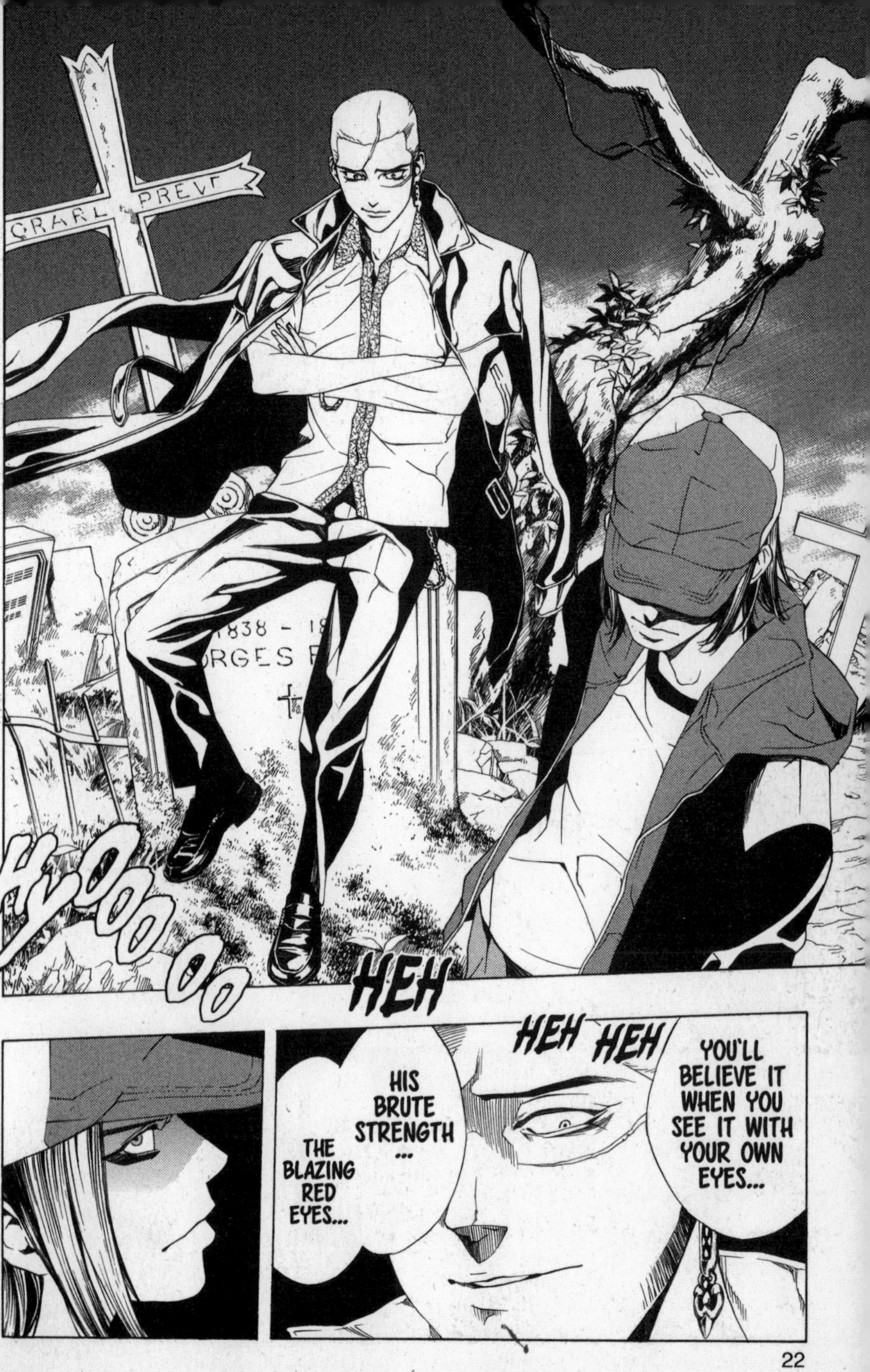

GRARL
PREVI
1838 - 18
RGES F
HYOOOOO
HEH
HEH HEH
YOU'LL BELIEVE IT WHEN YOU SEE IT WITH YOUR OWN EYES...
HIS BRUTE STRENGTH ...
THE BLAZING RED EYES...

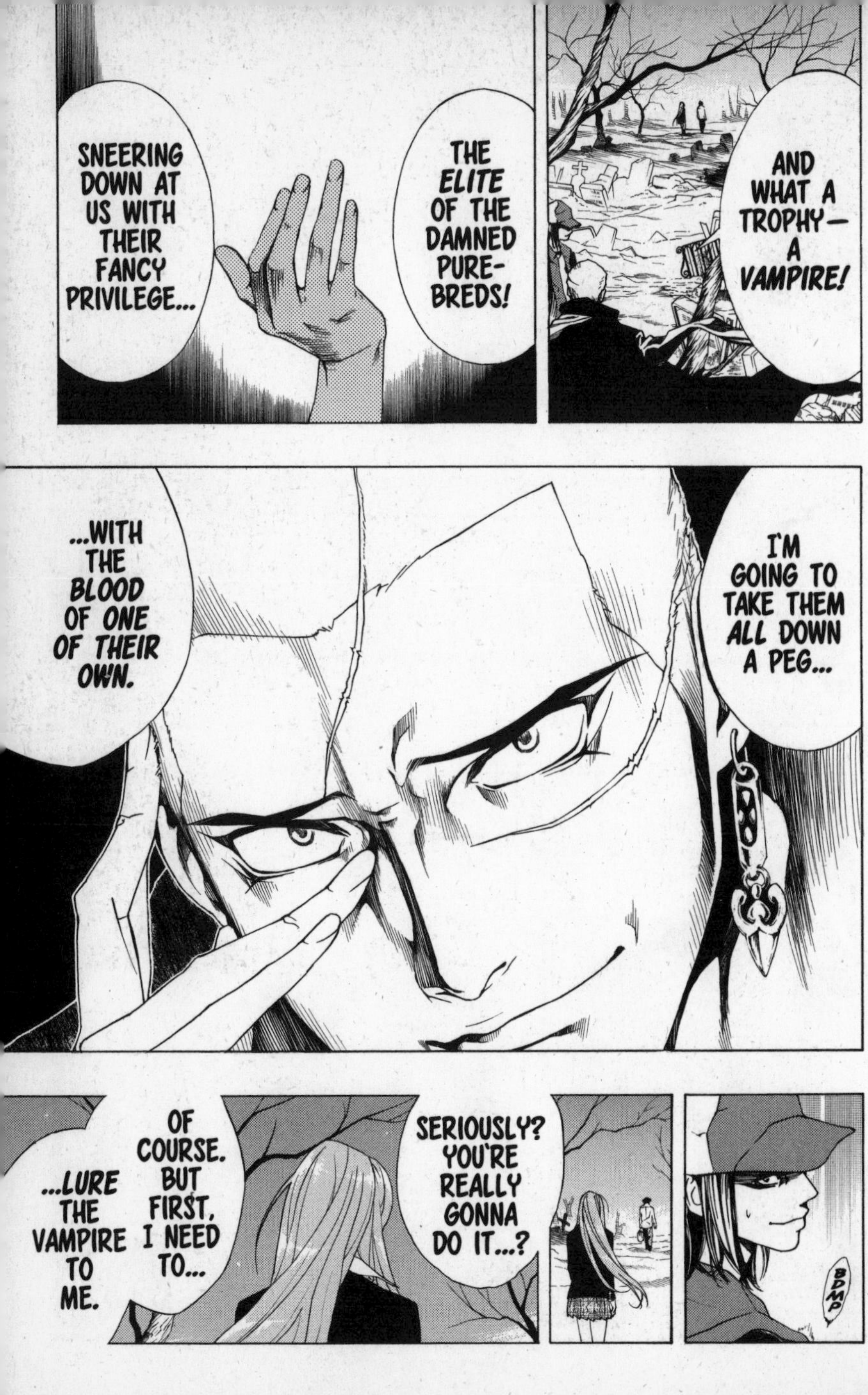
AND WHAT A TROPHY—A VAMPIRE!
THE ELITE OF THE DAMNED PUREBREDS!
SNEERING DOWN AT US WITH THEIR FANCY PRIVILEGE...
I'M GOING TO TAKE THEM ALL DOWN A PEG...
...WITH THE BLOOD OF ONE OF THEIR OWN.
BDMP
SERIOUSLY? YOU'RE REALLY GONNA DO IT...?
OF COURSE. BUT FIRST, I NEED TO...
...LURE THE VAMPIRE TO ME.

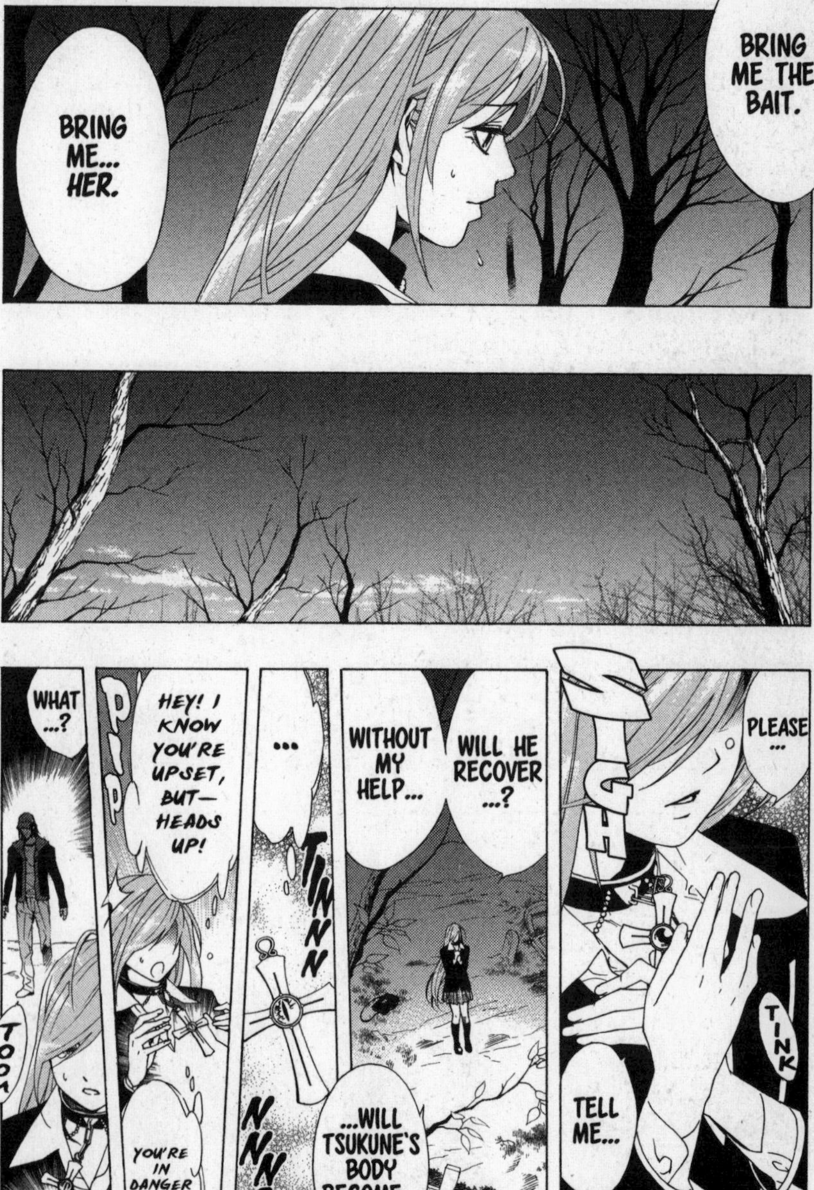
BRING ME THE BAIT.
BRING ME... HER.
PLEASE ...
SIGH
TINK
TELL ME...
WILL HE RECOVER ...?
WITHOUT MY HELP...
...WILL TSUKUNE'S BODY BECOME...
...
TINNN NNNG
HEY! I KNOW YOU'RE UPSET, BUT— HEADS UP!
PIP
YOU'RE IN DANGER!
WHAT ...?
TOOM

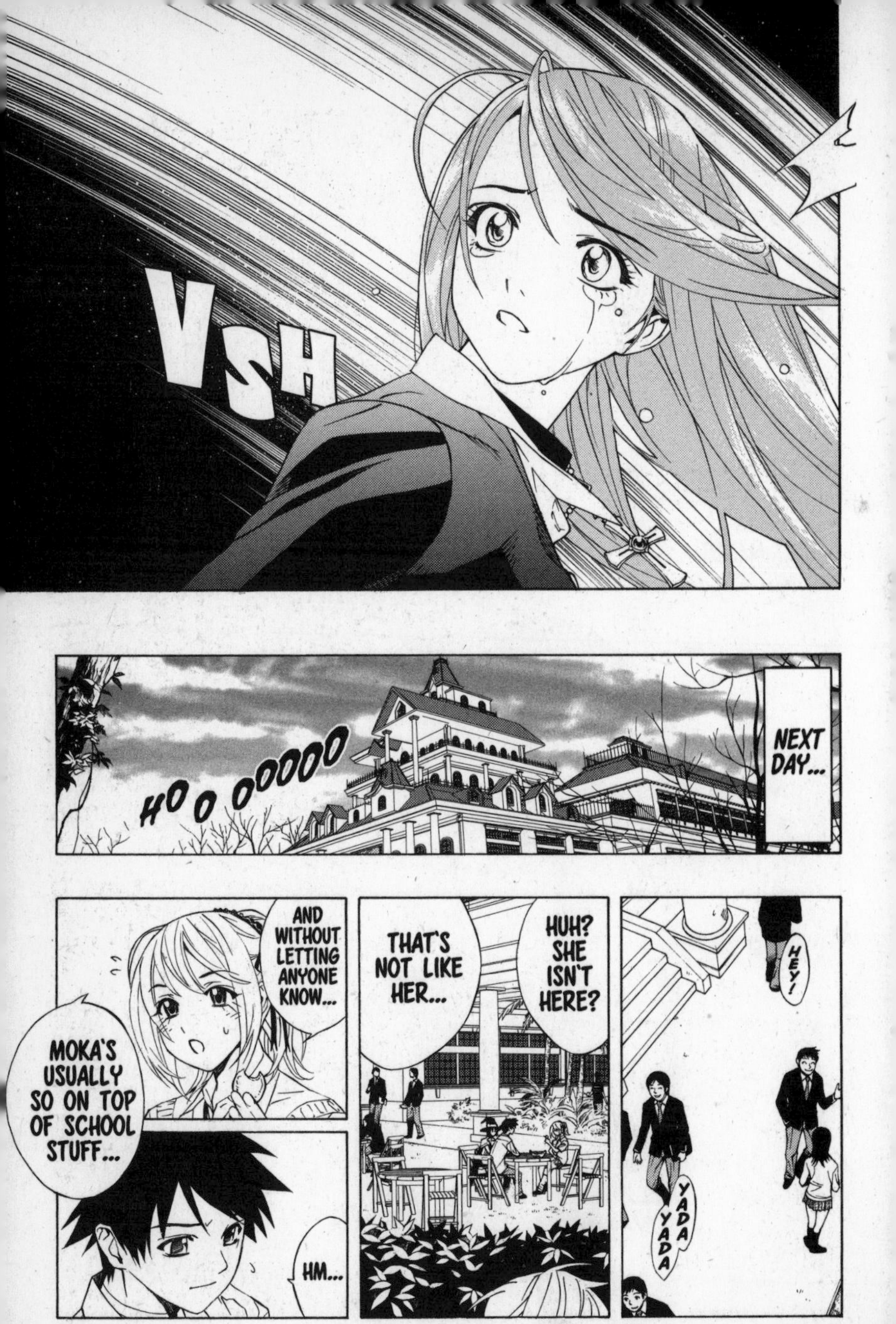
VSH
NEXT DAY...
HO O OOOOO
HEY!
YADA YADA
HUH? SHE ISN'T HERE?
THAT'S NOT LIKE HER...
AND WITHOUT LETTING ANYONE KNOW...
MOKA'S USUALLY SO ON TOP OF SCHOOL STUFF...
HM...

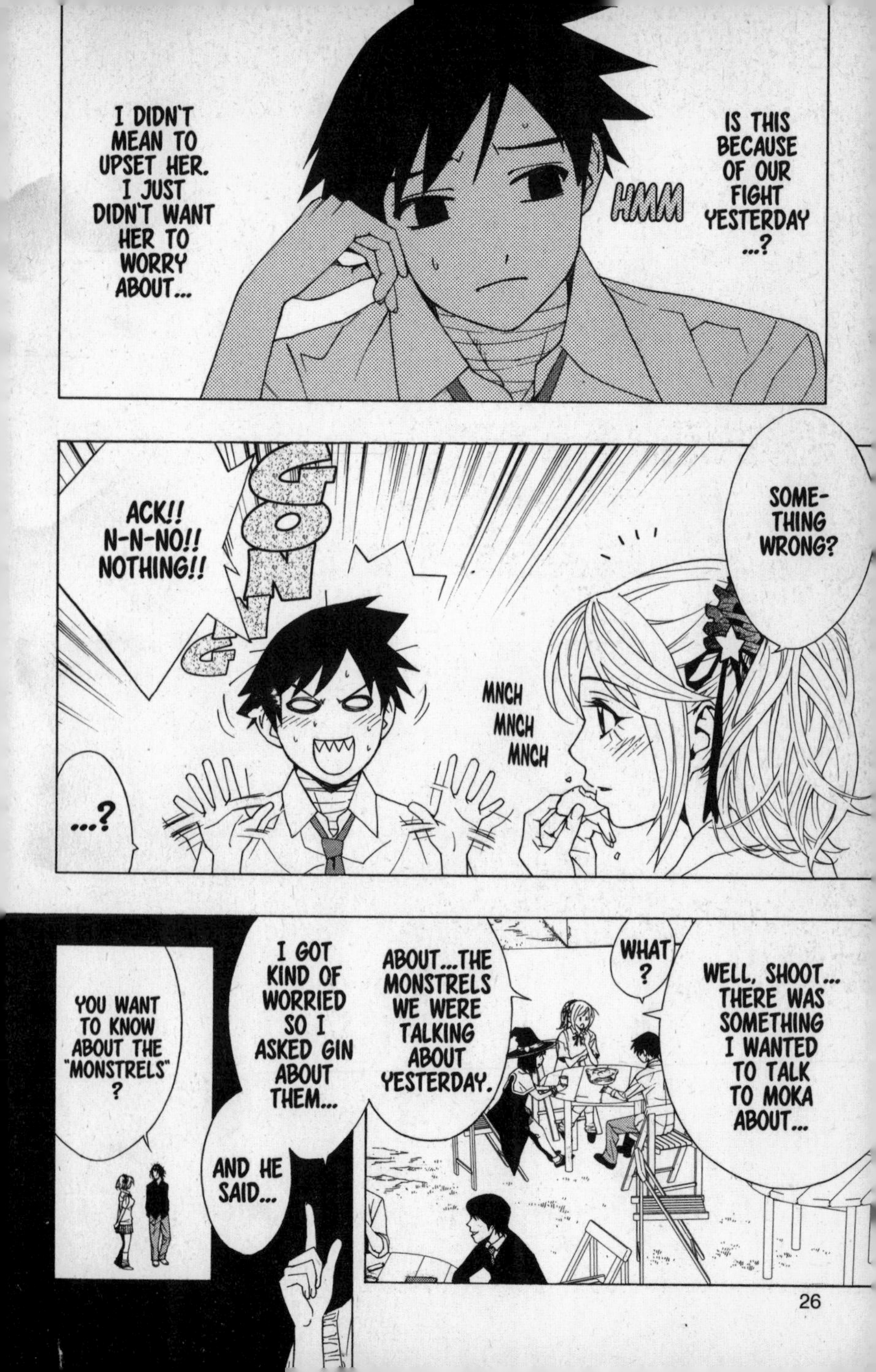
IS THIS BECAUSE OF OUR FIGHT YESTERDAY ...?
HMM
I DIDN'T MEAN TO UPSET HER. I JUST DIDN'T WANT HER TO WORRY ABOUT...
SOME-THING WRONG?
MNCH MNCH MNCH
GONG
ACK!! N-N-NO!! NOTHING!!
...?
WELL, SHOOT... THERE WAS SOMETHING I WANTED TO TALK TO MOKA ABOUT...
WHAT?
ABOUT...THE MONSTRELS WE WERE TALKING ABOUT YESTERDAY.
I GOT KIND OF WORRIED SO I ASKED GIN ABOUT THEM...
AND HE SAID...
YOU WANT TO KNOW ABOUT THE "MONSTRELS"?

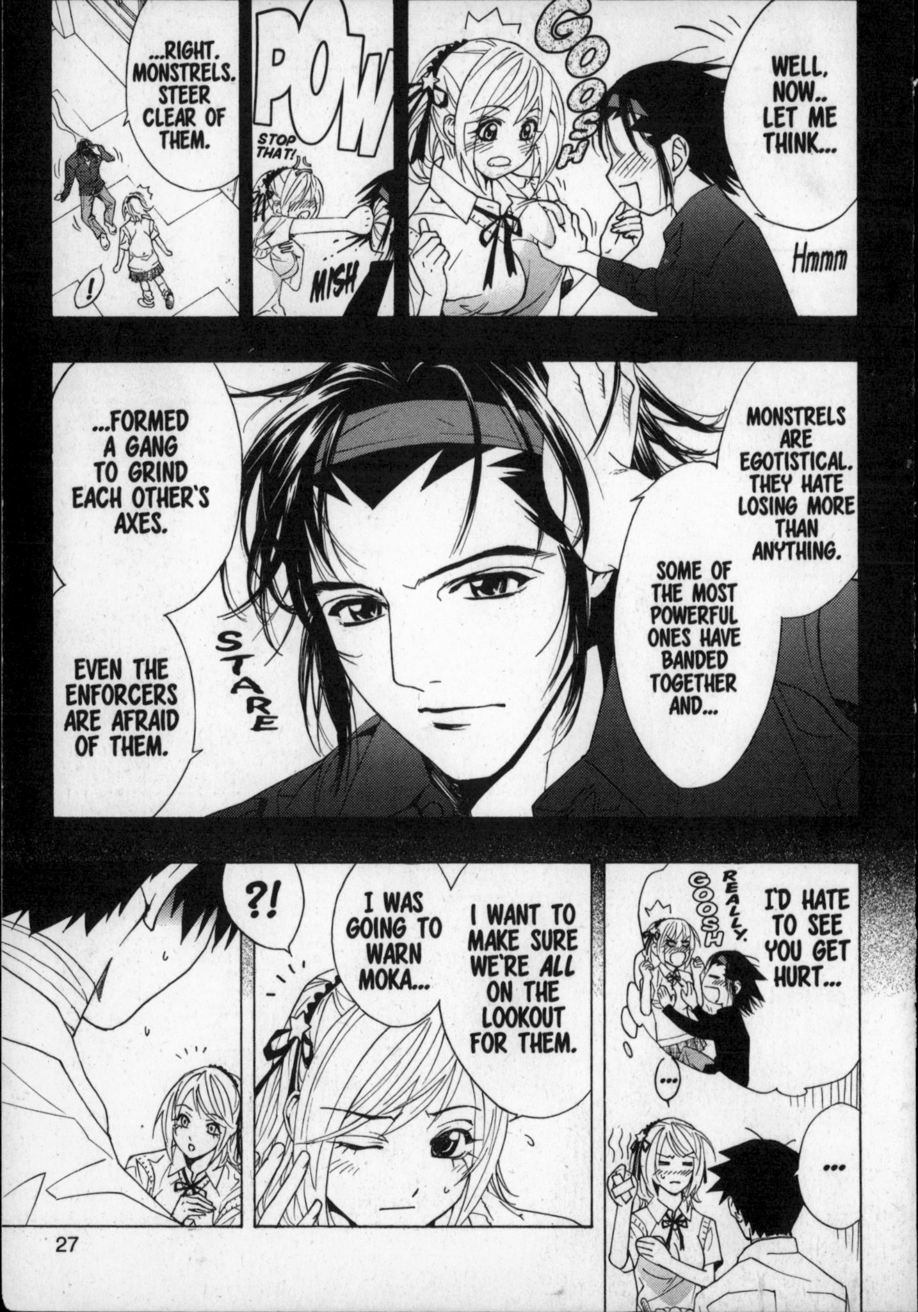

WELL, NOW.. LET ME THINK...
Hmmm
GOOSH
POW
STOP THAT!
MISH
...RIGHT. MONSTRELS. STEER CLEAR OF THEM.
!
MONSTRELS ARE EGOTISTICAL. THEY HATE LOSING MORE THAN ANYTHING.
SOME OF THE MOST POWERFUL ONES HAVE BANDED TOGETHER AND...
STARE
...FORMED A GANG TO GRIND EACH OTHER'S AXES.
EVEN THE ENFORCERS ARE AFRAID OF THEM.
I'D HATE TO SEE YOU GET HURT...
REALLY.
GOOSH
...
...
I WANT TO MAKE SURE WE'RE ALL ON THE LOOKOUT FOR THEM.
I WAS GOING TO WARN MOKA...
?!

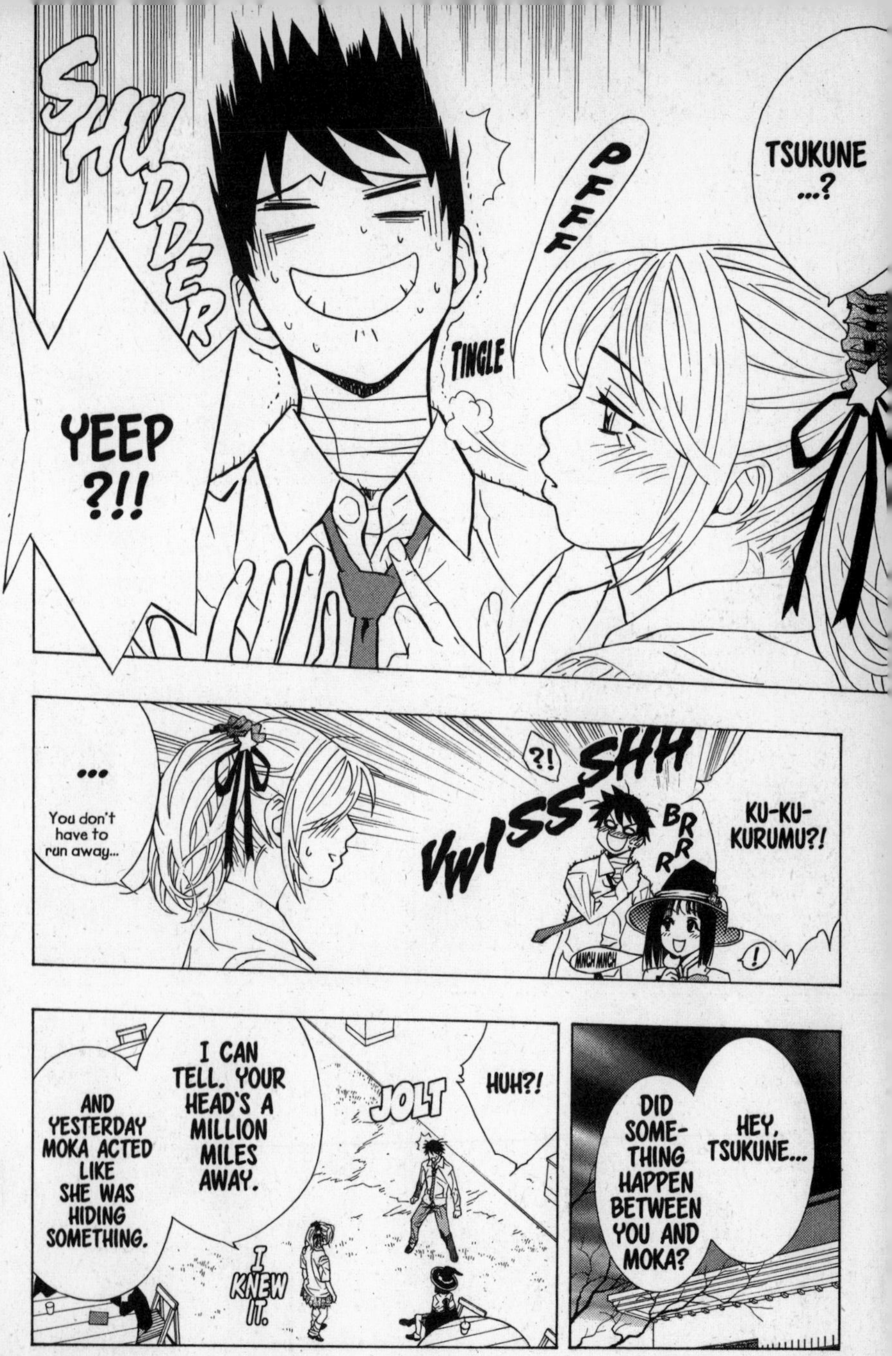
TSUKUNE ...?
PFFF
TINGLE
SHUDDER
YEEP ?!!
KU-KU-KURUMU?!
BRRR
?!
VWISSSHH
MNCH MNCH
!
...
You don't have to run away...
HEY, TSUKUNE...
DID SOMETHING HAPPEN BETWEEN YOU AND MOKA?
HUH?!
JOLT
I CAN TELL. YOUR HEAD'S A MILLION MILES AWAY.
AND YESTERDAY MOKA ACTED LIKE SHE WAS HIDING SOMETHING.
I KNEW IT.

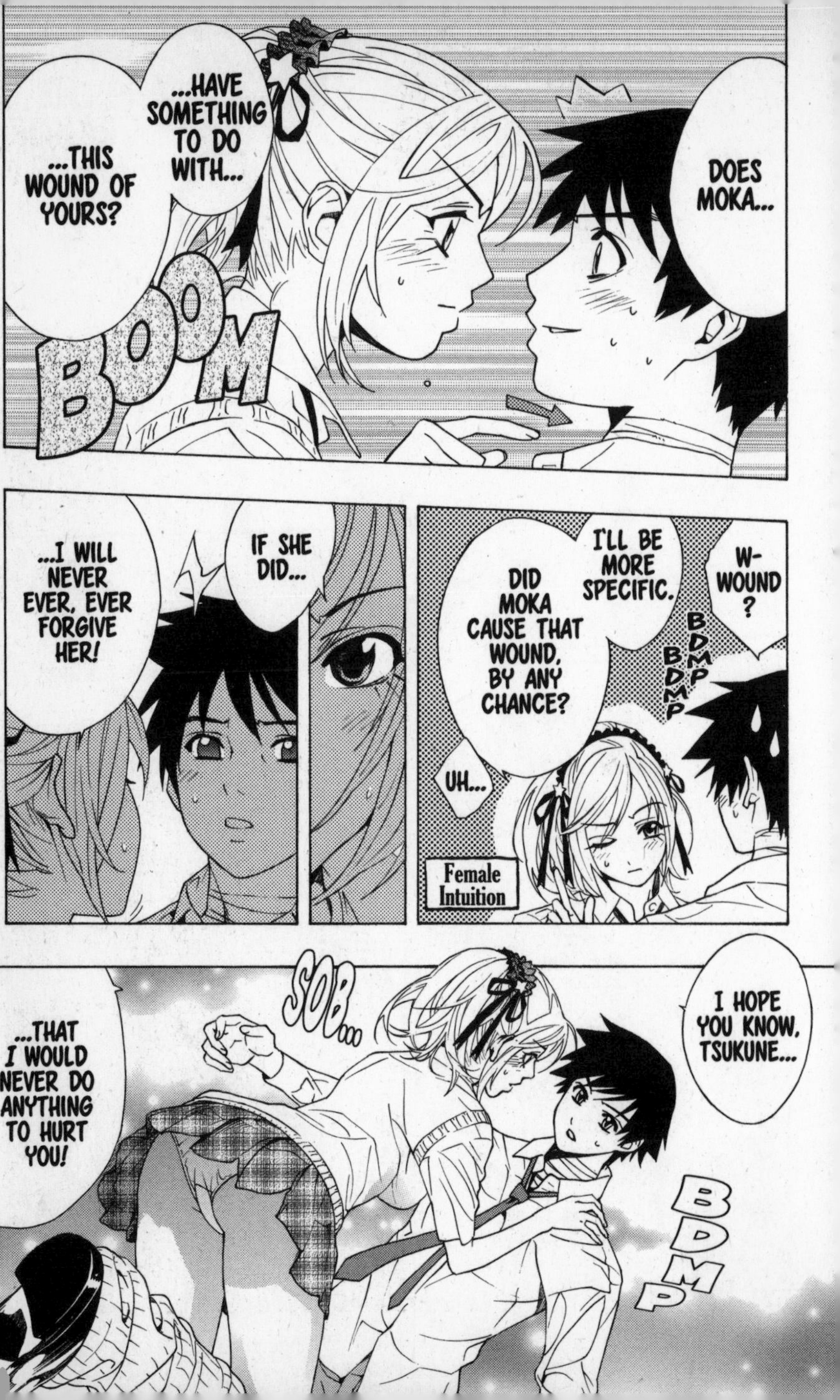
DOES MOKA...
...HAVE SOMETHING TO DO WITH...
...THIS WOUND OF YOURS?
BOOM
W-WOUND?
BDMP BDMP
I'LL BE MORE SPECIFIC.
DID MOKA CAUSE THAT WOUND, BY ANY CHANCE?
UH...
Female Intuition
IF SHE DID...
...I WILL NEVER EVER, EVER FORGIVE HER!
I HOPE YOU KNOW, TSUKUNE...
SOB...
...THAT I WOULD NEVER DO ANYTHING TO HURT YOU!
BDMP

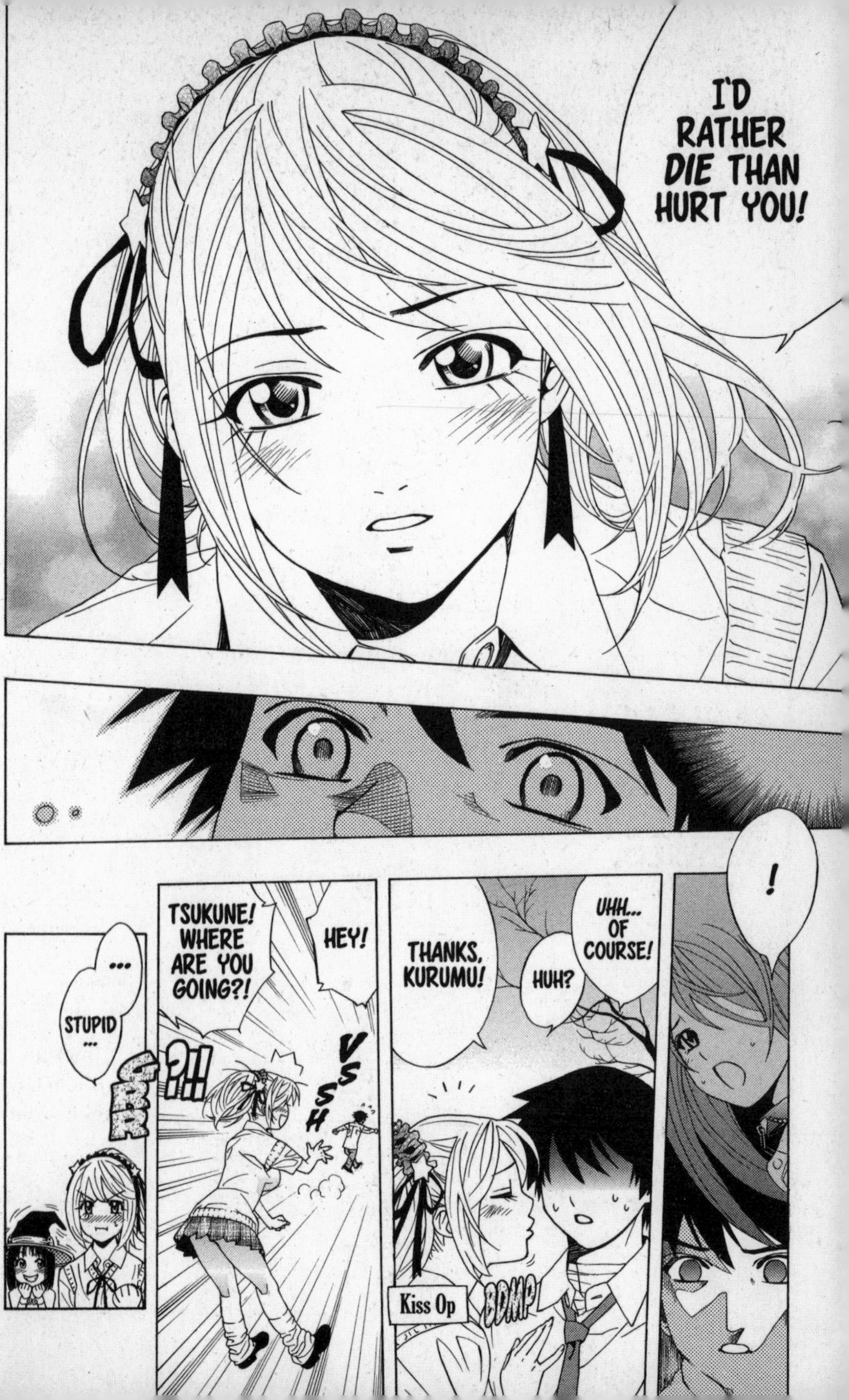
I'D RATHER DIE THAN HURT YOU!
!
UHH... OF COURSE!
HUH?
THANKS, KURUMU!
Kiss Op
BDMP
HEY!
TSUKUNE! WHERE ARE YOU GOING?!
VSSH
?!!
...
STUPID ...
GRR

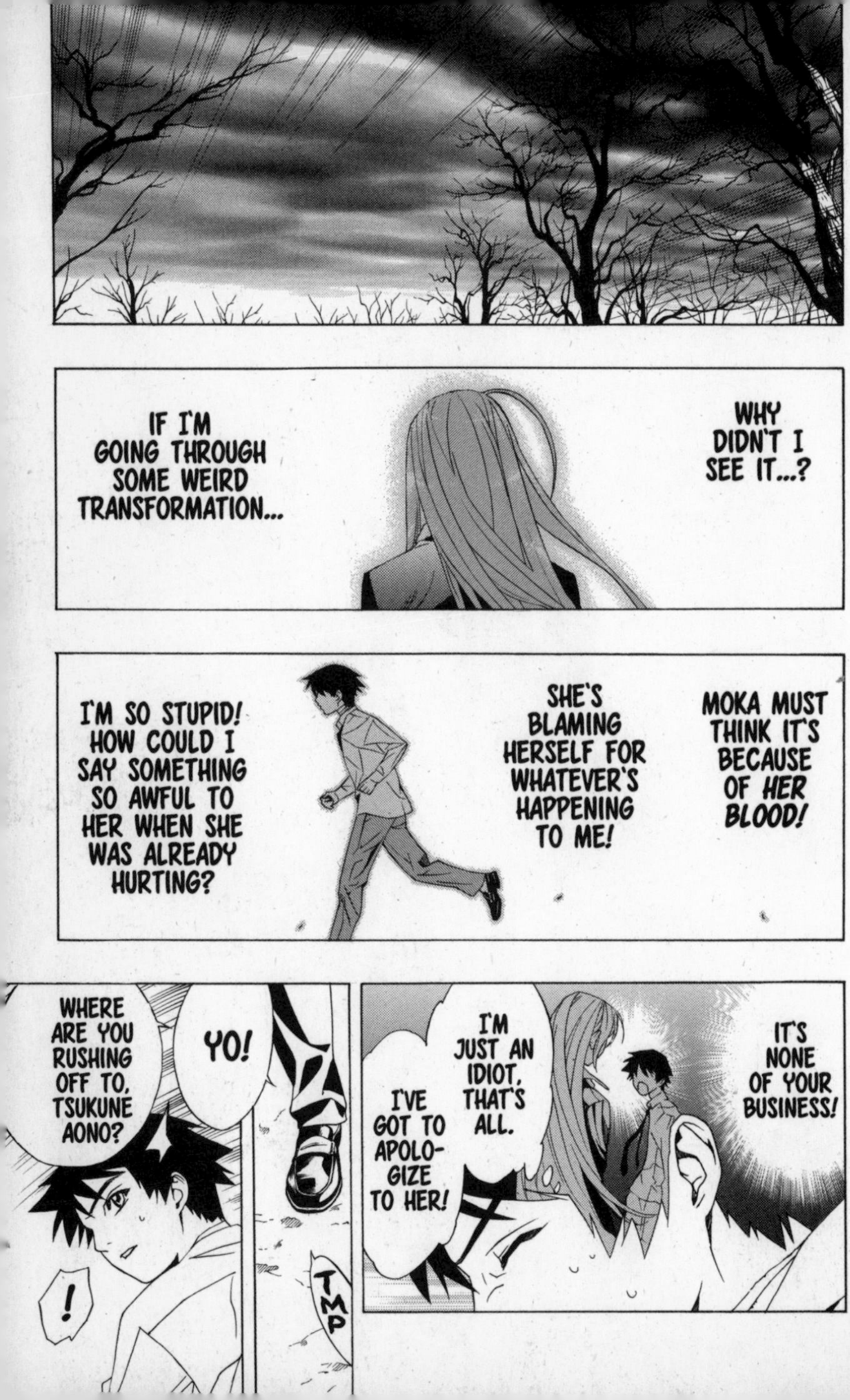
WHY DIDN'T I SEE IT...?
IF I'M GOING THROUGH SOME WEIRD TRANSFORMATION...
MOKA MUST THINK IT'S BECAUSE OF *HER BLOOD!*
SHE'S BLAMING HERSELF FOR WHATEVER'S HAPPENING TO ME!
I'M SO STUPID! HOW COULD I SAY SOMETHING SO AWFUL TO HER WHEN SHE WAS ALREADY HURTING?
TMP
!
YO!
WHERE ARE YOU RUSHING OFF TO, TSUKUNE AONO?
IT'S NONE OF YOUR BUSINESS!
I'M JUST AN IDIOT, THAT'S ALL.
I'VE GOT TO APOLOGIZE TO HER!

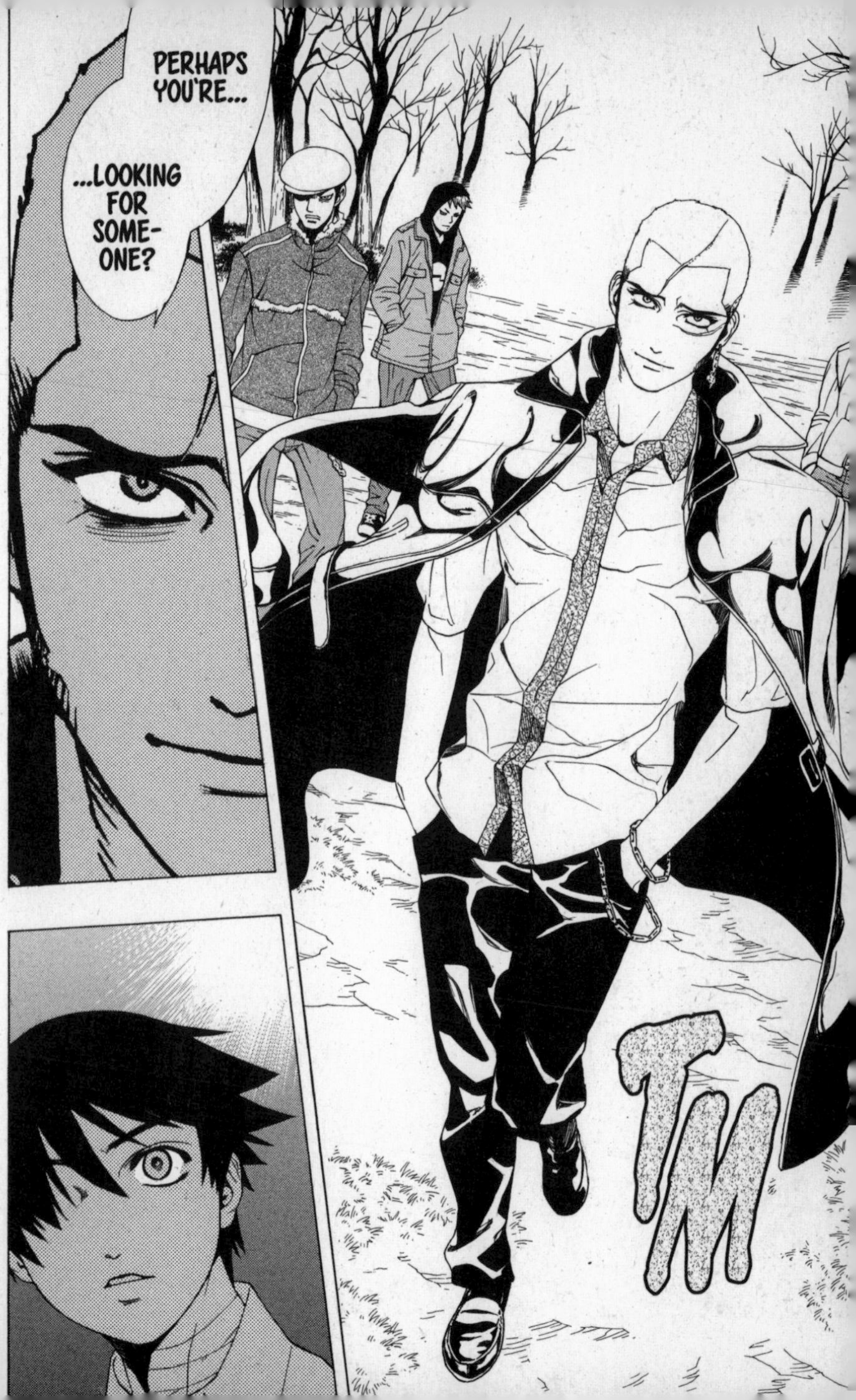
PERHAPS YOU'RE...
...LOOKING FOR SOME-ONE?
TM

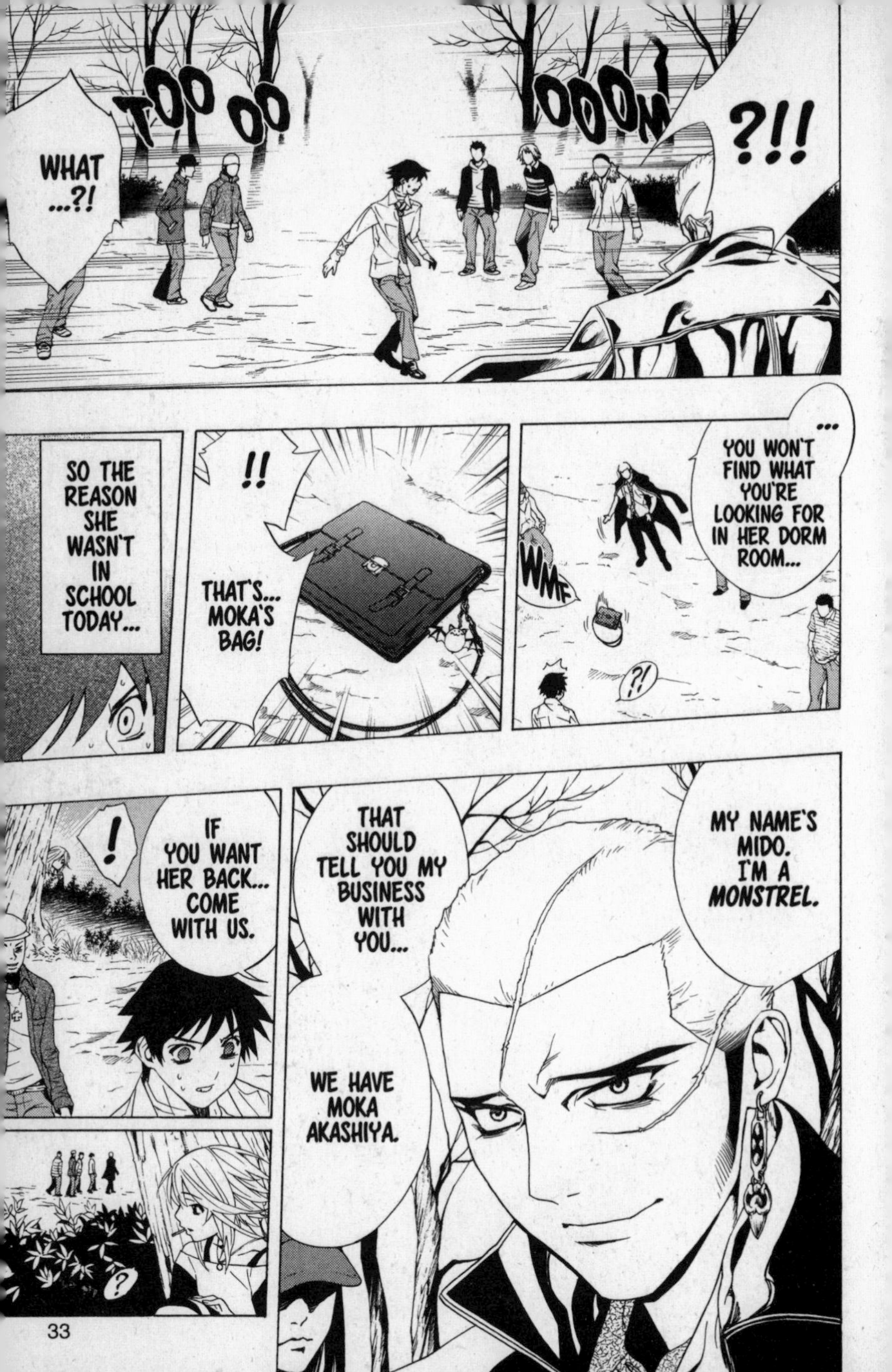

?!!
TOO OO OOOM
WHAT ...?!
... YOU WON'T FIND WHAT YOU'RE LOOKING FOR IN HER DORM ROOM...
WMF
?!
!!
THAT'S... MOKA'S BAG!
SO THE REASON SHE WASN'T IN SCHOOL TODAY...
MY NAME'S MIDO. I'M A MONSTREL.
THAT SHOULD TELL YOU MY BUSINESS WITH YOU...
WE HAVE MOKA AKASHIYA.
IF YOU WANT HER BACK... COME WITH US.
!
?

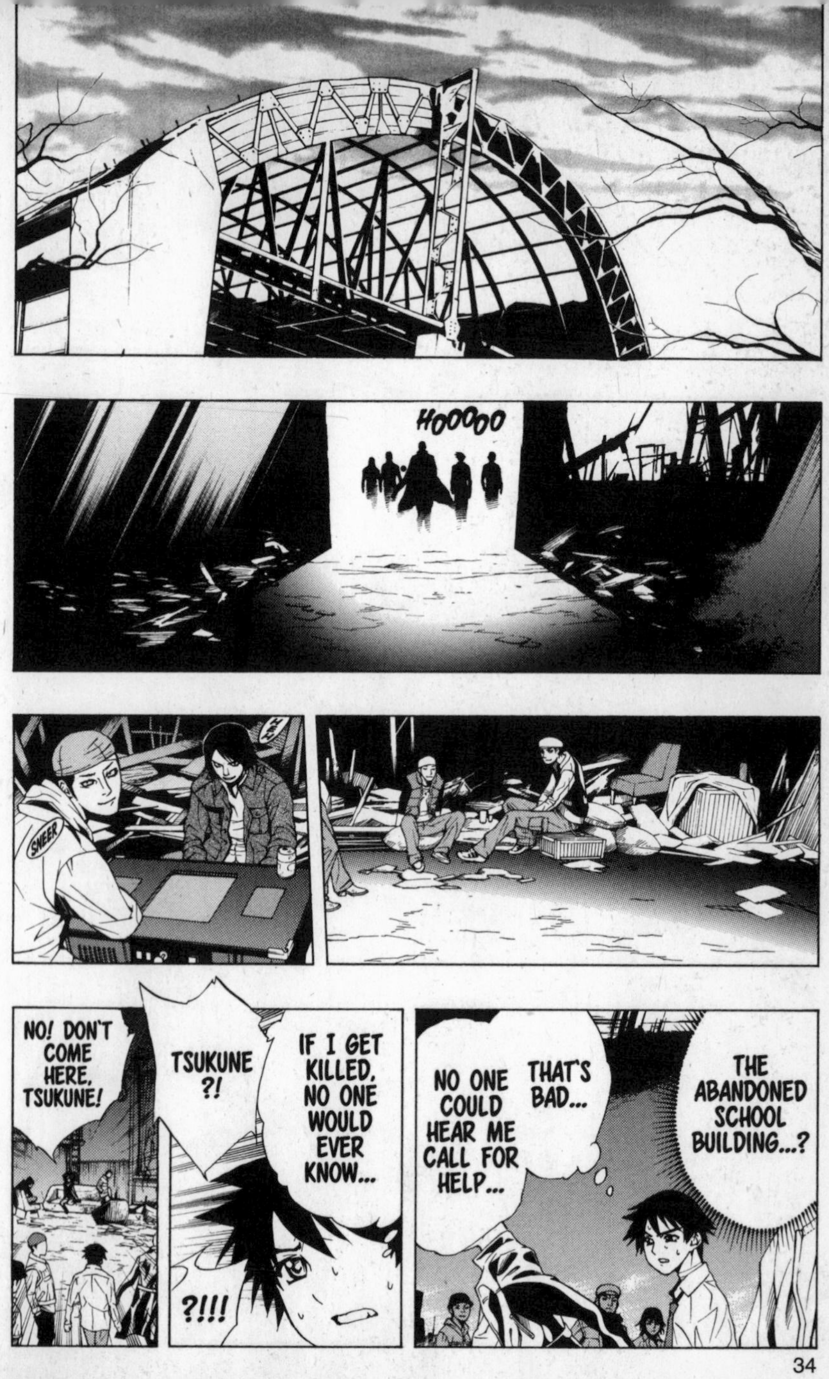
HOOOOO
HEH
SNEER
THE ABANDONED SCHOOL BUILDING...?
THAT'S BAD...
NO ONE COULD HEAR ME CALL FOR HELP...
IF I GET KILLED, NO ONE WOULD EVER KNOW...
TSUKUNE ?!
?!!!
NO! DON'T COME HERE, TSUKUNE!

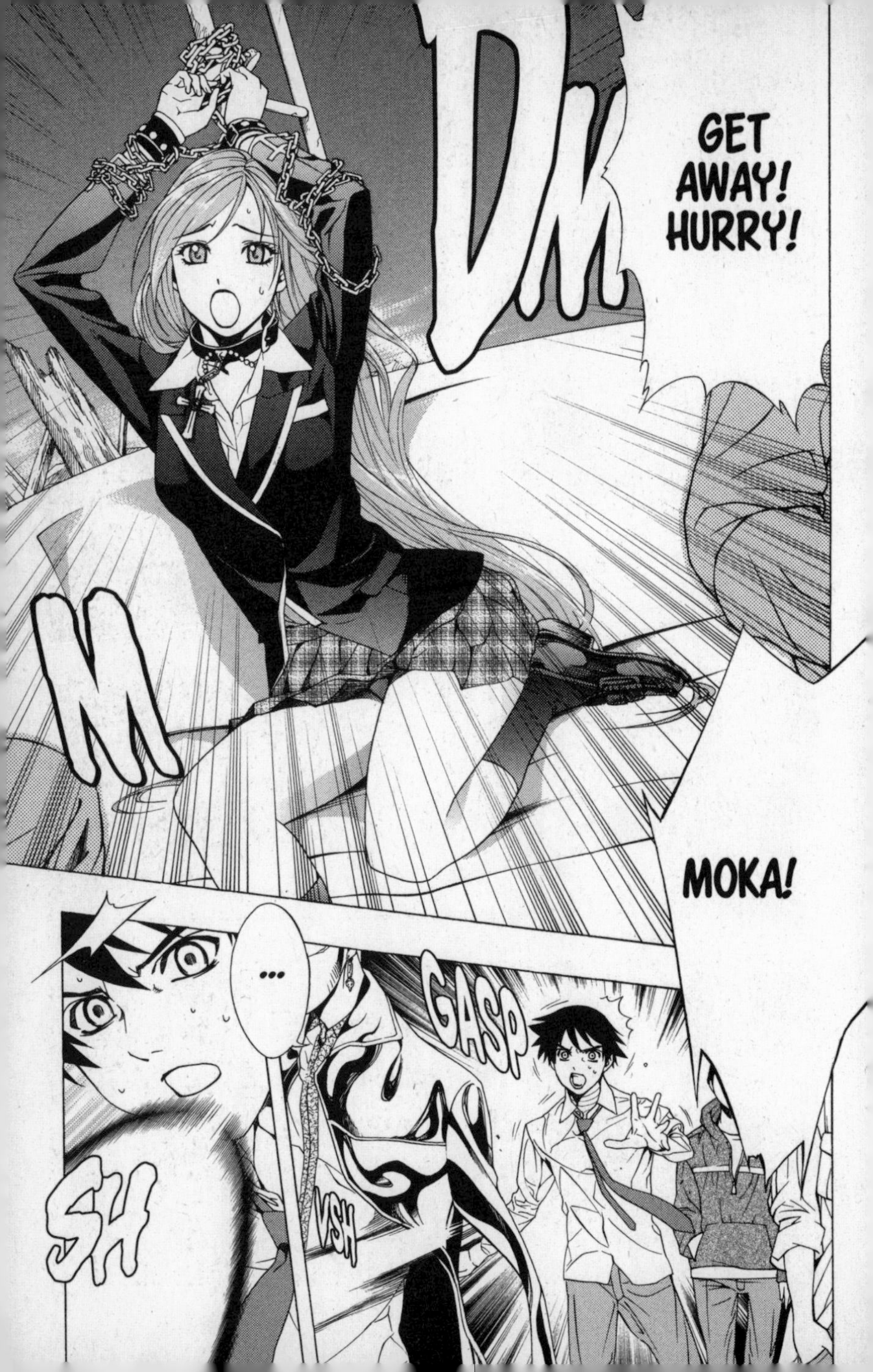
GET AWAY! HURRY!
DM
M
MOKA!
GASP
...
SH
VSH

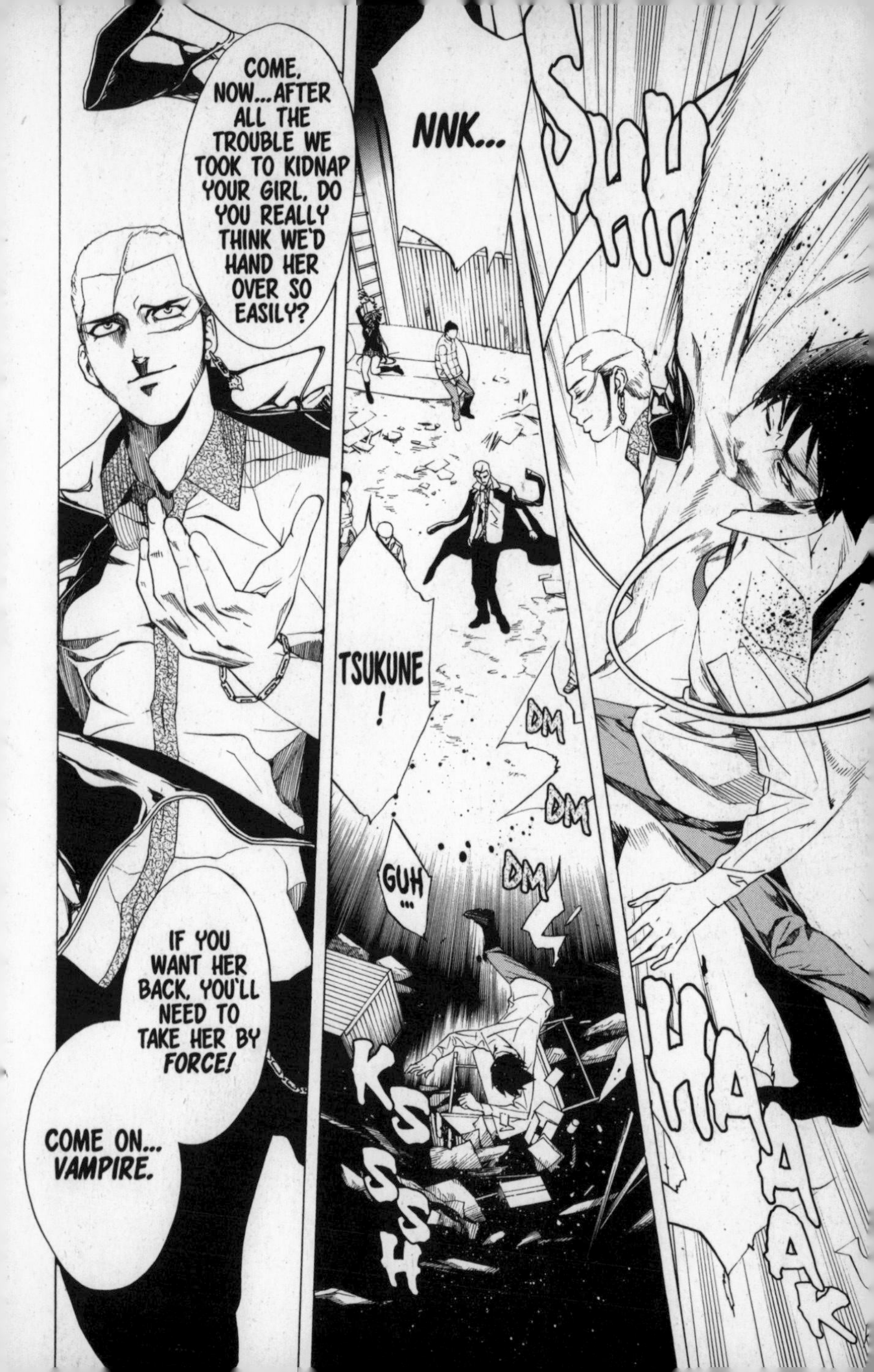
SHH
HAAAK
NNK...
TSUKUNE!
DM
DM
DM
GUH...
KSSSH
COME, NOW...AFTER ALL THE TROUBLE WE TOOK TO KIDNAP YOUR GIRL, DO YOU REALLY THINK WE'D HAND HER OVER SO EASILY?
IF YOU WANT HER BACK, YOU'LL NEED TO TAKE HER BY FORCE!
COME ON... VAMPIRE.

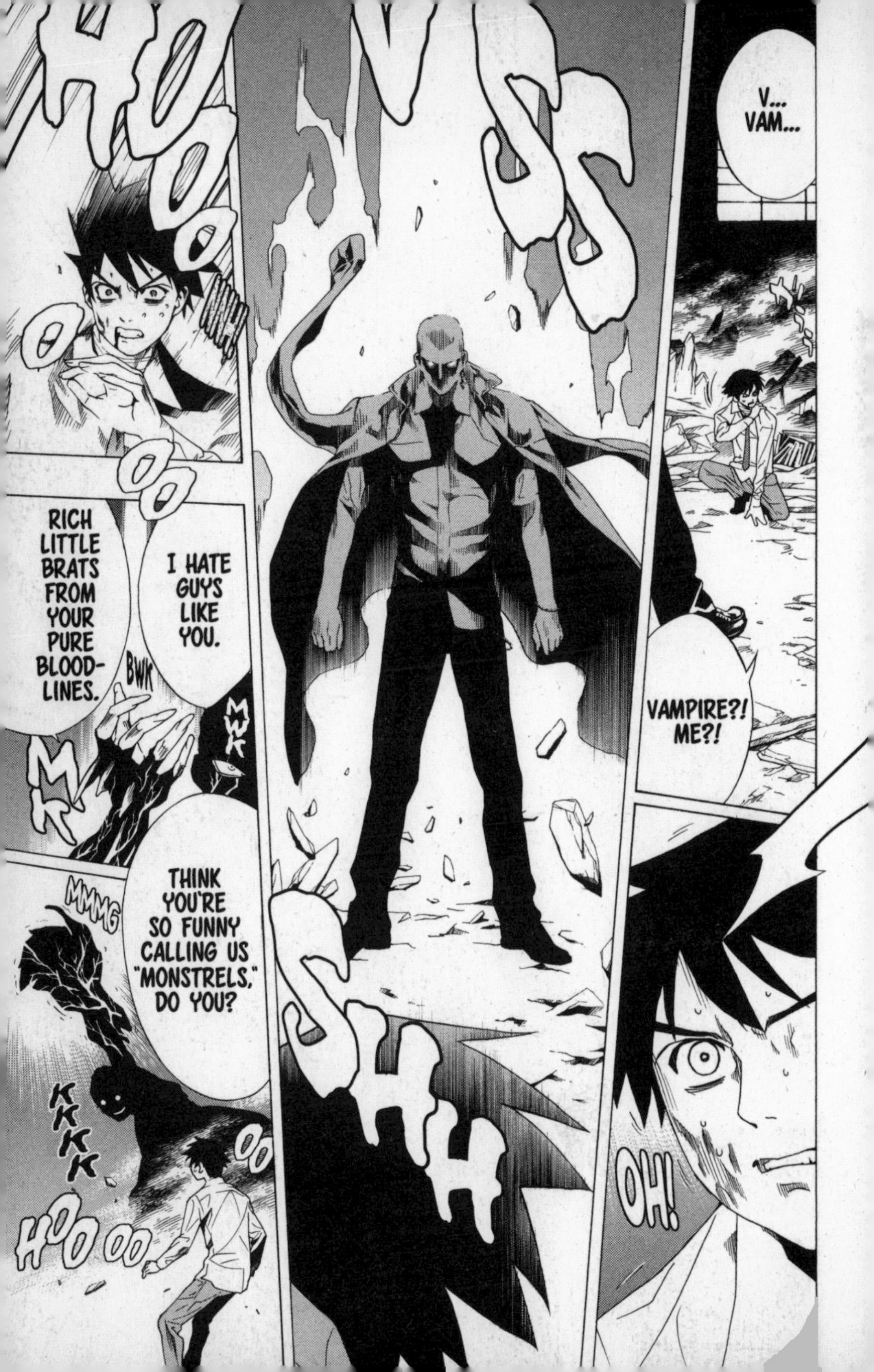
V... VAM...
VAMPIRE?! ME?!
OH!
I HATE GUYS LIKE YOU.
RICH LITTLE BRATS FROM YOUR PURE BLOOD-LINES.
BWK
MWK
MK
THINK YOU'RE SO FUNNY CALLING US "MONSTRELS," DO YOU?
MMMG
KKKK

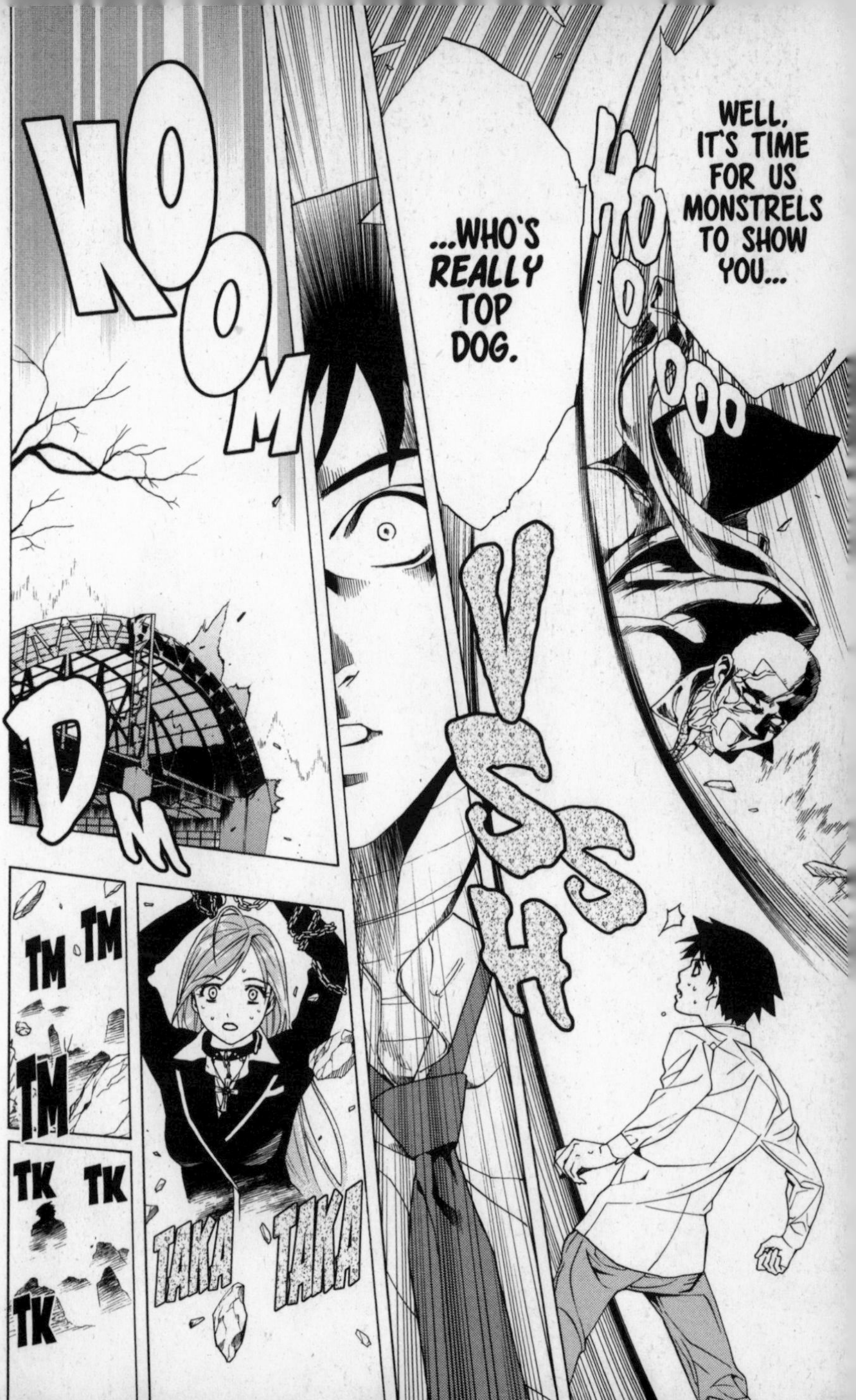
WELL, IT'S TIME FOR US MONSTRELS TO SHOW YOU...
HOOOOOO
...WHO'S REALLY TOP DOG.
VSSSH
KOOOM
DM
TM TM
TM
TK TK
TK
TAKA TAKA

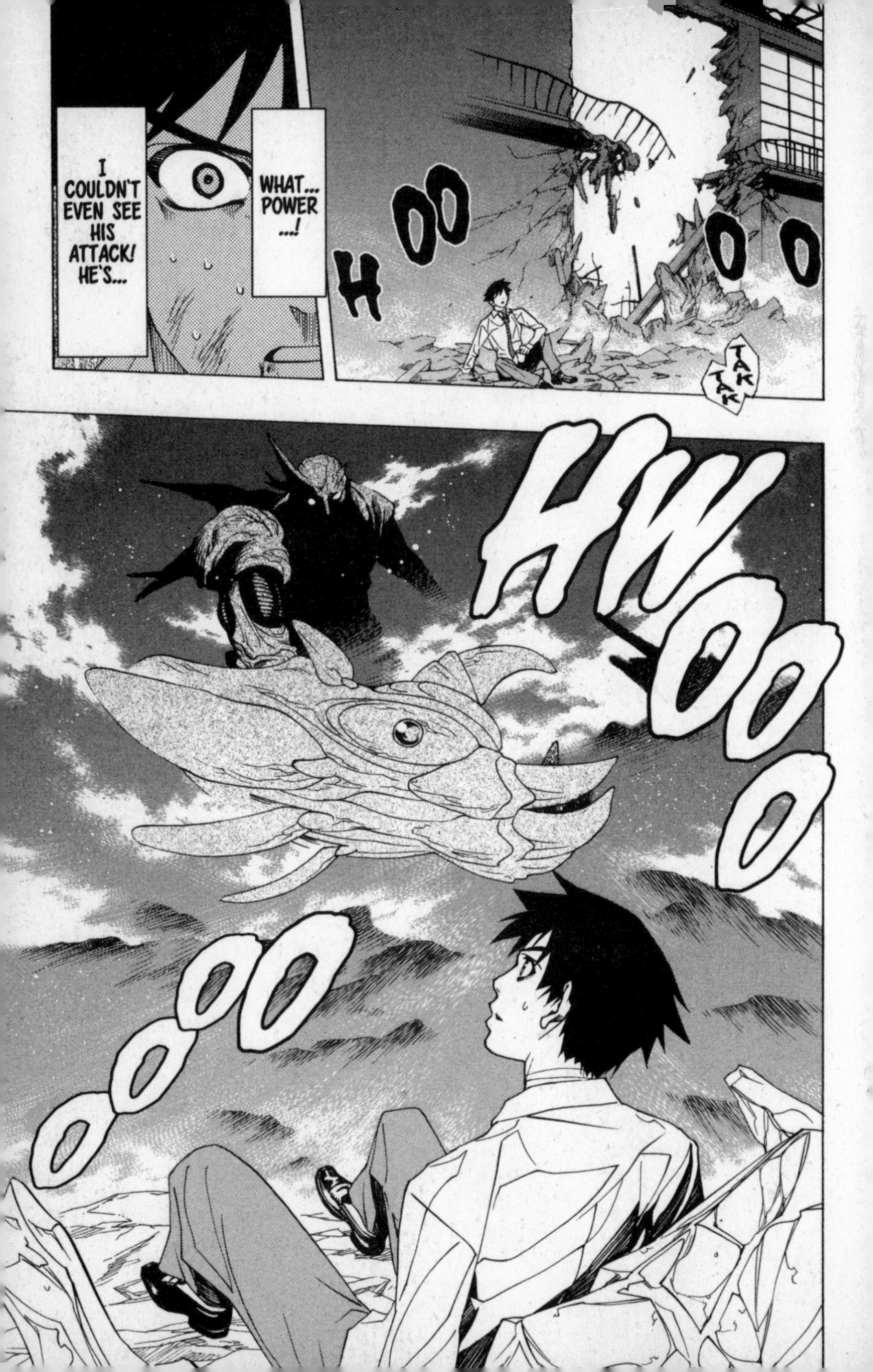

WHAT... POWER ...!
I COULDN'T EVEN SEE HIS ATTACK! HE'S...
HOOOOO
TAK TAK
HWOOOOOOOOO

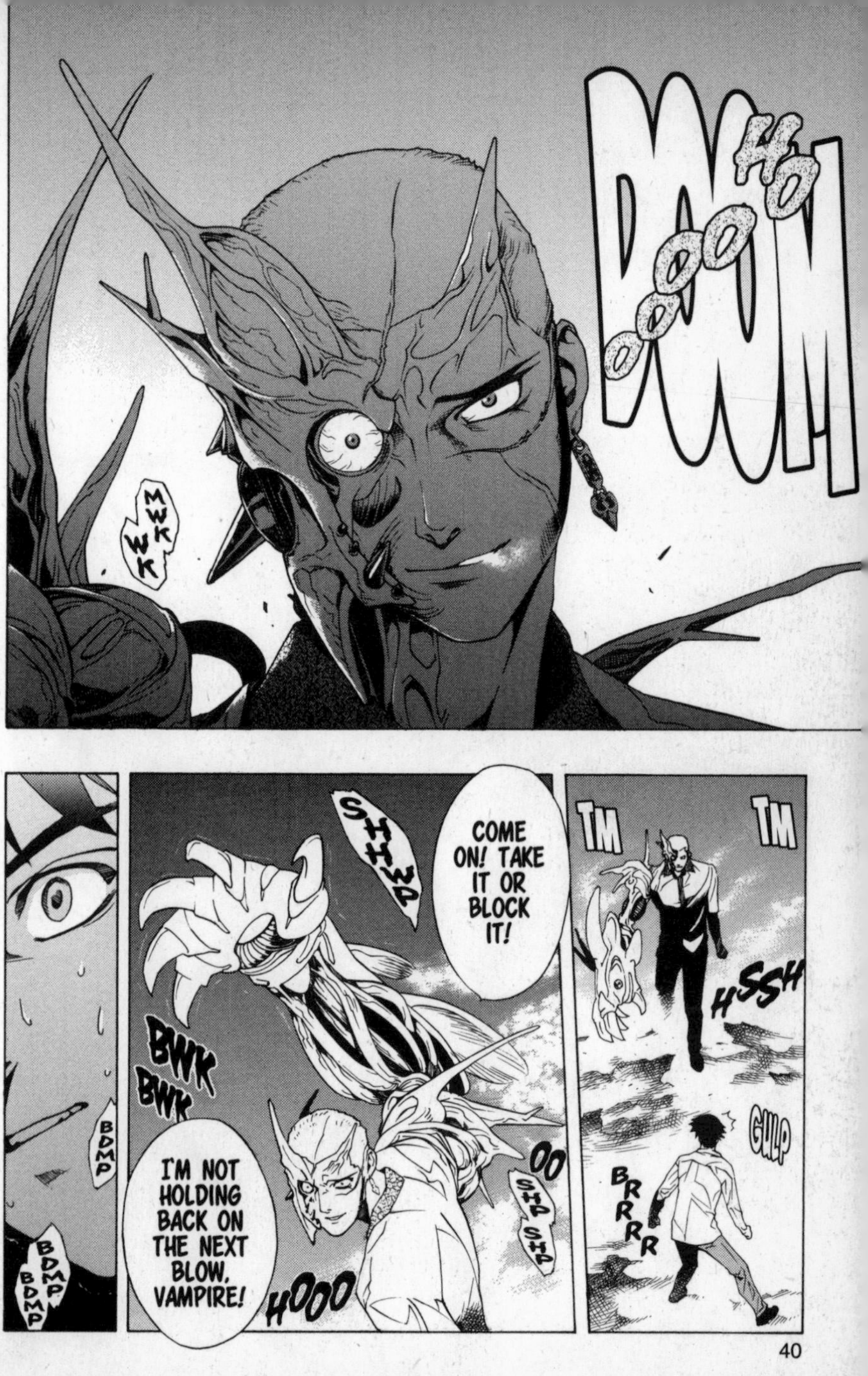
DOOM
MWK
TM TM
HSSH
GULP
BRRRR
COME ON! TAKE IT OR BLOCK IT!
SHHWP
BWK BWK
I'M NOT HOLDING BACK ON THE NEXT BLOW, VAMPIRE!
OO SHP SHP
HOOO
BDMP
BDMP BDMP

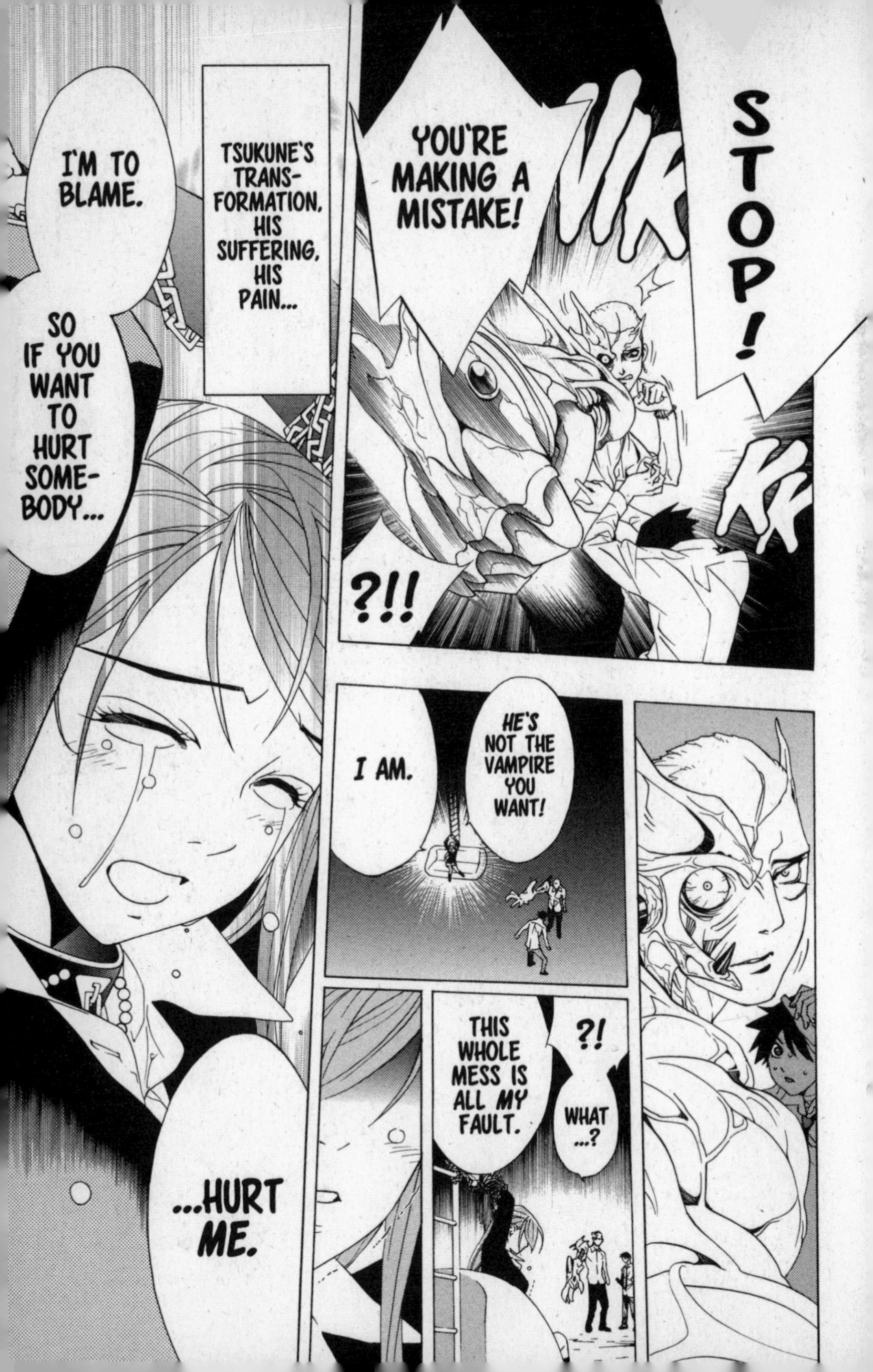
STOP!
YOU'RE MAKING A MISTAKE!
?!!
HE'S NOT THE VAMPIRE YOU WANT!
I AM.
?!
WHAT ...?
THIS WHOLE MESS IS ALL MY FAULT.
TSUKUNE'S TRANSFORMATION, HIS SUFFERING, HIS PAIN...
I'M TO BLAME.
SO IF YOU WANT TO HURT SOMEBODY...
...HURT ME.

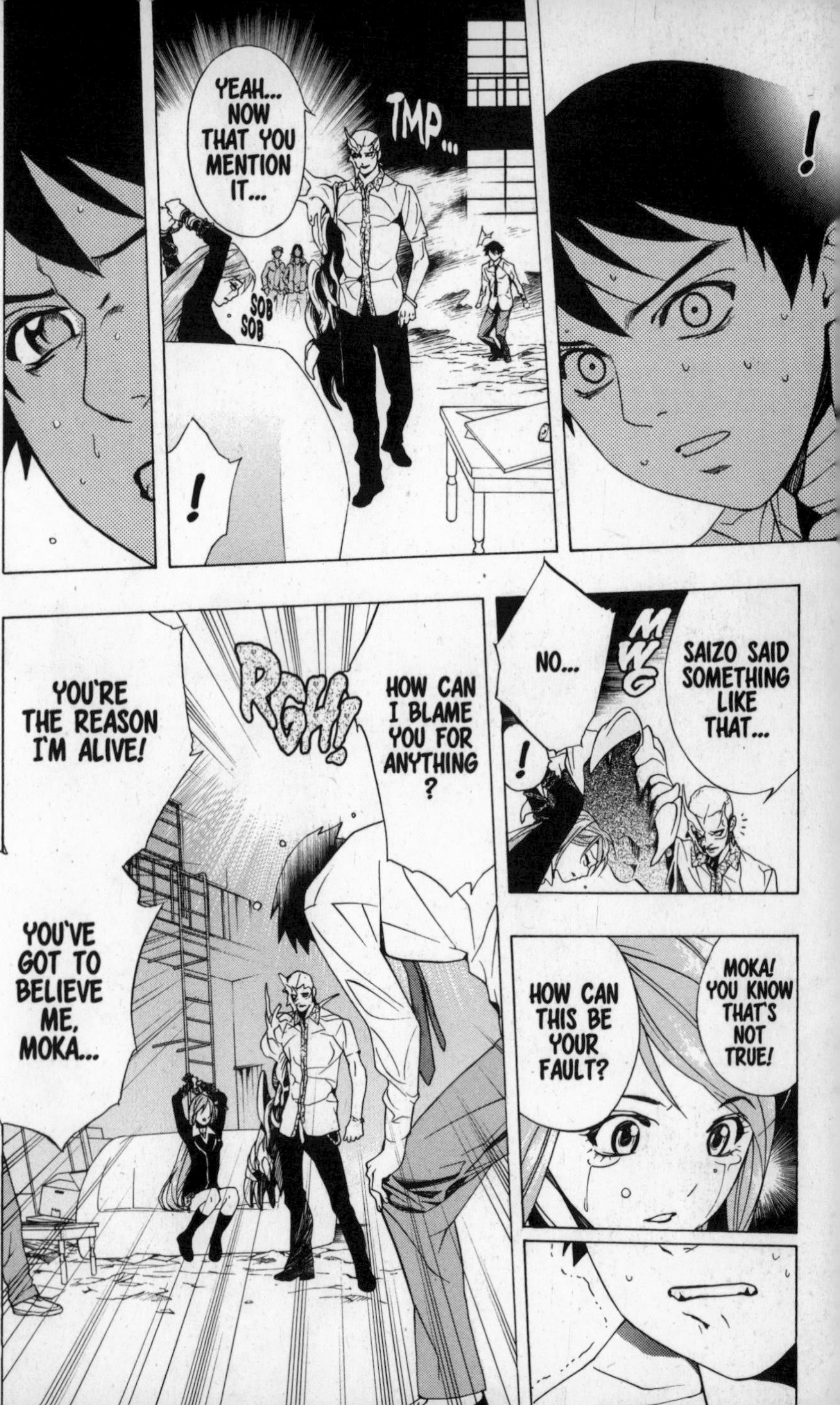
!
TMP...
YEAH... NOW THAT YOU MENTION IT...
SOB SOB
!
SAIZO SAID SOMETHING LIKE THAT...
MWG
NO...
!
MOKA! YOU KNOW THAT'S NOT TRUE!
HOW CAN THIS BE YOUR FAULT?
HOW CAN I BLAME YOU FOR ANYTHING?
RGH!
YOU'RE THE REASON I'M ALIVE!
YOU'VE GOT TO BELIEVE ME, MOKA...

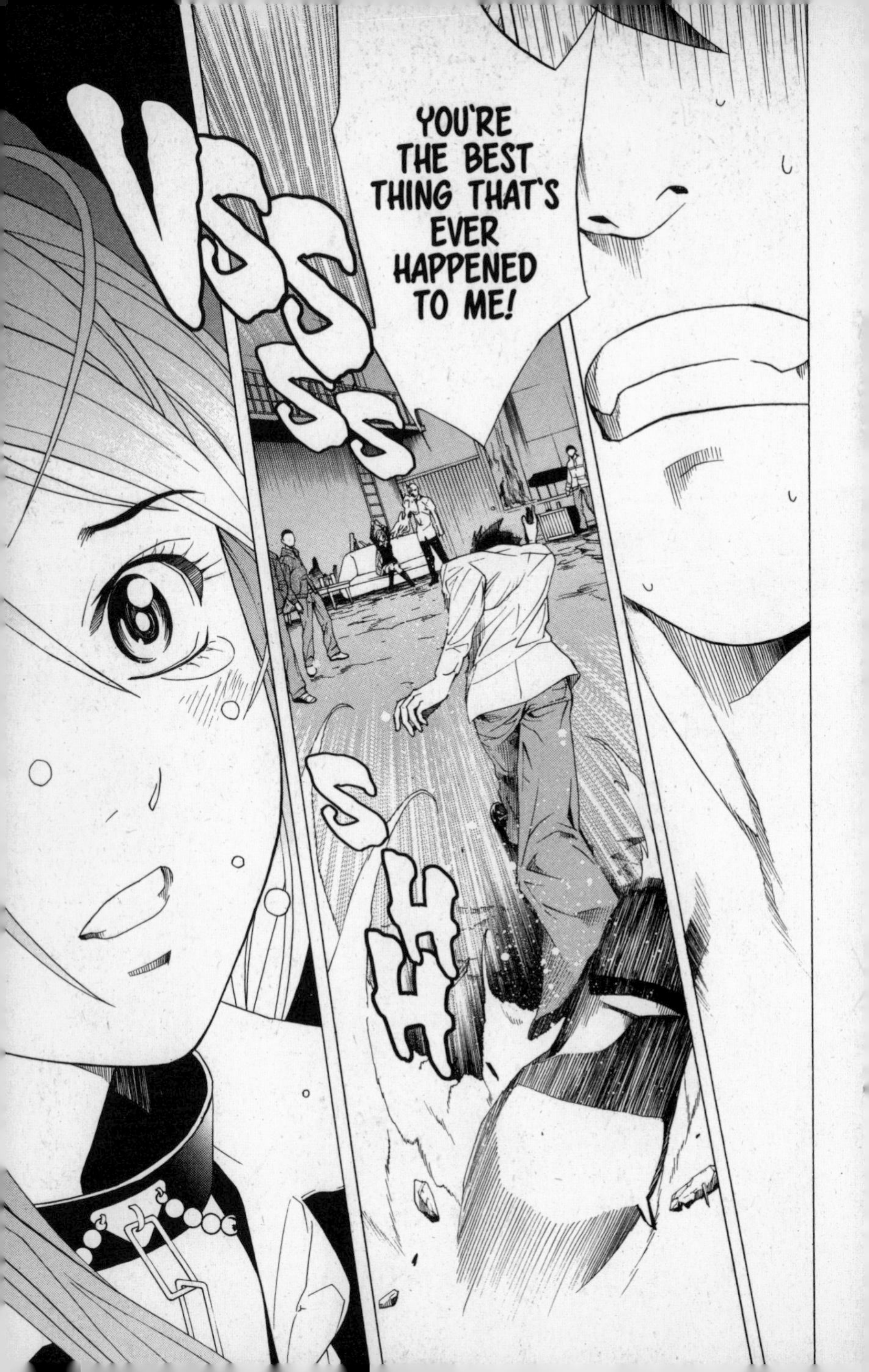
YOU'RE THE BEST THING THAT'S EVER HAPPENED TO ME!
VASSSS
SSH

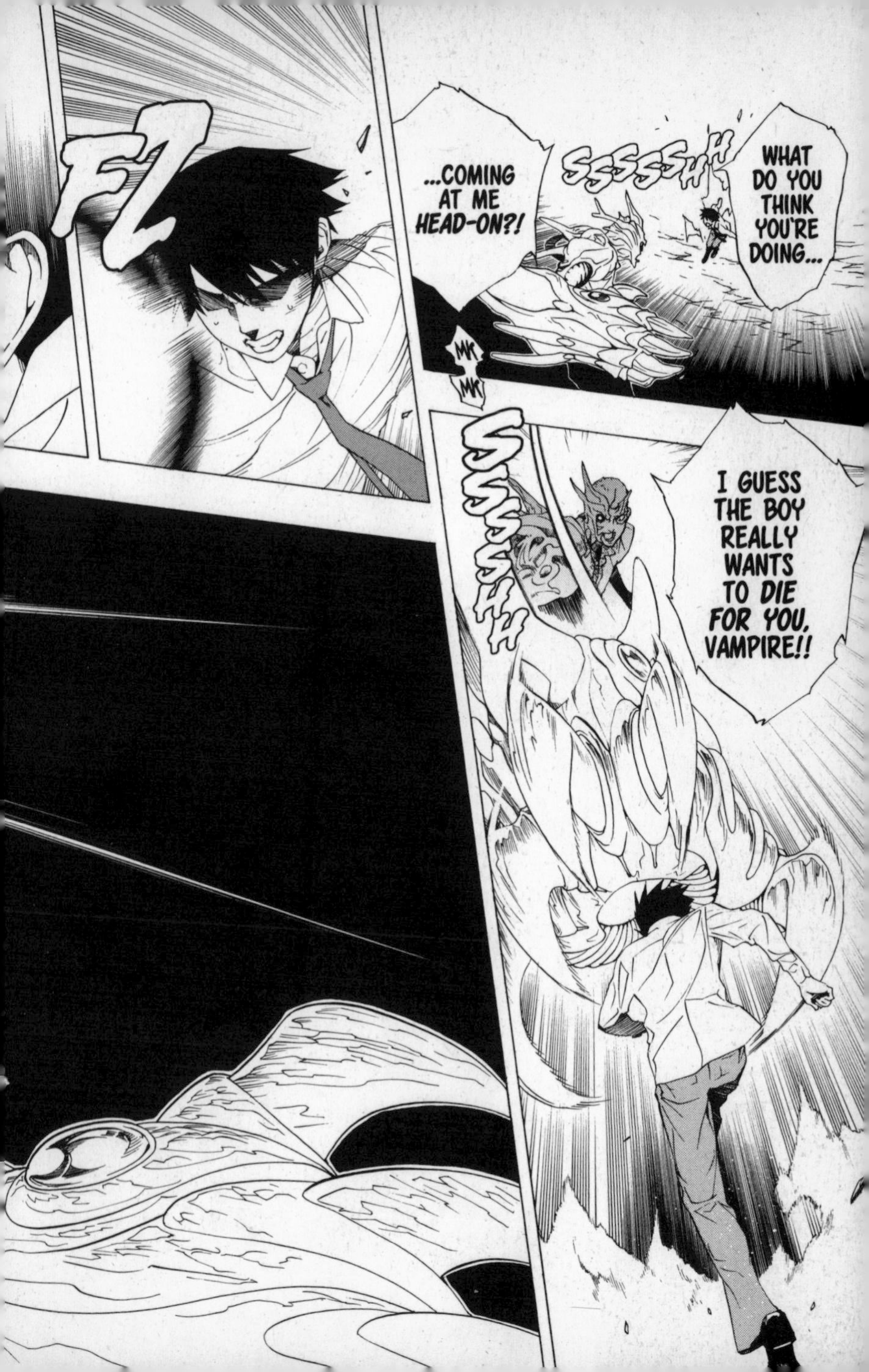
WHAT DO YOU THINK YOU'RE DOING...
SSSSSHH
...COMING AT ME HEAD-ON?!
MK MK
FZ
I GUESS THE BOY REALLY WANTS TO DIE FOR YOU, VAMPIRE!!
SSSSSHH

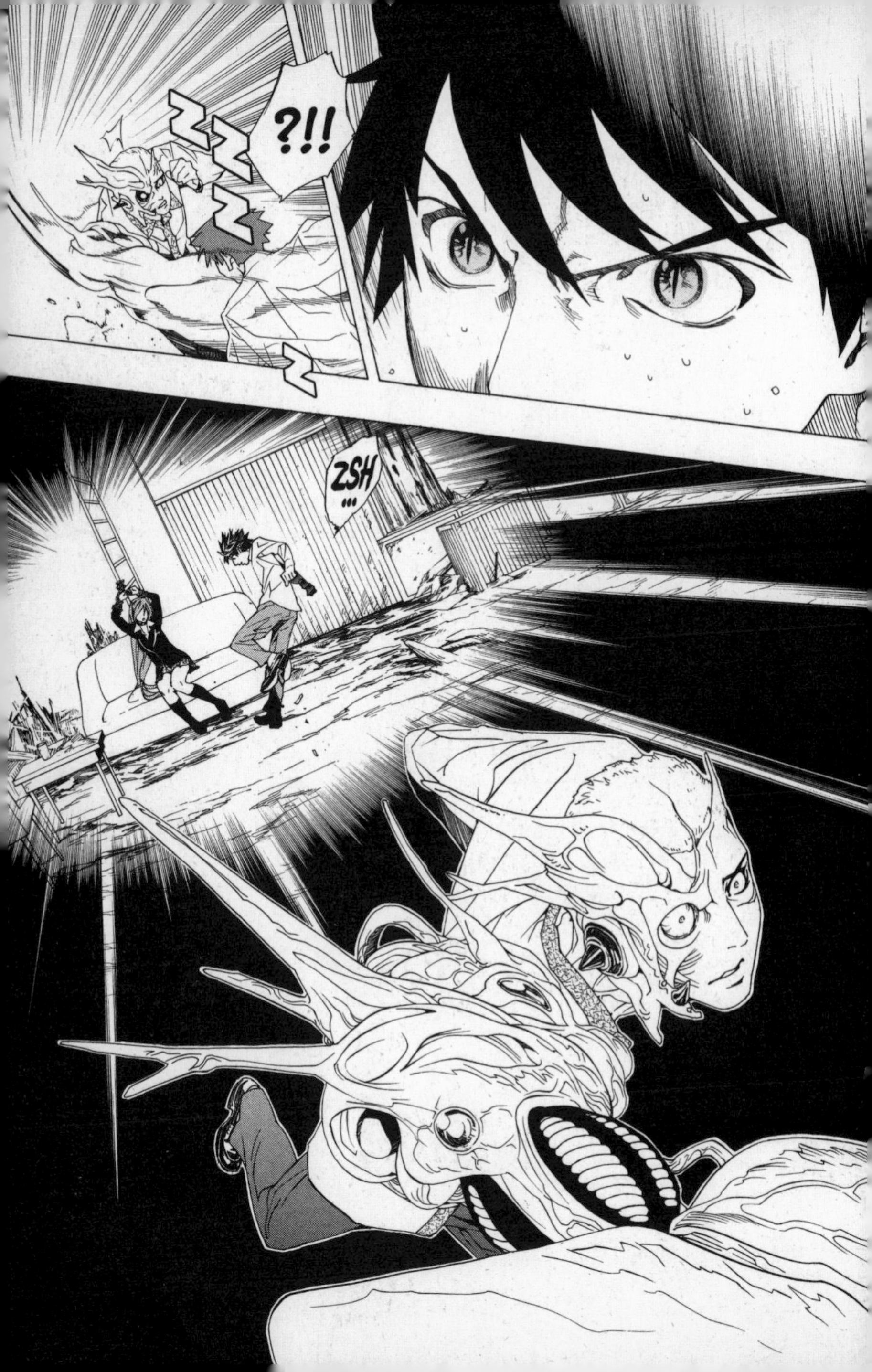
?!!
ZZZ
Z
ZSH
...

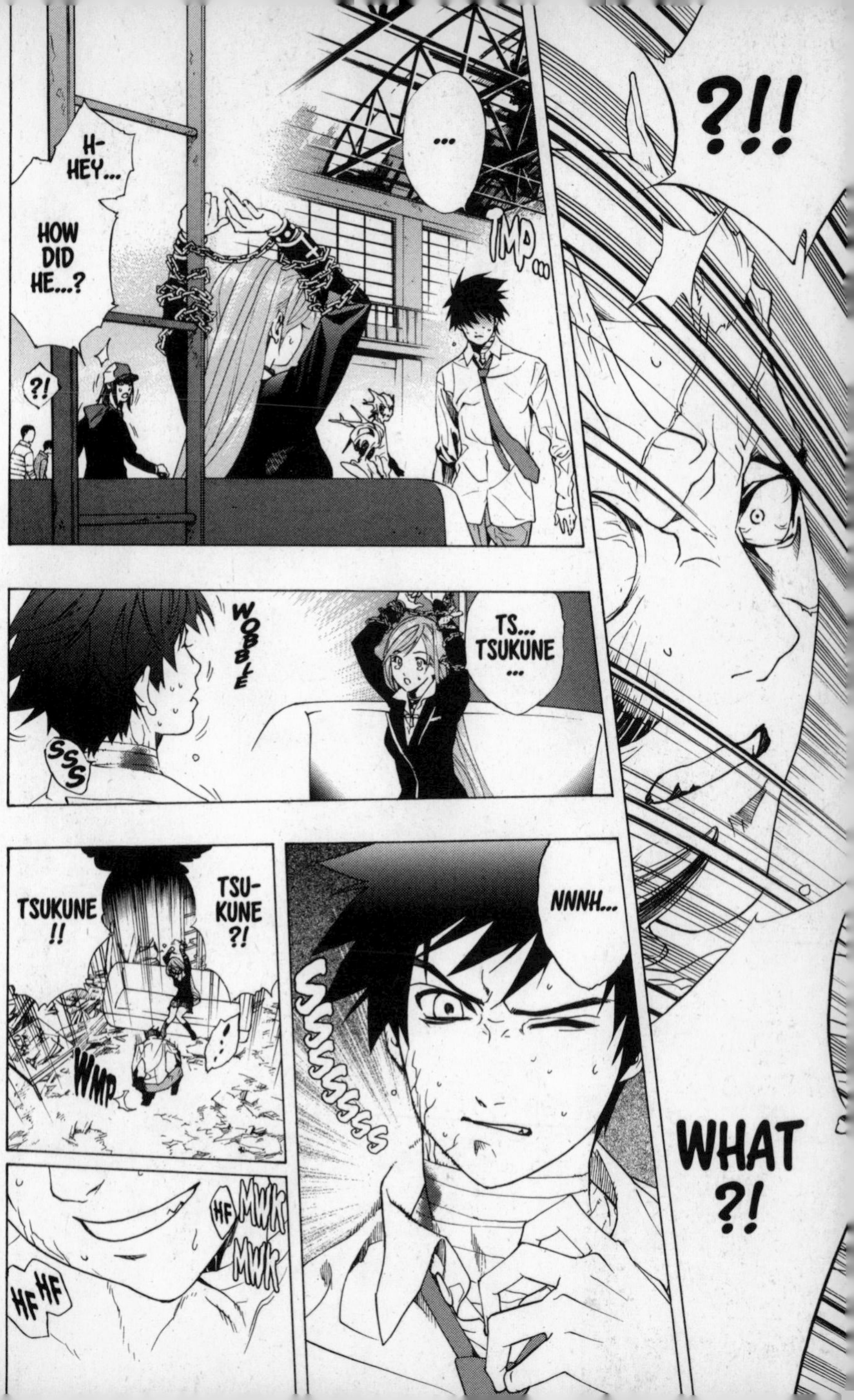
?!!
...
IMP...
H-
HEY...
HOW
DID
HE...?
?!
TS...
TSUKUNE
...
WOBBLE
SSS
WHAT
?!
NNNH...
SSSSSSS
TSU-
KUNE
?!
TSUKUNE
!!
WMP
...
MWK
MWK
HF
HF
HF

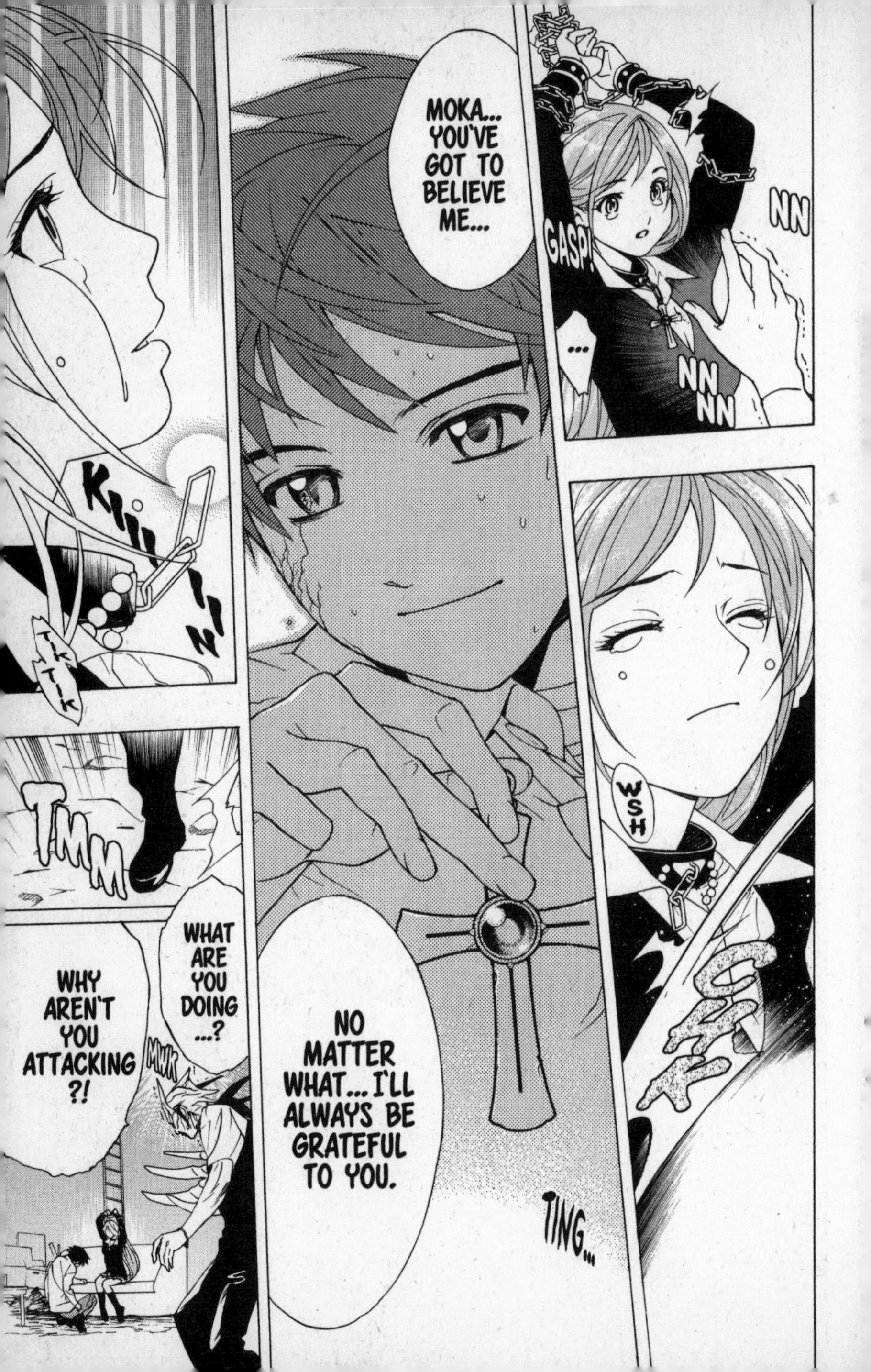
NN
NN NN
GASP!
...
MOKA... YOU'VE GOT TO BELIEVE ME...
KIIIIIIN
TIK TIK
WSH
NO MATTER WHAT... I'LL ALWAYS BE GRATEFUL TO YOU.
TING...
TMM
WHAT ARE YOU DOING ...?
WHY AREN'T YOU ATTACKING ?!
MWK

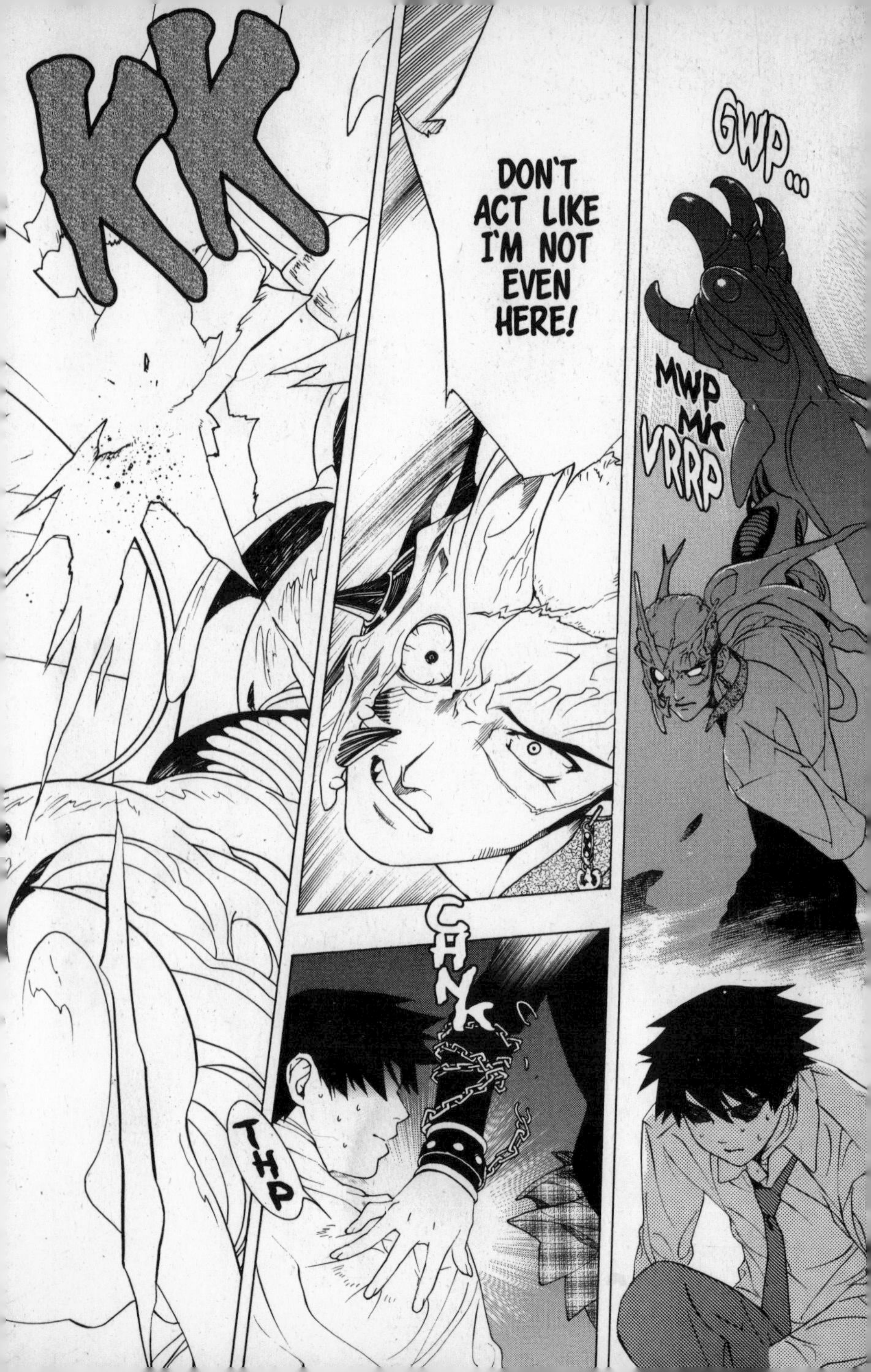
GWP...
MWP MK VRRP
DON'T ACT LIKE I'M NOT EVEN HERE!
KK
CHNK
THP

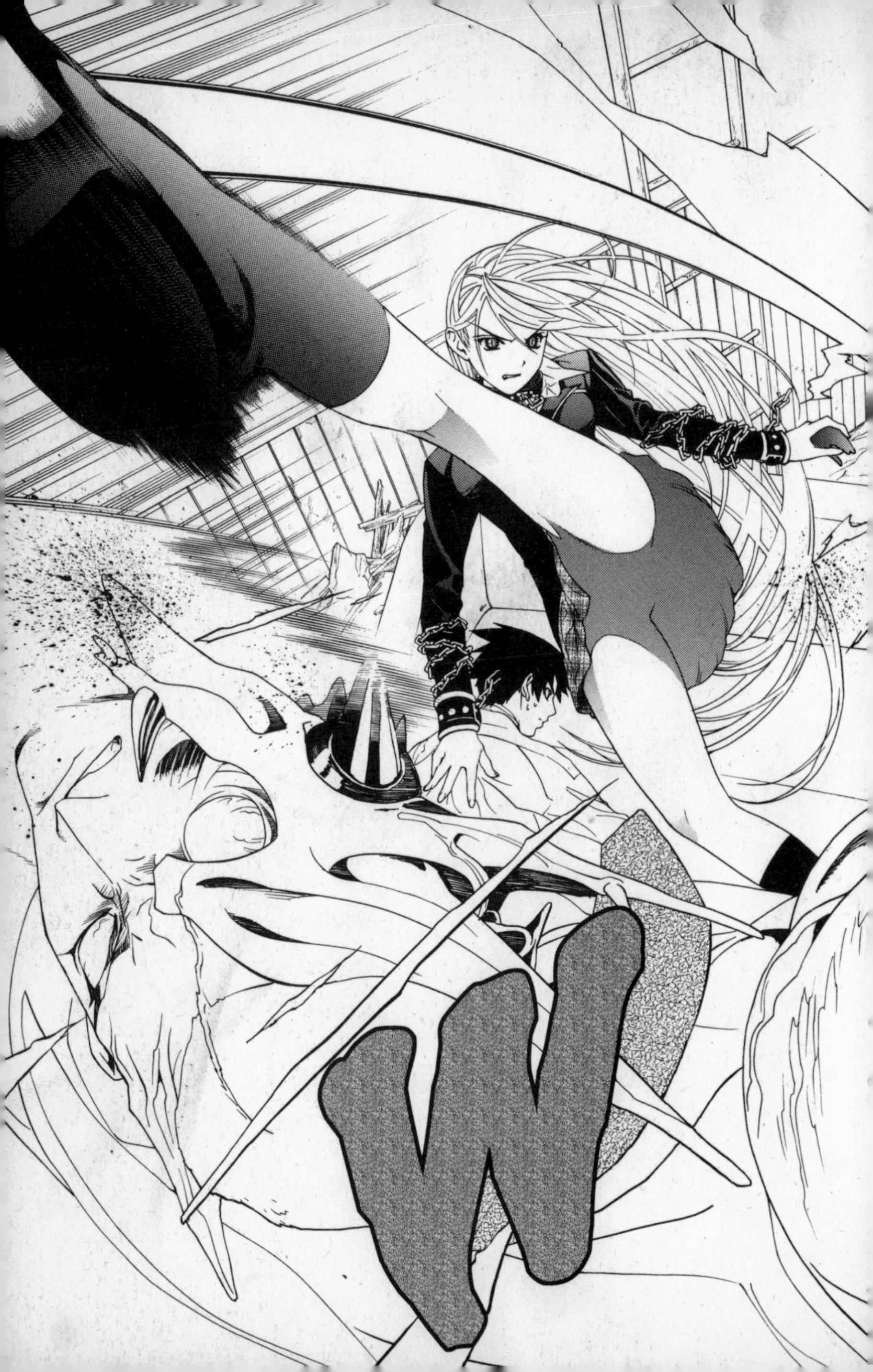
W

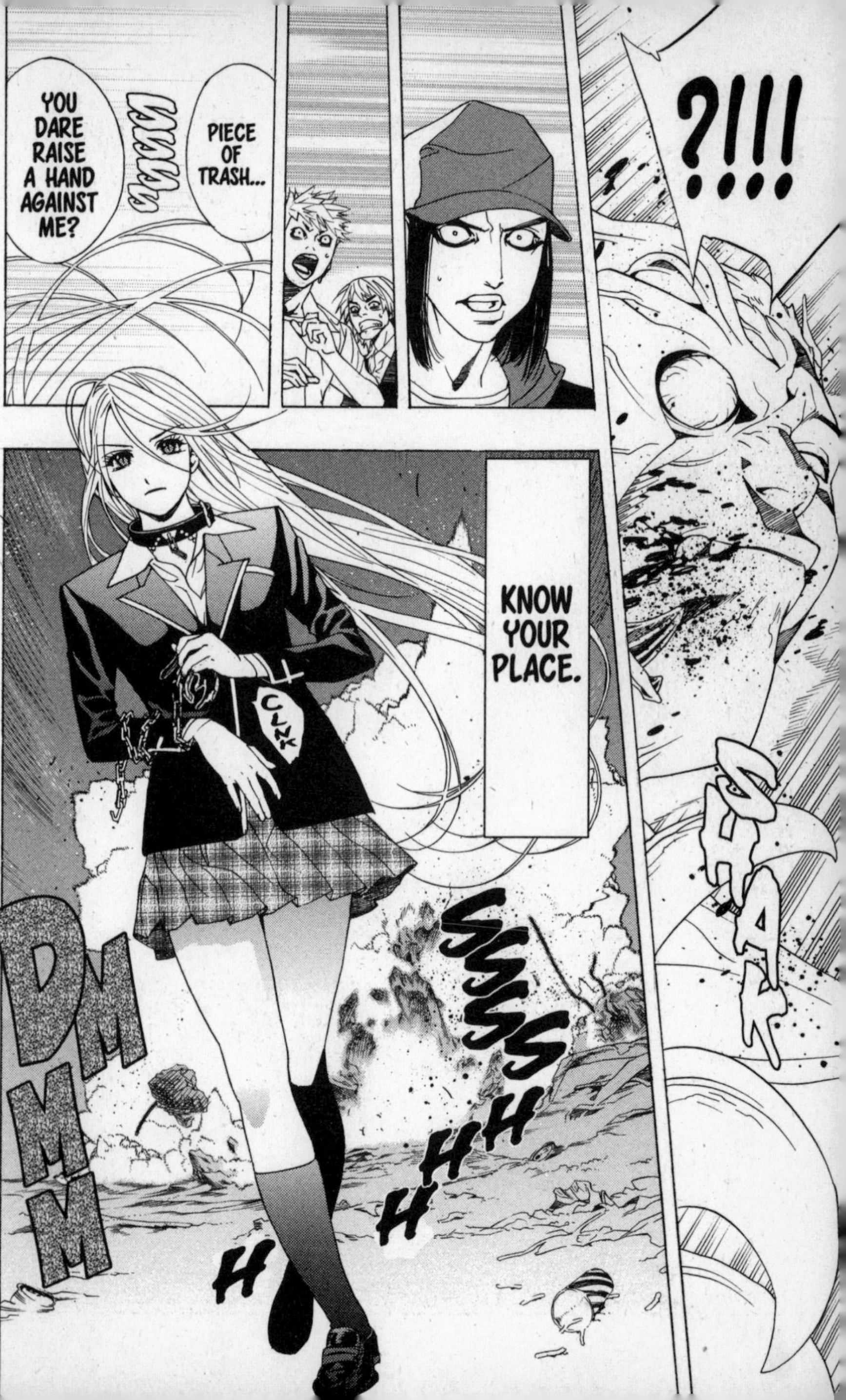
?!!!
PIECE OF TRASH...
YOU DARE RAISE A HAND AGAINST ME?
KNOW YOUR PLACE.
CLNK
SSSSHHHHH
DMMM

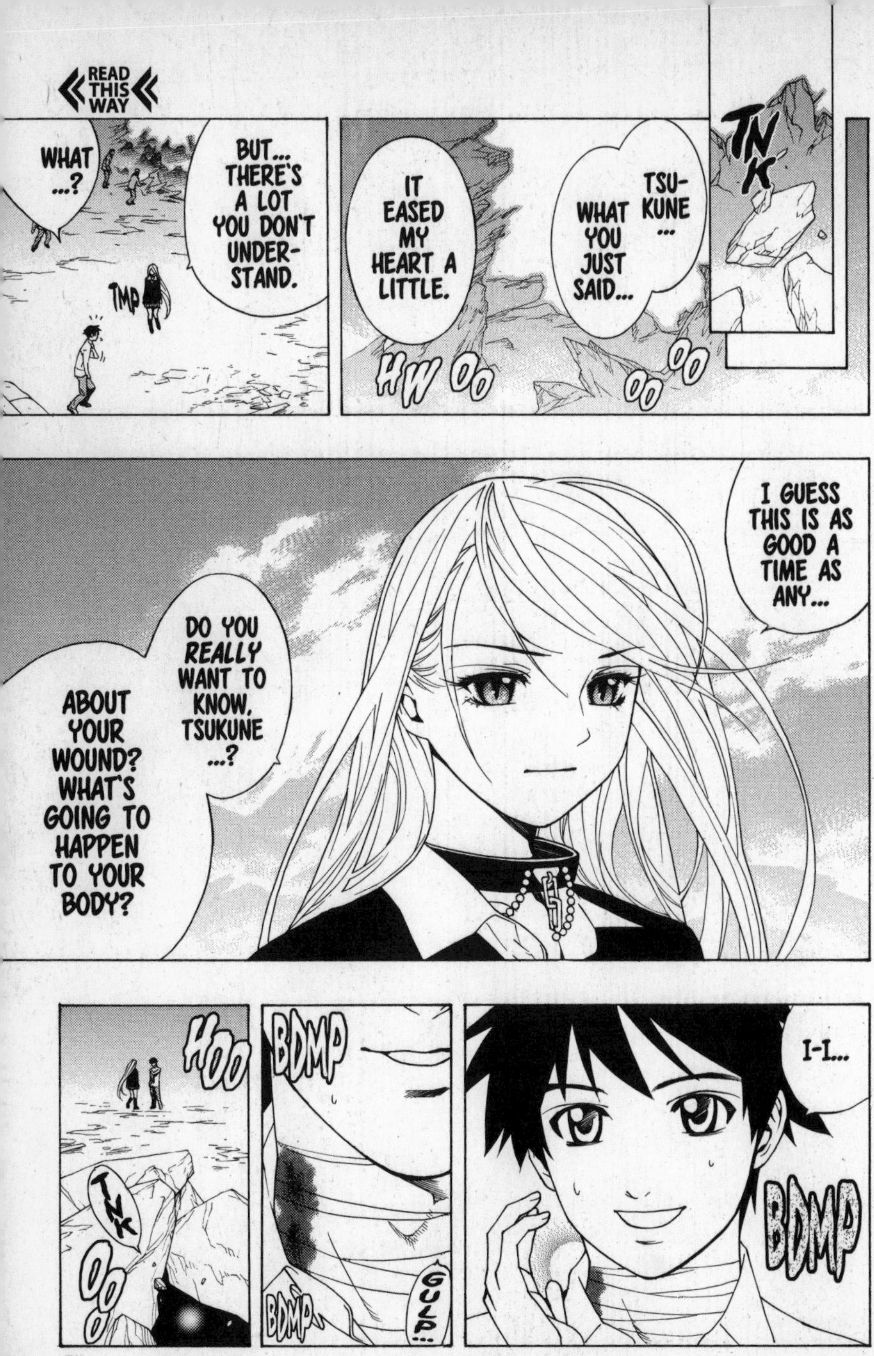
READ THIS WAY
TNK
TSUKUNE... WHAT YOU JUST SAID...
IT EASED MY HEART A LITTLE.
HWOOOOOO
BUT... THERE'S A LOT YOU DON'T UNDERSTAND.
WHAT...?
TMP
I GUESS THIS IS AS GOOD A TIME AS ANY...
DO YOU REALLY WANT TO KNOW, TSUKUNE...?
ABOUT YOUR WOUND? WHAT'S GOING TO HAPPEN TO YOUR BODY?
I-I...
BDMP
BDMP
GULP...
BDMP
HOO
TNK
OOO

22: A Kiss

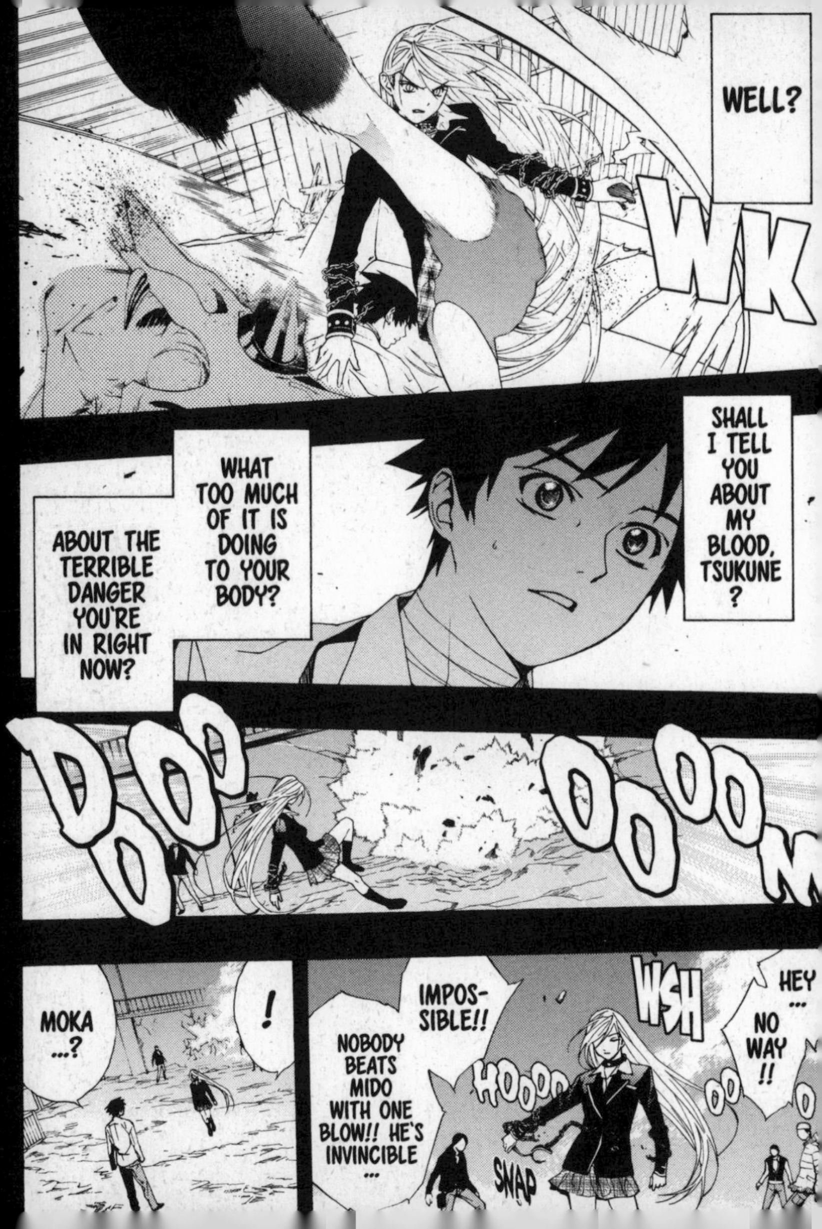
WELL?
WK
SHALL I TELL YOU ABOUT MY BLOOD, TSUKUNE?
WHAT TOO MUCH OF IT IS DOING TO YOUR BODY?
ABOUT THE TERRIBLE DANGER YOU'RE IN RIGHT NOW?
DOOOOOOOOOM
HEY... NO WAY!!
WSH
IMPOSSIBLE!!
NOBODY BEATS MIDO WITH ONE BLOW!! HE'S INVINCIBLE...
HOOOOOOO
SNAP
!
MOKA...?

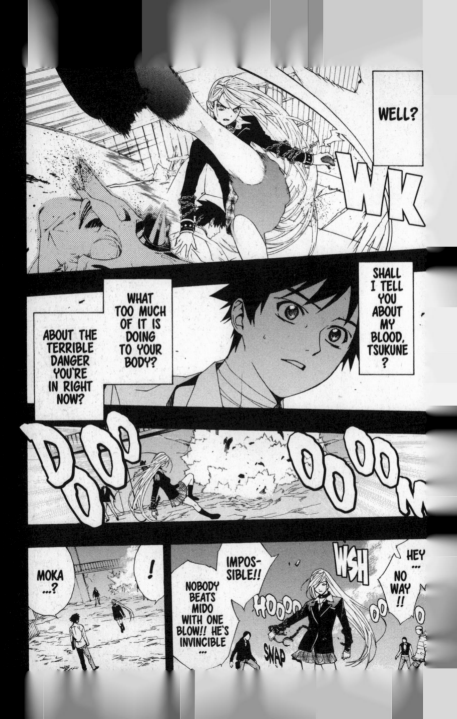

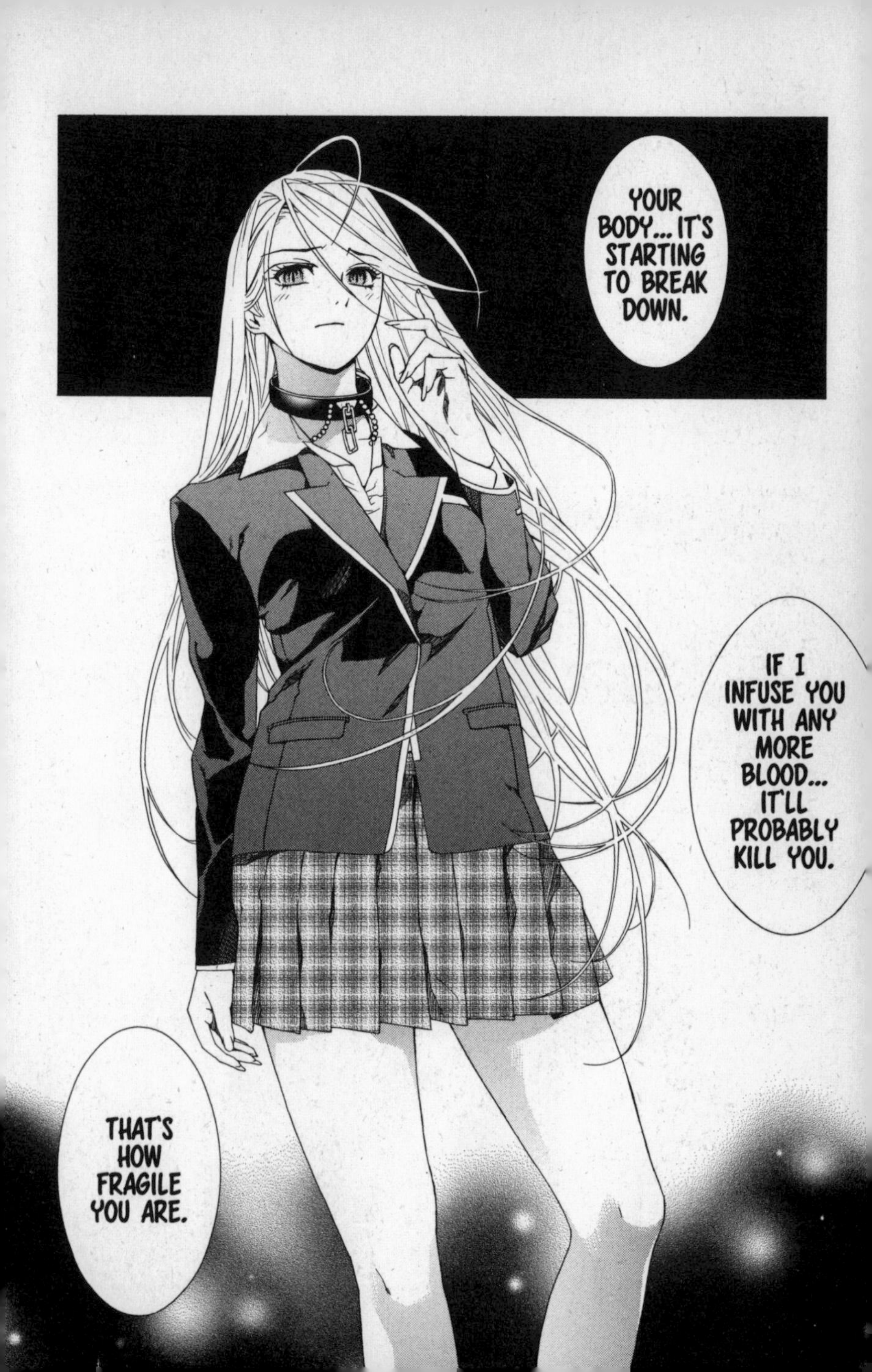
YOUR BODY... IT'S STARTING TO BREAK DOWN.
IF I INFUSE YOU WITH ANY MORE BLOOD... IT'LL PROBABLY KILL YOU.
THAT'S HOW FRAGILE YOU ARE.

READ THIS WAY

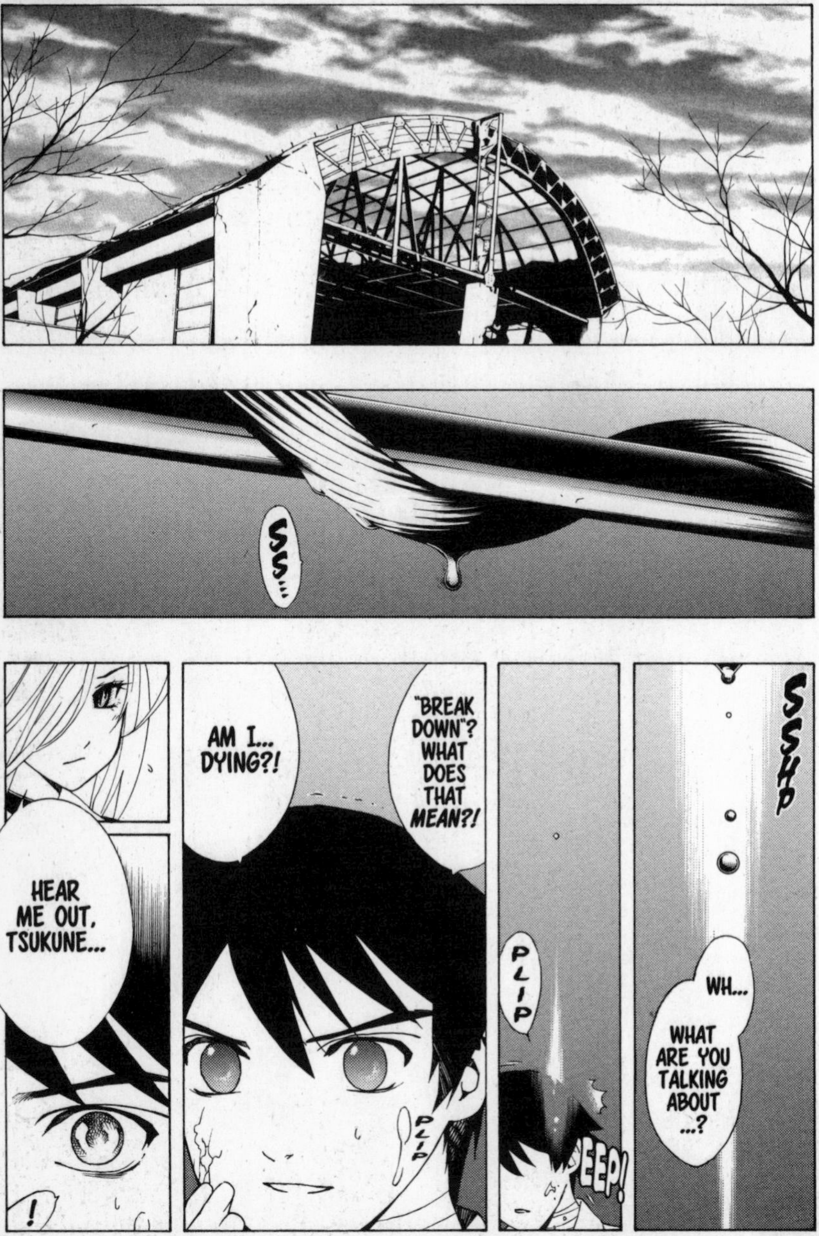
SS...
SSHP
WH...
WHAT ARE YOU TALKING ABOUT ...?
PLIP
EEP!
"BREAK DOWN"? WHAT DOES THAT MEAN?!
AM I... DYING?!
PLIP
HEAR ME OUT, TSUKUNE...
!

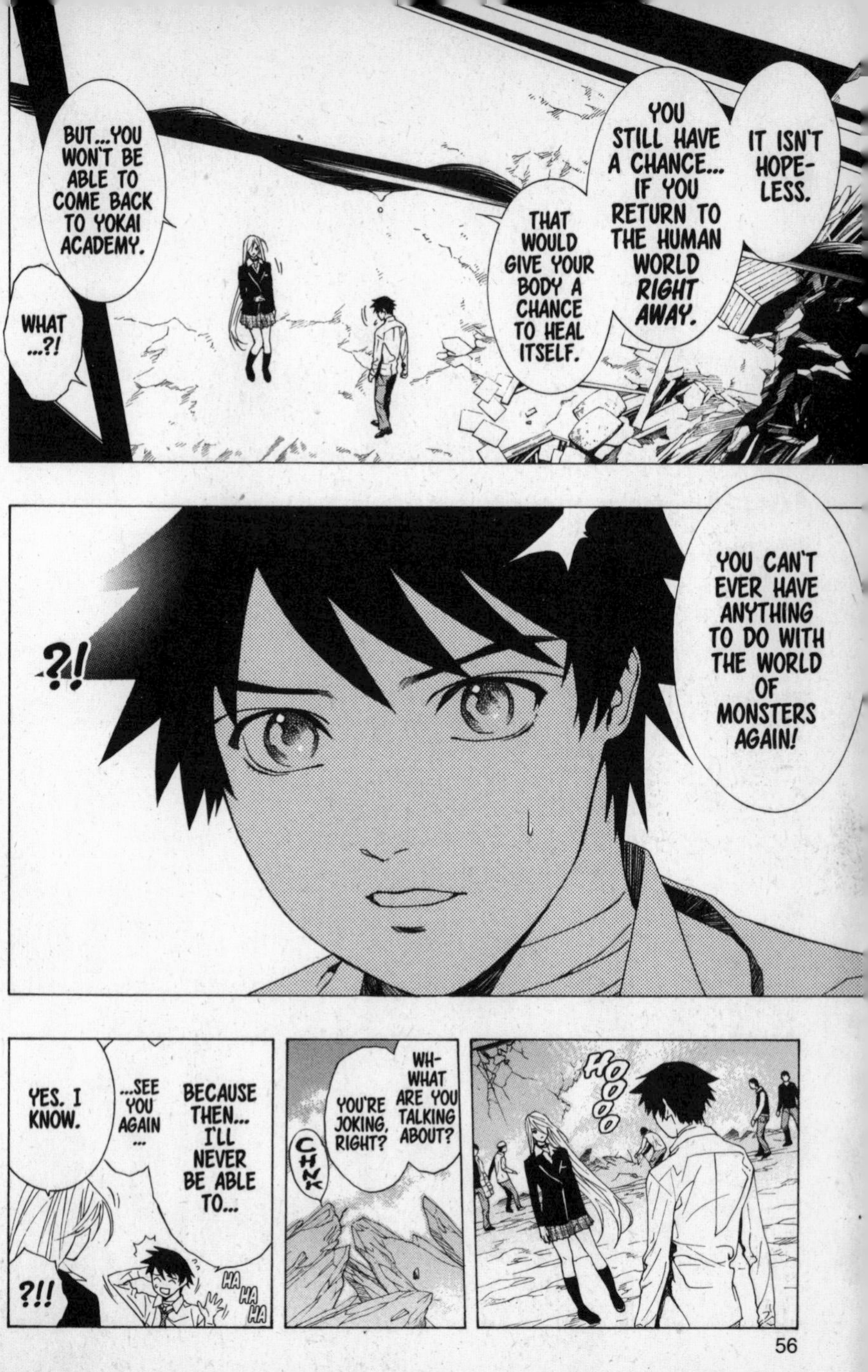
IT ISN'T HOPE-LESS.
YOU STILL HAVE A CHANCE... IF YOU RETURN TO THE HUMAN WORLD RIGHT AWAY.
THAT WOULD GIVE YOUR BODY A CHANCE TO HEAL ITSELF.
BUT...YOU WON'T BE ABLE TO COME BACK TO YOKAI ACADEMY.
WHAT ...?!
YOU CAN'T EVER HAVE ANYTHING TO DO WITH THE WORLD OF MONSTERS AGAIN!
?!
HOOOO
WH-WHAT ARE YOU TALKING ABOUT?
YOU'RE JOKING, RIGHT?
CHNK
BECAUSE THEN... I'LL NEVER BE ABLE TO...
...SEE YOU AGAIN ...
YES. I KNOW.
?!!
HA HA HA

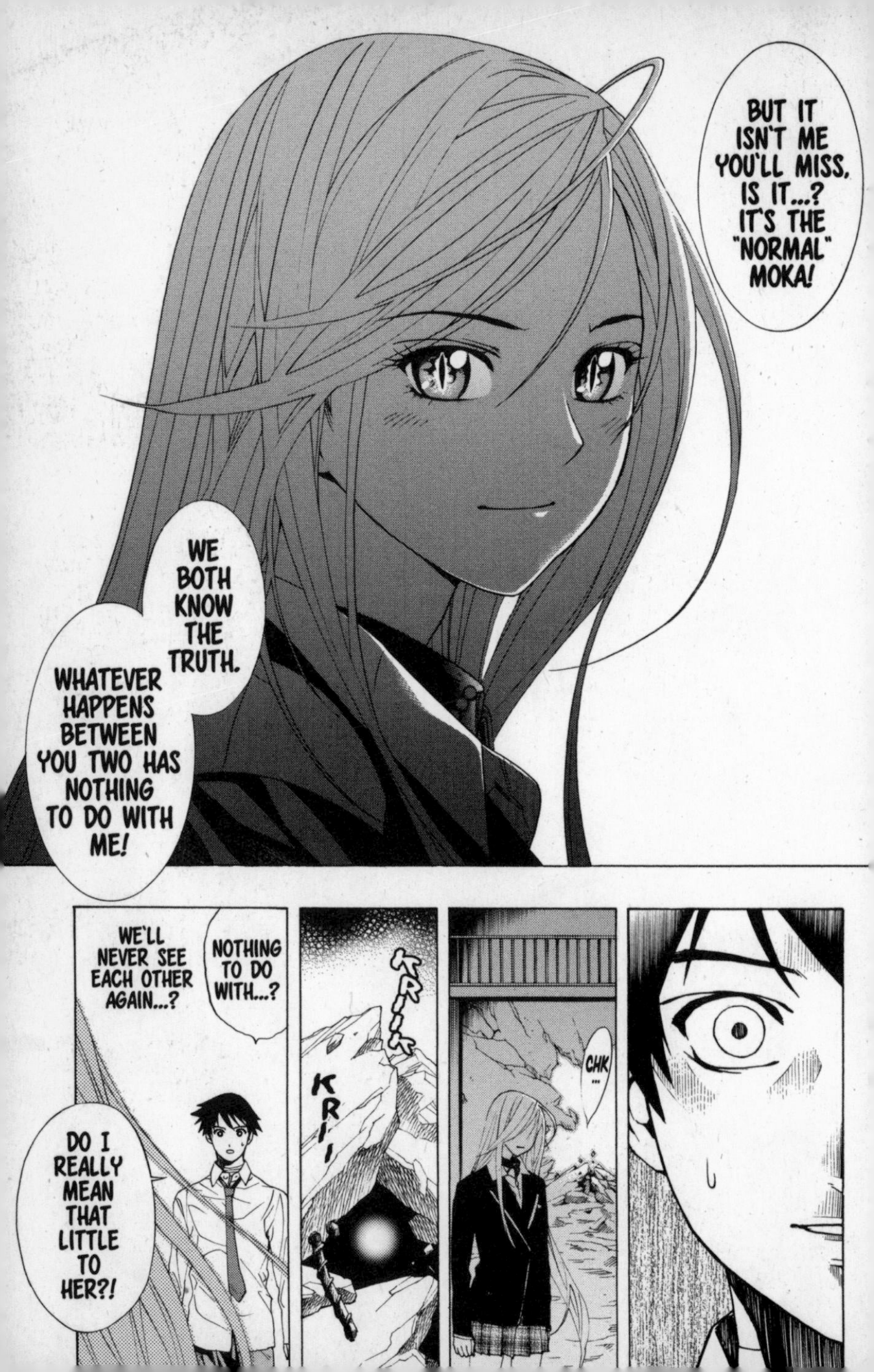
BUT IT ISN'T ME YOU'LL MISS, IS IT...? IT'S THE "NORMAL" MOKA!
WE BOTH KNOW THE TRUTH.
WHATEVER HAPPENS BETWEEN YOU TWO HAS NOTHING TO DO WITH ME!
CHK...
KRIIK
KRIII
NOTHING TO DO WITH...?
WE'LL NEVER SEE EACH OTHER AGAIN...?
DO I REALLY MEAN THAT LITTLE TO HER?!

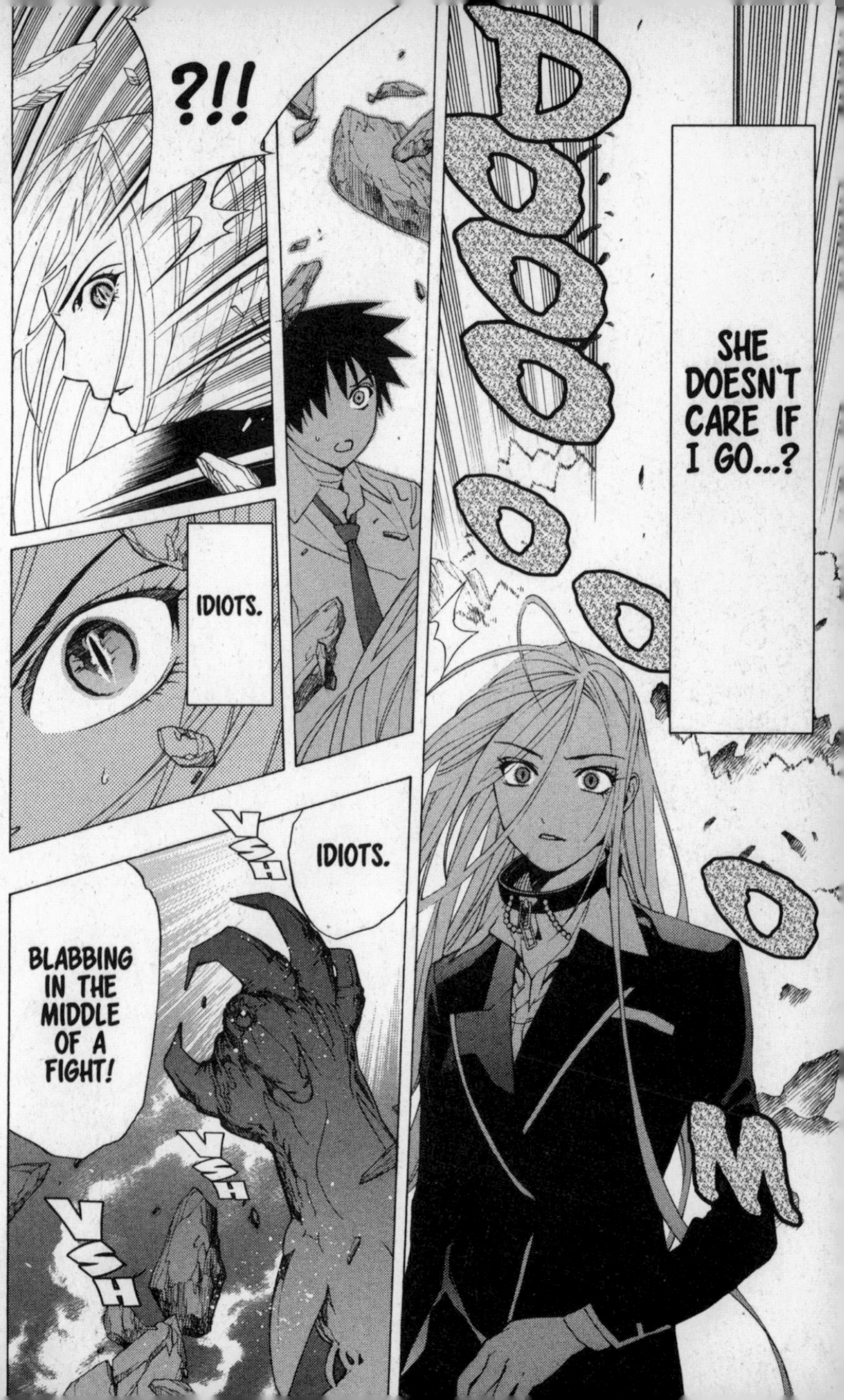
SHE DOESN'T CARE IF I GO...?
DOOOOOOOOM
?!!
IDIOTS.
IDIOTS.
BLABBING IN THE MIDDLE OF A FIGHT!
VSH
VSH
VSH

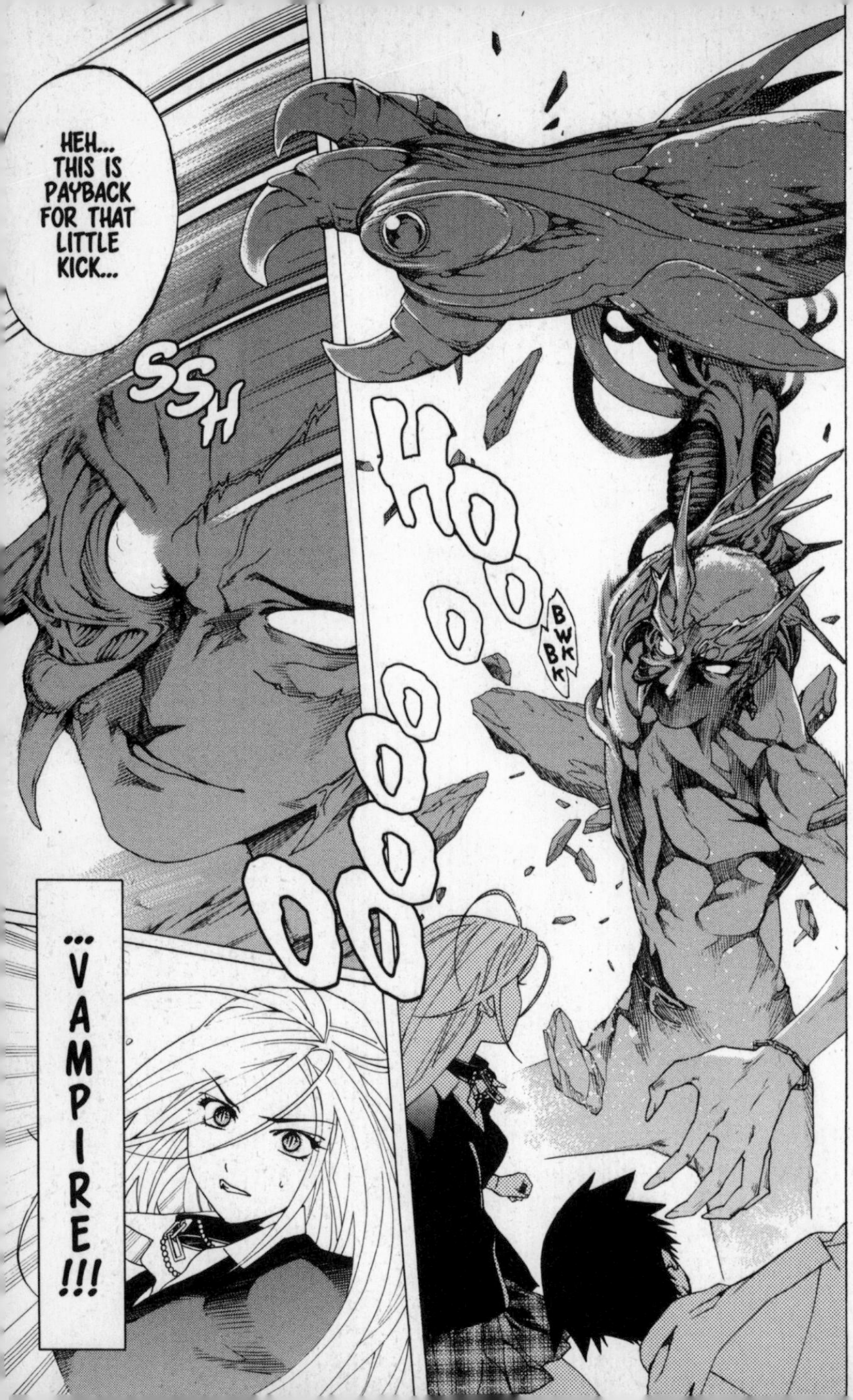
HEH... THIS IS PAYBACK FOR THAT LITTLE KICK...
SSH
HOOOOOOOOOO
BWK BKK
...VAMPIRE!!!

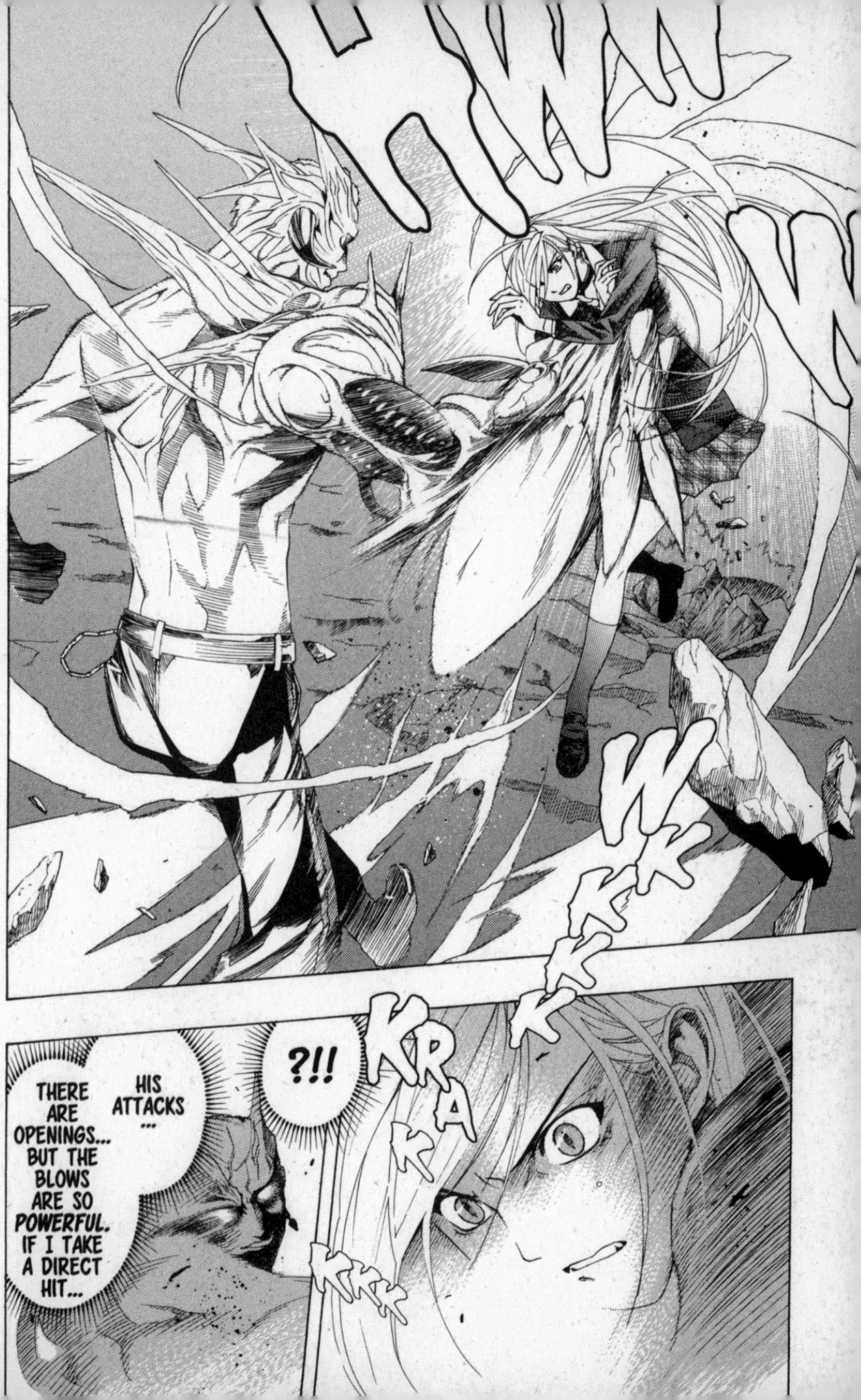
WHAM
WKKK
KRAKK
?!!
HIS ATTACKS...
THERE ARE OPENINGS... BUT THE BLOWS ARE SO POWERFUL. IF I TAKE A DIRECT HIT...
KKK

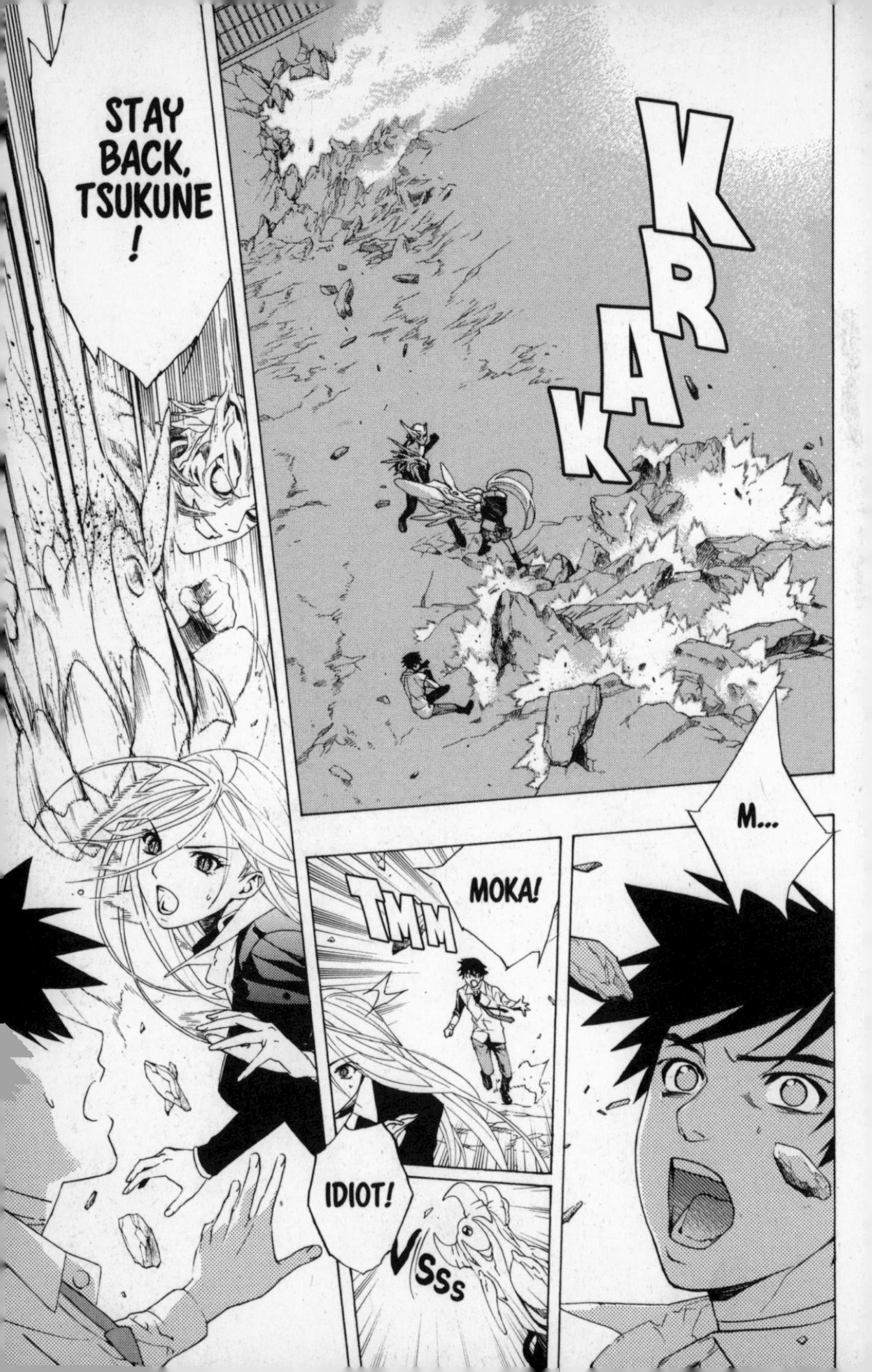
KRAK
STAY BACK, TSUKUNE!
M...
MOKA!
TMM
IDIOT!
VSss

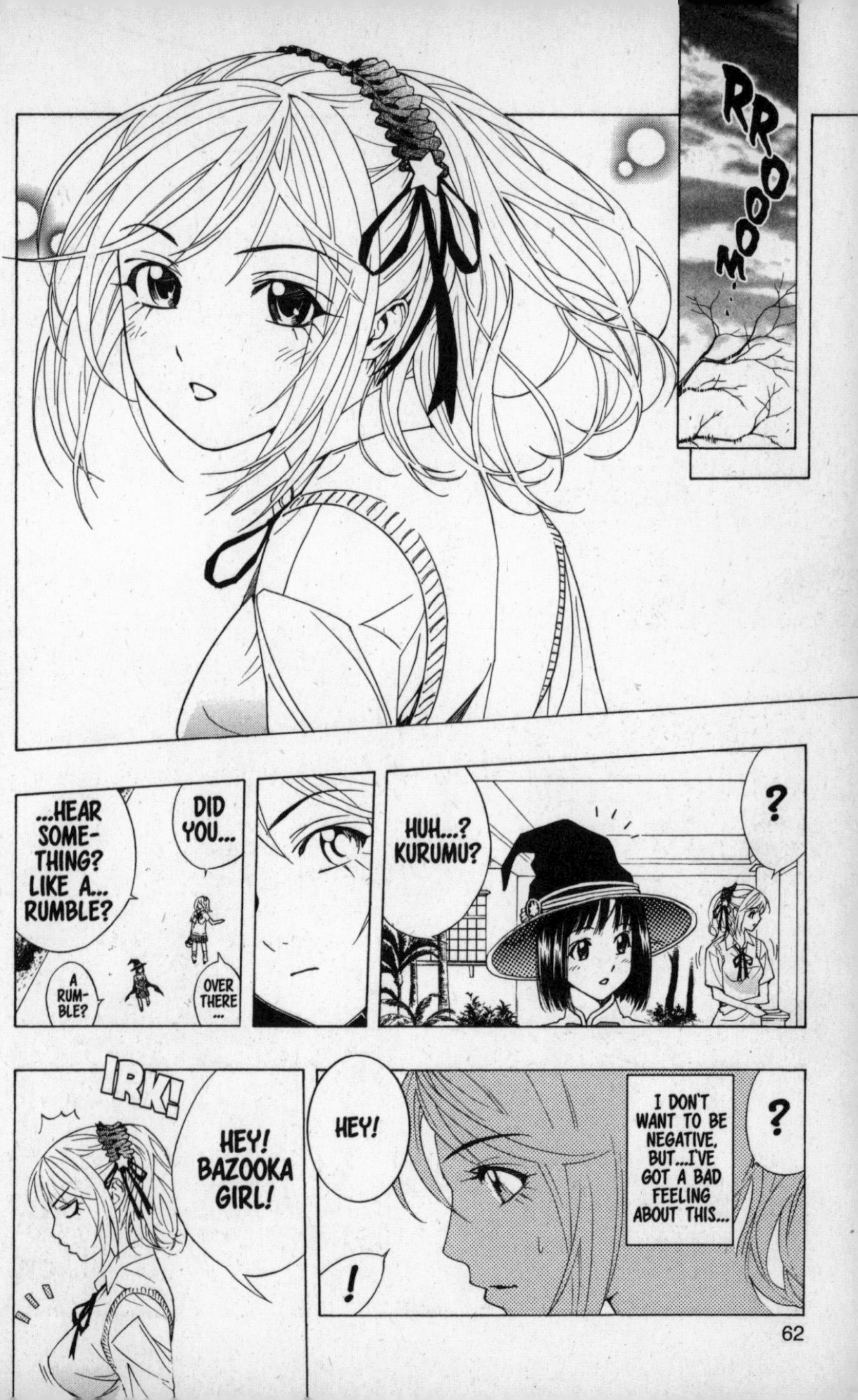
RROOOOM...
?
HUH...? KURUMU?
DID YOU...
...HEAR SOMETHING? LIKE A... RUMBLE?
OVER THERE...
A RUMBLE?
?
I DON'T WANT TO BE NEGATIVE, BUT...I'VE GOT A BAD FEELING ABOUT THIS...
HEY!
!
HEY! BAZOOKA GIRL!
IRK!

READ THIS WAY

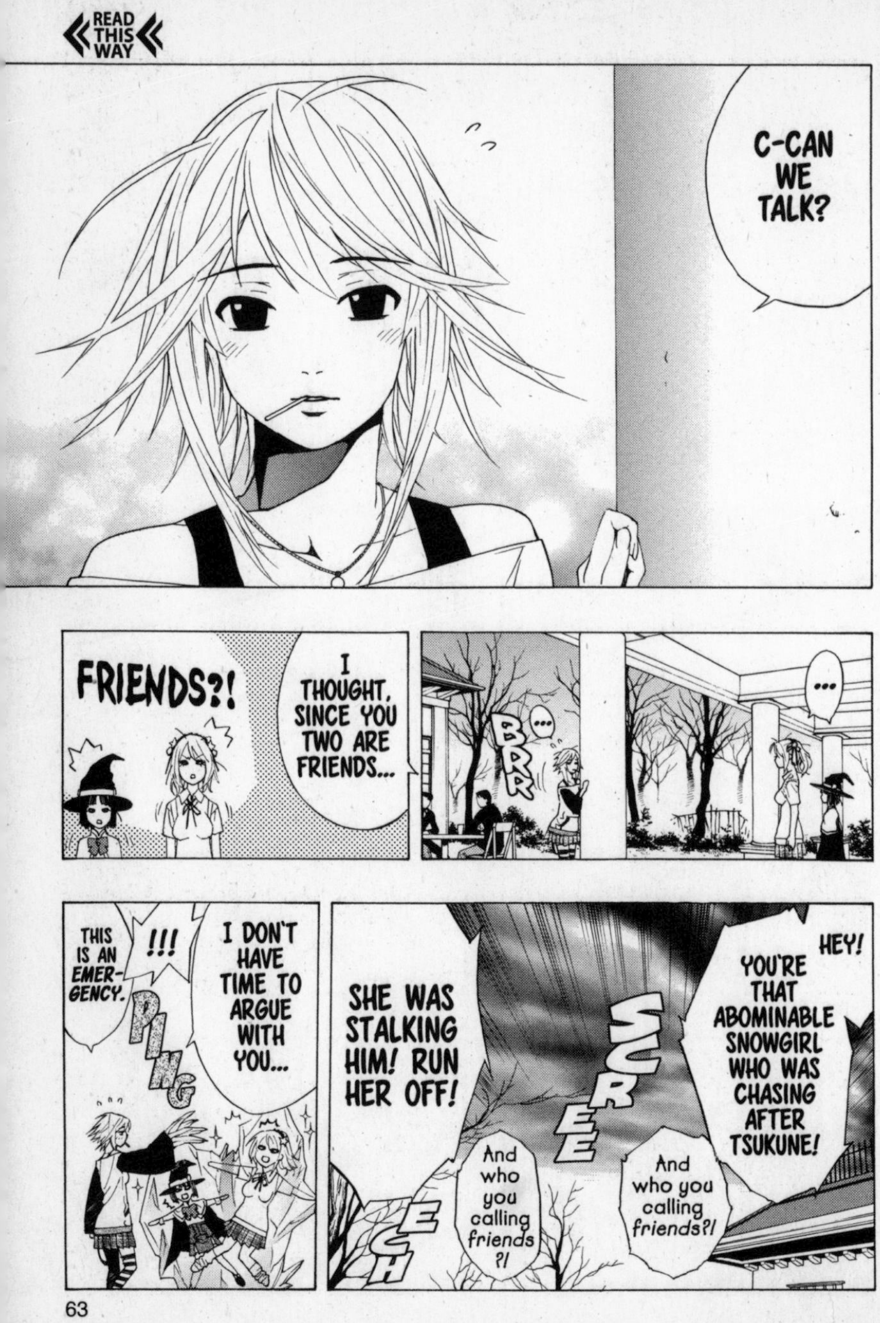

C-CAN WE TALK?
...
...
BRR
I THOUGHT, SINCE YOU TWO ARE FRIENDS...
FRIENDS?!
HEY! YOU'RE THAT ABOMINABLE SNOWGIRL WHO WAS CHASING AFTER TSUKUNE!
SCREE
And who you calling friends?!
And who you calling friends ?!
SHE WAS STALKING HIM! RUN HER OFF!
ECH
I DON'T HAVE TIME TO ARGUE WITH YOU...
!!!
THIS IS AN EMER-GENCY.
PING

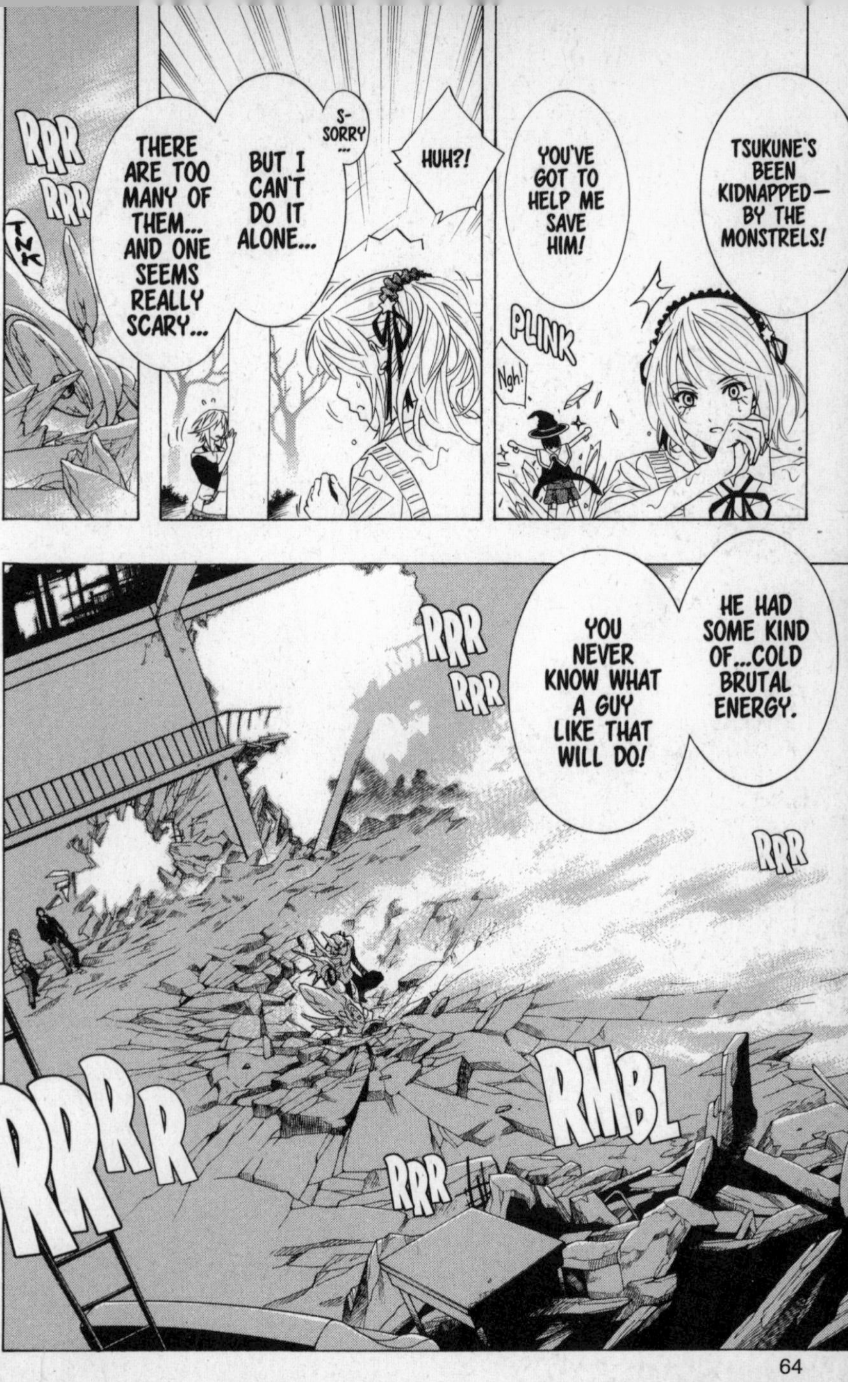
TSUKUNE'S BEEN KIDNAPPED—BY THE MONSTRELS!
YOU'VE GOT TO HELP ME SAVE HIM!
PLINK
Ngh!
HUH?!
S-SORRY...
BUT I CAN'T DO IT ALONE...
THERE ARE TOO MANY OF THEM... AND ONE SEEMS REALLY SCARY...
RRR
RRR
TNK
HE HAD SOME KIND OF...COLD BRUTAL ENERGY.
YOU NEVER KNOW WHAT A GUY LIKE THAT WILL DO!
RRR
RRR
RRR
RMBL
RRR
RRRR

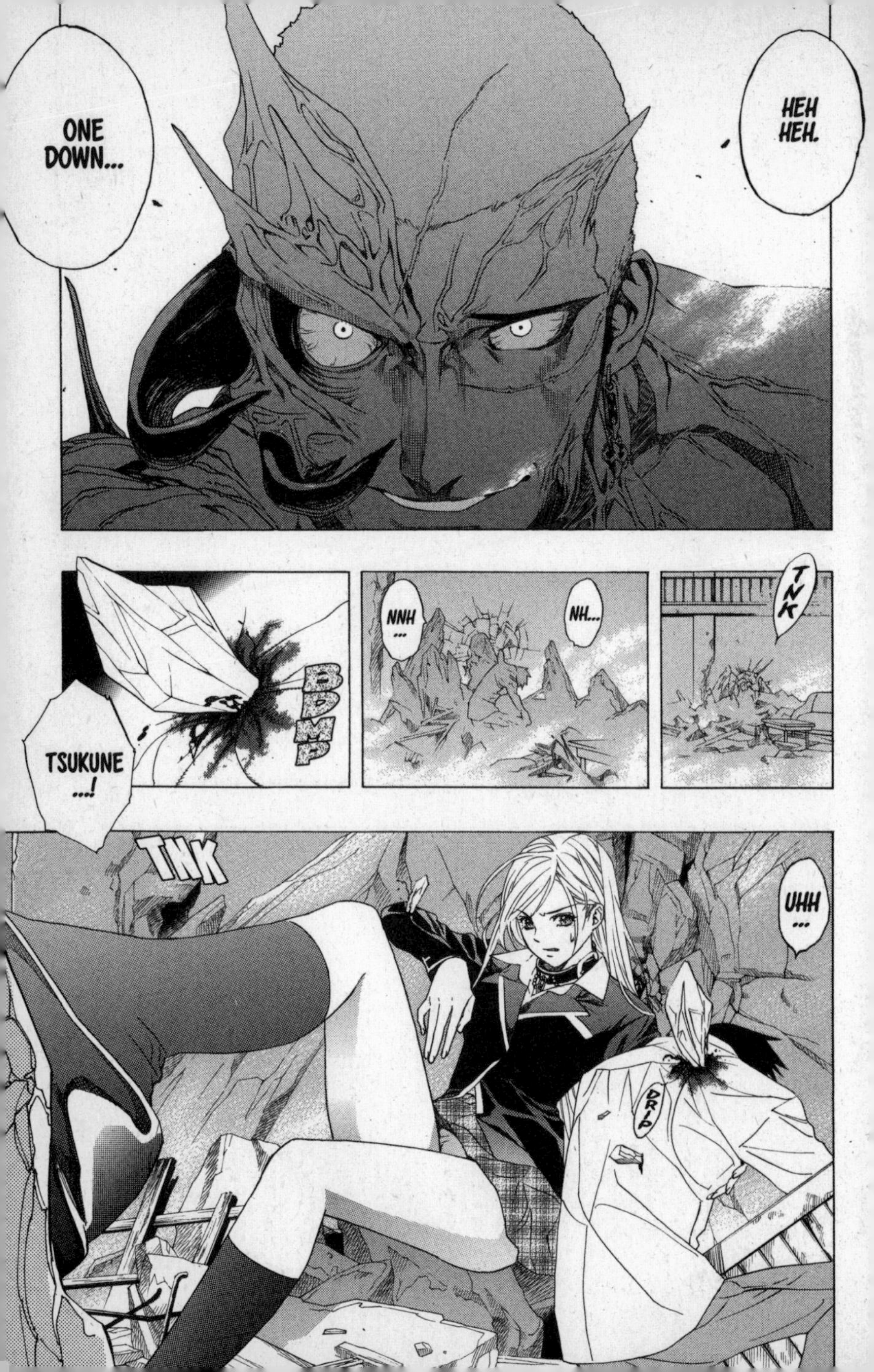
HEH HEH.
ONE DOWN...
TNK
NH...
NNH...
BDMP
TSUKUNE...!
UHH...
TNK
DRIP

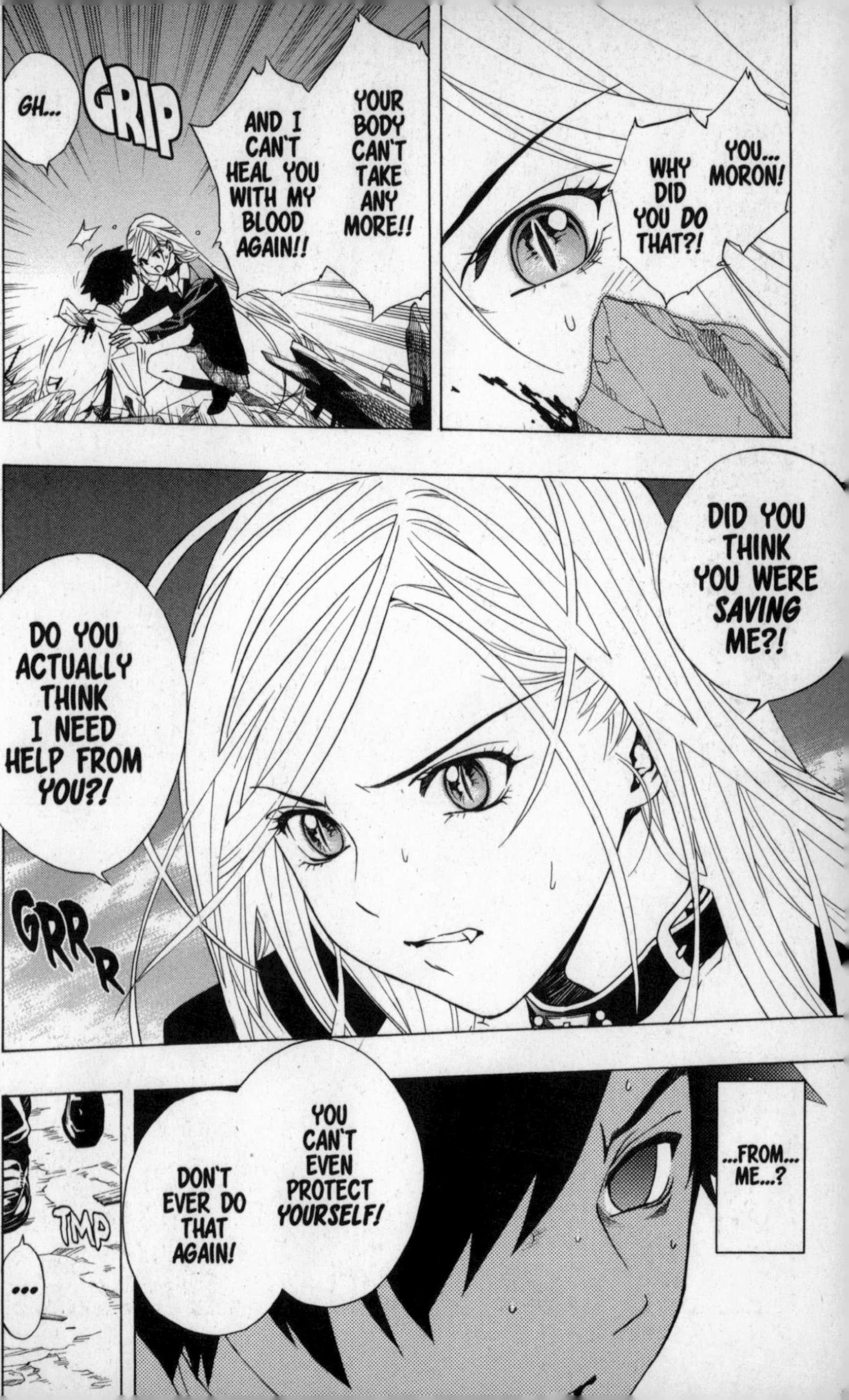
YOU... MORON!
WHY DID YOU DO THAT?!
YOUR BODY CAN'T TAKE ANY MORE!!
AND I CAN'T HEAL YOU WITH MY BLOOD AGAIN!!
GRIP
GH...
DID YOU THINK YOU WERE SAVING ME?!
DO YOU ACTUALLY THINK I NEED HELP FROM YOU?!
GRRR
...FROM... ME...?
YOU CAN'T EVEN PROTECT YOURSELF!
DON'T EVER DO THAT AGAIN!
TMP
...

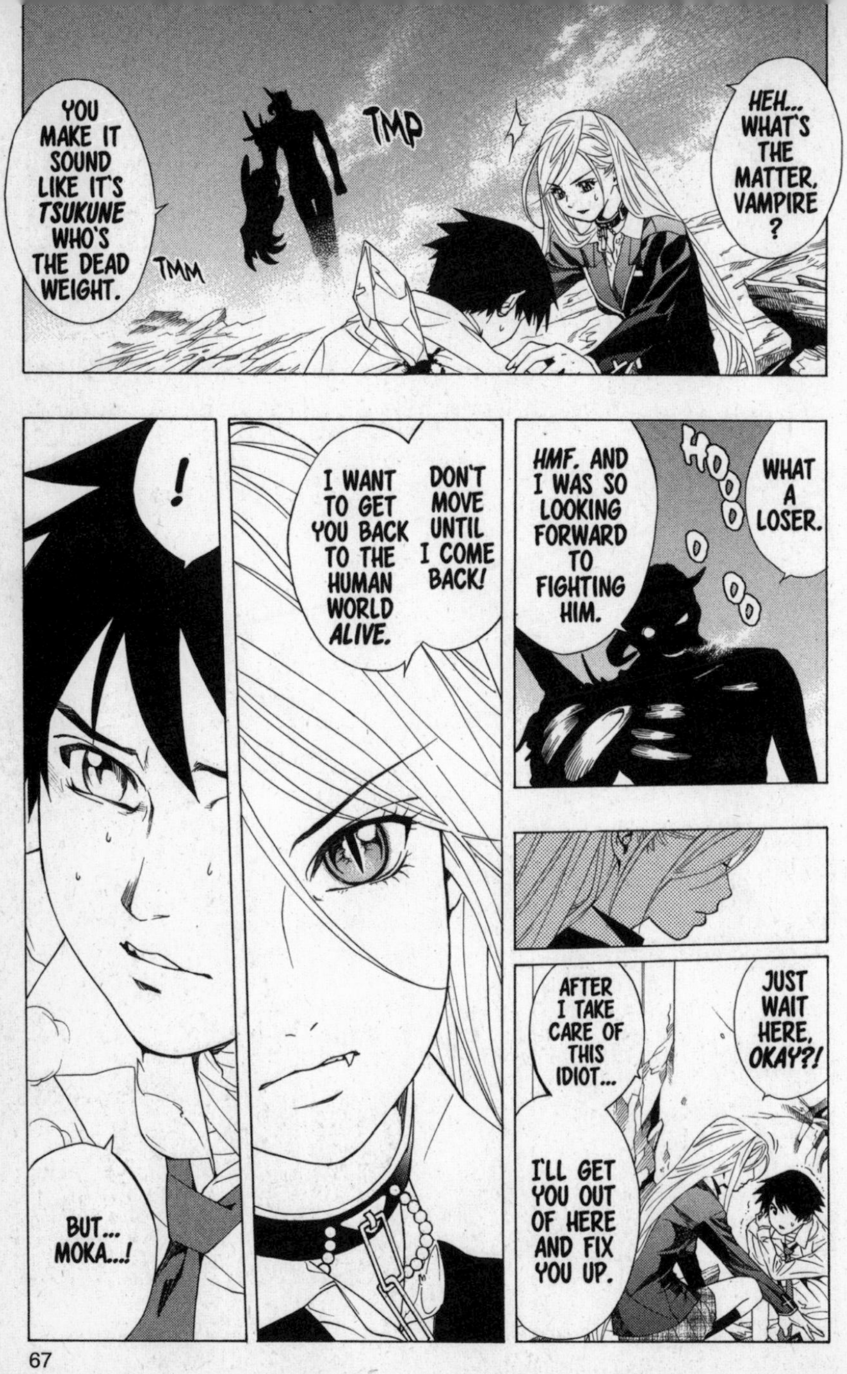
HEH... WHAT'S THE MATTER, VAMPIRE?
TMP
TMM
YOU MAKE IT SOUND LIKE IT'S *TSUKUNE* WHO'S THE DEAD WEIGHT.
WHAT A LOSER.
HOOOOOO
HMF. AND I WAS SO LOOKING FORWARD TO FIGHTING HIM.
JUST WAIT HERE, *OKAY?!*
AFTER I TAKE CARE OF THIS IDIOT...
I'LL GET YOU OUT OF HERE AND FIX YOU UP.
DON'T MOVE UNTIL I COME BACK!
I WANT TO GET YOU BACK TO THE HUMAN WORLD *ALIVE.*
!
BUT... MOKA...!

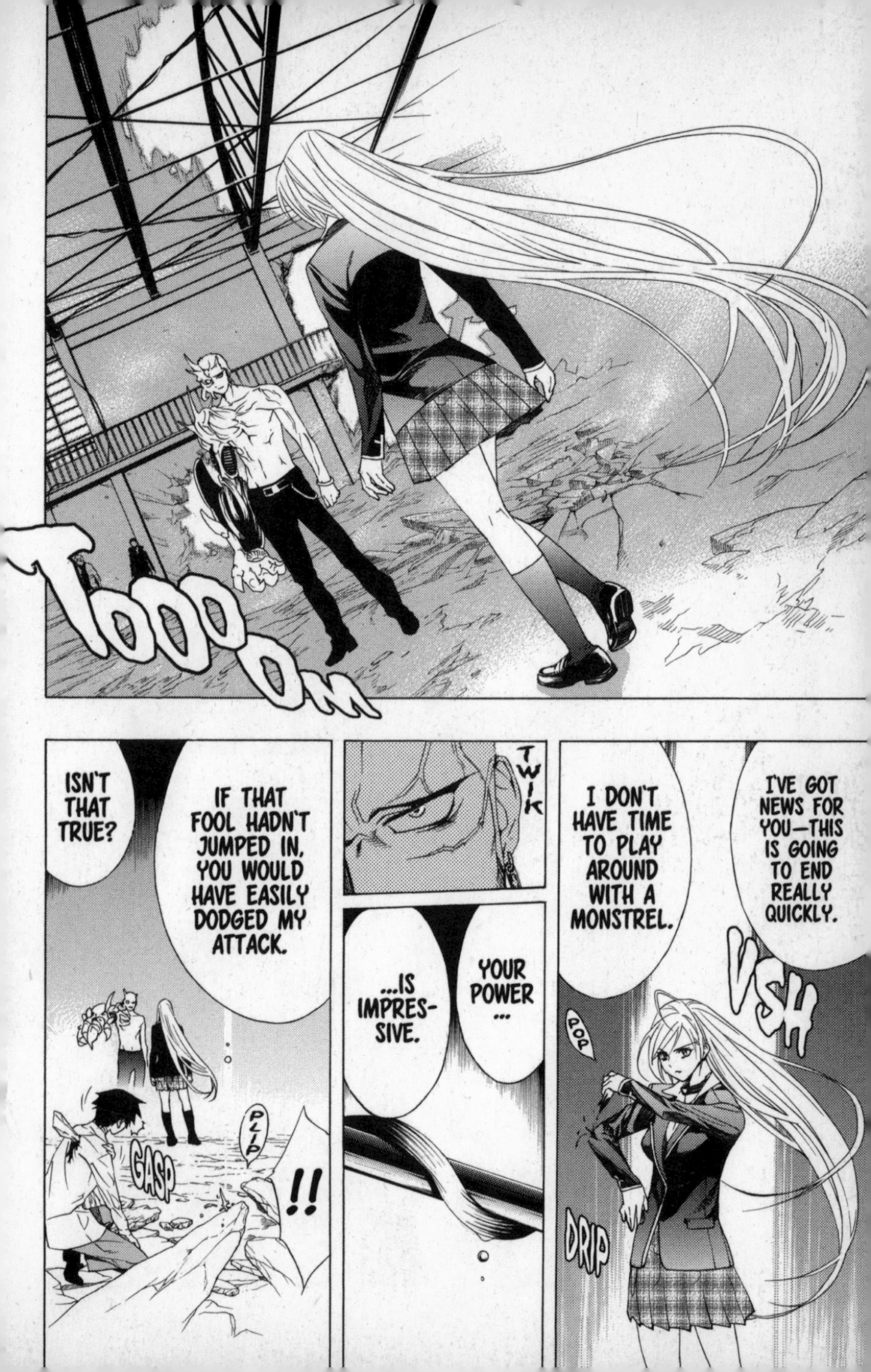
TOOOOM
I'VE GOT NEWS FOR YOU—THIS IS GOING TO END REALLY QUICKLY.
I DON'T HAVE TIME TO PLAY AROUND WITH A MONSTREL.
VSH
POP
DRIP
TWIK
YOUR POWER...
...IS IMPRESSIVE.
IF THAT FOOL HADN'T JUMPED IN, YOU WOULD HAVE EASILY DODGED MY ATTACK.
ISN'T THAT TRUE?
PLIP
GASP
!!

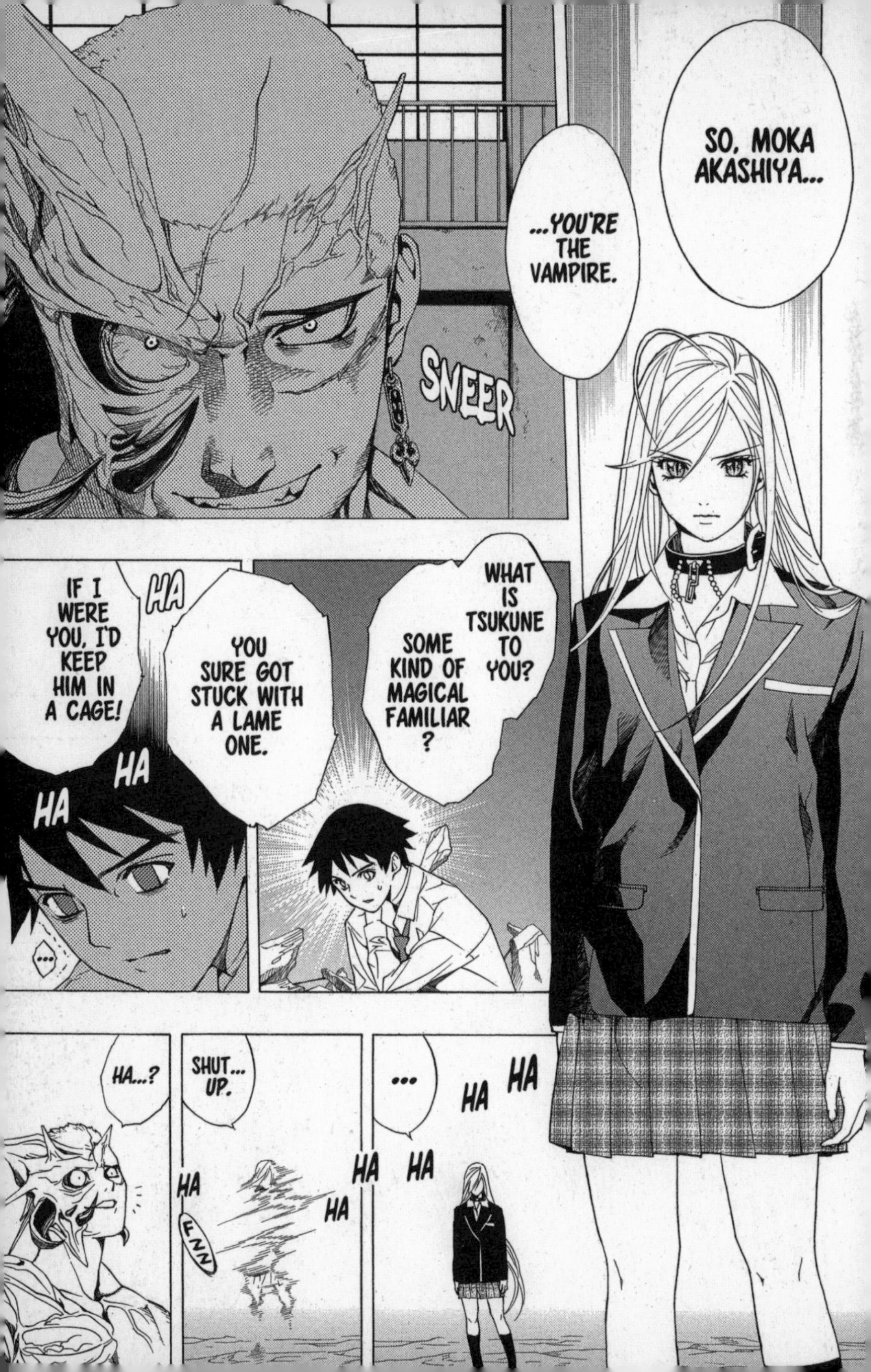
SO, MOKA AKASHIYA...
...YOU'RE THE VAMPIRE.
SNEER
WHAT IS TSUKUNE TO YOU?
SOME KIND OF MAGICAL FAMILIAR?
YOU SURE GOT STUCK WITH A LAME ONE.
HA
IF I WERE YOU, I'D KEEP HIM IN A CAGE!
HA
HA
...
HA HA
...
HA HA
HA
SHUT... UP.
HA
FZZ
HA...?

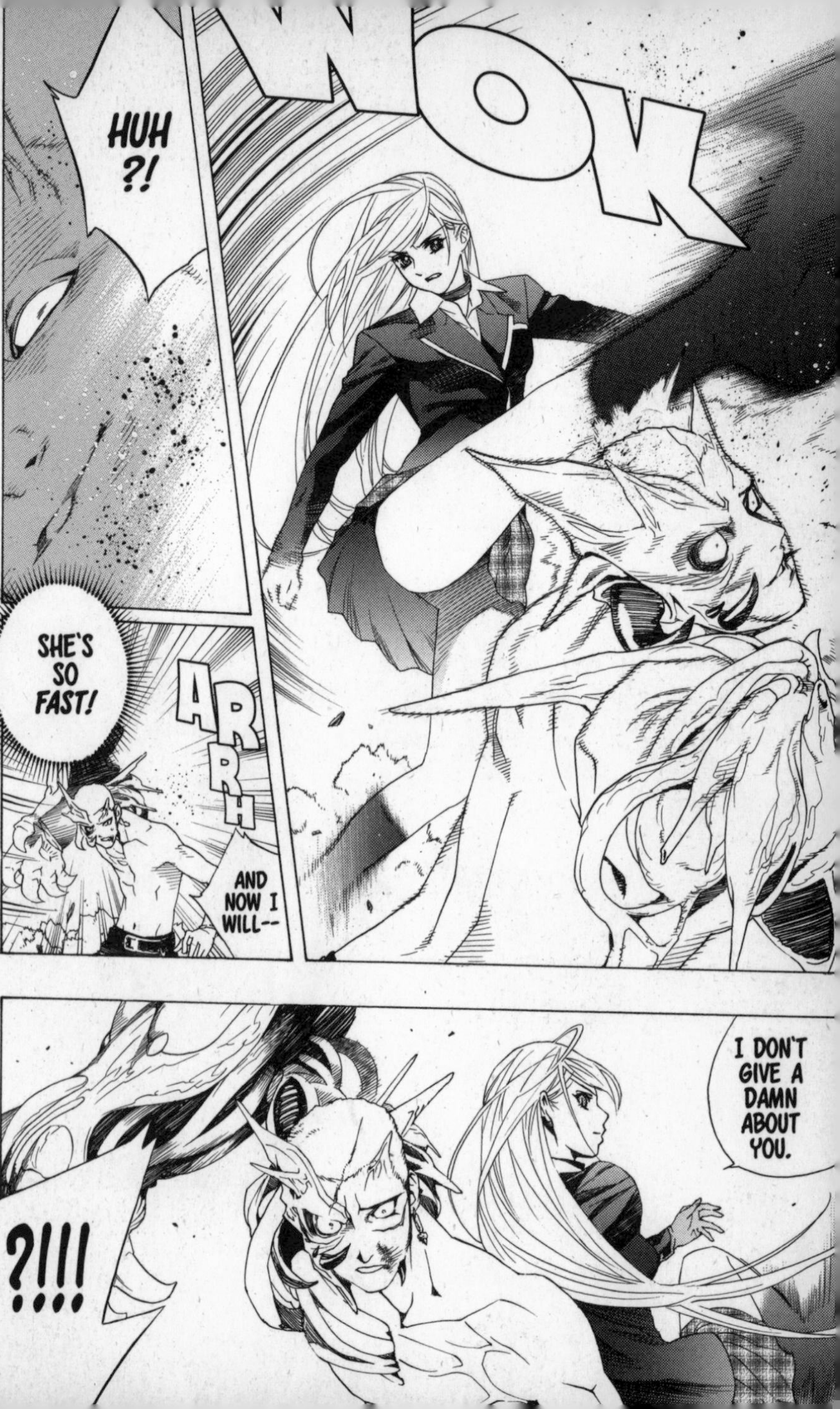
WOK
HUH ?!
SHE'S SO FAST!
ARRH
AND NOW I WILL--
I DON'T GIVE A DAMN ABOUT YOU.
?!!!

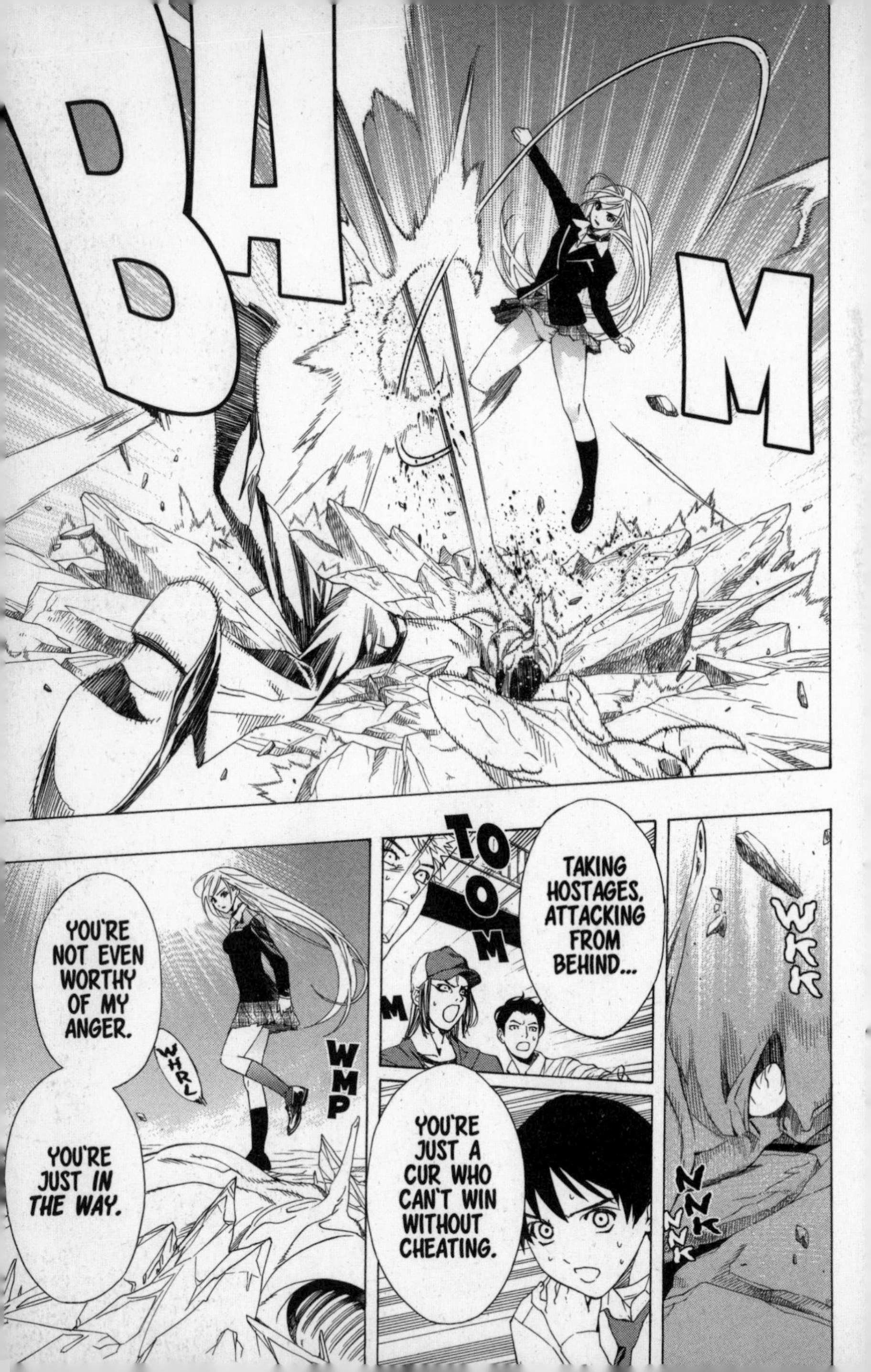
BAM
WKK
NNK
NNK
TOOM
TAKING HOSTAGES, ATTACKING FROM BEHIND...
YOU'RE JUST A CUR WHO CAN'T WIN WITHOUT CHEATING.
YOU'RE NOT EVEN WORTHY OF MY ANGER.
WHRL
WMP
YOU'RE JUST IN THE WAY.

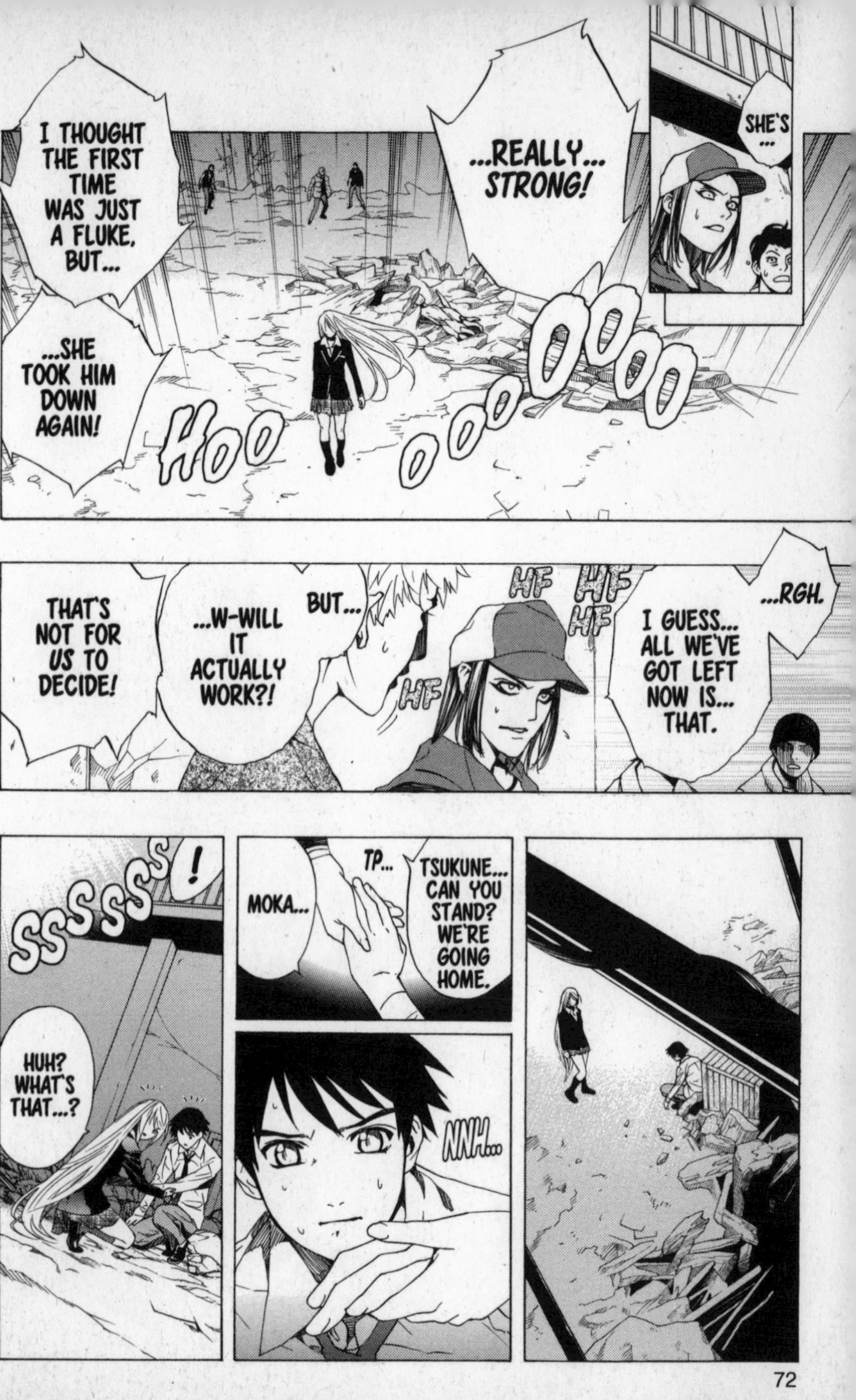
SHE'S ...
...REALLY... STRONG!
I THOUGHT THE FIRST TIME WAS JUST A FLUKE, BUT...
...SHE TOOK HIM DOWN AGAIN!
HOOOOOOOOOOO
...RGH.
I GUESS... ALL WE'VE GOT LEFT NOW IS... THAT.
HF HF HF HF
BUT...
...W-WILL IT ACTUALLY WORK?!
THAT'S NOT FOR US TO DECIDE!
TSUKUNE... CAN YOU STAND? WE'RE GOING HOME.
TP...
MOKA...
NNH...
SSSSSS!
HUH? WHAT'S THAT...?

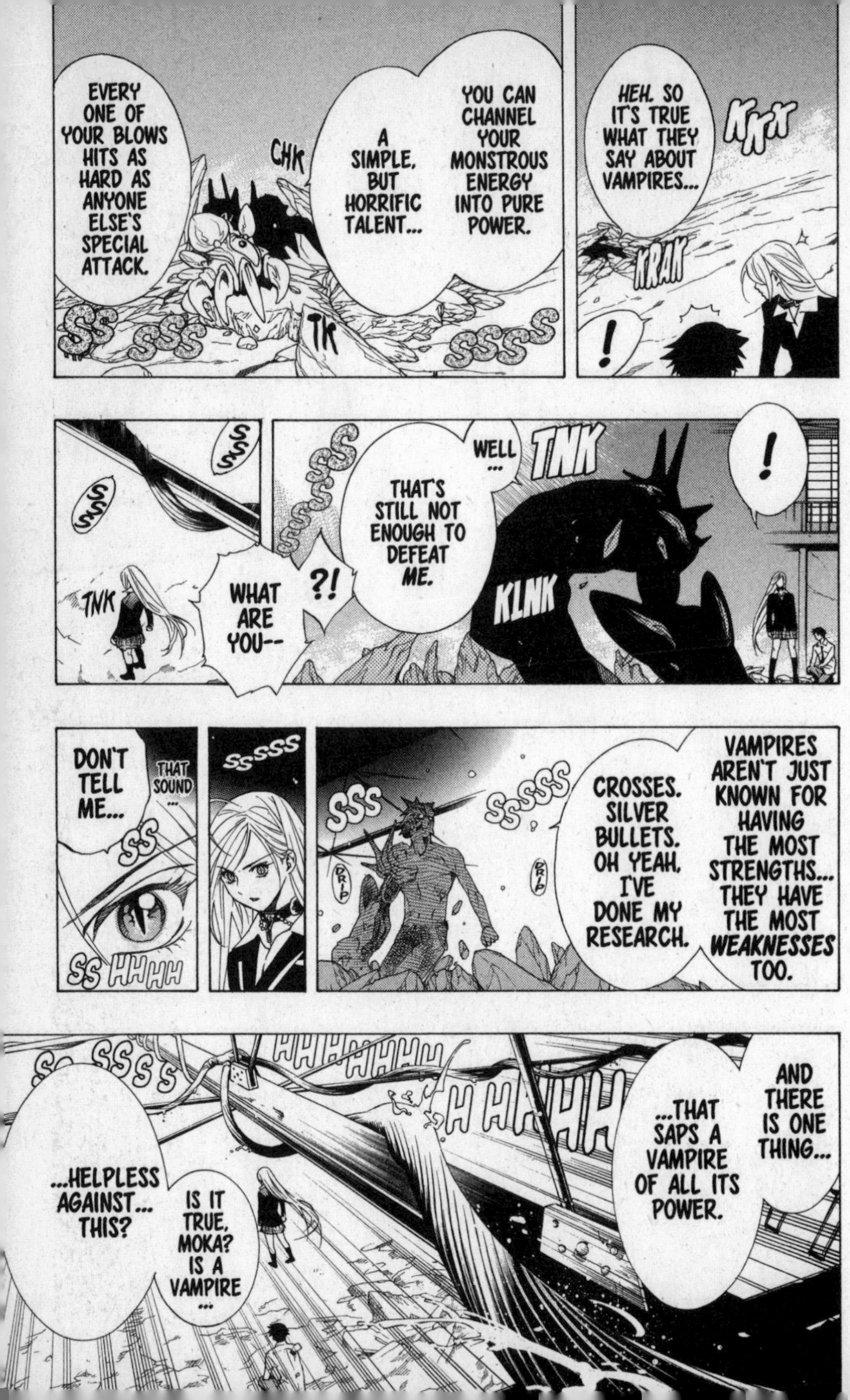

KKKT
HEH. SO IT'S TRUE WHAT THEY SAY ABOUT VAMPIRES...
KRAK
!
YOU CAN CHANNEL YOUR MONSTROUS ENERGY INTO PURE POWER.
A SIMPLE, BUT HORRIFIC TALENT...
CHK
EVERY ONE OF YOUR BLOWS HITS AS HARD AS ANYONE ELSE'S SPECIAL ATTACK.
TK
!
TNK
WELL...
THAT'S STILL NOT ENOUGH TO DEFEAT ME.
KLNK
?!
WHAT ARE YOU--
TNK
VAMPIRES AREN'T JUST KNOWN FOR HAVING THE MOST STRENGTHS... THEY HAVE THE MOST WEAKNESSES TOO.
CROSSES. SILVER BULLETS. OH YEAH, I'VE DONE MY RESEARCH.
DRIP
DRIP
THAT SOUND...
DON'T TELL ME...
SS HHHH
AND THERE IS ONE THING...
...THAT SAPS A VAMPIRE OF ALL ITS POWER.
IS IT TRUE, MOKA? IS A VAMPIRE...
...HELPLESS AGAINST... THIS?

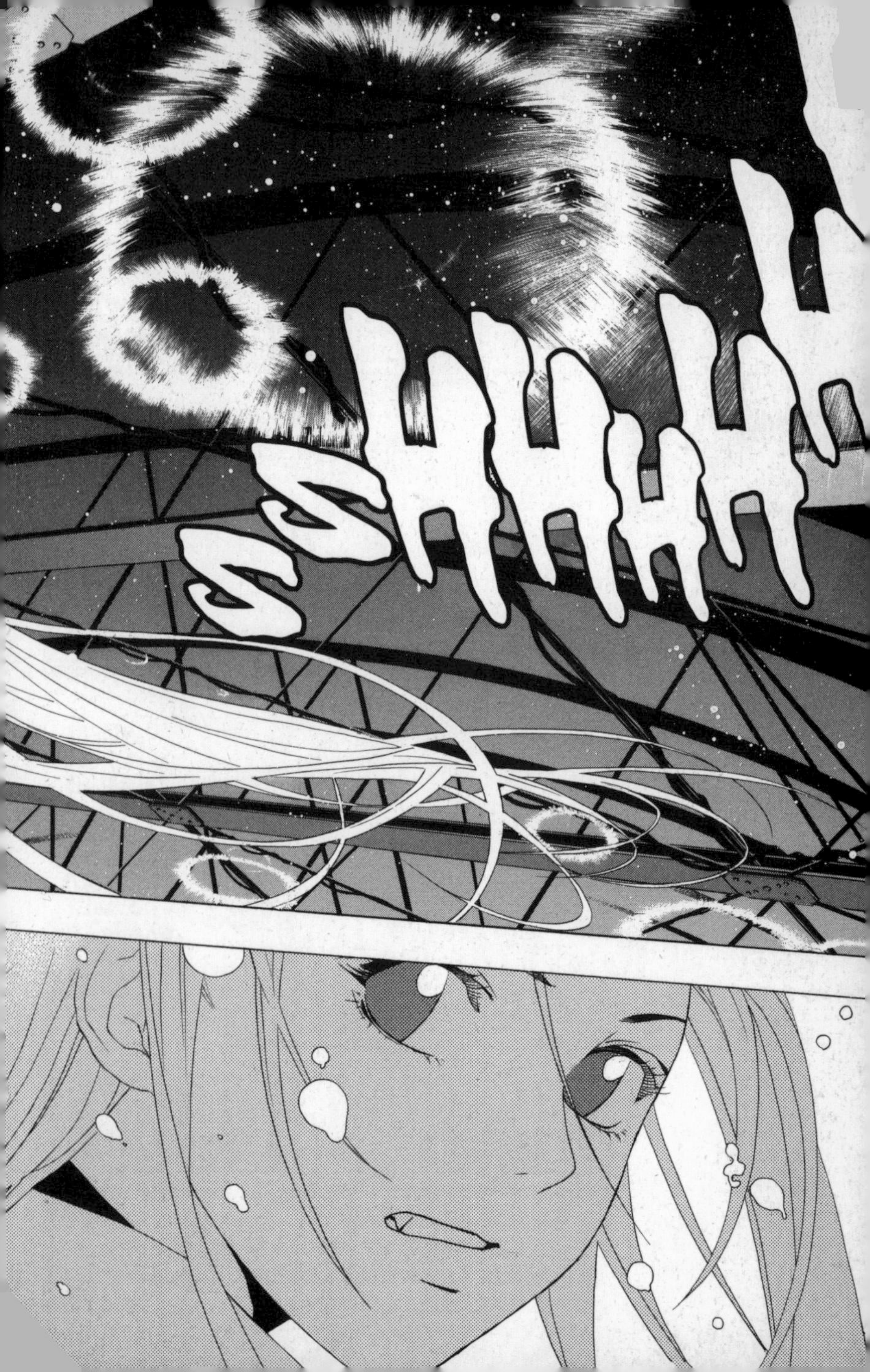

SSHHHH

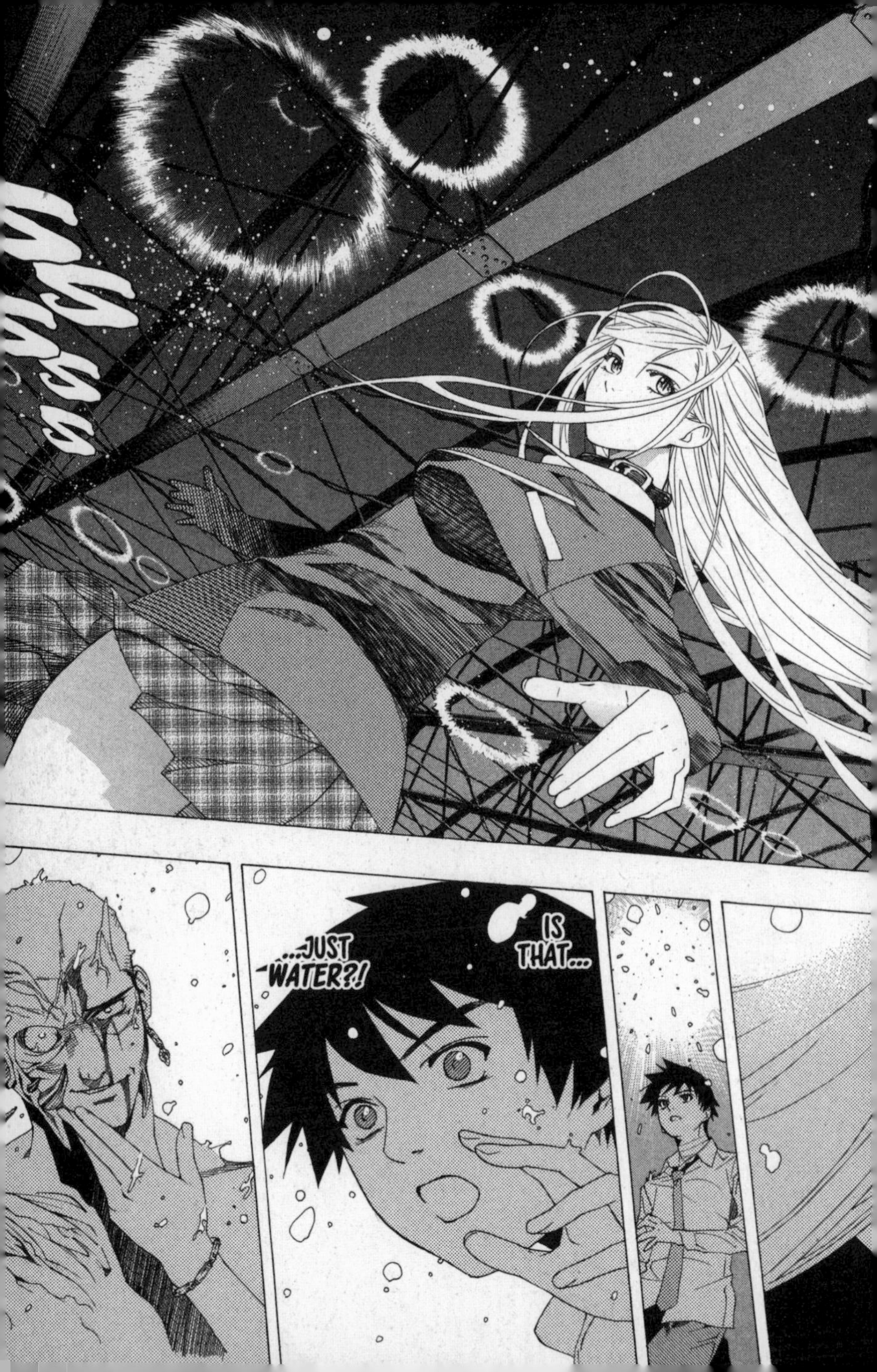
IS THAT...
...JUST WATER?!

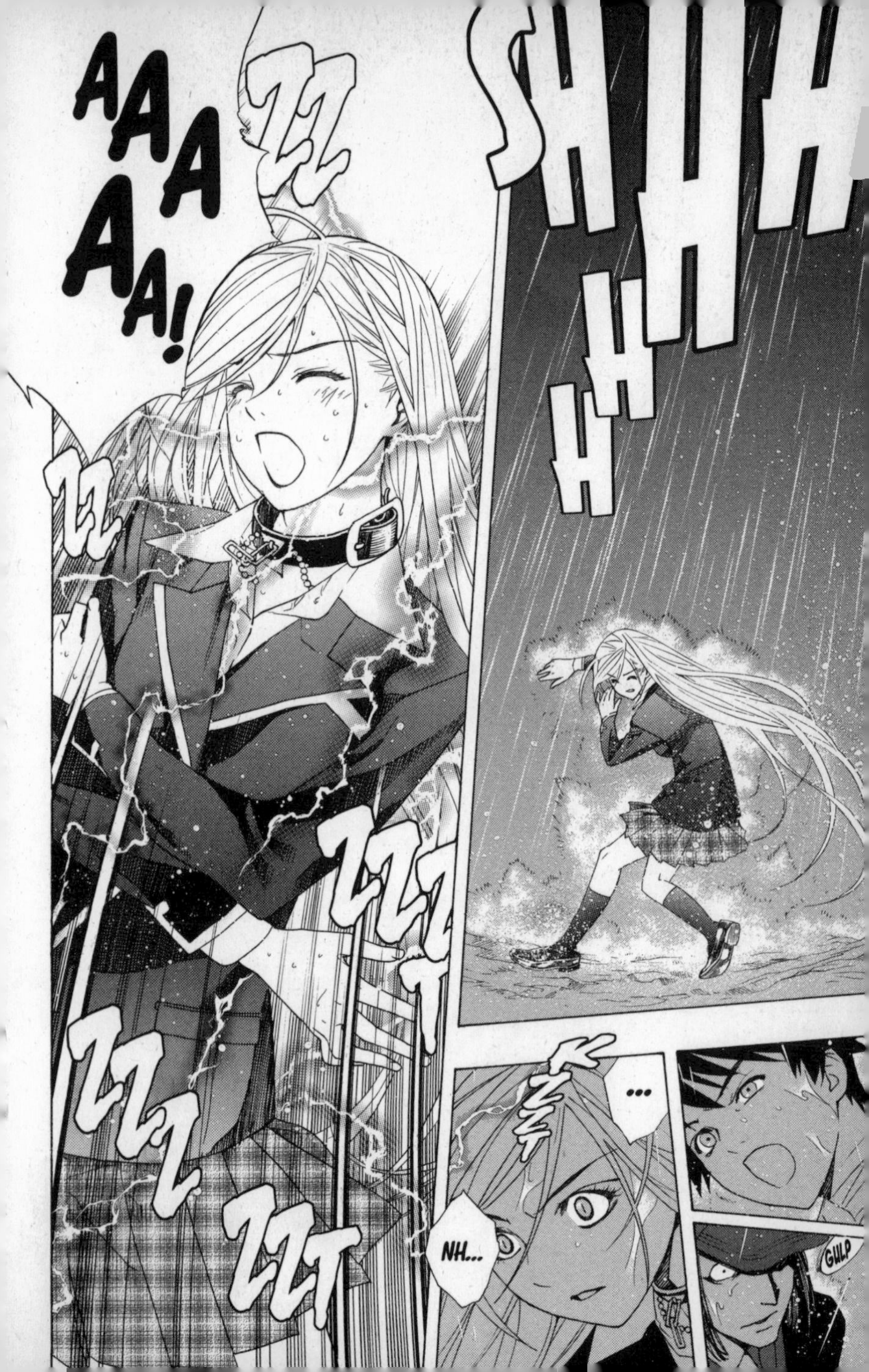
SHHHHHHH
AAAAAAA!
ZZ
ZZ
ZZZT
ZZZ
ZZZT
...
NH...
GULP

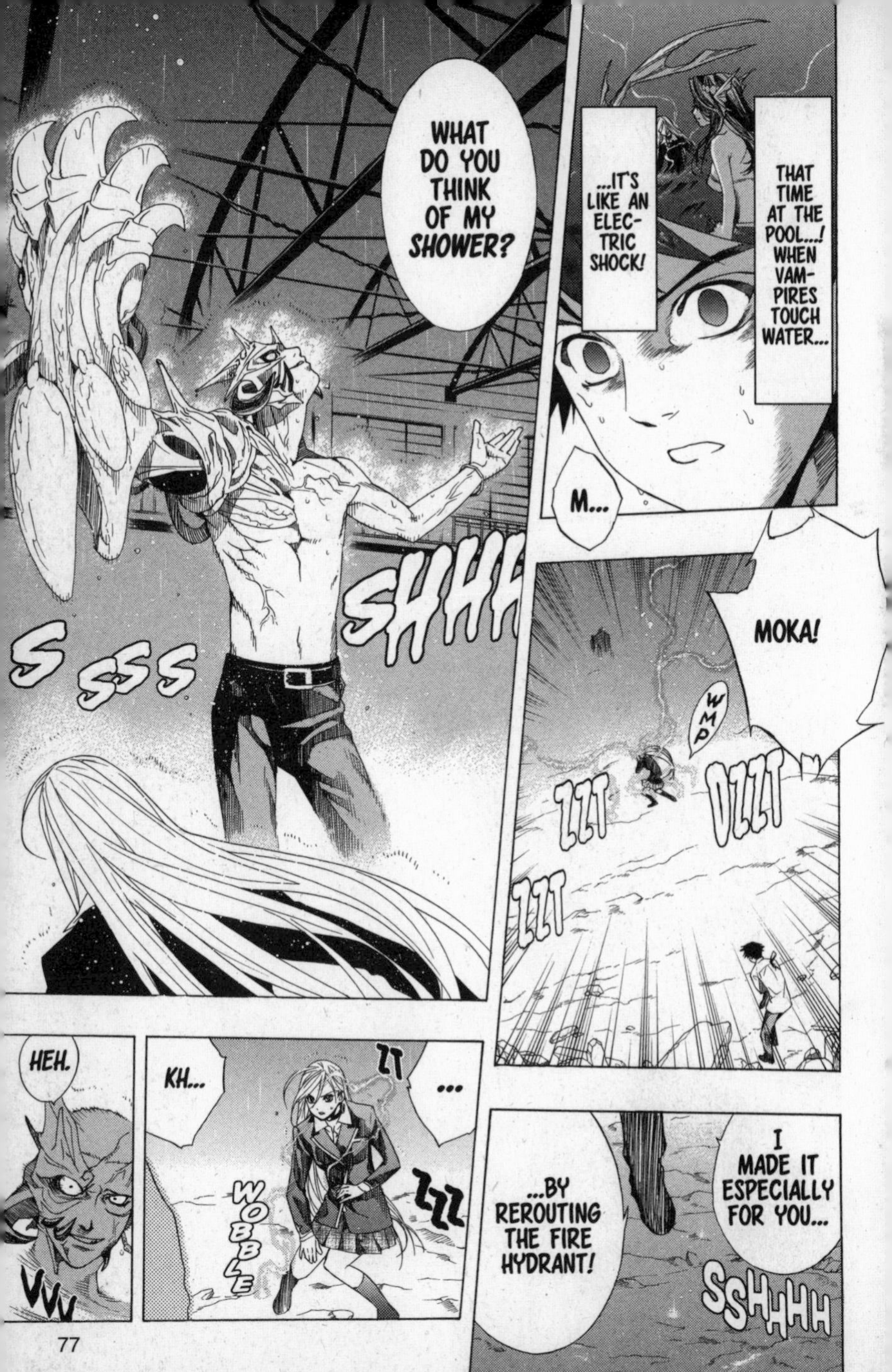

THAT TIME AT THE POOL...! WHEN VAMPIRES TOUCH WATER...
...IT'S LIKE AN ELECTRIC SHOCK!
M...
WHAT DO YOU THINK OF MY SHOWER?
SHHH
S SSS
MOKA!
WMP
DZZT
ZZT
ZZT
I MADE IT ESPECIALLY FOR YOU...
...BY REROUTING THE FIRE HYDRANT!
SSHHHHH
...
ZT
ZZZ
WOBBLE
KH...
HEH.
VVV

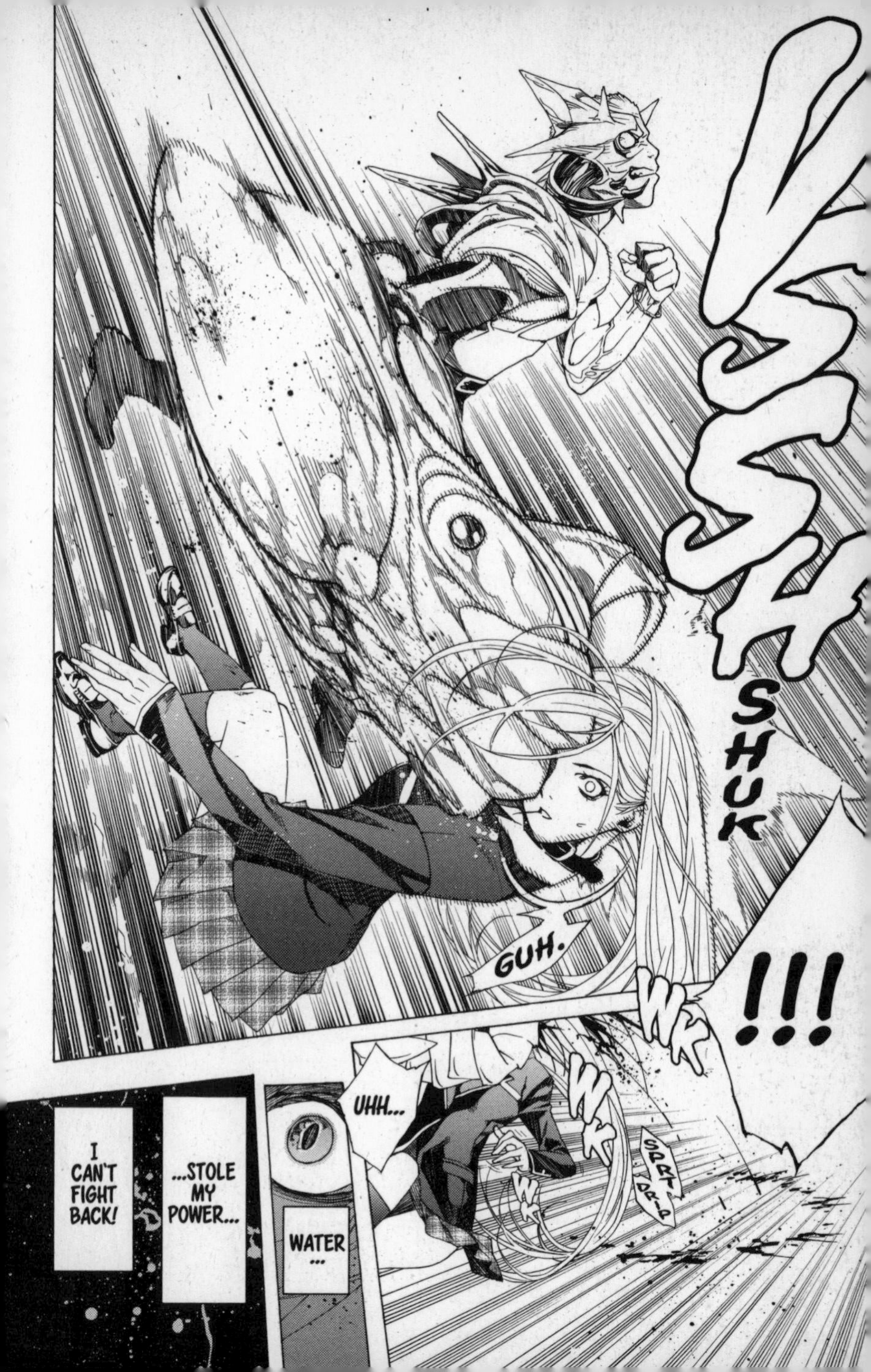
SHUK
!!!
GUH.
WK WK WK
SPRT DRIP
UHH...
WATER ...
...STOLE MY POWER...
I CAN'T FIGHT BACK!

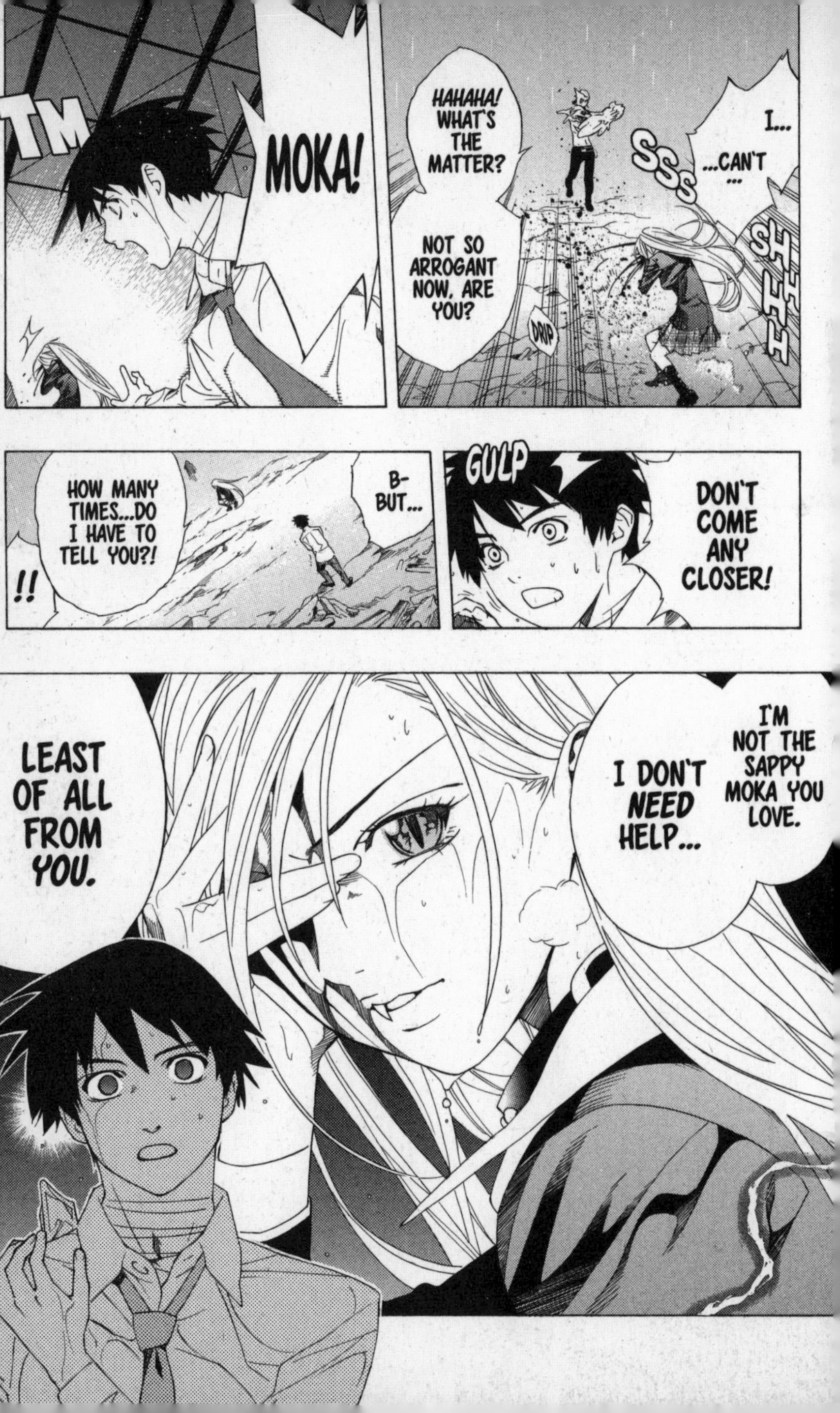
HAHAHA! WHAT'S THE MATTER?
NOT SO ARROGANT NOW, ARE YOU?
DRIP
I... ...CAN'T ...
SSS
SHHHH
TM
MOKA!
GULP
DON'T COME ANY CLOSER!
B-BUT...
!!
HOW MANY TIMES...DO I HAVE TO TELL YOU?!
I'M NOT THE SAPPY MOKA YOU LOVE.
I DON'T NEED HELP...
LEAST OF ALL FROM YOU.

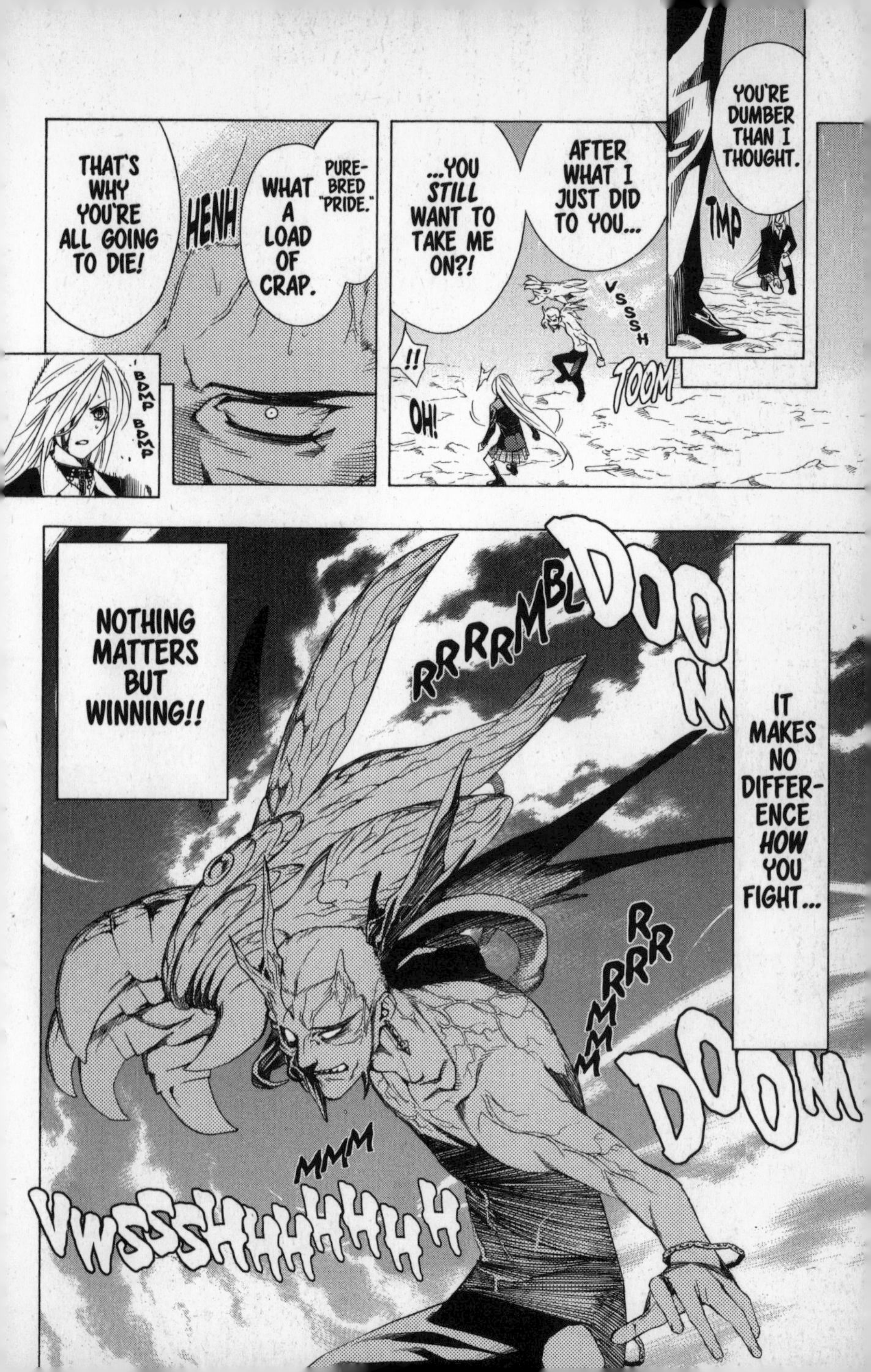
YOU'RE DUMBER THAN I THOUGHT.
IMP
AFTER WHAT I JUST DID TO YOU...
...YOU STILL WANT TO TAKE ME ON?!
VSSSH
TOOM
!!
OH!
PURE-BRED "PRIDE."
WHAT A LOAD OF CRAP.
HENH
THAT'S WHY YOU'RE ALL GOING TO DIE!
BDMP BDMP
IT MAKES NO DIFFERENCE HOW YOU FIGHT...
DOOM
RRRRMBL
NOTHING MATTERS BUT WINNING!!
MMMMRRRRR
DOOM
MMM
VWSSSHHHHHHH

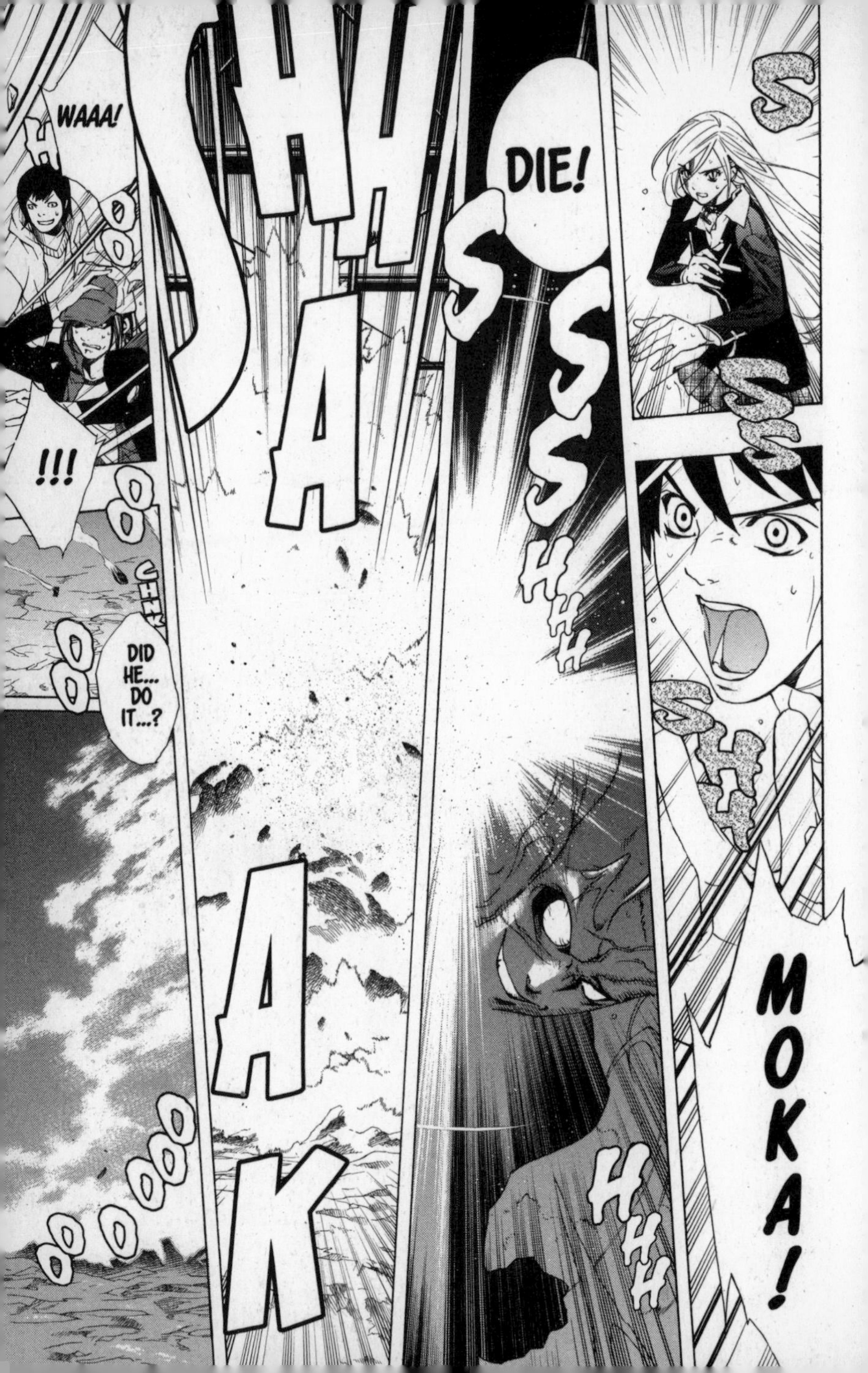

SSSS
SHH
MOKA!
DIE!
SSSSHHHHHH
SHHAAAK
WAAA!
HOOO
!!!
OOO
CHNK
DID HE... DO IT...?
OOOOOOOOO

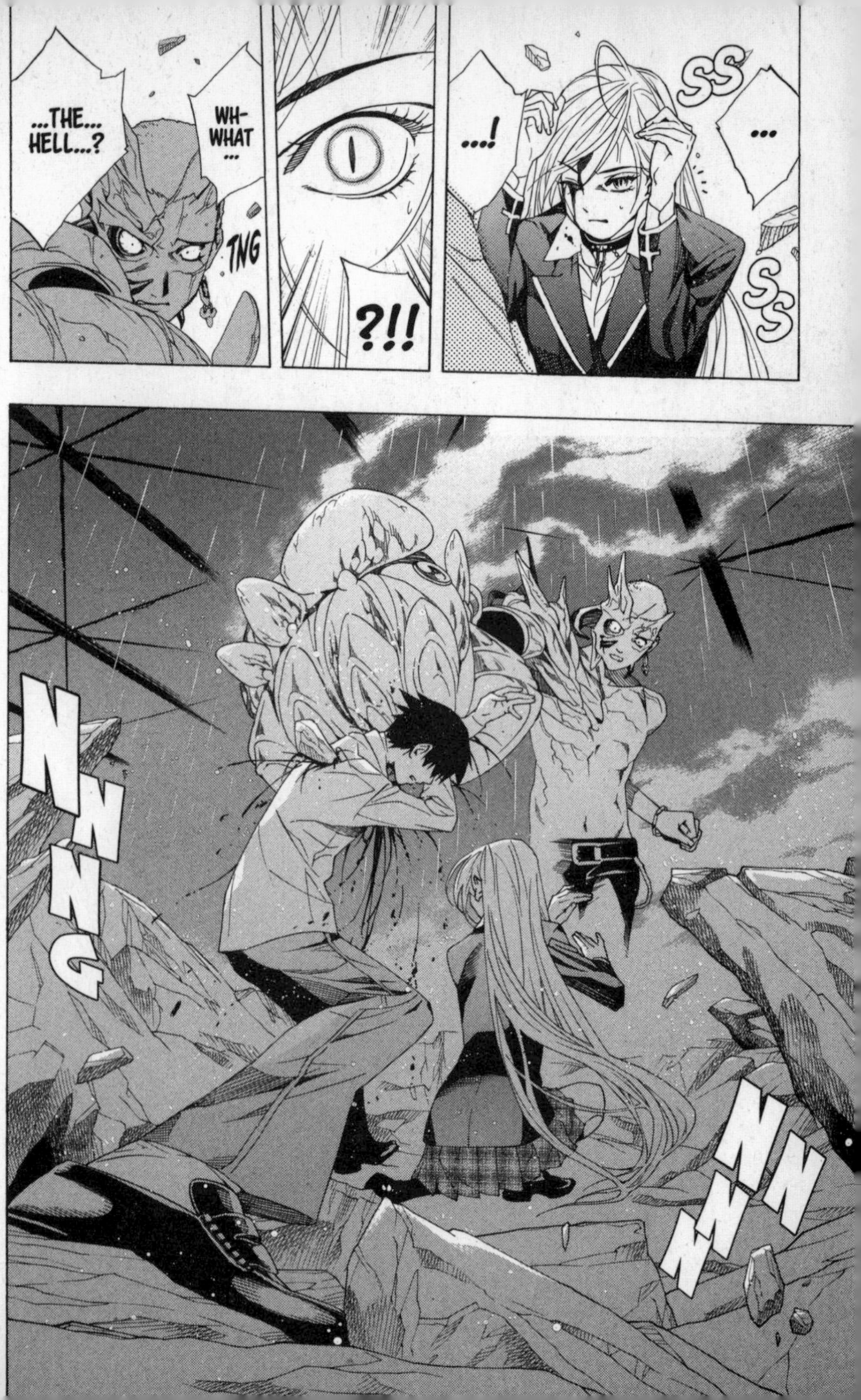

...
SS
SS
...!
?!!
WH-
WHAT
...
...THE...
HELL...?
TNG
NNNN
NNNNG

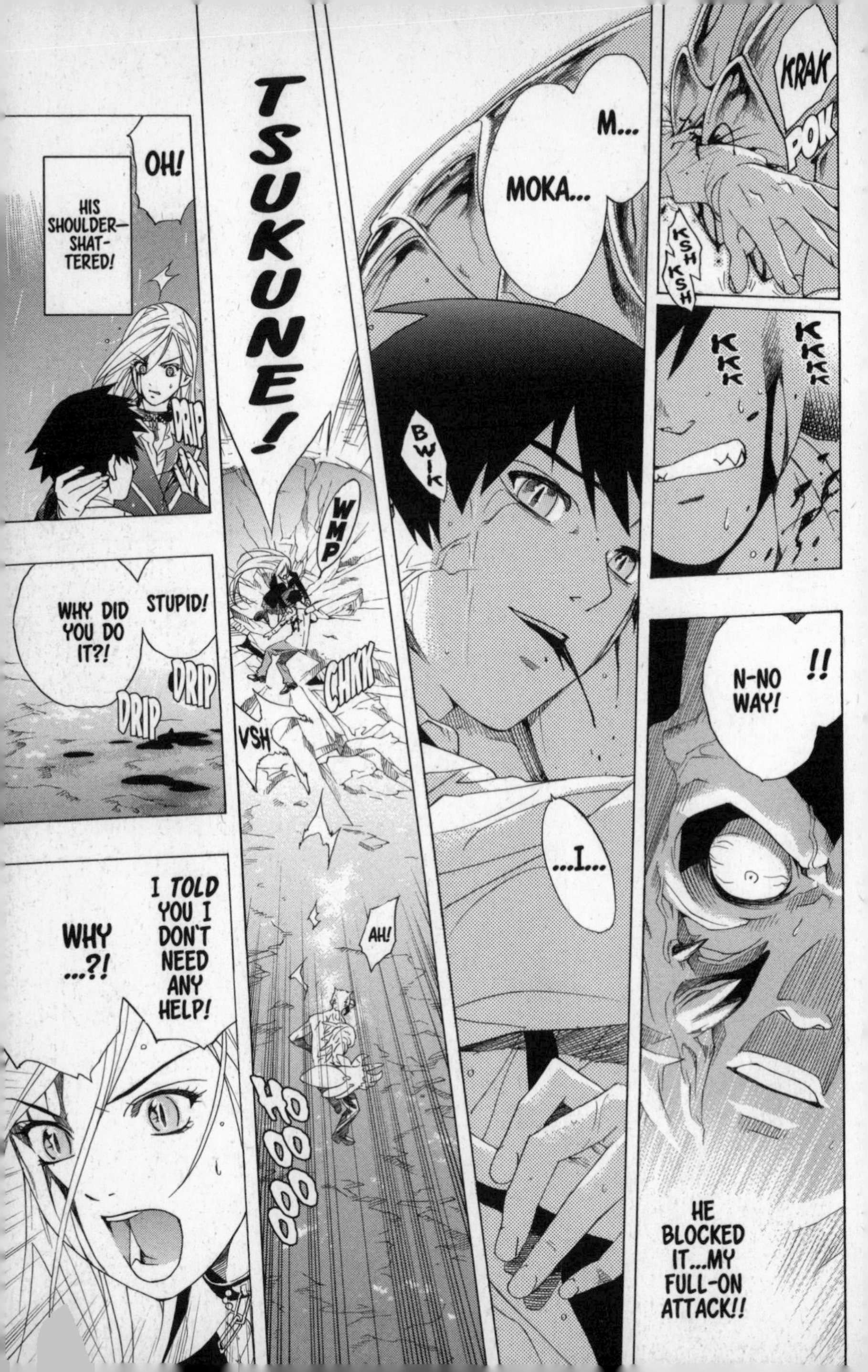
KRAK
POK
KSH KSH
M...
MOKA...
KKK
KKKK
TSUKUNE!
BWIK
N-NO WAY!
!!
...I...
WMP
CHKK
VSH
AH!
HE BLOCKED IT...MY FULL-ON ATTACK!!
HOOOOOO
OH!
HIS SHOULDER-SHAT-TERED!
DRIP
STUPID!
WHY DID YOU DO IT?!
DRIP
DRIP
I TOLD YOU I DON'T NEED ANY HELP!
WHY ...?!

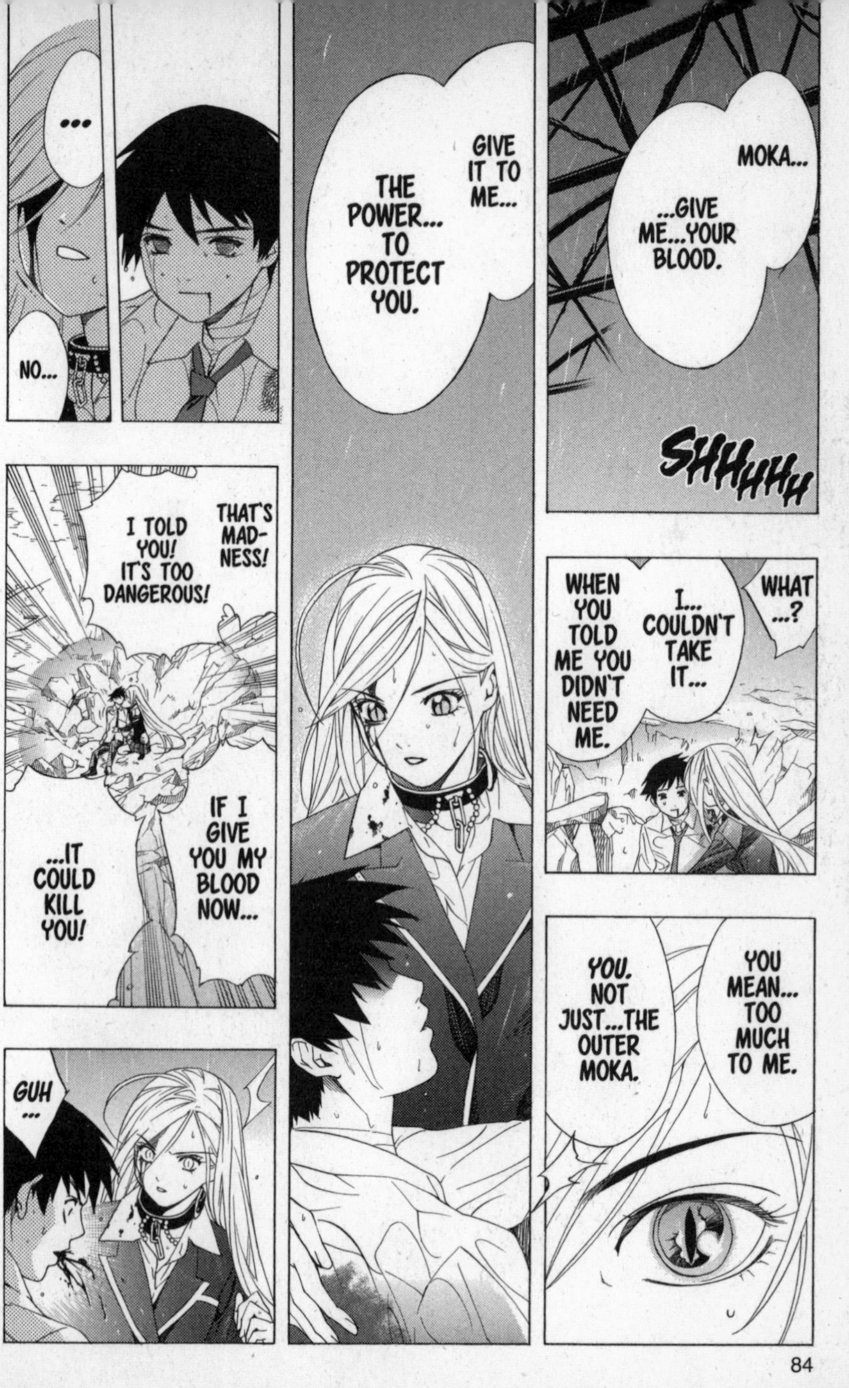
MOKA...
...GIVE ME...YOUR BLOOD.
SHHHHHH
GIVE IT TO ME...
THE POWER... TO PROTECT YOU.
...
NO...
WHAT ...?
I... COULDN'T TAKE IT...
WHEN YOU TOLD ME YOU DIDN'T NEED ME.
THAT'S MAD-NESS!
I TOLD YOU! IT'S TOO DANGEROUS!
IF I GIVE YOU MY BLOOD NOW...
...IT COULD KILL YOU!
YOU MEAN... TOO MUCH TO ME.
YOU. NOT JUST...THE OUTER MOKA.
GUH ...

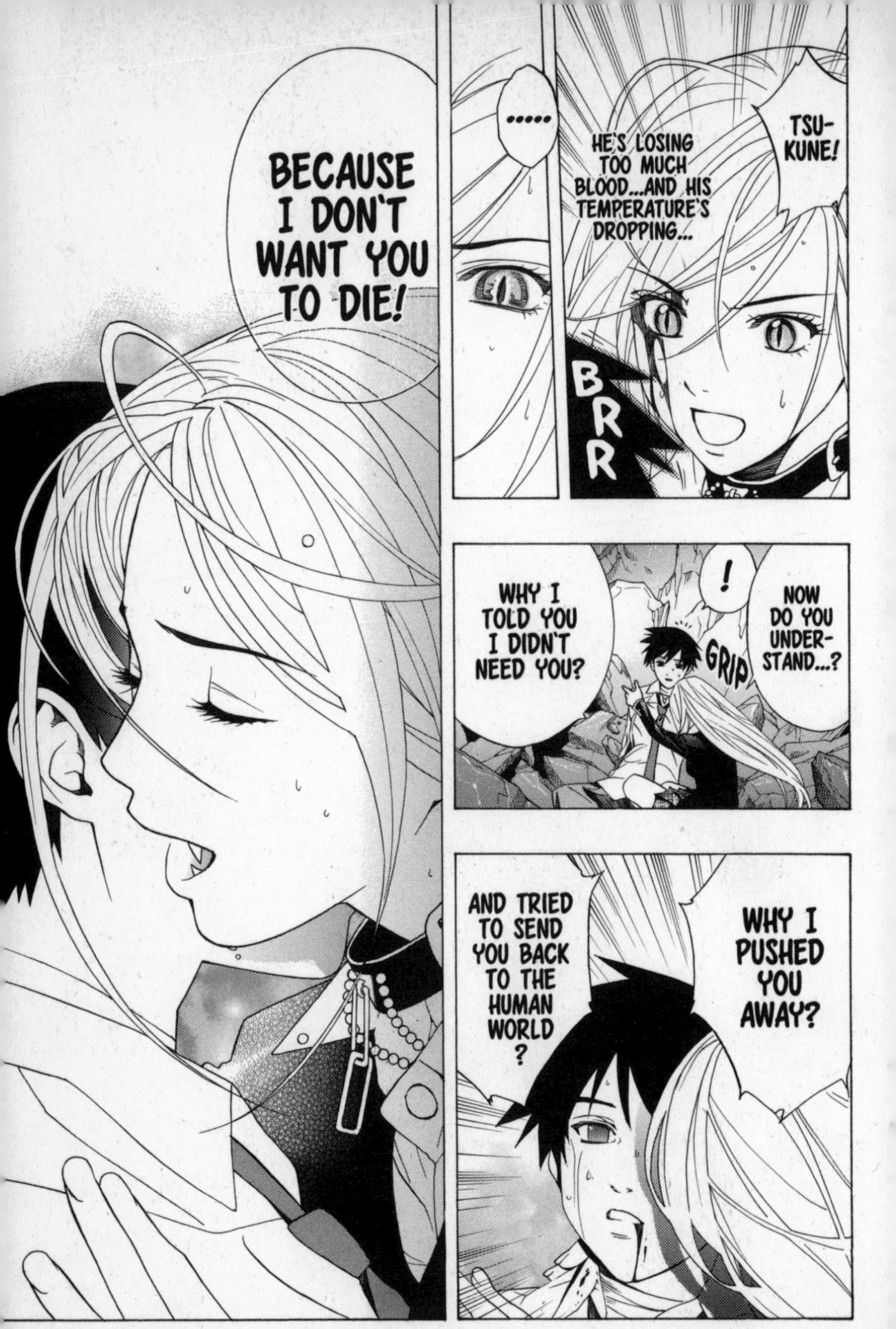

TSU-KUNE!
HE'S LOSING TOO MUCH BLOOD...AND HIS TEMPERATURE'S DROPPING...
BRRR
......
!
NOW DO YOU UNDERSTAND...?
GRIP
WHY I TOLD YOU I DIDN'T NEED YOU?
WHY I PUSHED YOU AWAY?
AND TRIED TO SEND YOU BACK TO THE HUMAN WORLD?
BECAUSE I DON'T WANT YOU TO DIE!

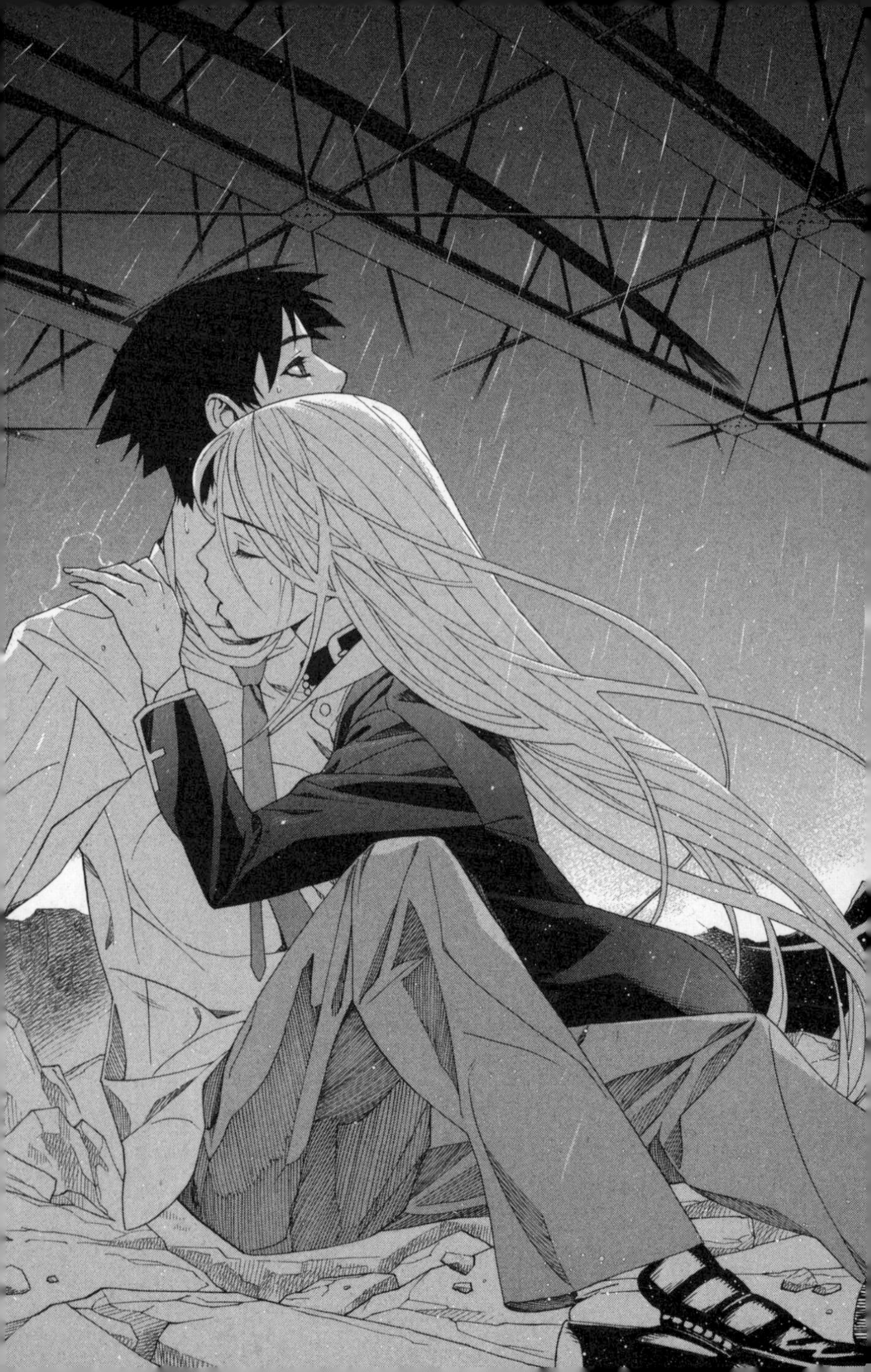

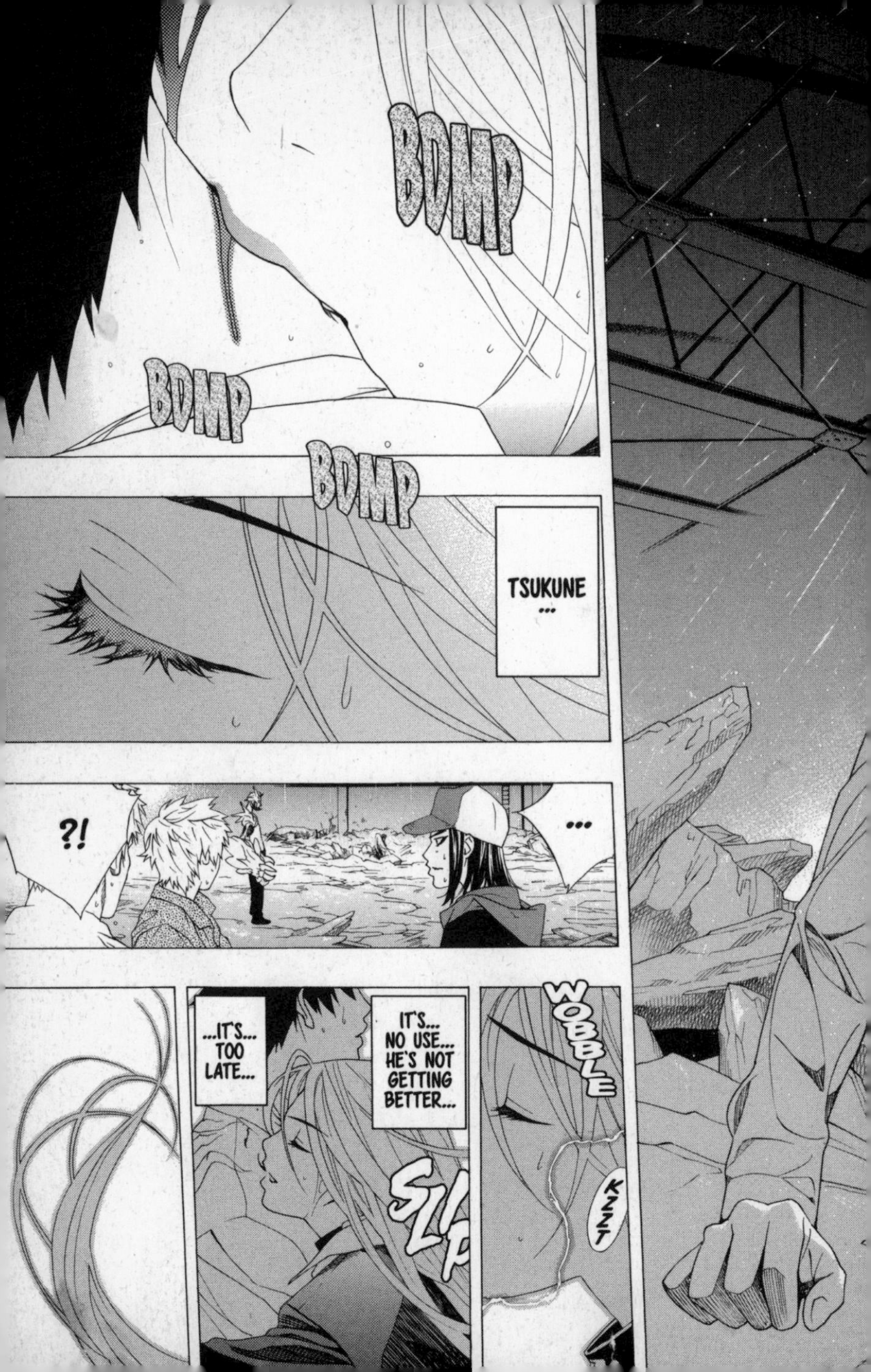
BDMP
BDMP
BDMP
TSUKUNE ...
...
?!
WOBBLE
IT'S... NO USE... HE'S NOT GETTING BETTER...
...IT'S... TOO LATE...
KZZT
SLIP

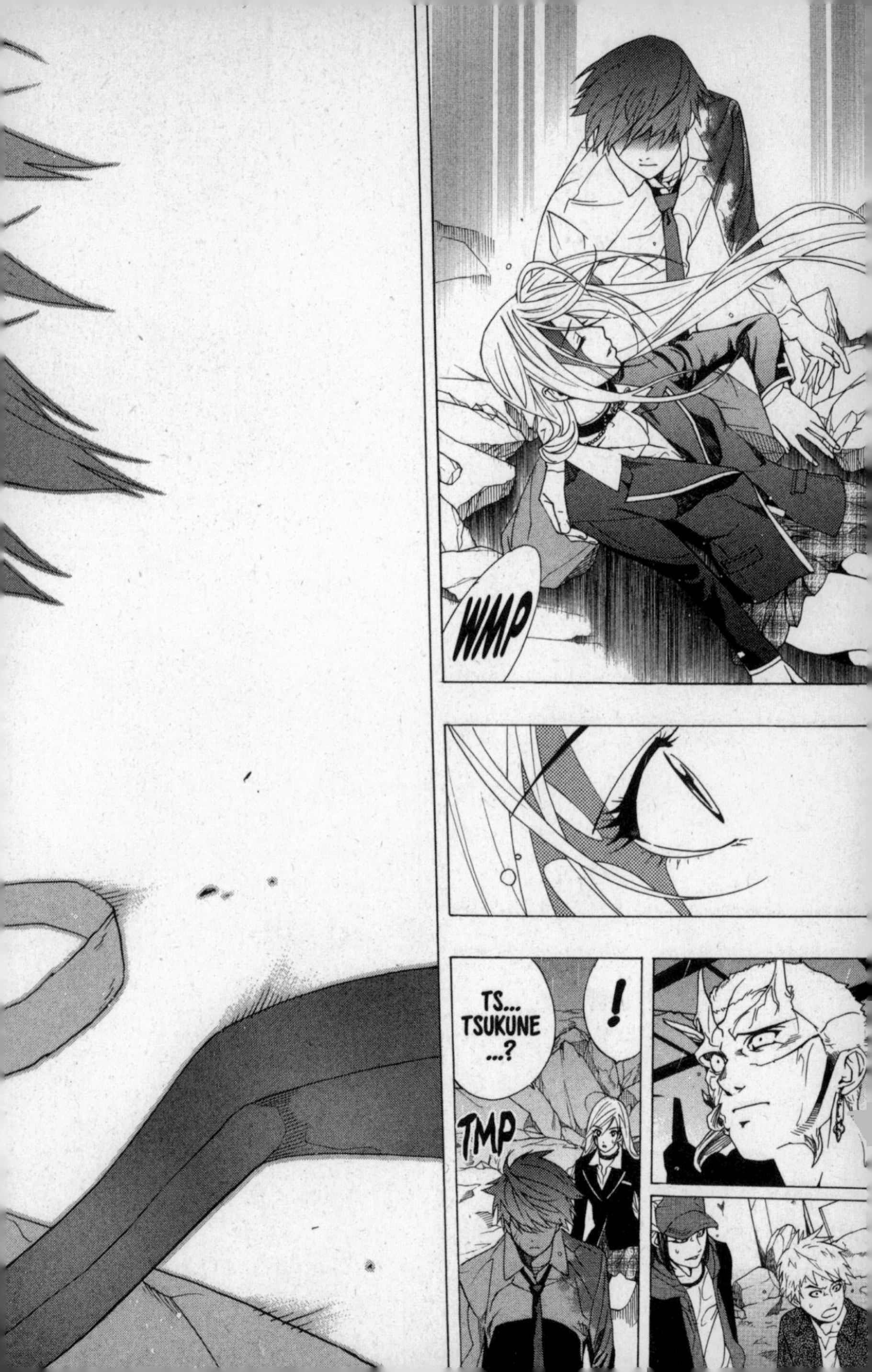
WMP
!
TS... TSUKUNE ...?
TMP

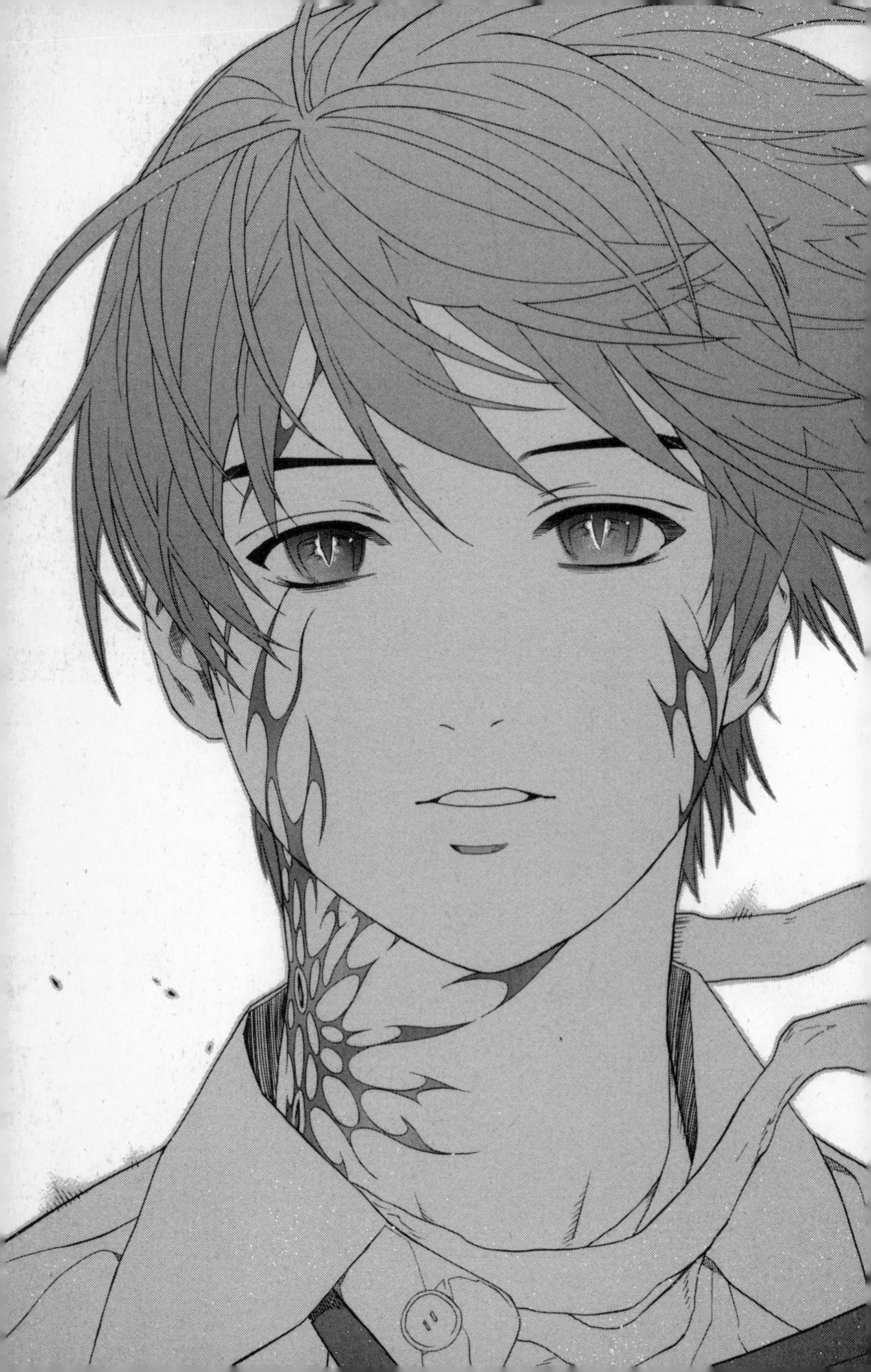

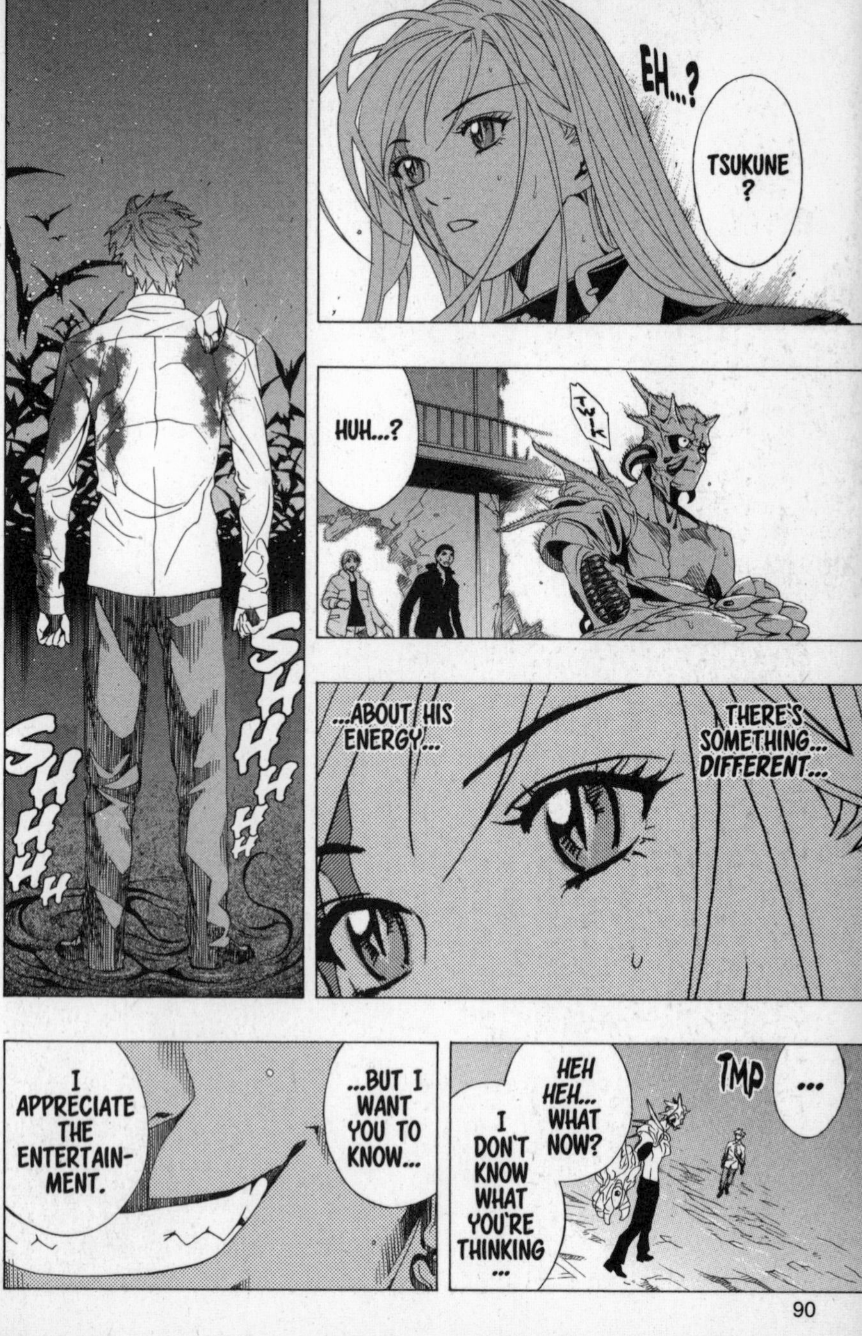
EH...?
TSUKUNE ?
TWIK
HUH...?
THERE'S SOMETHING... DIFFERENT...
...ABOUT HIS ENERGY...
SHHHHHH
SHHHHH
TMP
...
HEH HEH... WHAT NOW?
I DON'T KNOW WHAT YOU'RE THINKING ...
...BUT I WANT YOU TO KNOW...
I APPRECIATE THE ENTERTAIN-MENT.

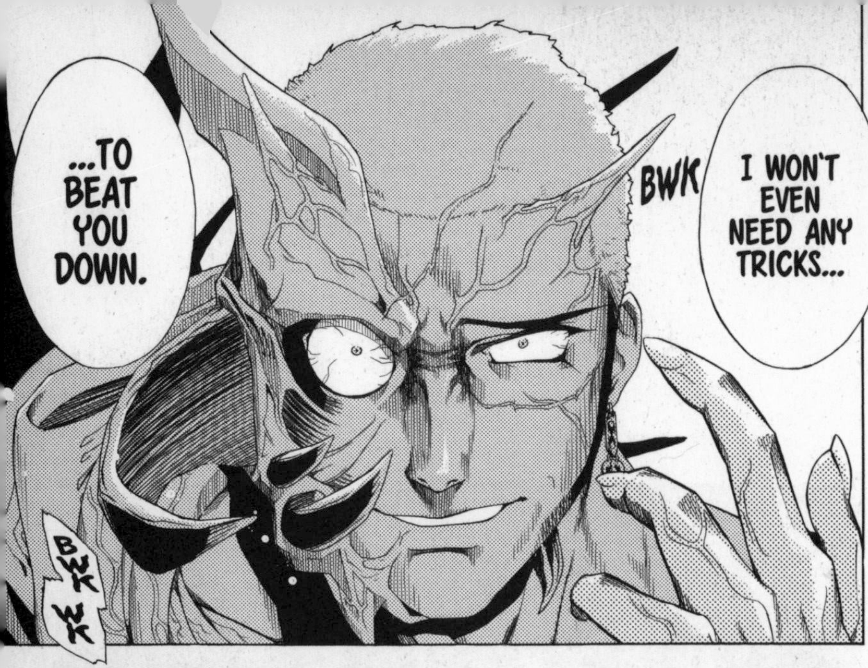
I WON'T EVEN NEED ANY TRICKS...
BWK
...TO BEAT YOU DOWN.
BWK WK

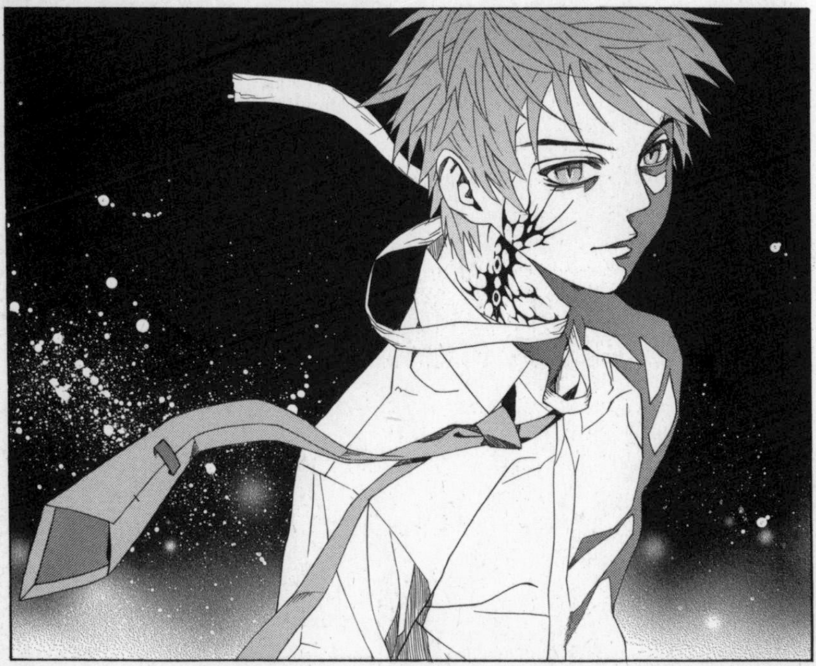

23: Ghoul

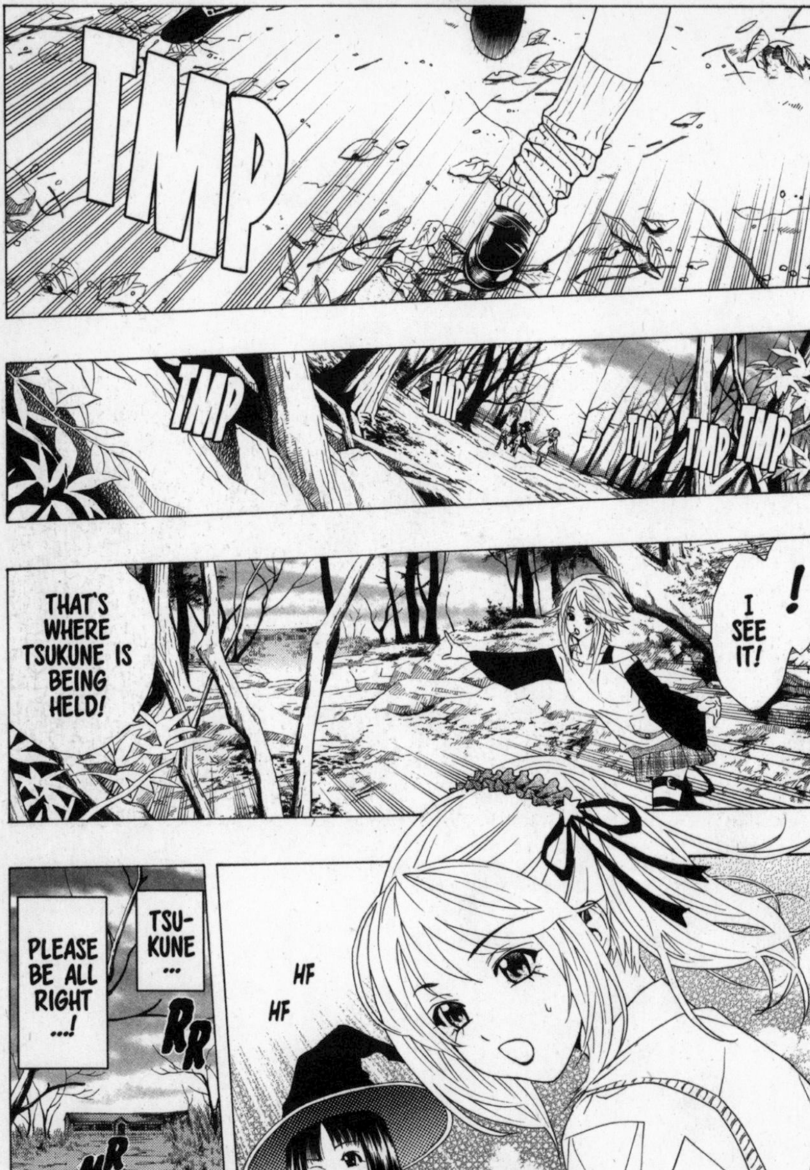
TMP
TMP
TMP
TMP
TMP
TMP
I SEE IT!
!
THAT'S WHERE TSUKUNE IS BEING HELD!
HF
HF
TSU-KUNE ...
PLEASE BE ALL RIGHT ...!
RR
LBMR

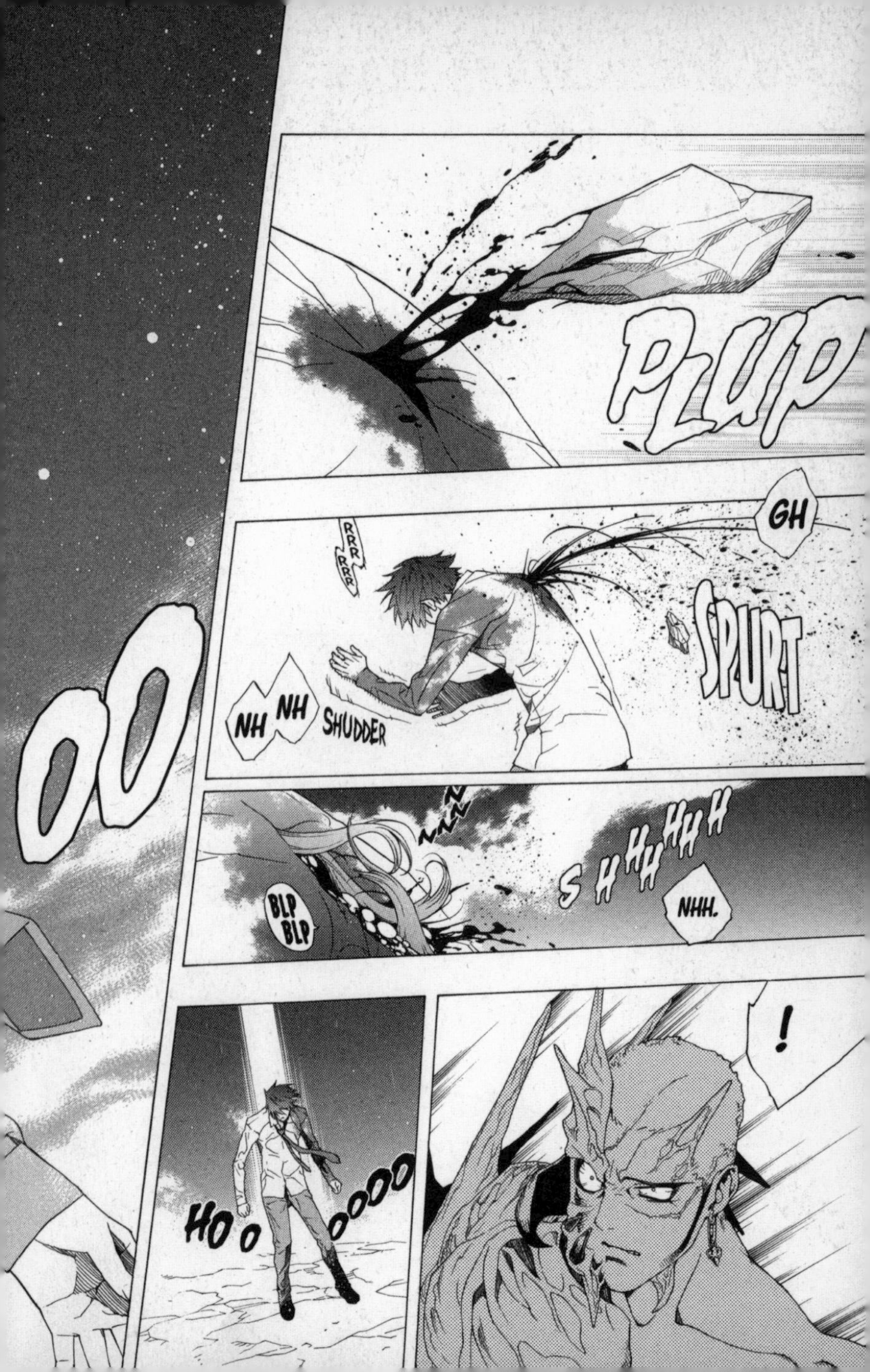
PLUP
GH
SPURT
RRR RRR
SHUDDER
NH
NH
NNNN
SHHHHHHH
NHH.
BLP BLP
OO
!
HOOOOOO

23 : Ghoul

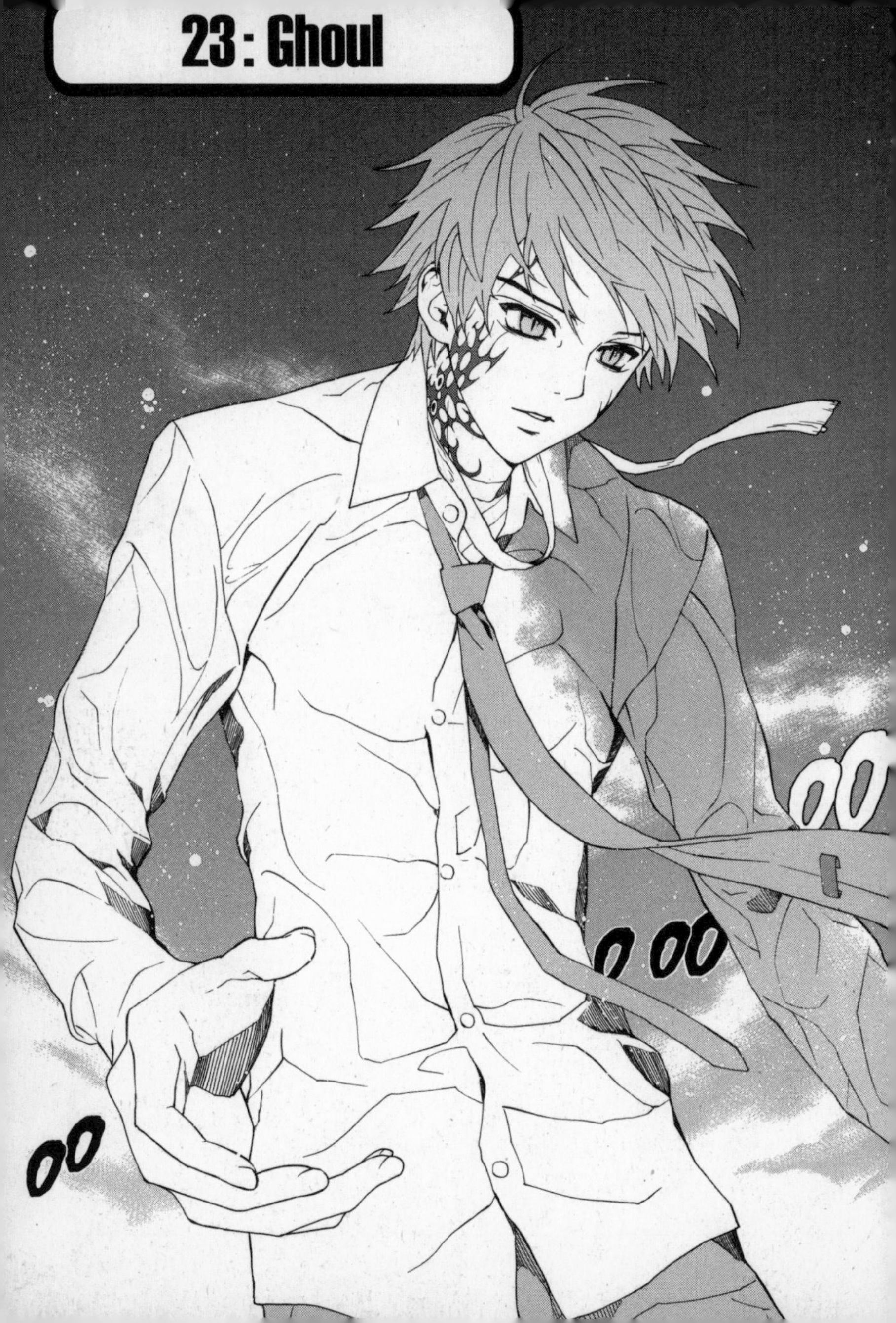

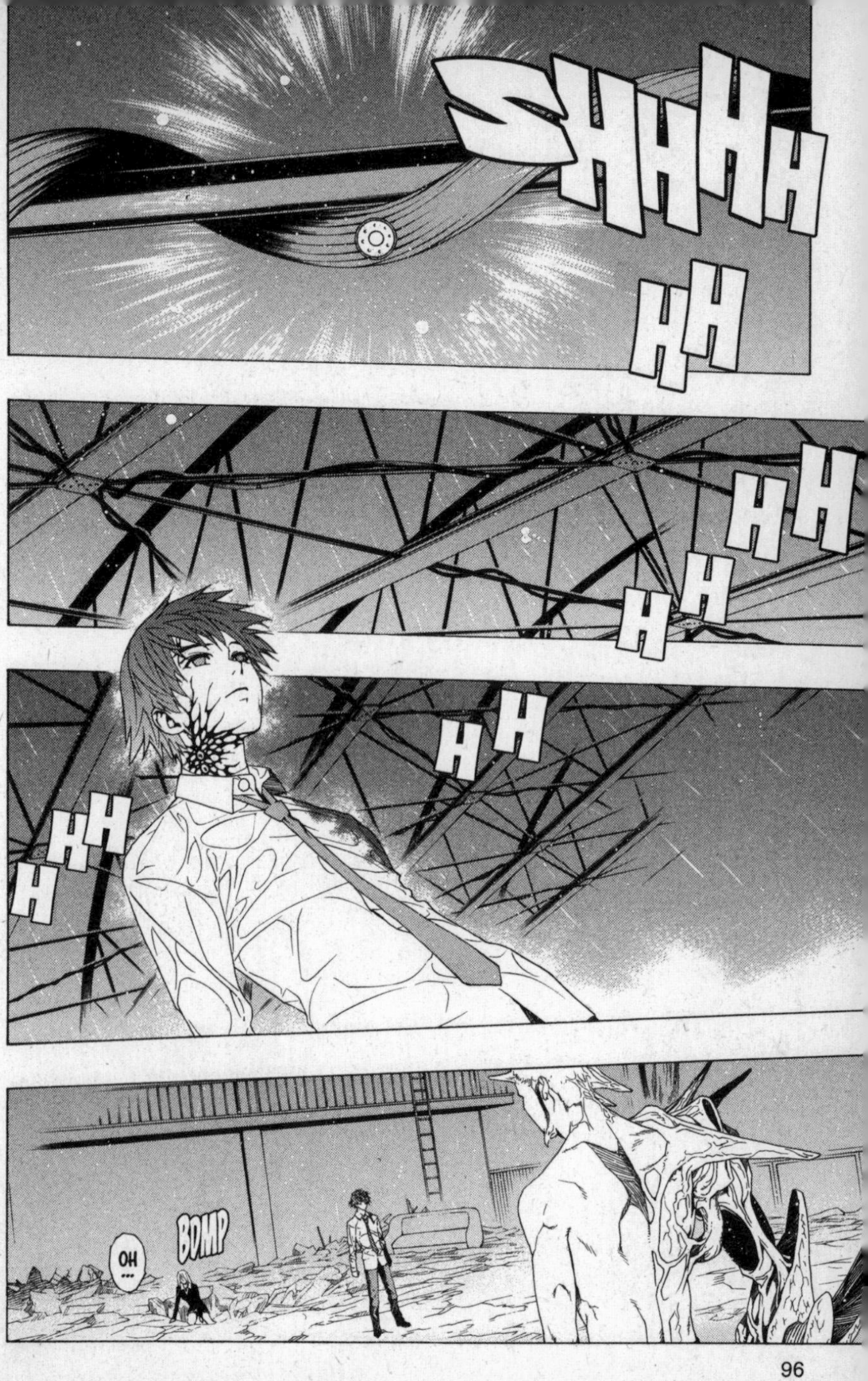
SHHHHHH
HHH
HHHH
HH
HHH
BOMP
OH...

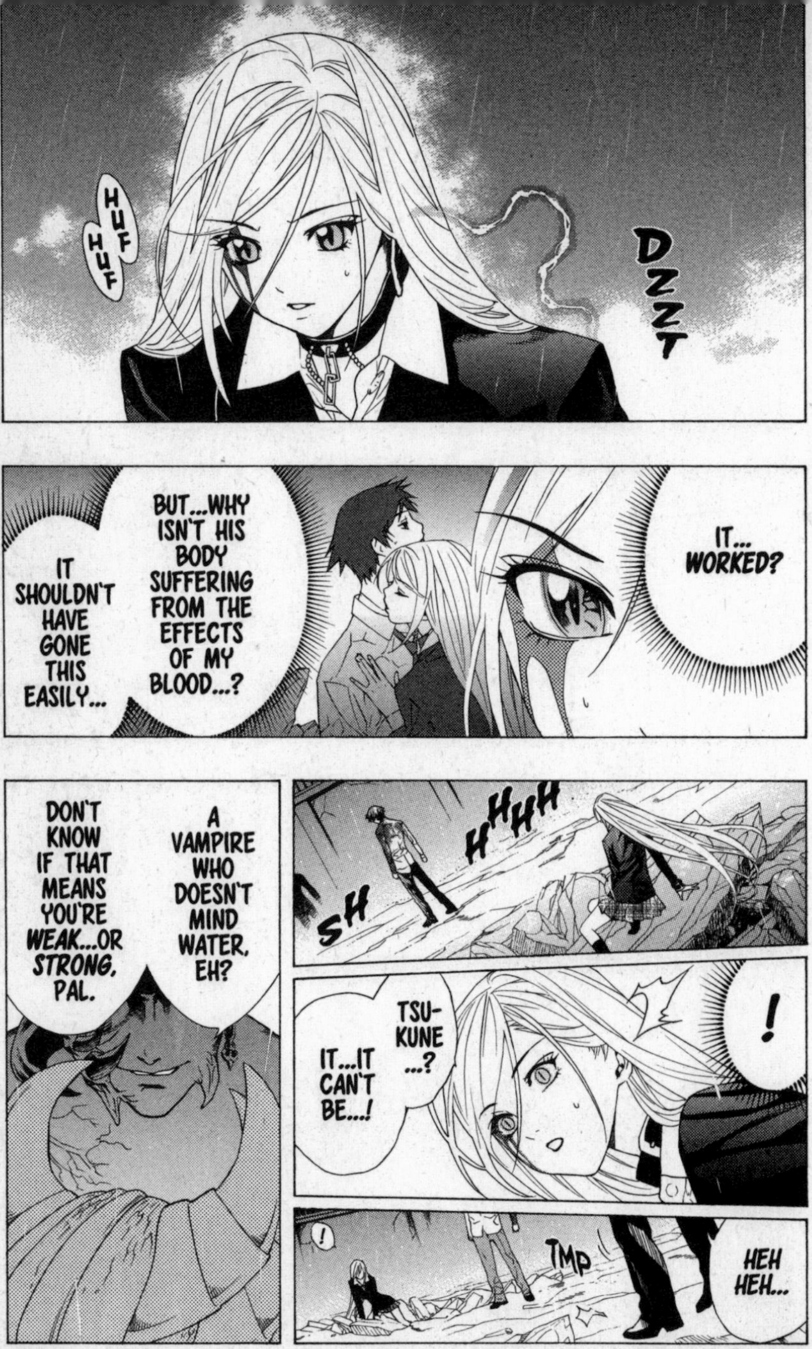
DZZT
HUF HUF
IT... WORKED?
BUT...WHY ISN'T HIS BODY SUFFERING FROM THE EFFECTS OF MY BLOOD...?
IT SHOULDN'T HAVE GONE THIS EASILY...
SHHHHHH
!
TSU-KUNE...?
IT...IT CAN'T BE...!
HEH HEH...
TMP
!
A VAMPIRE WHO DOESN'T MIND WATER, EH?
DON'T KNOW IF THAT MEANS YOU'RE WEAK...OR STRONG, PAL.

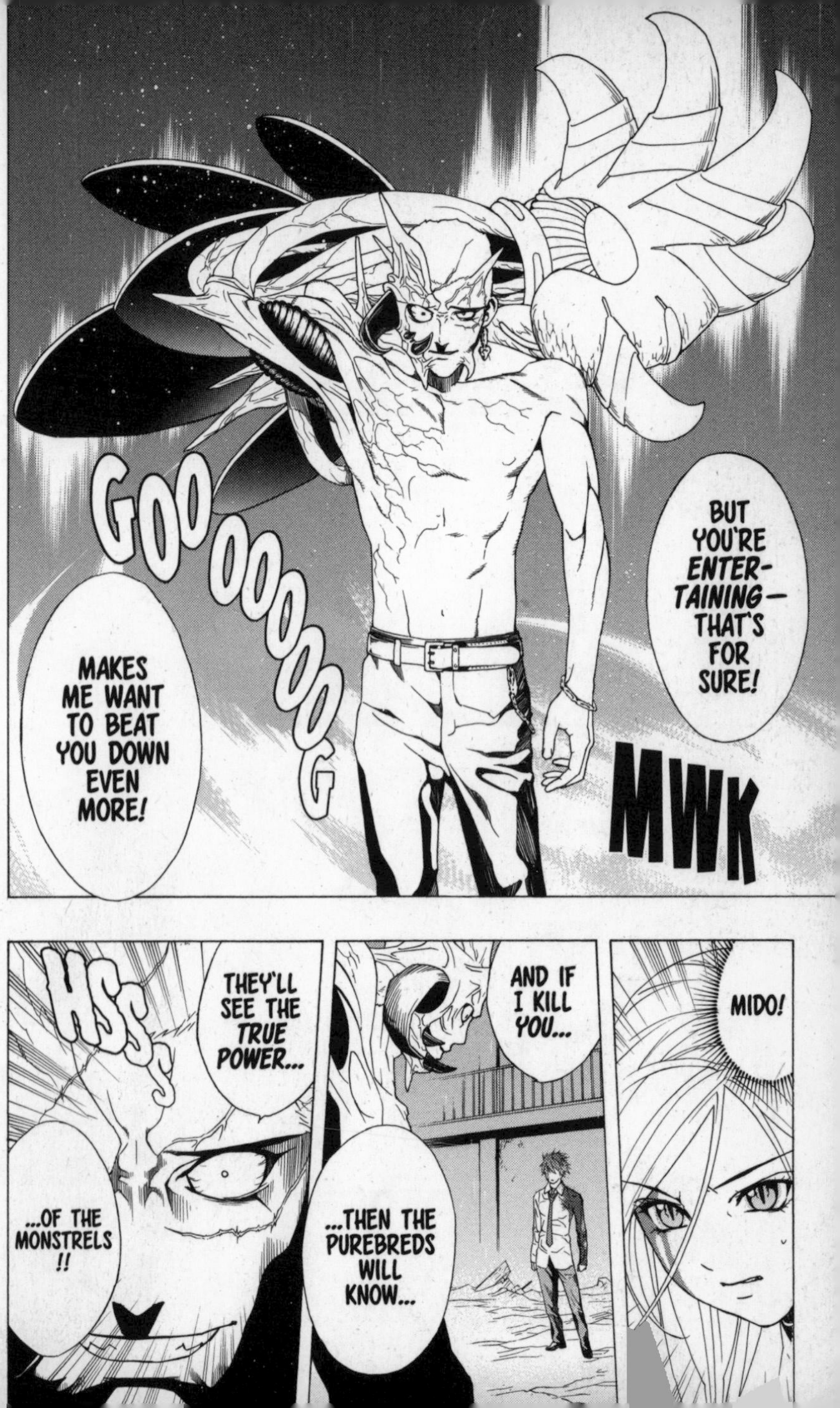
BUT YOU'RE ENTER-TAINING—THAT'S FOR SURE!
MWK
GOOOOOOOG
MAKES ME WANT TO BEAT YOU DOWN EVEN MORE!
MIDO!
AND IF I KILL YOU...
...THEN THE PUREBREDS WILL KNOW...
THEY'LL SEE THE TRUE POWER...
HSSS
...OF THE MONSTRELS !!

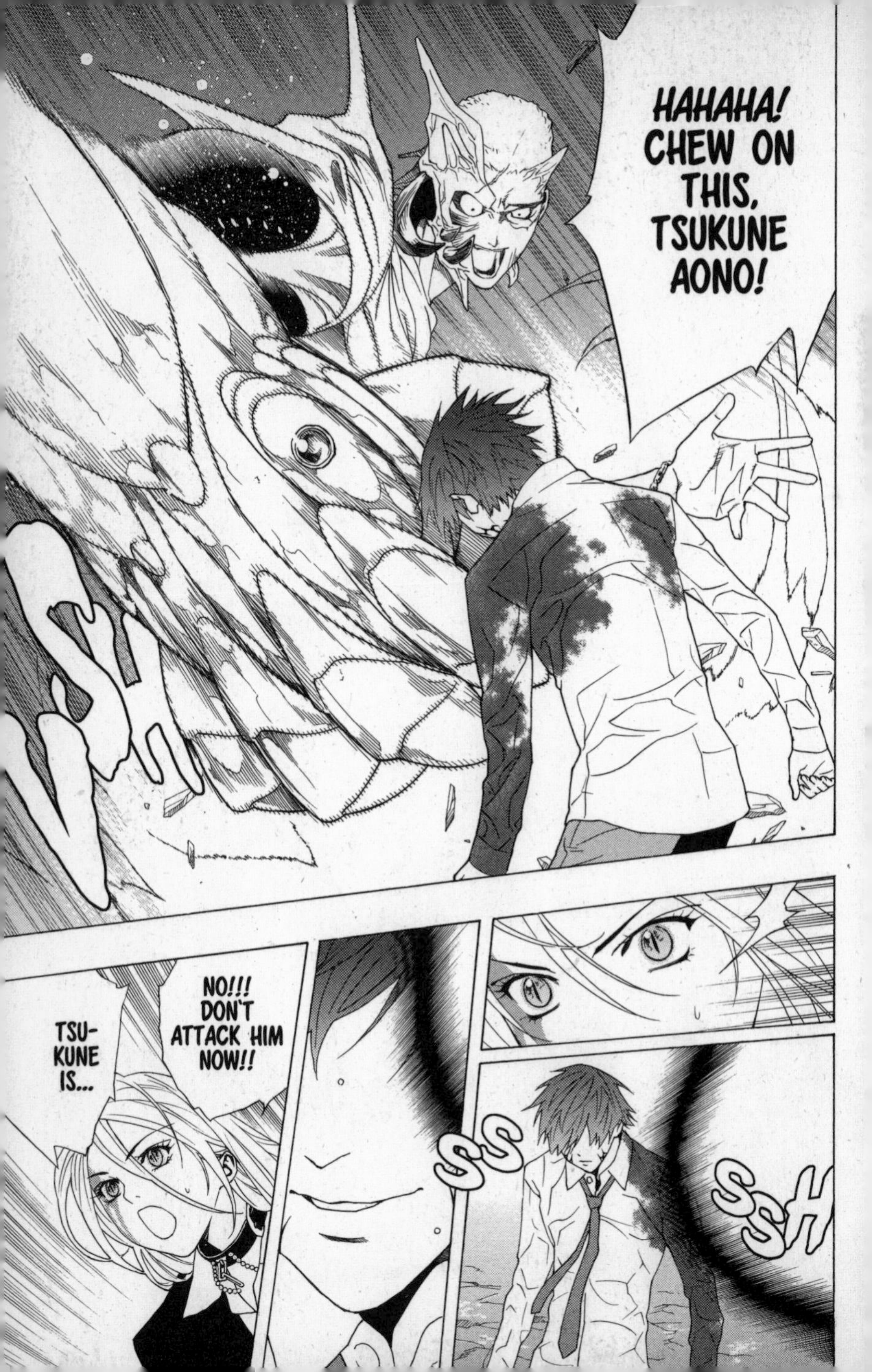
HAHAHA! CHEW ON THIS, TSUKUNE AONO!
SSH
SS
NO!!! DON'T ATTACK HIM NOW!!
TSU-KUNE IS...

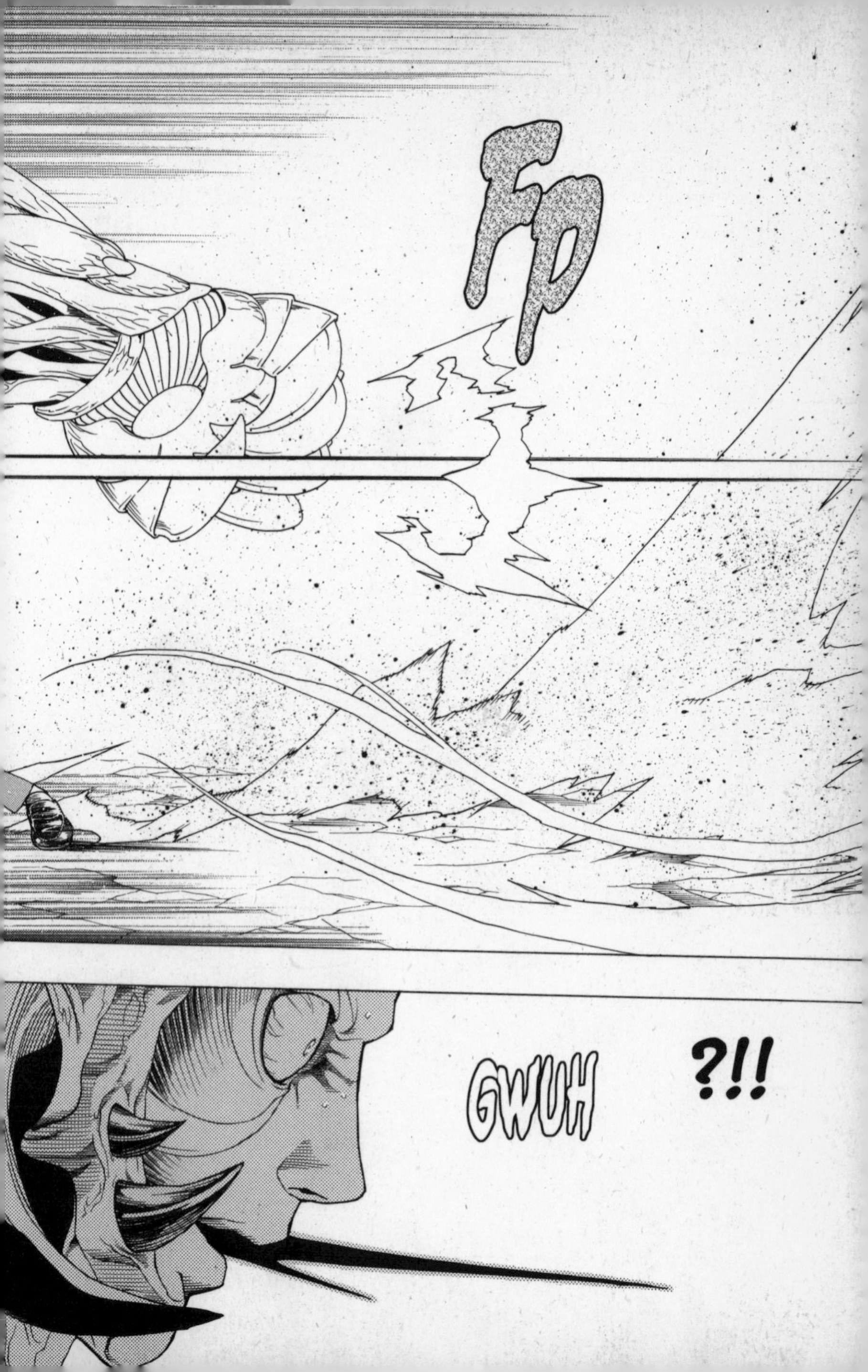

Fp
GWUH
?!!

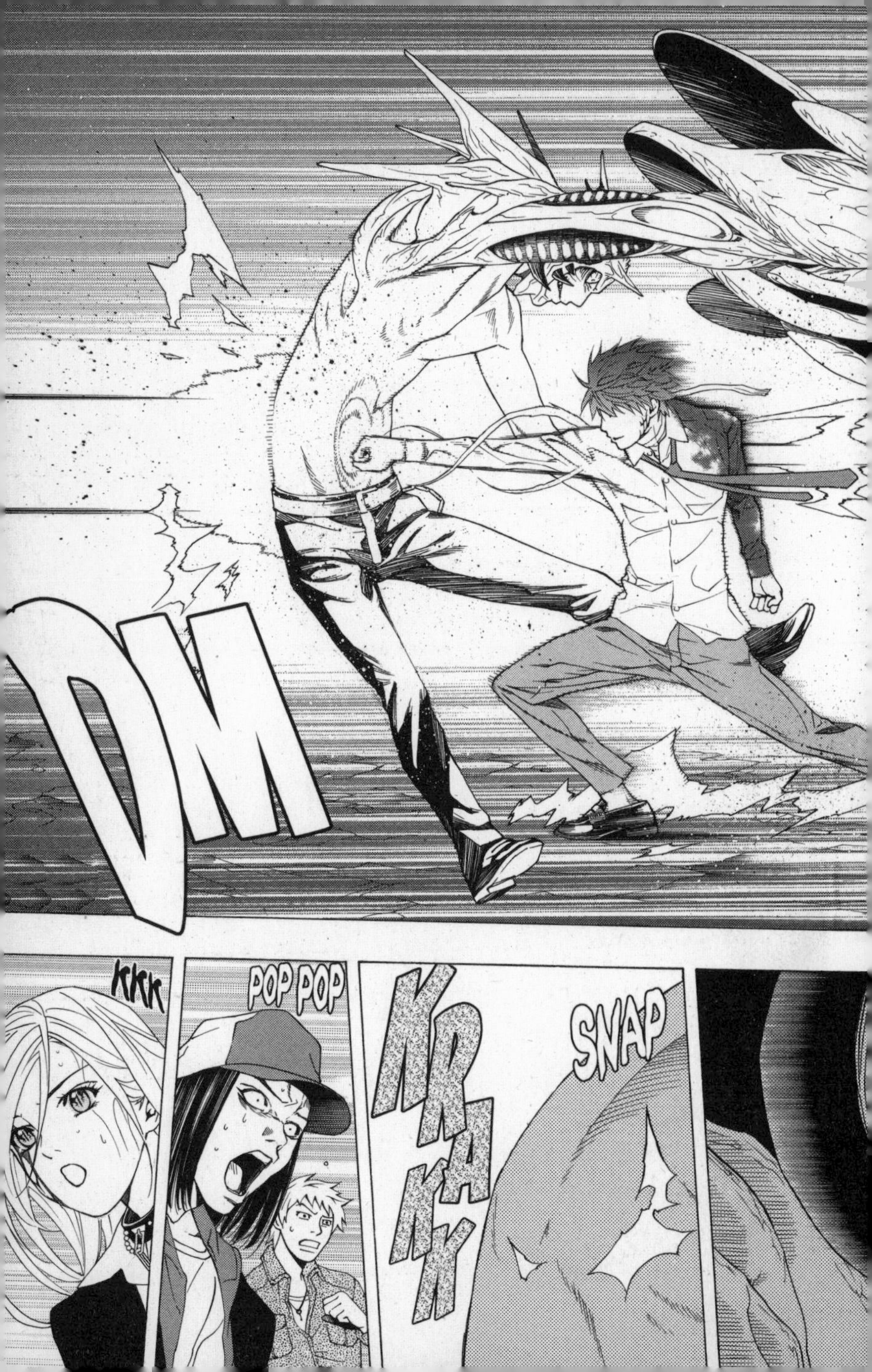
DM
SNAP
KRAKAKK
POP POP
KKK

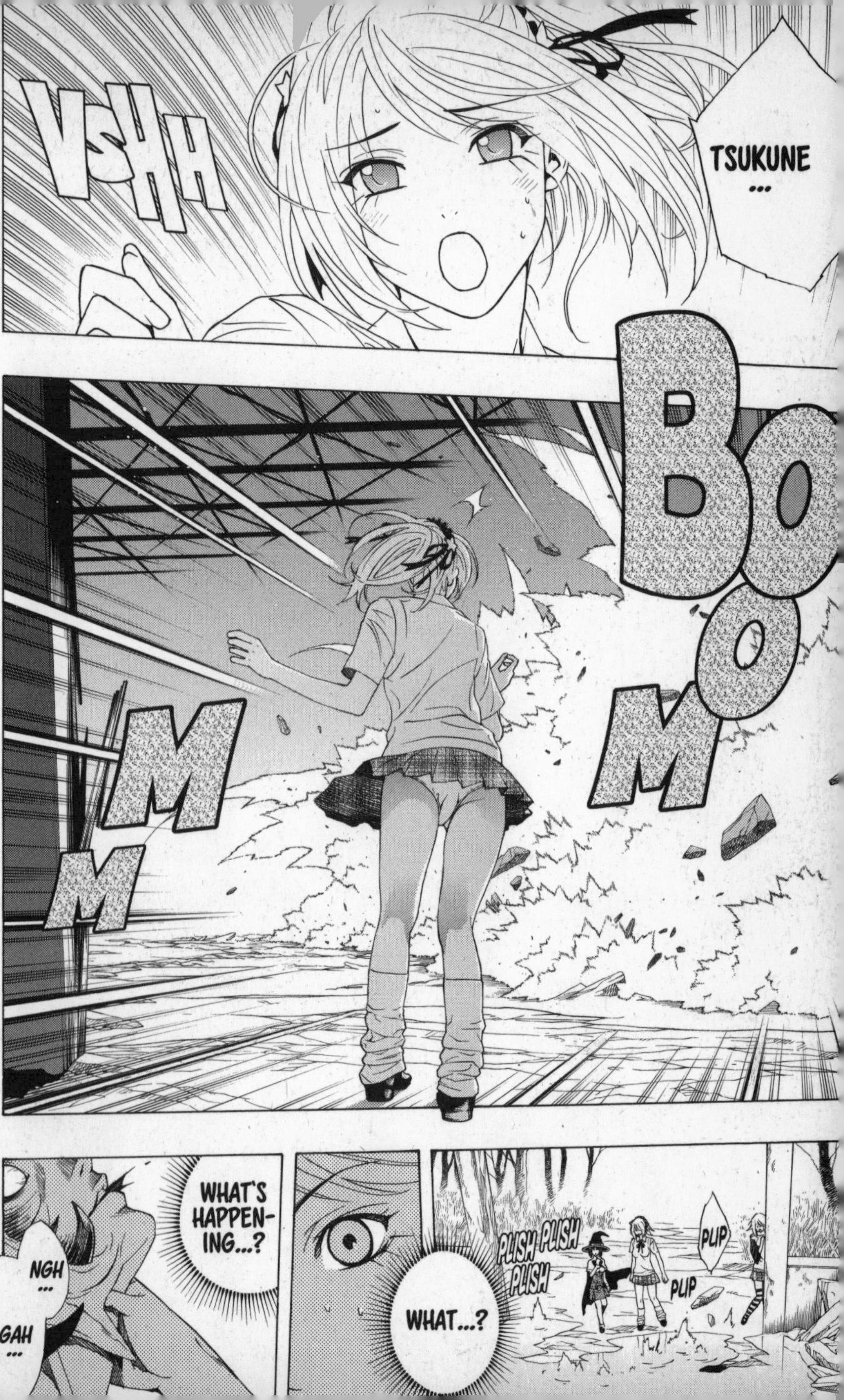
TSUKUNE ...
VSHH
BOOOMMMM
PLIP
PLIP
PLISH PLISH PLISH
WHAT...?
WHAT'S HAPPEN-ING...?
NGH ...
GAH ...

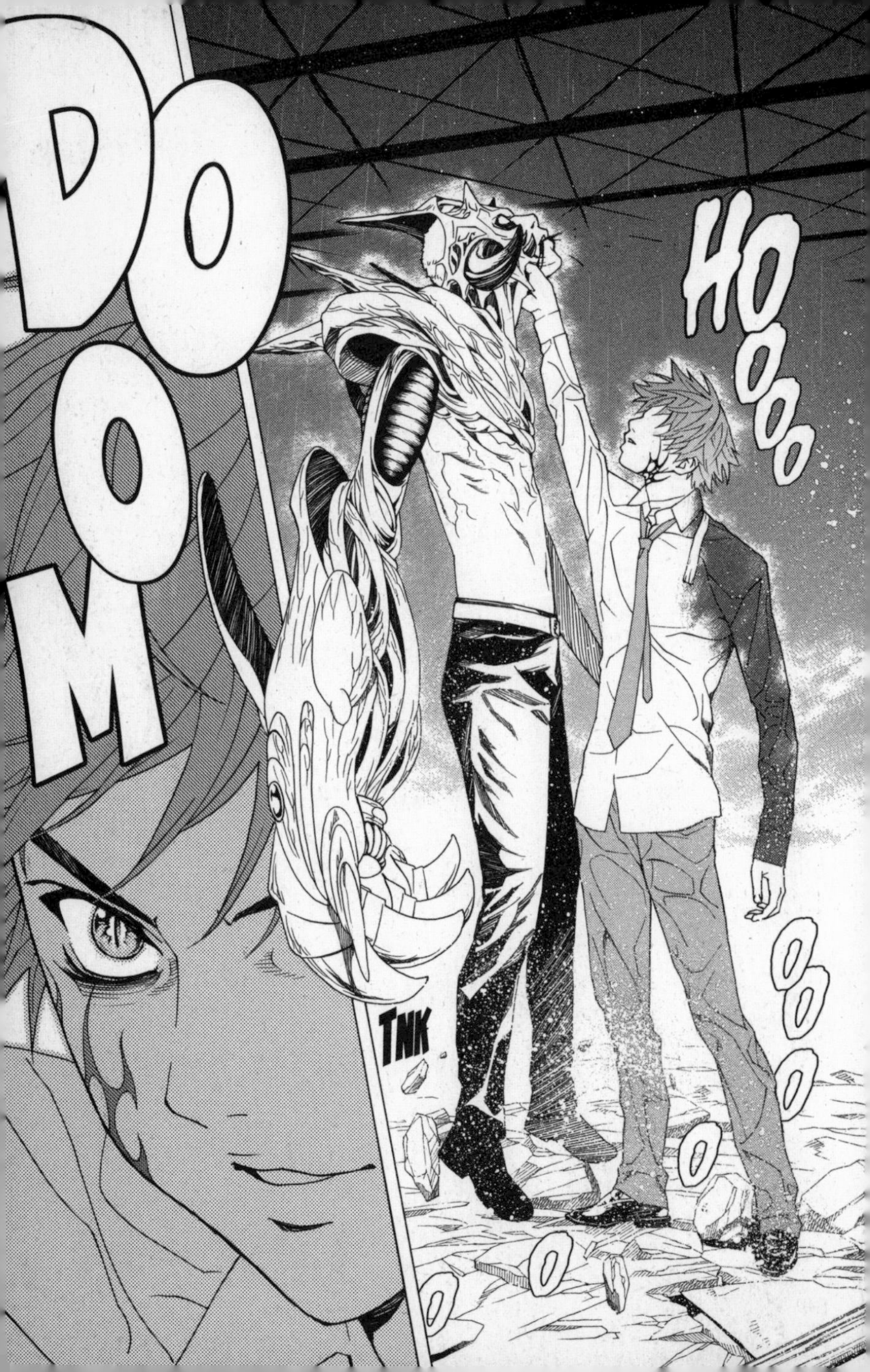
DOOOM
HOOOOOOOOOOOOOO
TNK

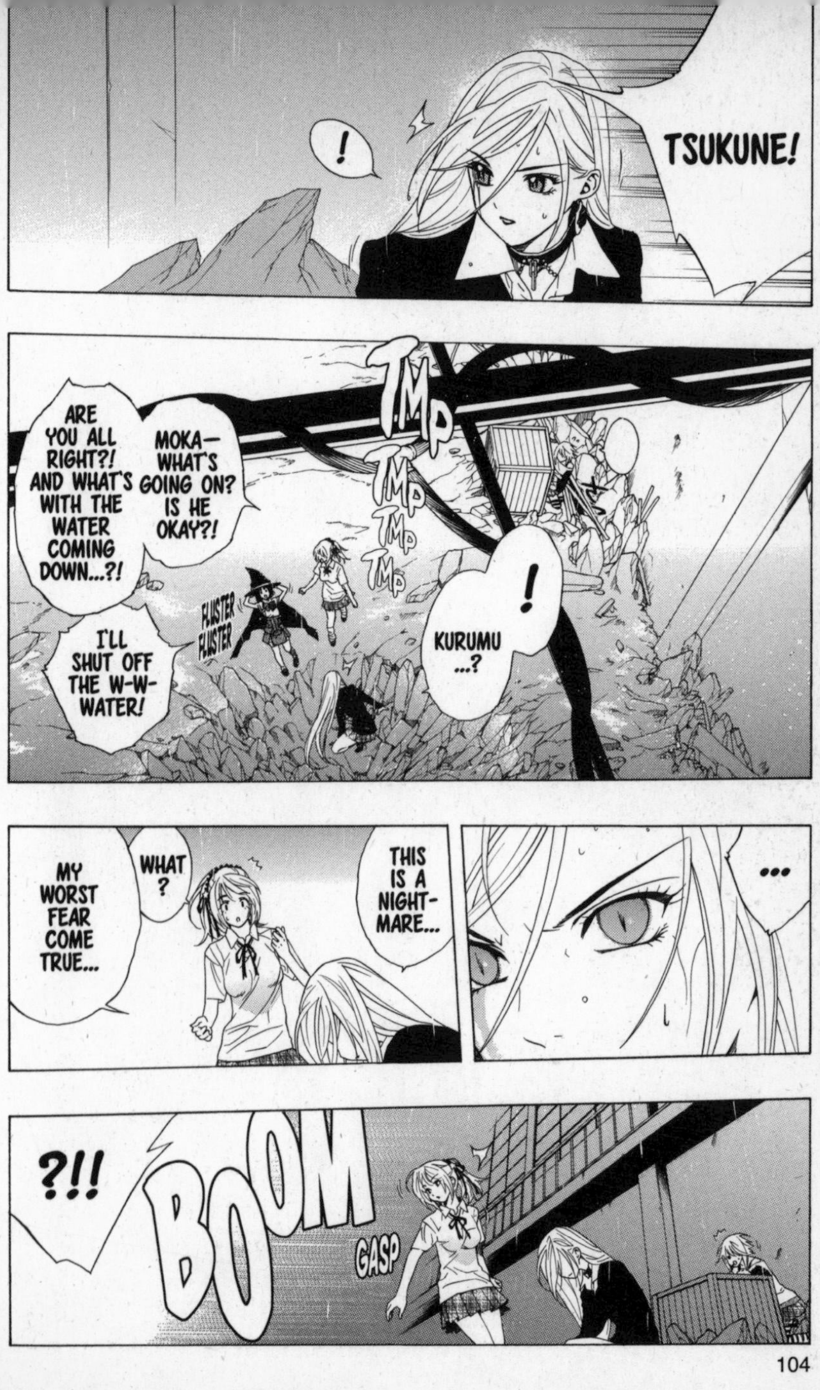
TSUKUNE!
!
!
KURUMU ...?
TMP TMP TMP TMP TMP
MOKA—WHAT'S GOING ON? IS HE OKAY?!
ARE YOU ALL RIGHT?! AND WHAT'S WITH THE WATER COMING DOWN...?!
FLUSTER FLUSTER
I'LL SHUT OFF THE W-W-WATER!
...
THIS IS A NIGHTMARE...
WHAT?
MY WORST FEAR COME TRUE...
GASP
BOOM
?!!

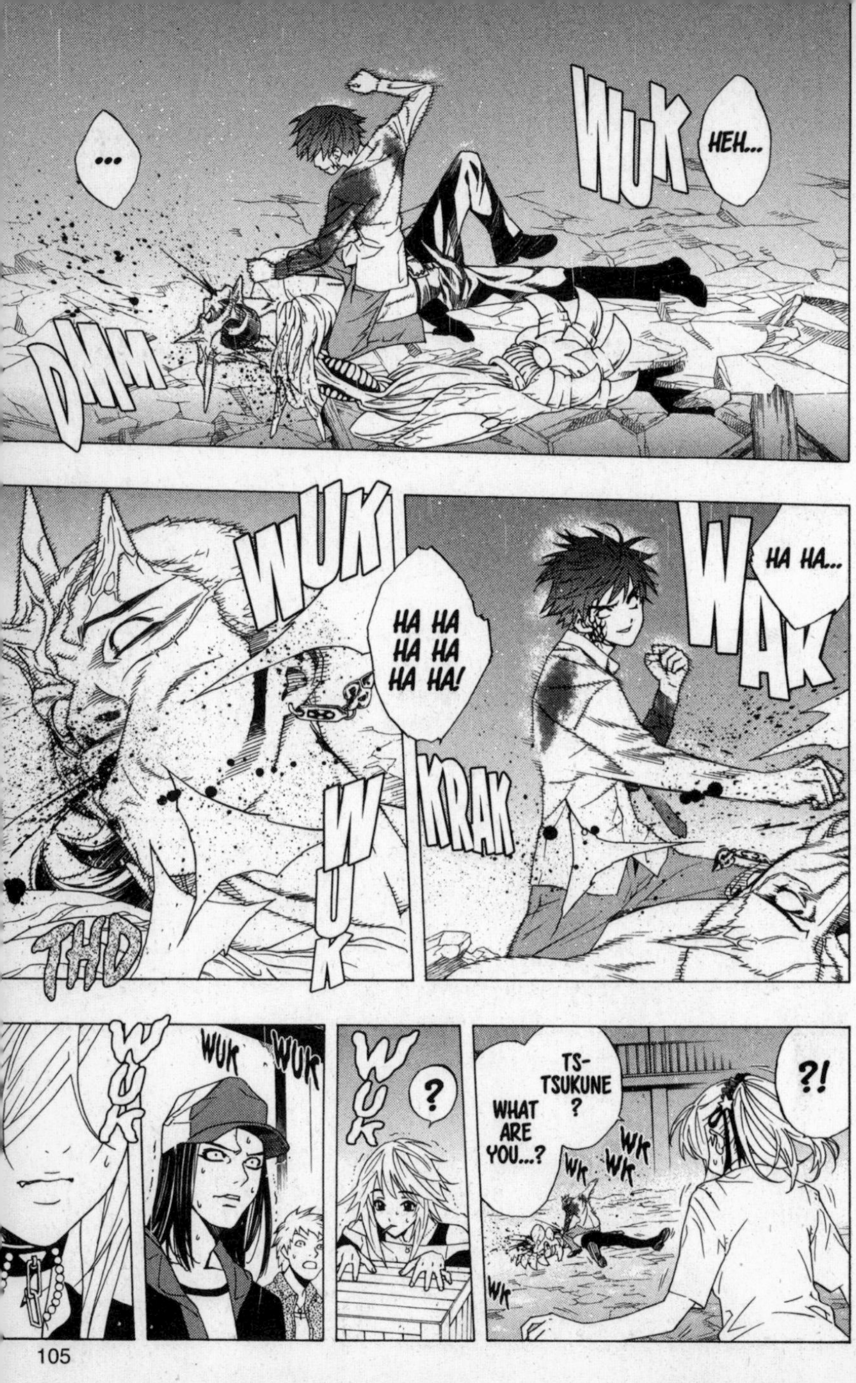
WUK
HEH...
...
DMM
WAK
HA HA...
HA HA HA HA HA HA!
KRAK
WUK
WUK
THD
?!
TS-TSUKUNE?
WHAT ARE YOU...?
WK
WK
WK
WK
WUK
?
WUK
WUK
WUK

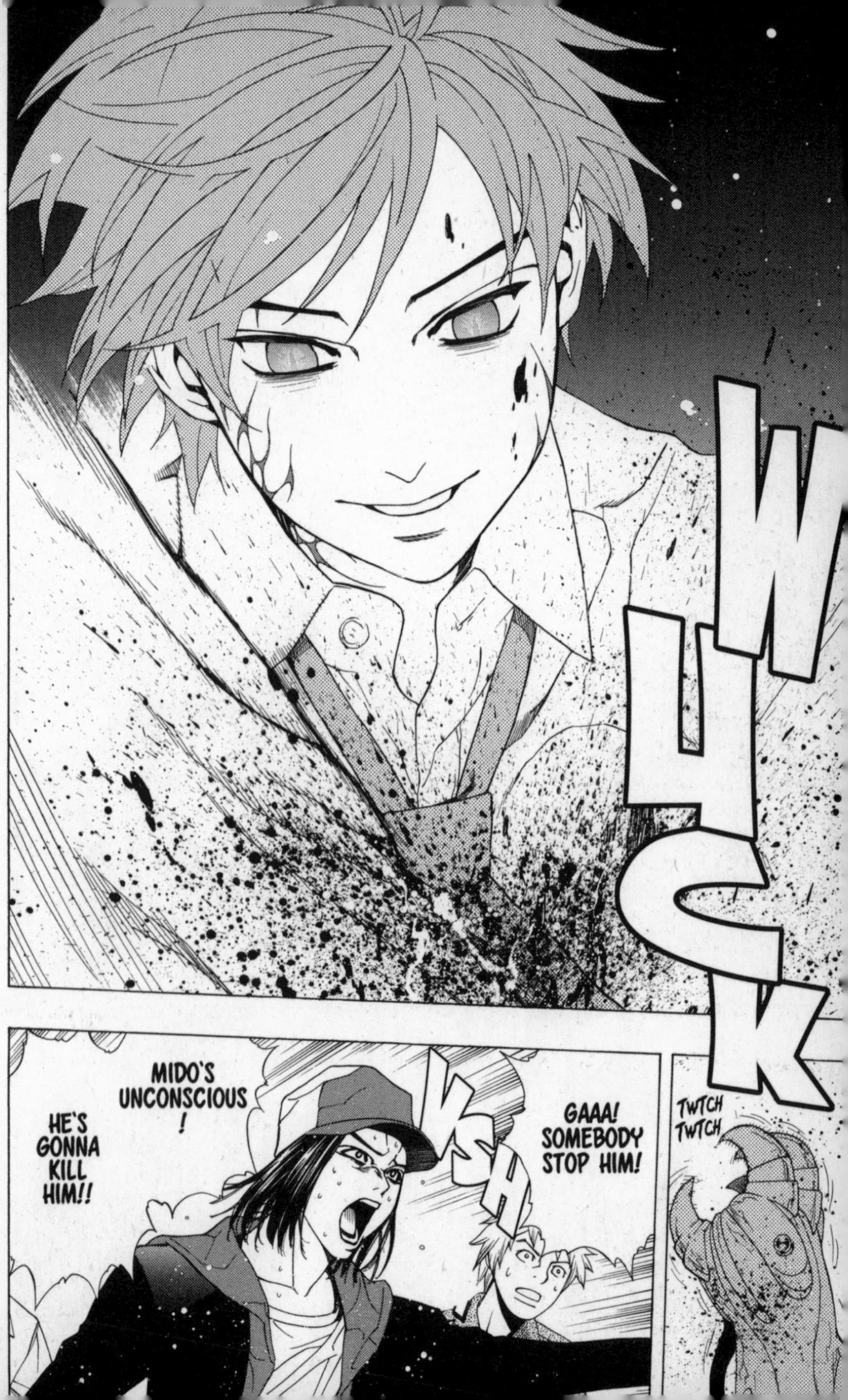
WHACK
MIDO'S UNCONSCIOUS!
HE'S GONNA KILL HIM!!
VSH
GAAA! SOMEBODY STOP HIM!
TWTCH TWTCH

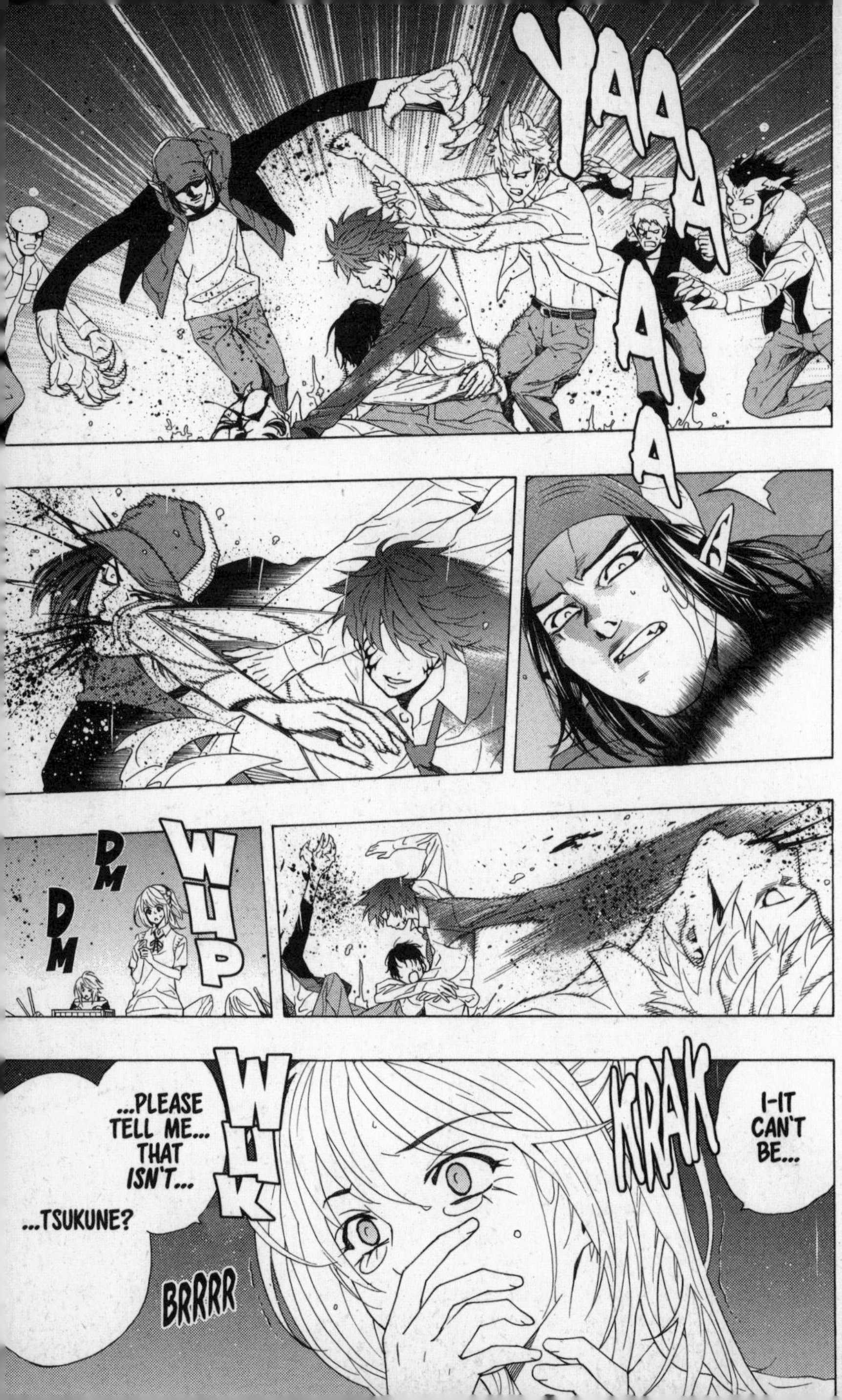
YAAAAAA
DM
DM
WUP
KRAK
I-IT CAN'T BE...
WUK
...PLEASE TELL ME... THAT ISN'T...
...TSUKUNE?
BRRRR

HIS BODY ...
...WAS SO WEAKENED ...
?!!
...THAT THE BLOOD I INFUSED HIM WITH...HAS TURNED HIM INTO A COMPLETE VAMPIRE!
AND NOT JUST PHYSIC-ALLY...
FEROCITY IS IN OUR BLOOD...
IT'S IN OUR NATURE TO BE HUNTERS, KILLERS... AND NOW...
...THAT'S TSUKUNE'S NATURE TOO!
TSUKUNE HAS TURNED INTO A GHOUL...
A KILLING MACHINE DOOMED TO WANDER THE WORLD IN SEARCH OF HUMAN FLESH!

Bite-Size Encyclopedia

Ghoul

Created when an evil spirit possesses a corpse. Favorite food: human meat. Feeds on children and cadavers exhumed from graves.
Weakness: the divine and spiritual. They avoid religious symbols.

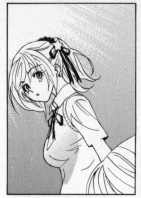

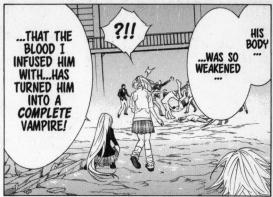

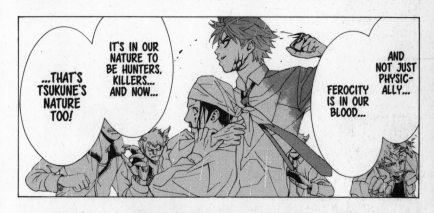

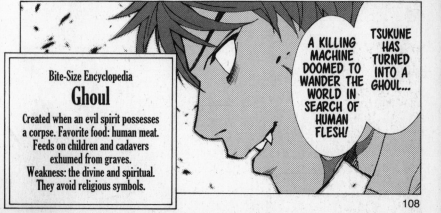

READ THIS WAY

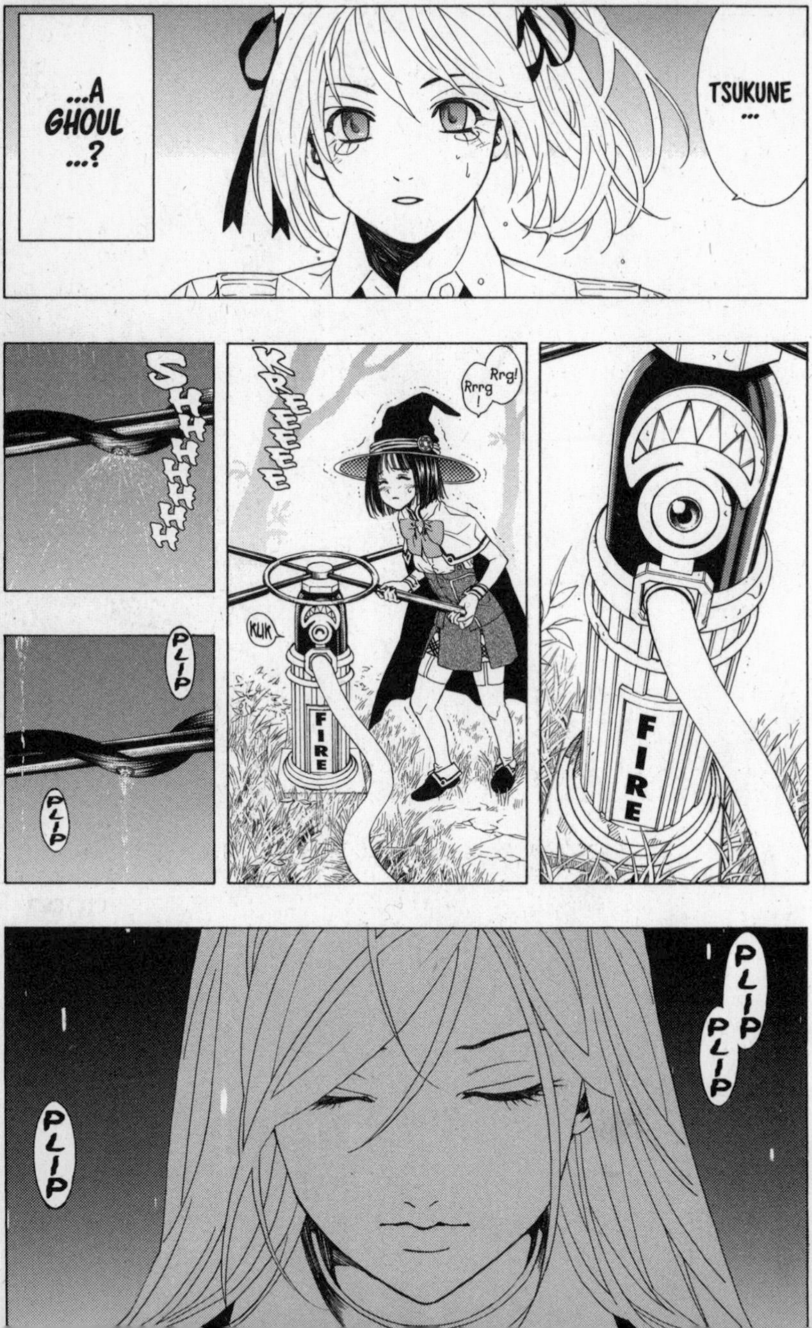

TSUKUNE ...
...A GHOUL ...?
KREEEE
Rrg!
Rrrg!
KUK
SHHHHHHH
PLIP
PLIP
PLIP
PLIP
PLIP

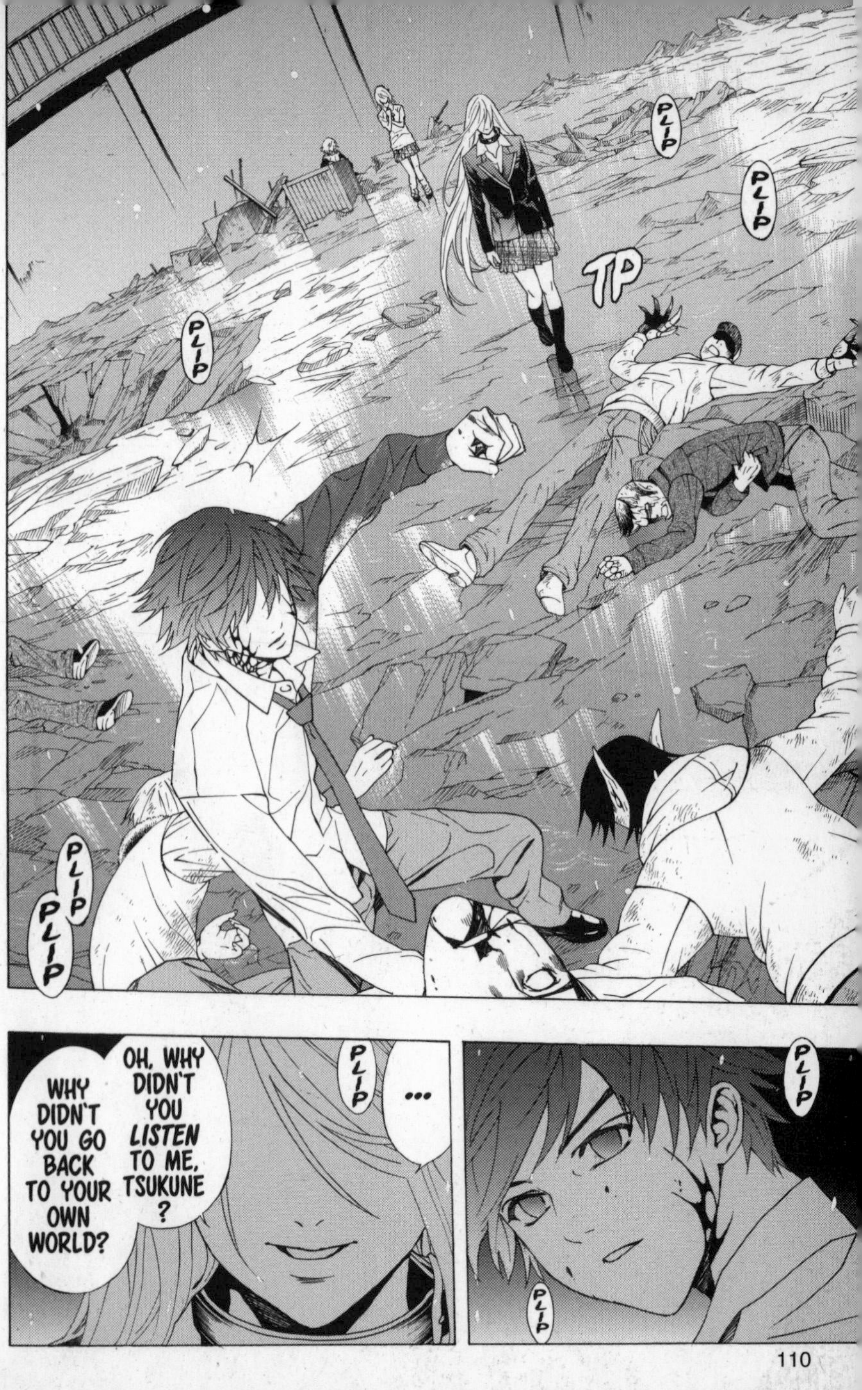
PLIP
PLIP
TP
PLIP
PLIP
PLIP
PLIP
PLIP
...
PLIP
OH, WHY DIDN'T YOU LISTEN TO ME, TSUKUNE?
WHY DIDN'T YOU GO BACK TO YOUR OWN WORLD?

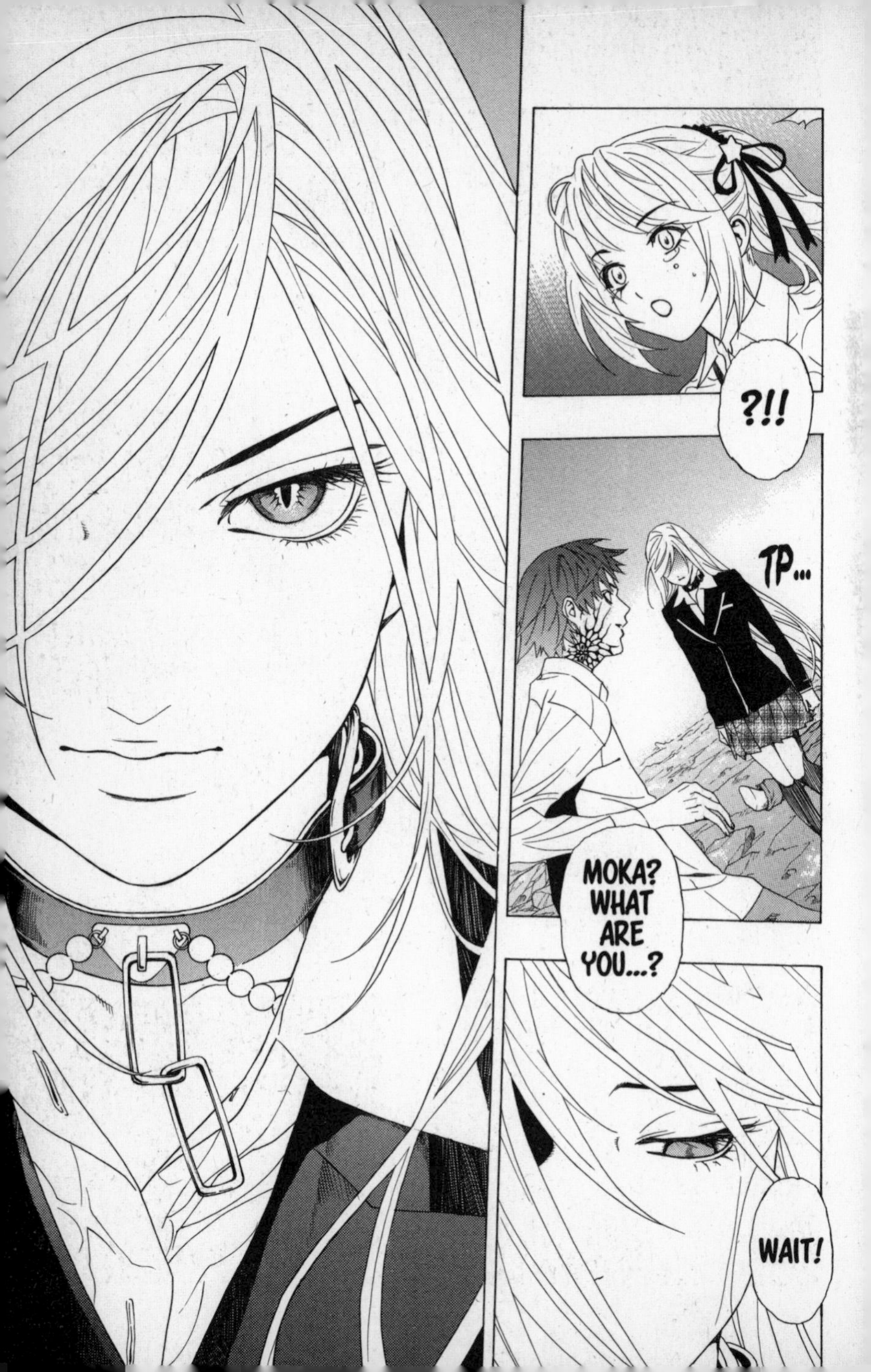
?!!
TP...
MOKA? WHAT ARE YOU...?
WAIT!

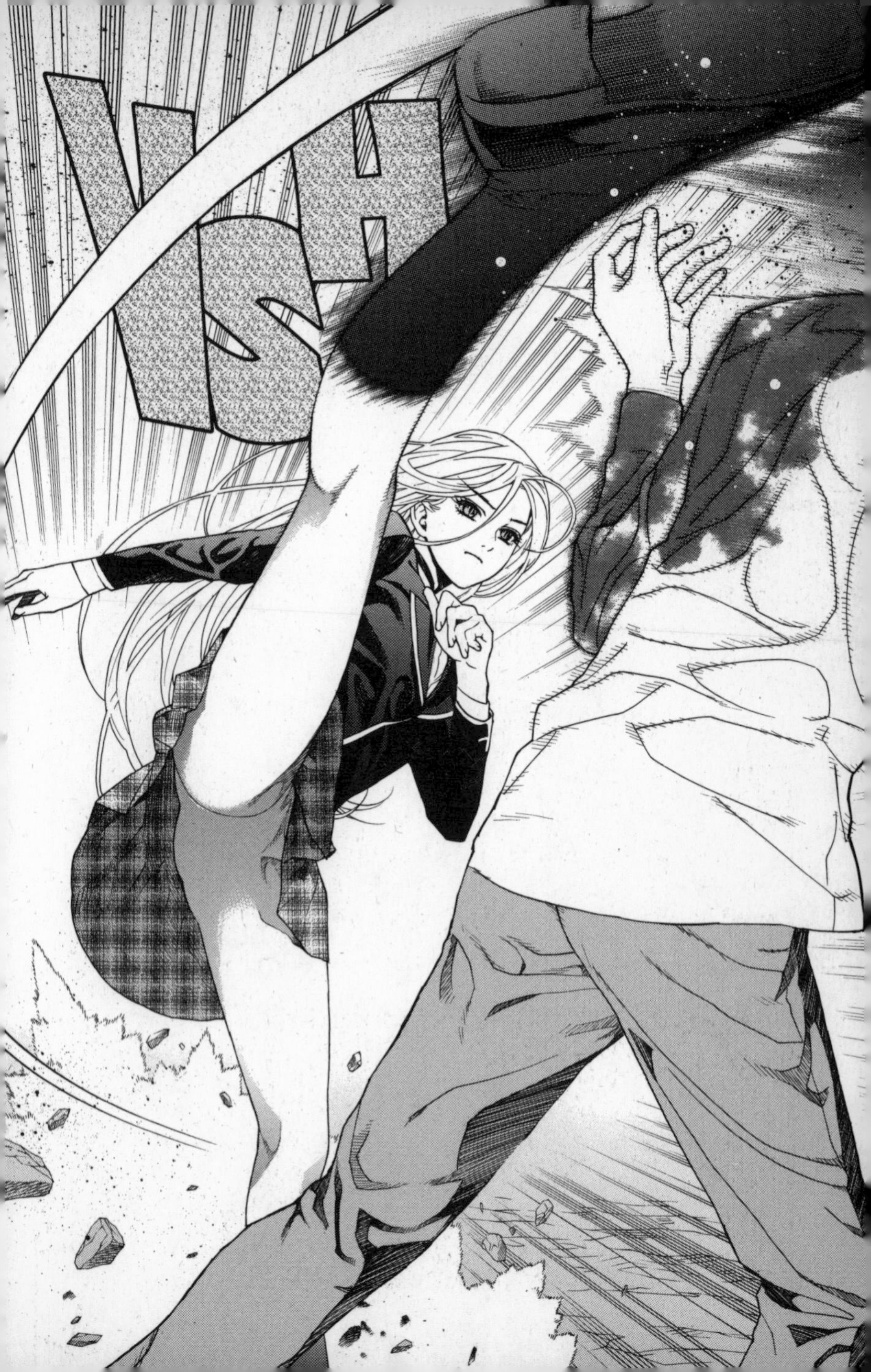
VISH

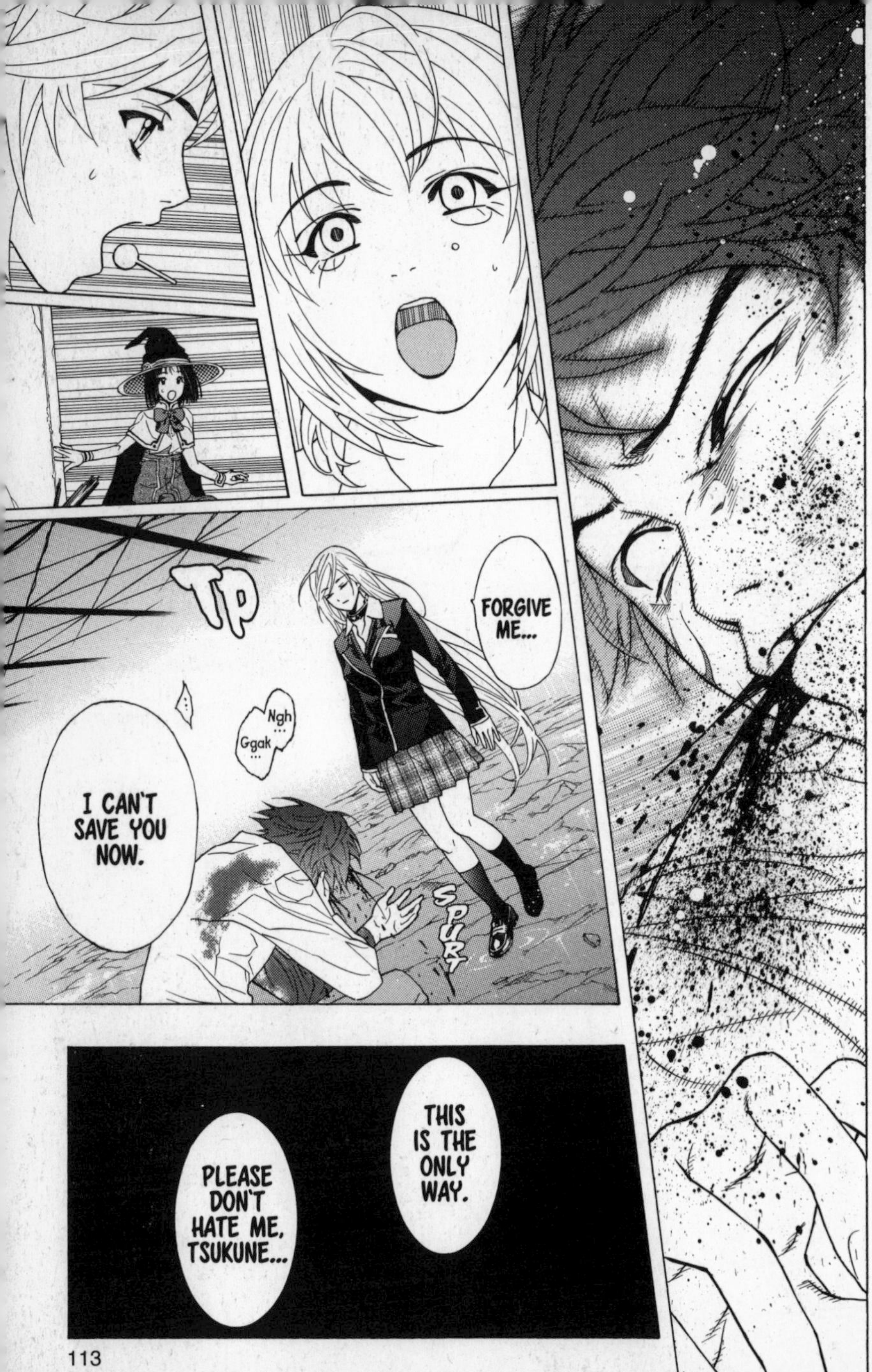
TP
FORGIVE ME...
Ngh...
Ggak...
I CAN'T SAVE YOU NOW.
SPURT
THIS IS THE ONLY WAY.
PLEASE DON'T HATE ME, TSUKUNE...

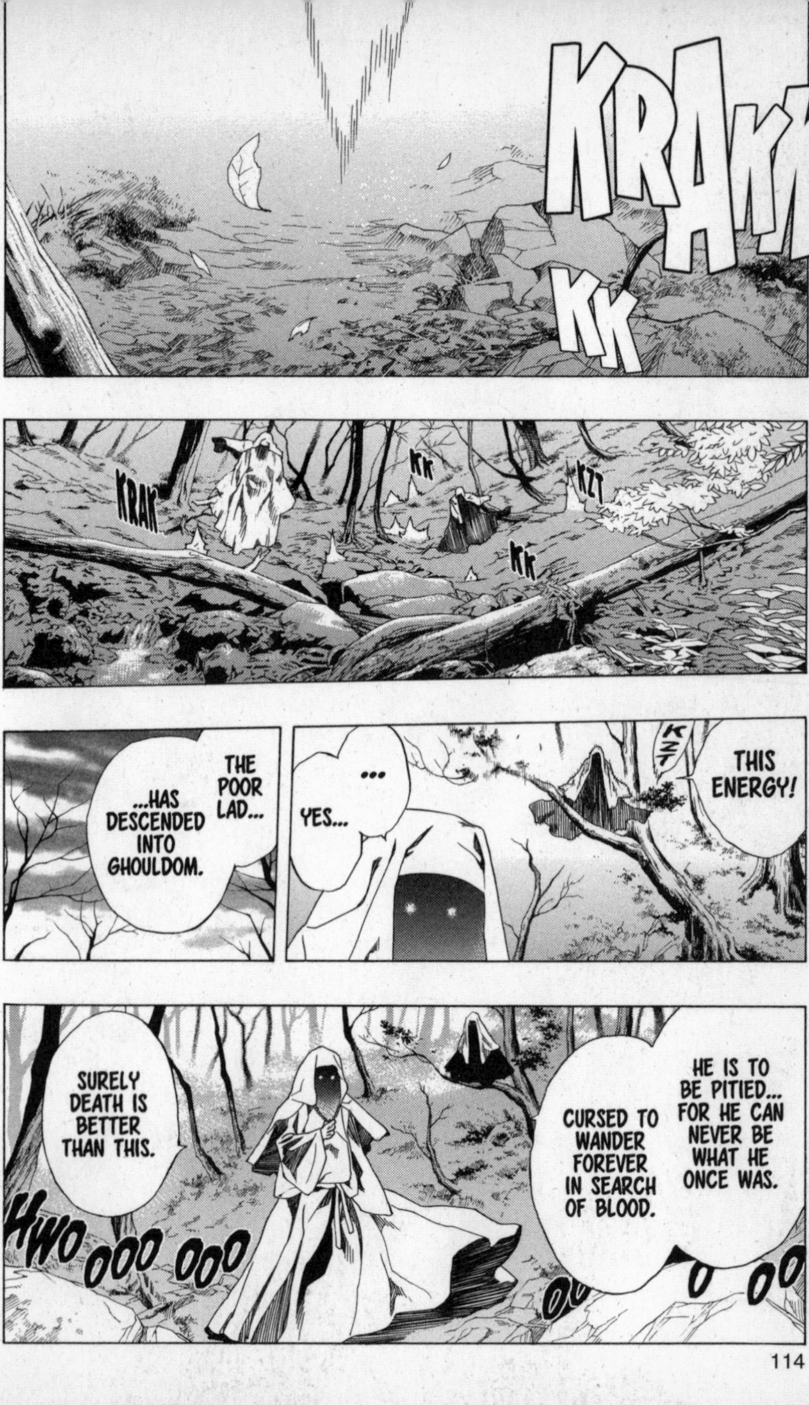
KRAKK
KK
KZT
KK
KK
KRAK
KZT
THIS ENERGY!
...
YES...
THE POOR LAD...
...HAS DESCENDED INTO GHOULDOM.
HE IS TO BE PITIED... FOR HE CAN NEVER BE WHAT HE ONCE WAS.
CURSED TO WANDER FOREVER IN SEARCH OF BLOOD.
SURELY DEATH IS BETTER THAN THIS.
HWO OOO OOO
OO O OO

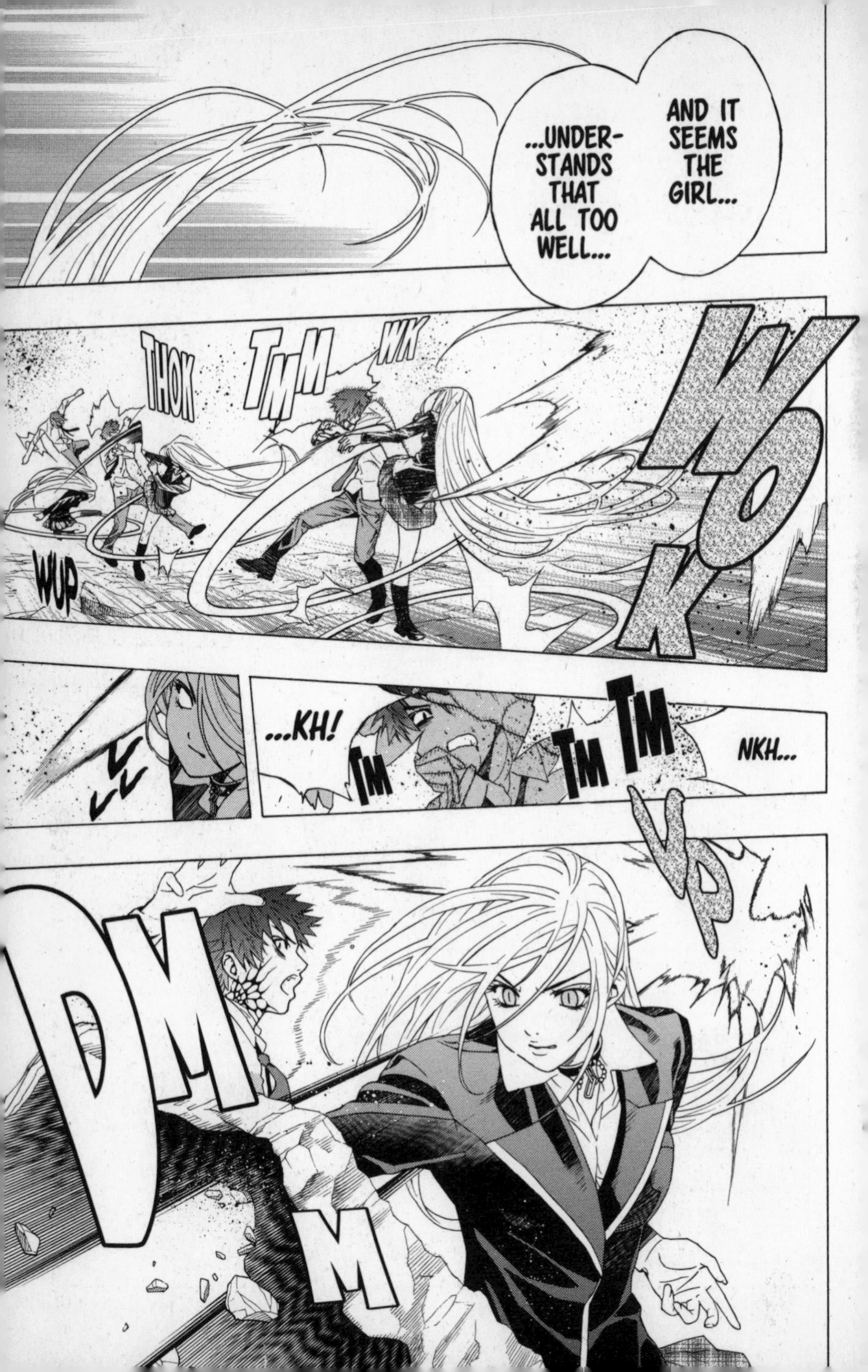

AND IT SEEMS THE GIRL...
...UNDER-STANDS THAT ALL TOO WELL...
WOK
WK
TMM
THOK
WUP
NKH...
TM TM
TM
...KH!
VP
DMM

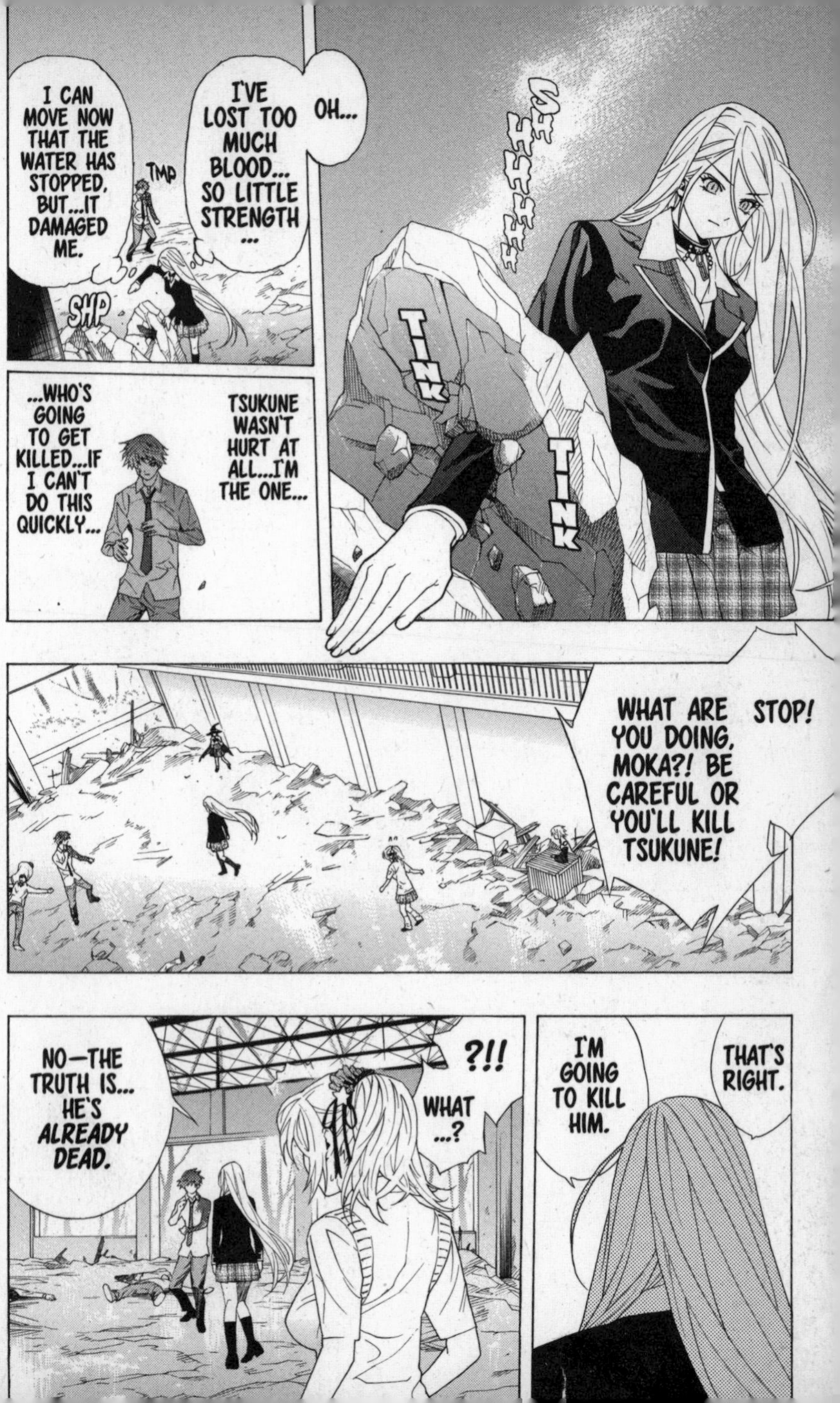

SHHHHHHH
OH...
I'VE LOST TOO MUCH BLOOD... SO LITTLE STRENGTH...
I CAN MOVE NOW THAT THE WATER HAS STOPPED, BUT...IT DAMAGED ME.
TMP
SHP
TINK
TINK
TSUKUNE WASN'T HURT AT ALL...I'M THE ONE...
...WHO'S GOING TO GET KILLED...IF I CAN'T DO THIS QUICKLY...
STOP!
WHAT ARE YOU DOING, MOKA?! BE CAREFUL OR YOU'LL KILL TSUKUNE!
THAT'S RIGHT.
I'M GOING TO KILL HIM.
?!!
WHAT...?
NO—THE TRUTH IS... HE'S ALREADY DEAD.

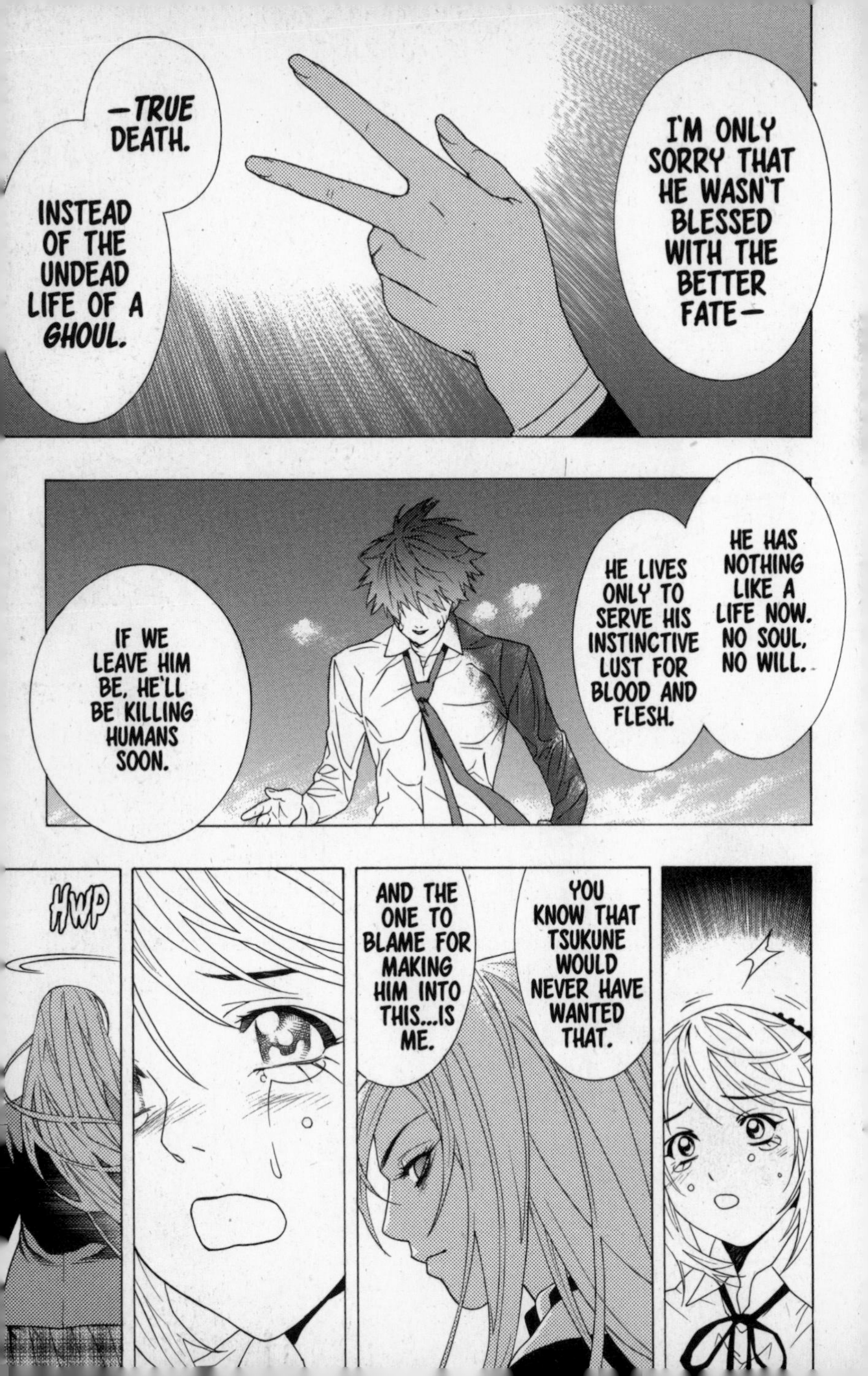
I'M ONLY SORRY THAT HE WASN'T BLESSED WITH THE BETTER FATE—
—TRUE DEATH.
INSTEAD OF THE UNDEAD LIFE OF A *GHOUL*.
HE HAS NOTHING LIKE A LIFE NOW. NO SOUL, NO WILL.
HE LIVES ONLY TO SERVE HIS INSTINCTIVE LUST FOR BLOOD AND FLESH.
IF WE LEAVE HIM BE, HE'LL BE KILLING HUMANS SOON.
YOU KNOW THAT TSUKUNE WOULD NEVER HAVE WANTED THAT.
AND THE ONE TO BLAME FOR MAKING HIM INTO THIS...IS ME.
HWP

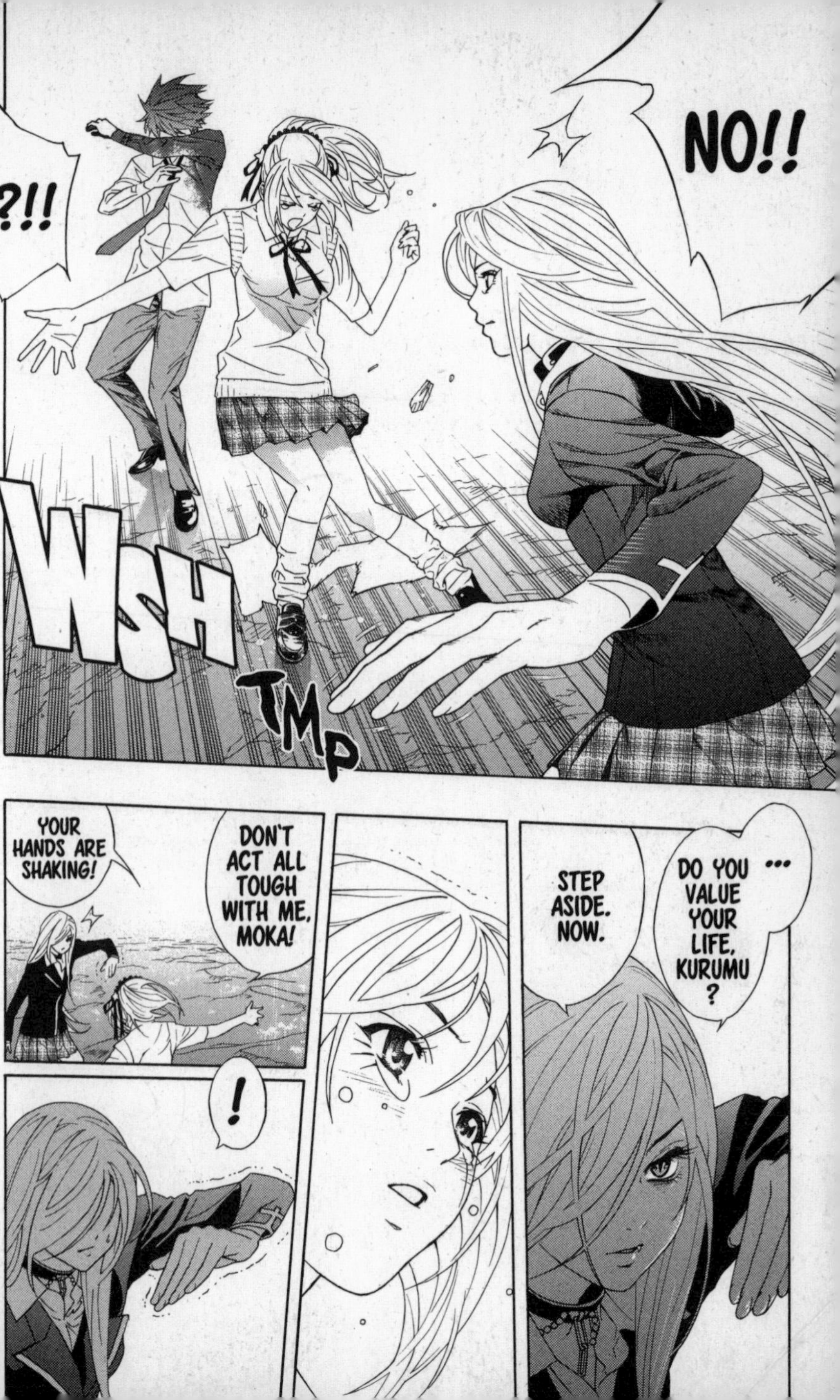
NO!!
?!!
WSH
TMP
DO YOU VALUE YOUR LIFE, KURUMU?
...
STEP ASIDE. NOW.
DON'T ACT ALL TOUGH WITH ME, MOKA!
YOUR HANDS ARE SHAKING!
!

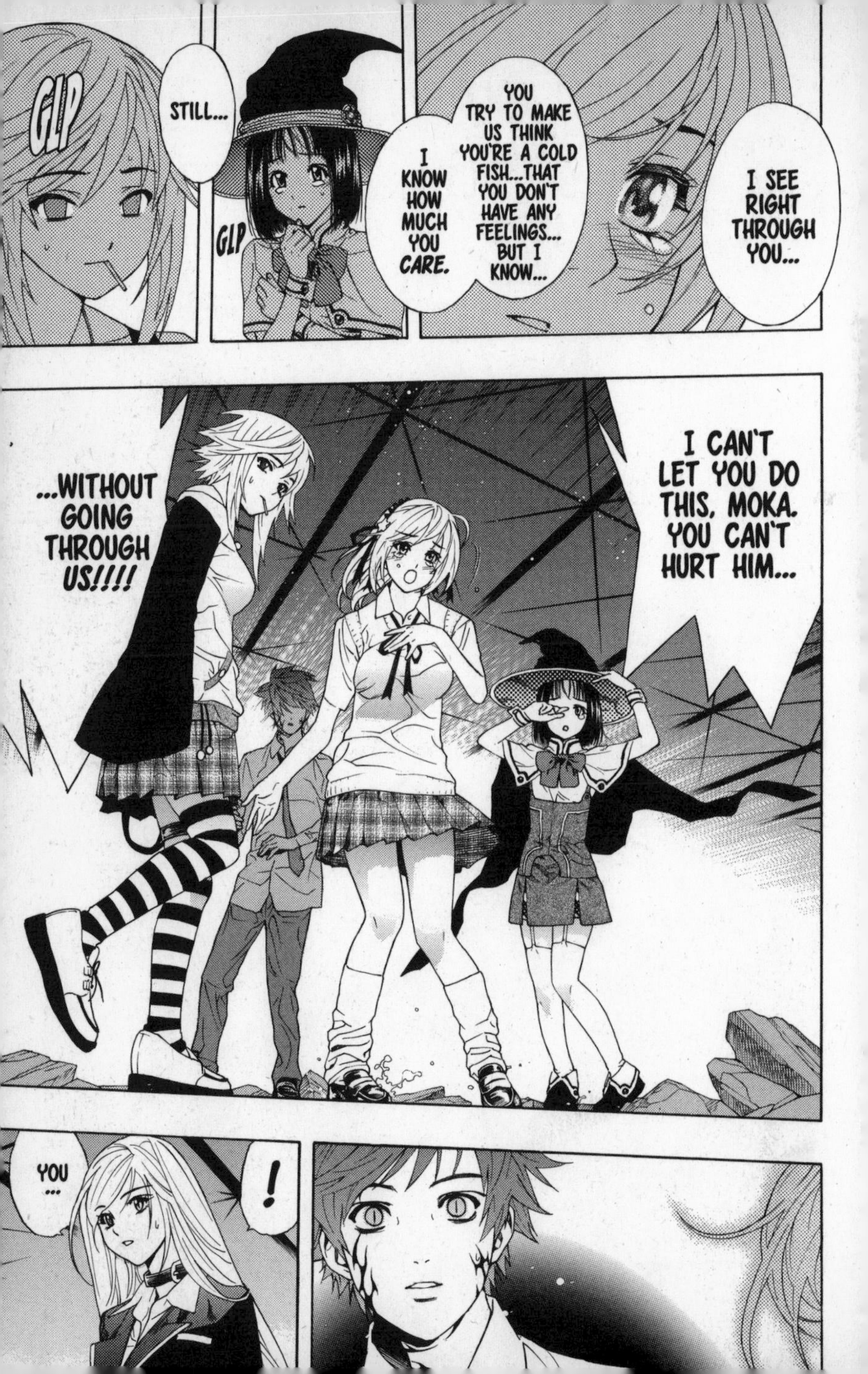

I SEE RIGHT THROUGH YOU...
YOU TRY TO MAKE US THINK YOU'RE A COLD FISH...THAT YOU DON'T HAVE ANY FEELINGS... BUT I KNOW...
I KNOW HOW MUCH YOU CARE.
GLP
STILL...
GLP
I CAN'T LET YOU DO THIS, MOKA. YOU CAN'T HURT HIM...
...WITHOUT GOING THROUGH US!!!!
!
YOU ...

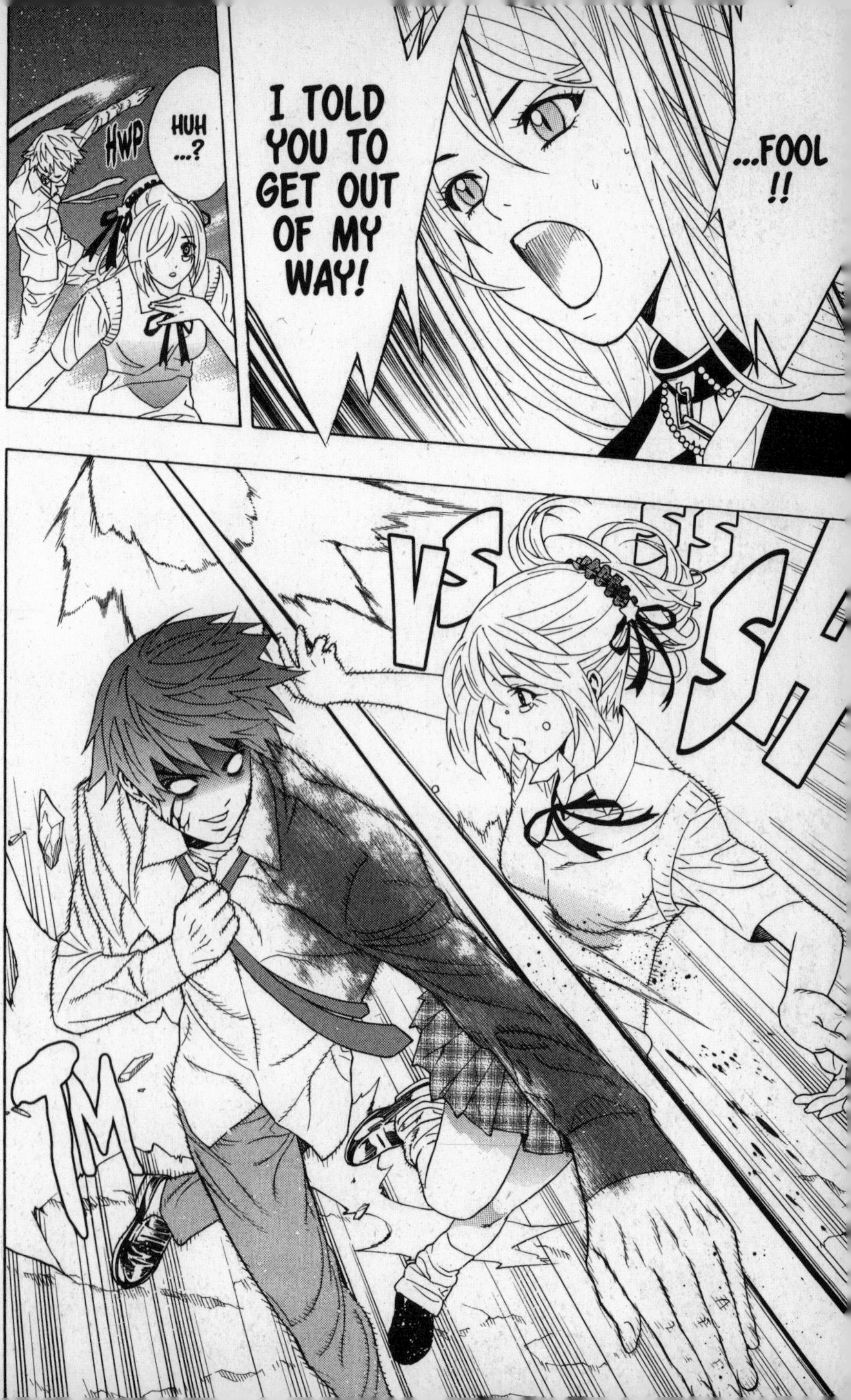

...FOOL !!
I TOLD YOU TO GET OUT OF MY WAY!
HUH ...?
HWP

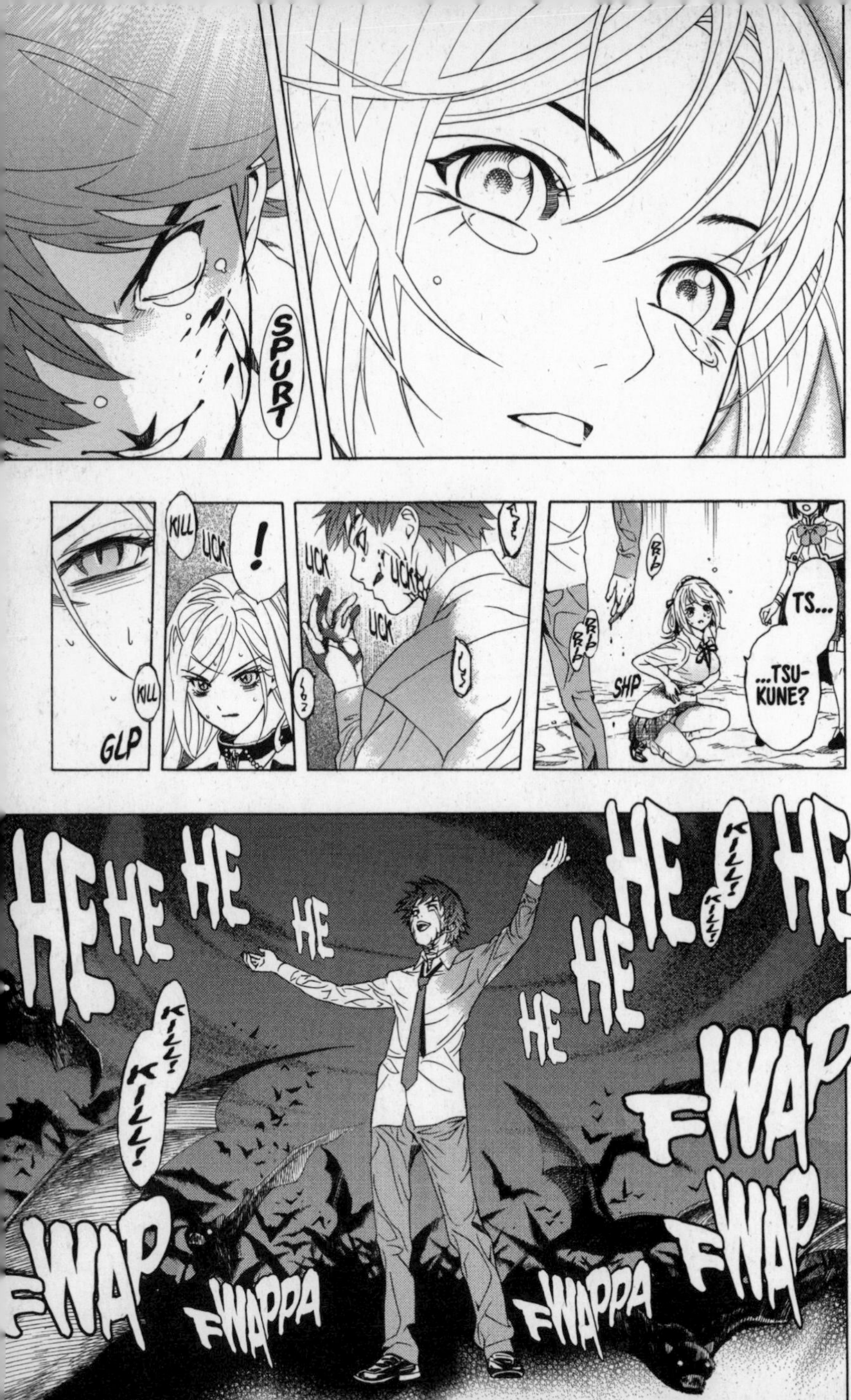
SPURT
TS...
...TSU-KUNE?
SHP
LICK
LICK
LICK
!
LICK
KILL
KILL
GLP
HE HE HE HE
KILL! KILL!
HE HE HE HE
KILL! KILL!
FWAP
FWAP
FWAPPA
FWAPPA
FWAP

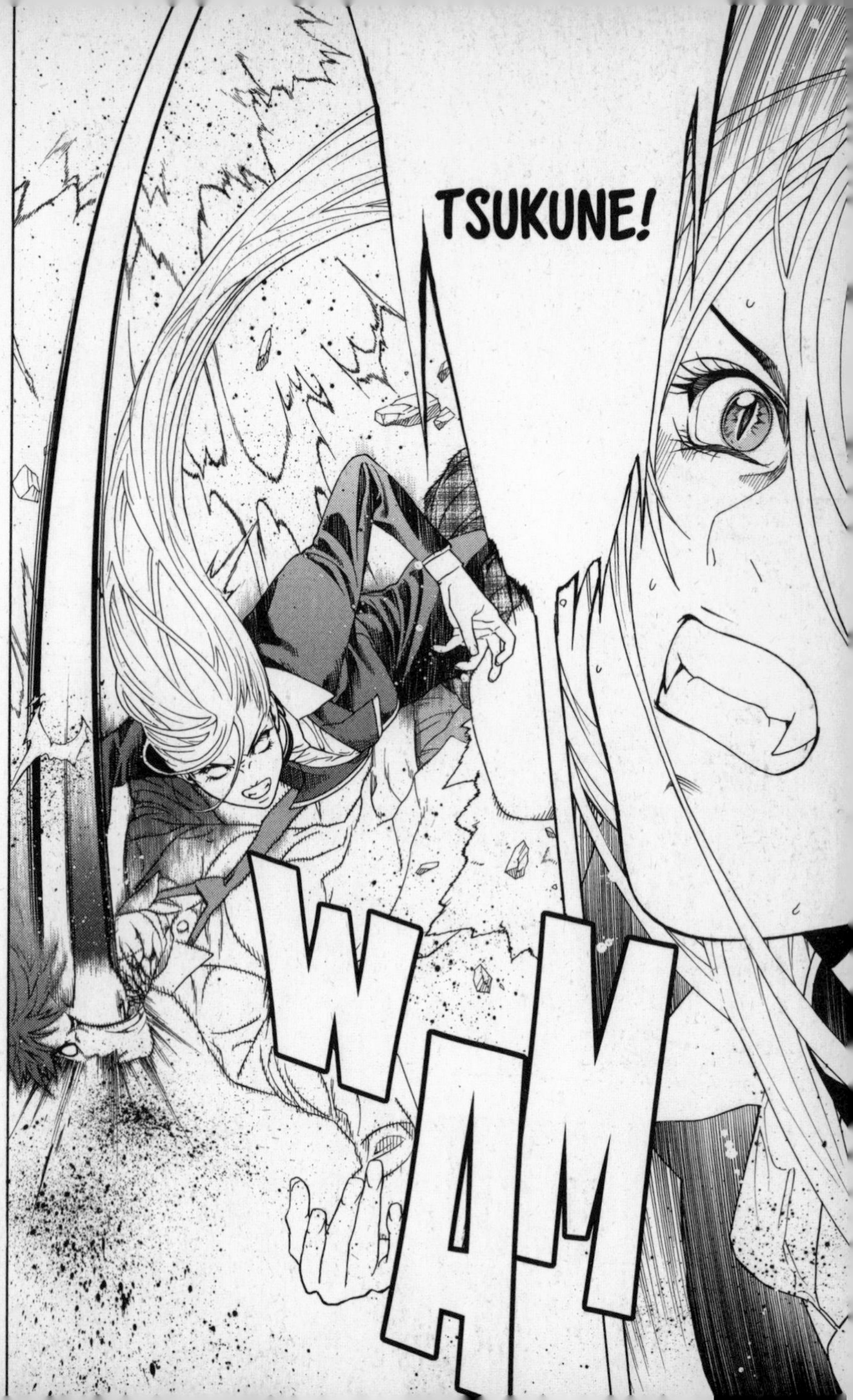
TSUKUNE!
WAM

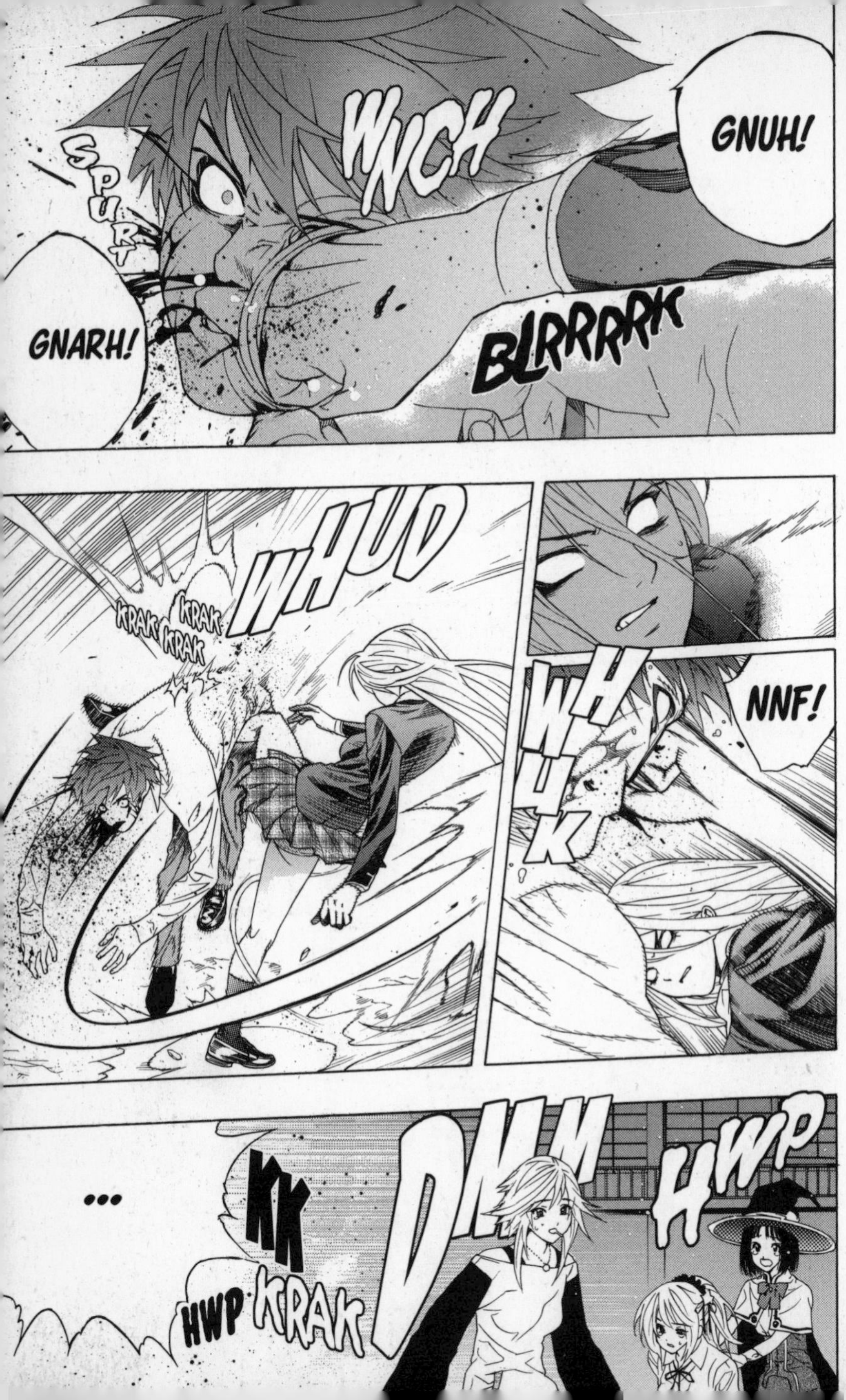
GNUH!
WNCH
SPURT
GNARH!
BLRRRRK
NNF!
WHUK
WHUD
KRAK
KRAK KRAK
HWP
DMM
KK
HWP KRAK
...

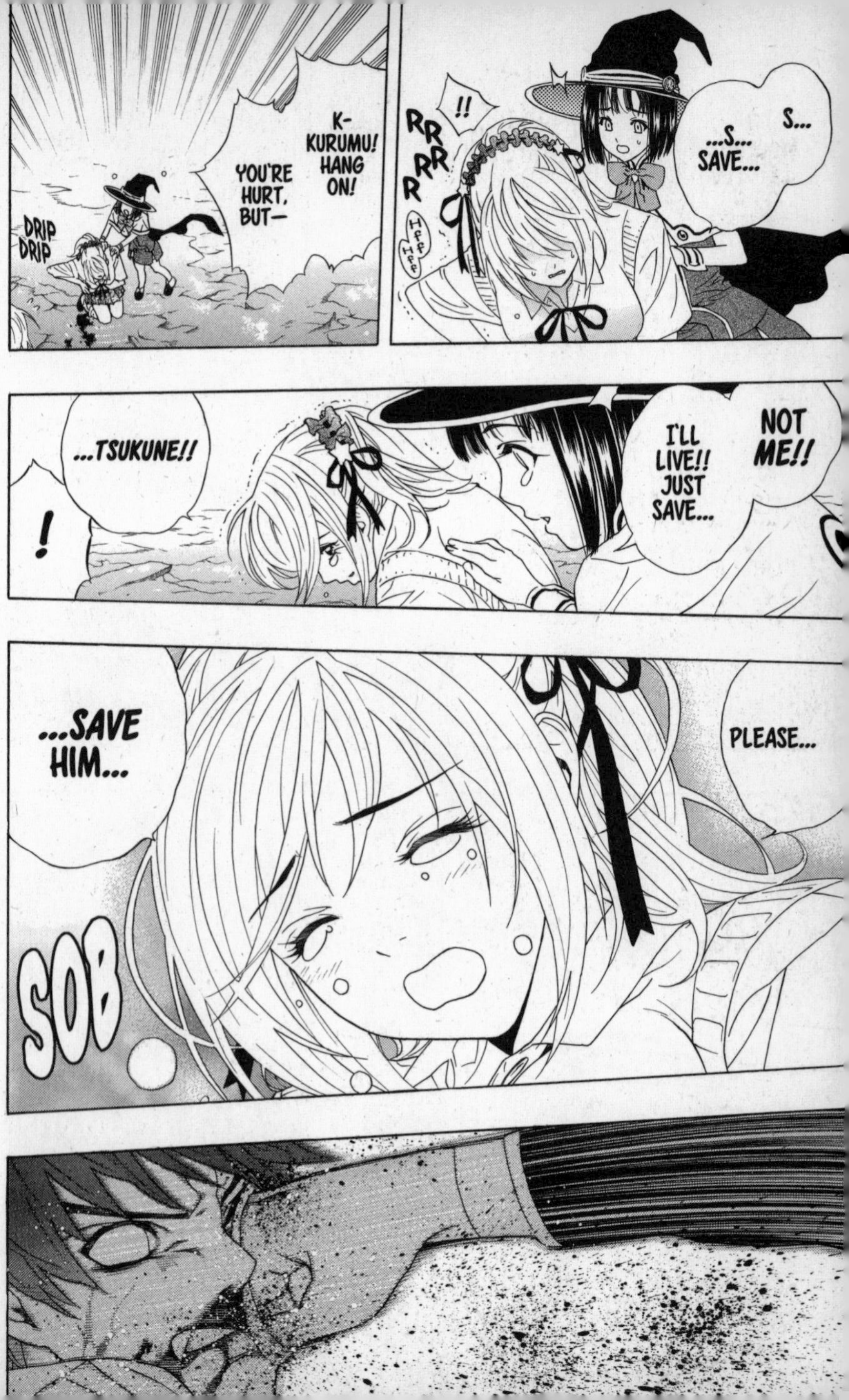
S...
...S... SAVE...
!!
RRRRR
Hff Hff
K-KURUMU! HANG ON!
YOU'RE HURT, BUT—
DRIP DRIP
NOT ME!!
I'LL LIVE!! JUST SAVE...
...TSUKUNE!!
!
PLEASE...
...SAVE HIM...
SOB

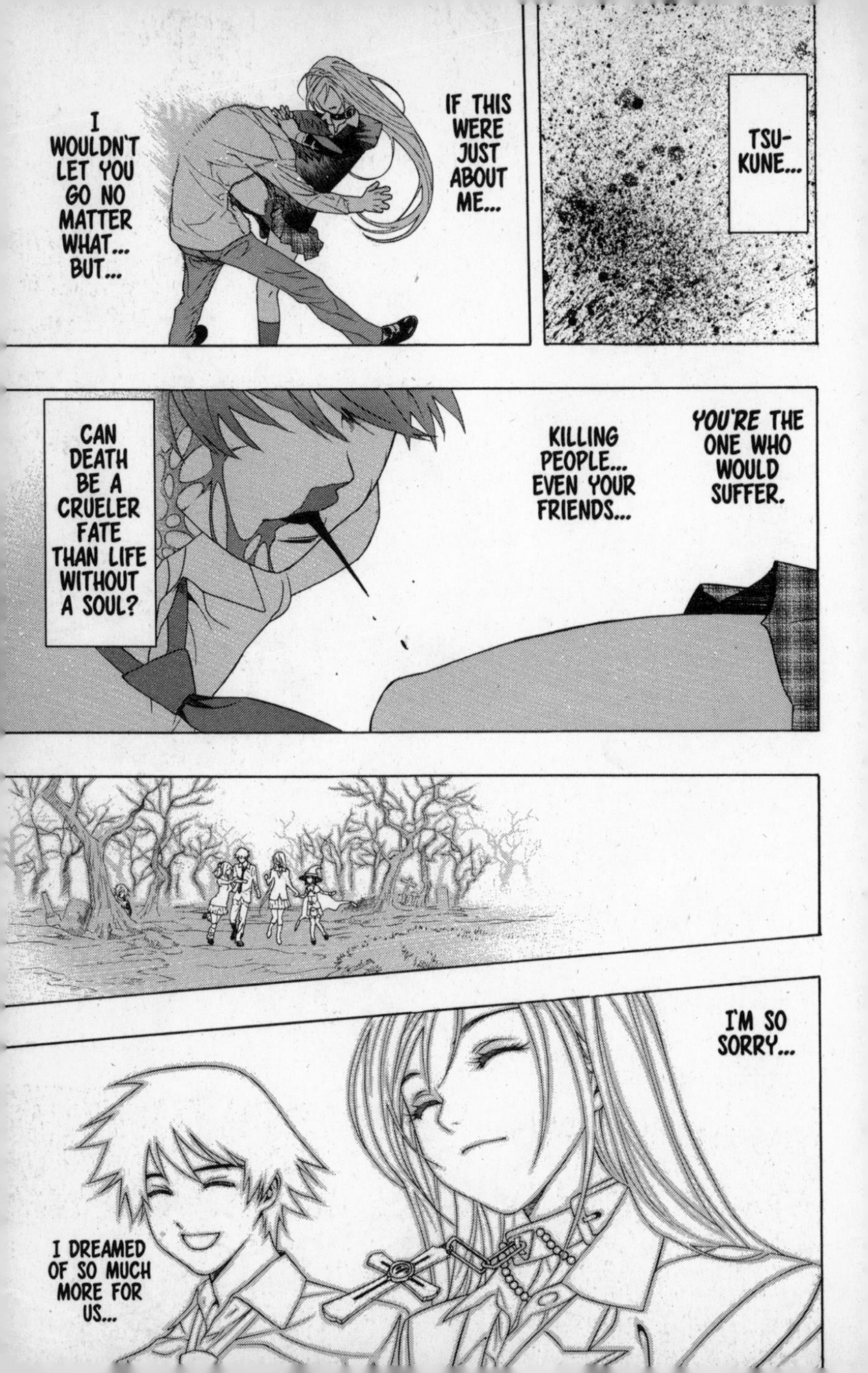
TSU-KUNE...
IF THIS WERE JUST ABOUT ME...
I WOULDN'T LET YOU GO NO MATTER WHAT... BUT...
YOU'RE THE ONE WHO WOULD SUFFER.
KILLING PEOPLE... EVEN YOUR FRIENDS...
CAN DEATH BE A CRUELER FATE THAN LIFE WITHOUT A SOUL?
I'M SO SORRY...
I DREAMED OF SO MUCH MORE FOR US...

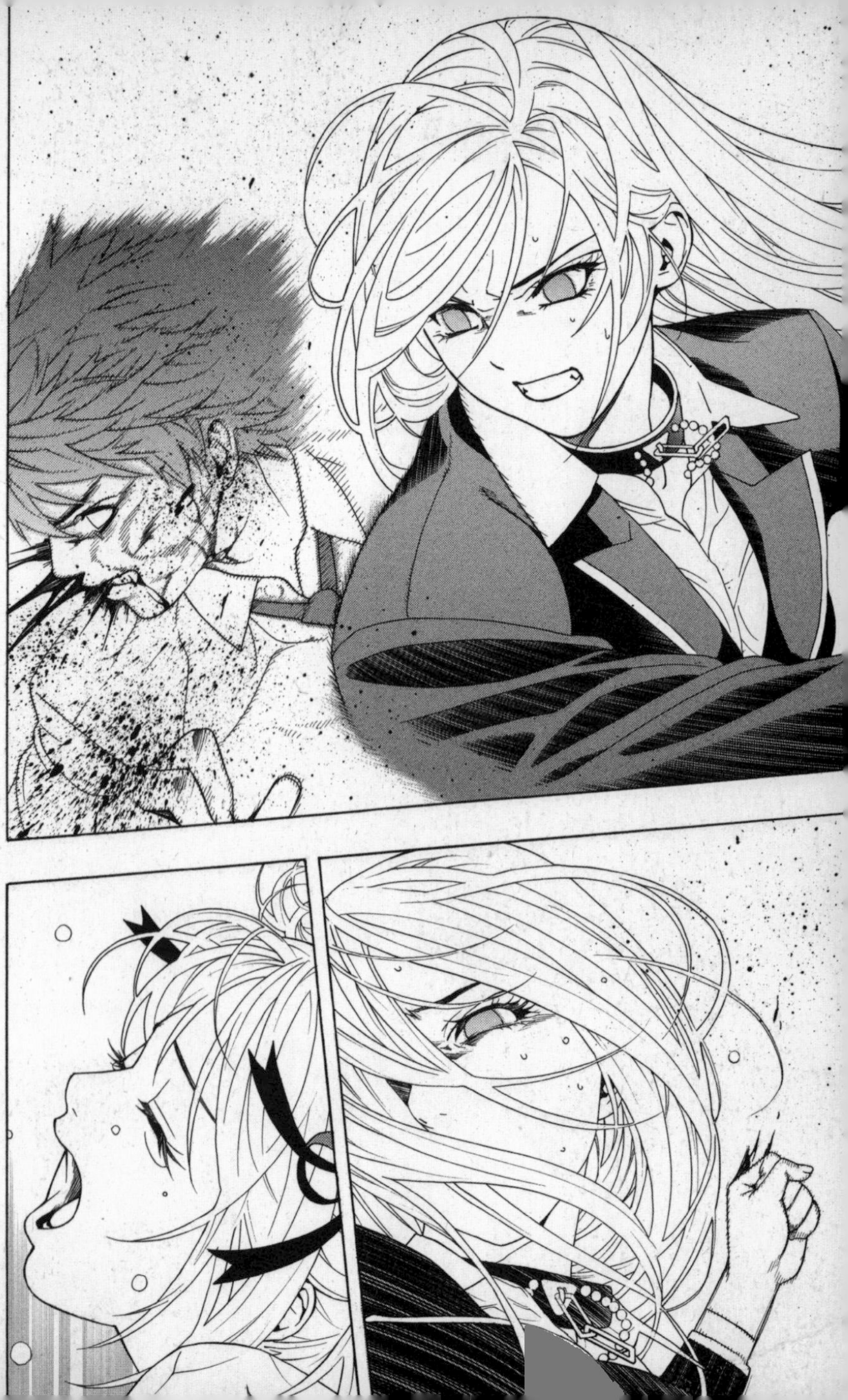

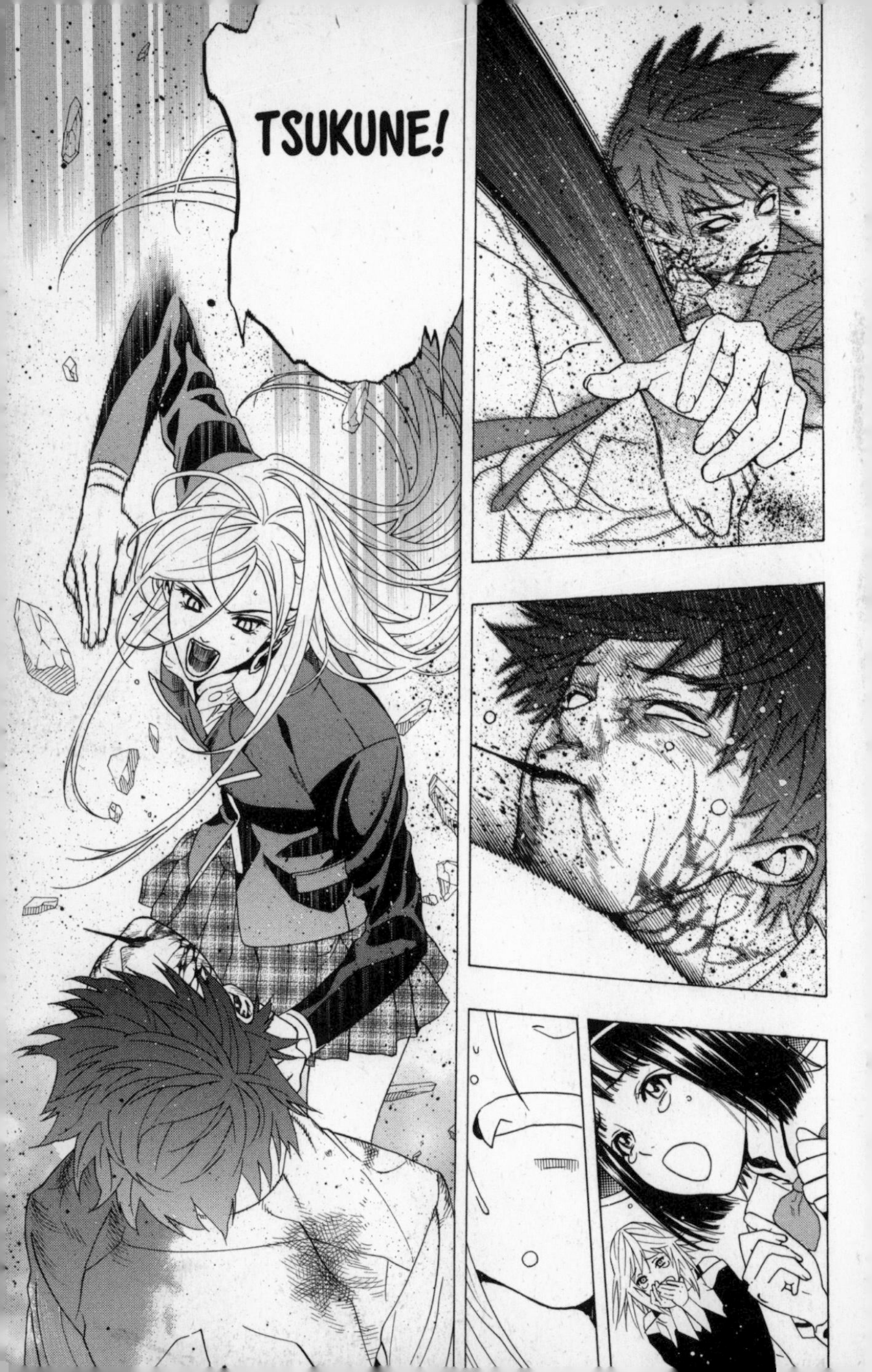
TSUKUNE!

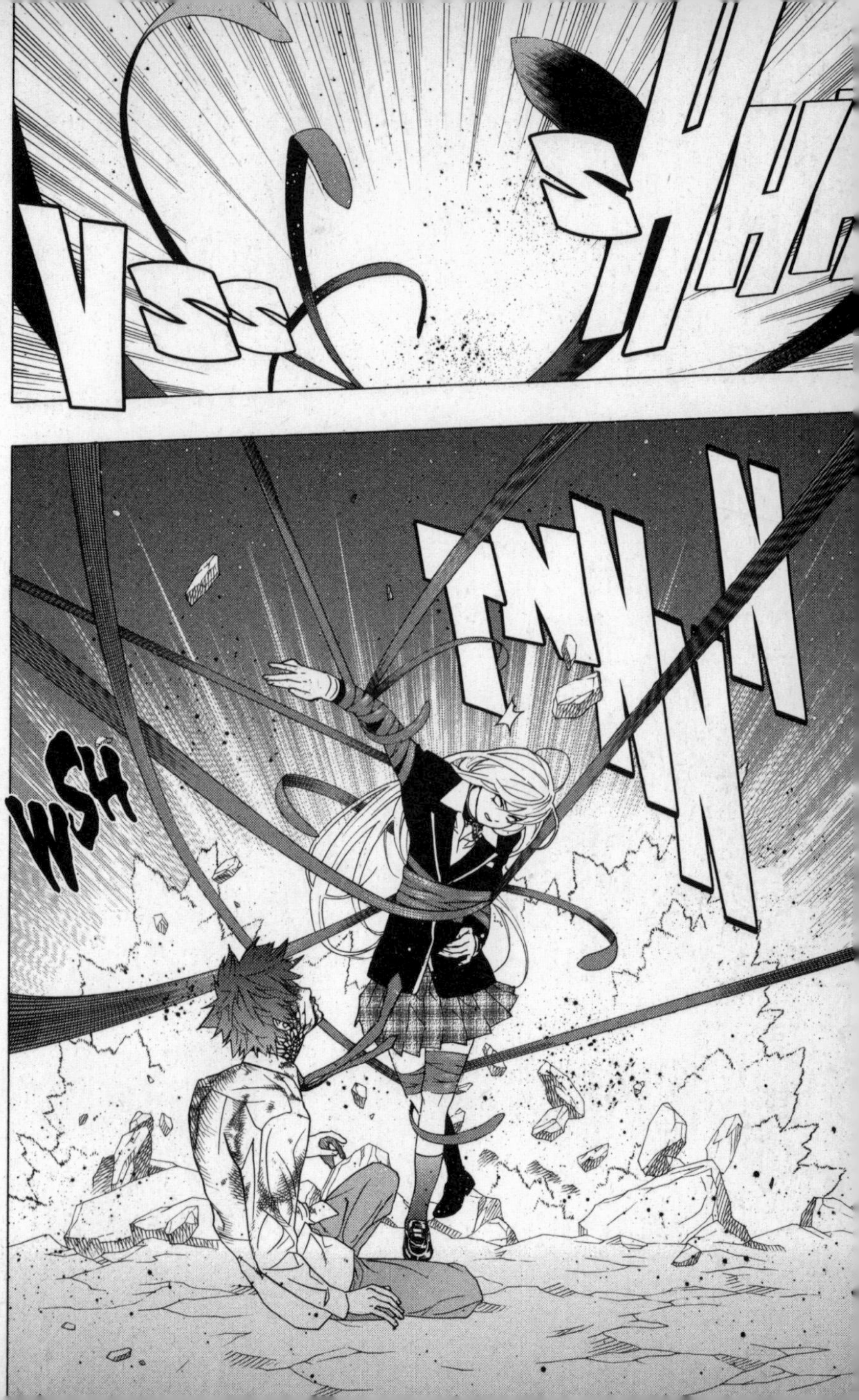
SHHH
VSSS
TNNNN
WSH

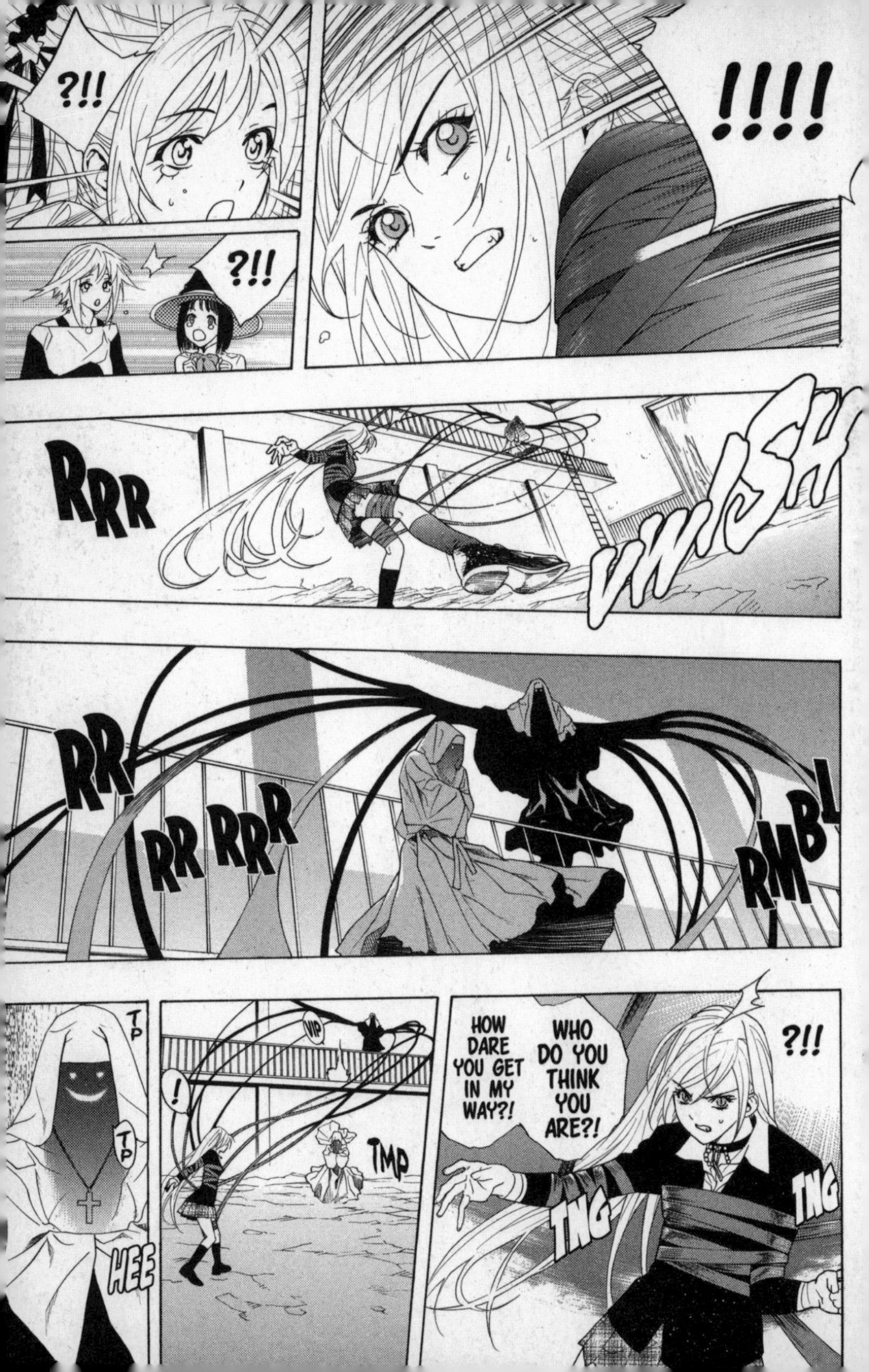
!!!!
?!!
?!!
RRR
RR
RR RRR
RMBL
?!!
WHO DO YOU THINK YOU ARE?!
HOW DARE YOU GET IN MY WAY?!
TNG
TNG
VIP
!
TMP
TP
TP
HEE

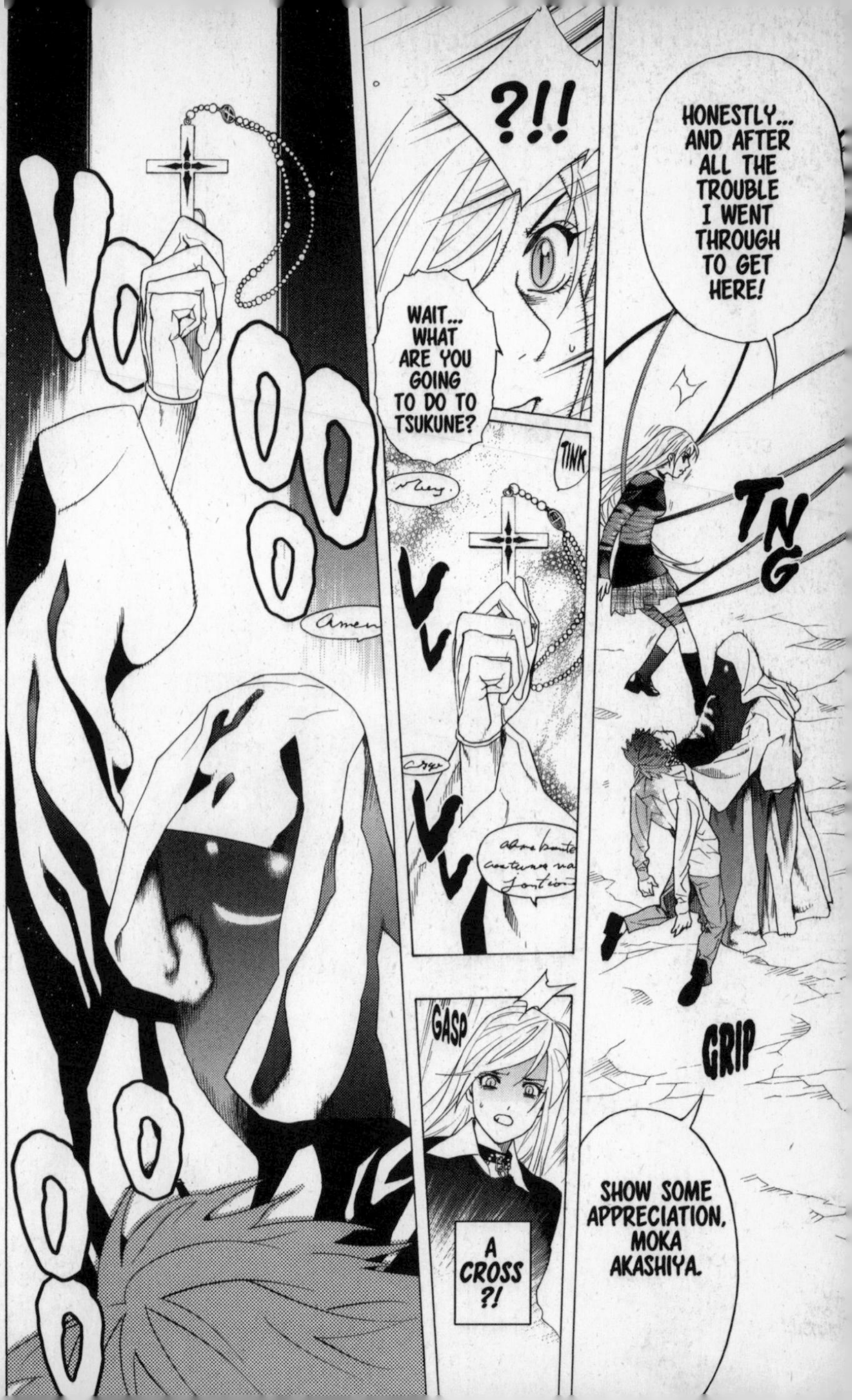
HONESTLY... AND AFTER ALL THE TROUBLE I WENT THROUGH TO GET HERE!
TNG
GRIP
SHOW SOME APPRECIATION, MOKA AKASHIYA.
?!!
WAIT... WHAT ARE YOU GOING TO DO TO TSUKUNE?
TINK
GASP
A CROSS?!
amen

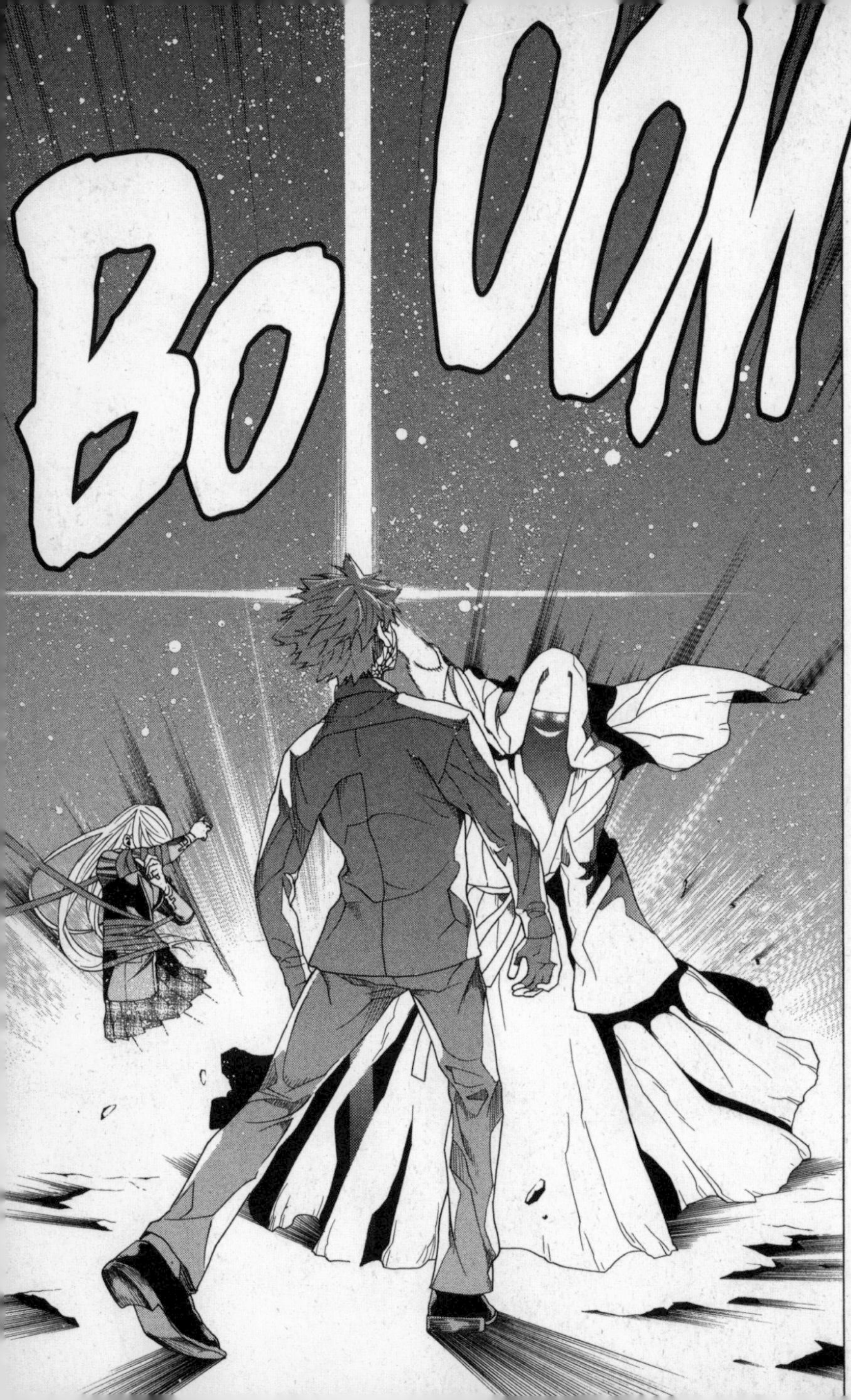
BOOOM

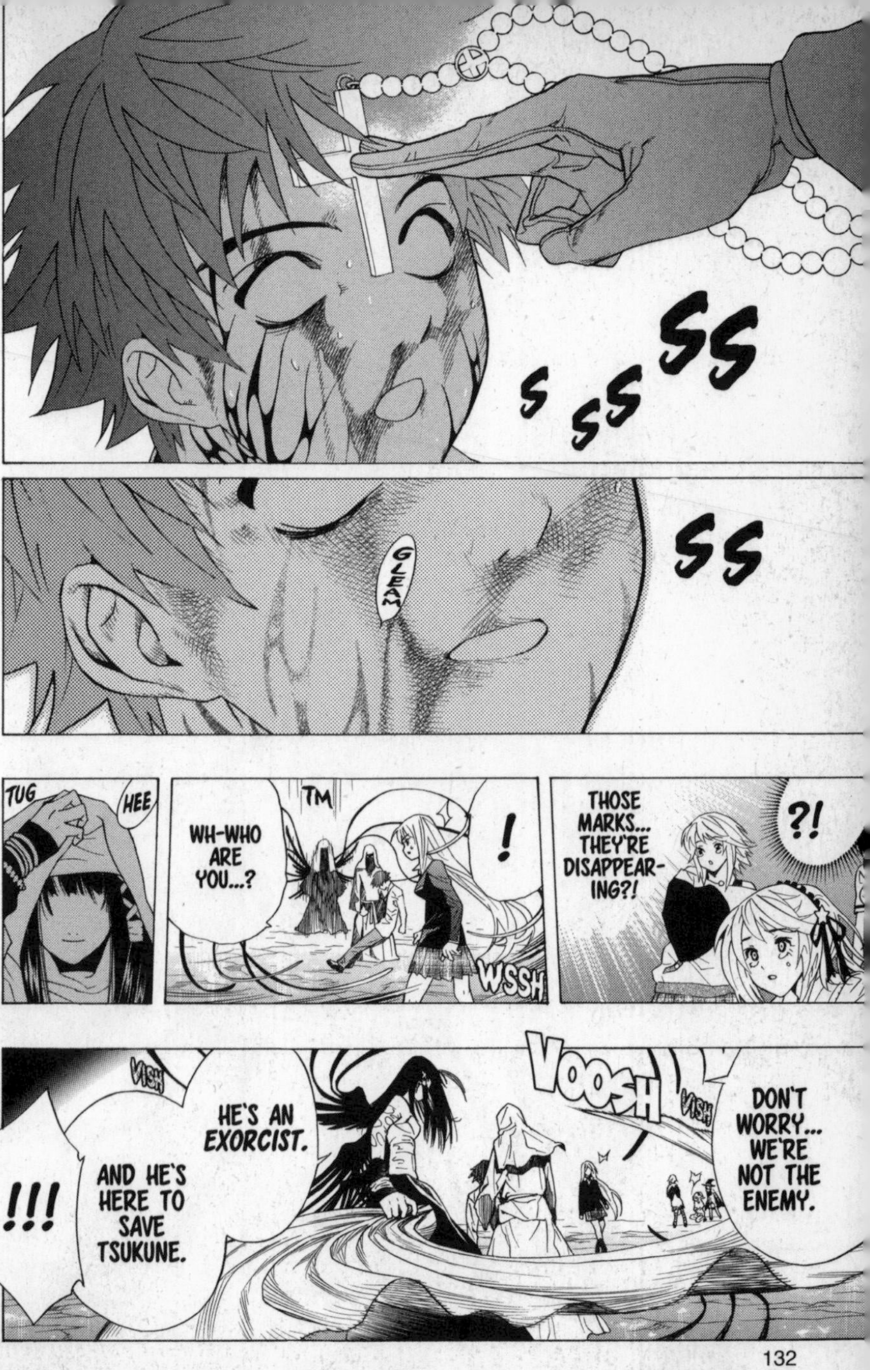
SSSSS
SS
GLEAM
?!
THOSE MARKS... THEY'RE DISAPPEARING?!
!
TM
WH-WHO ARE YOU...?
WSSH
HEE
TUG
VOOSH
VISH
DON'T WORRY... WE'RE NOT THE ENEMY.
HE'S AN EXORCIST.
AND HE'S HERE TO SAVE TSUKUNE.
VISH
!!!

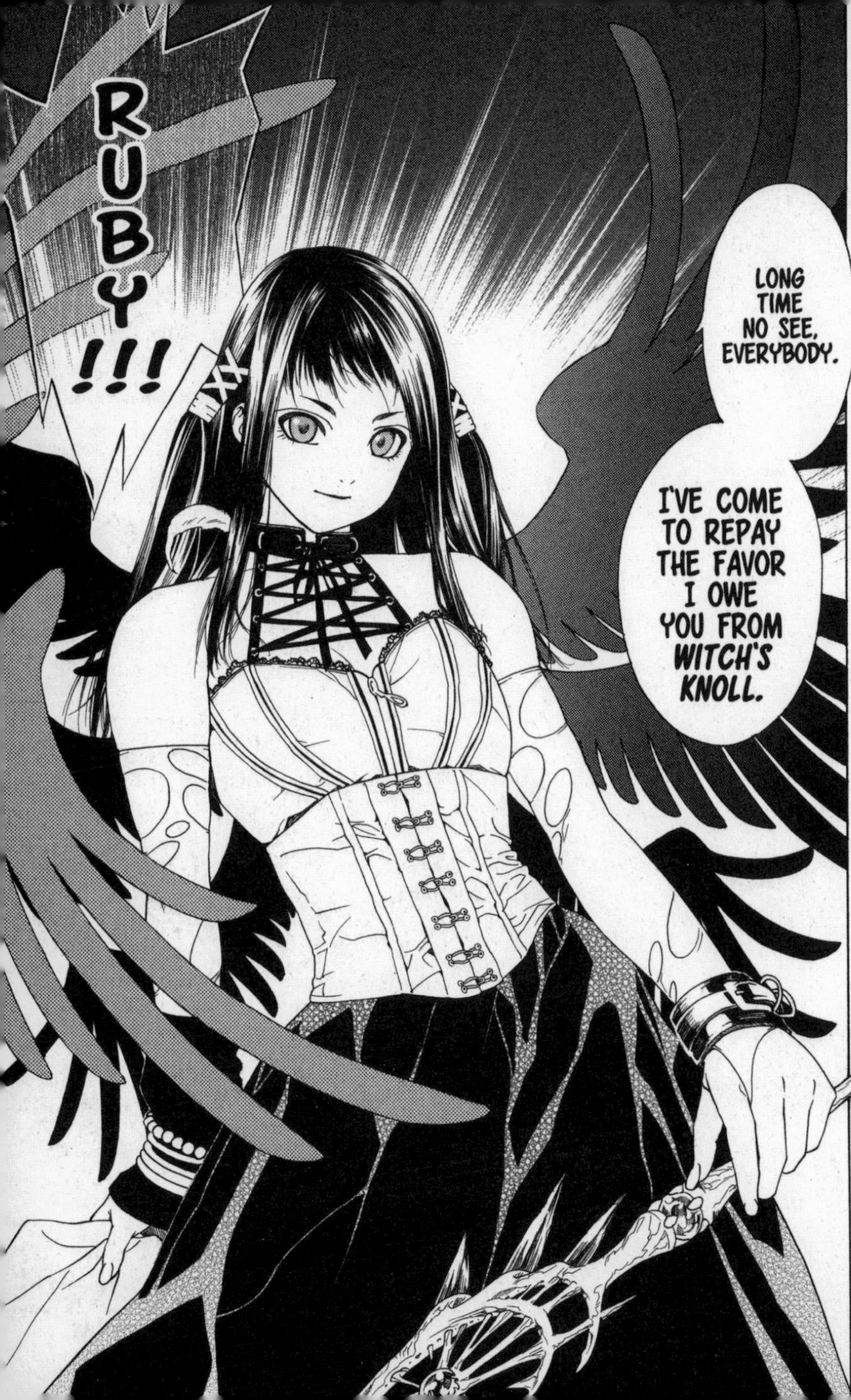
LONG TIME NO SEE, EVERYBODY.
I'VE COME TO REPAY THE FAVOR I OWE YOU FROM WITCH'S KNOLL.
RUBY!!!

ROSARIO+VAMPIRE

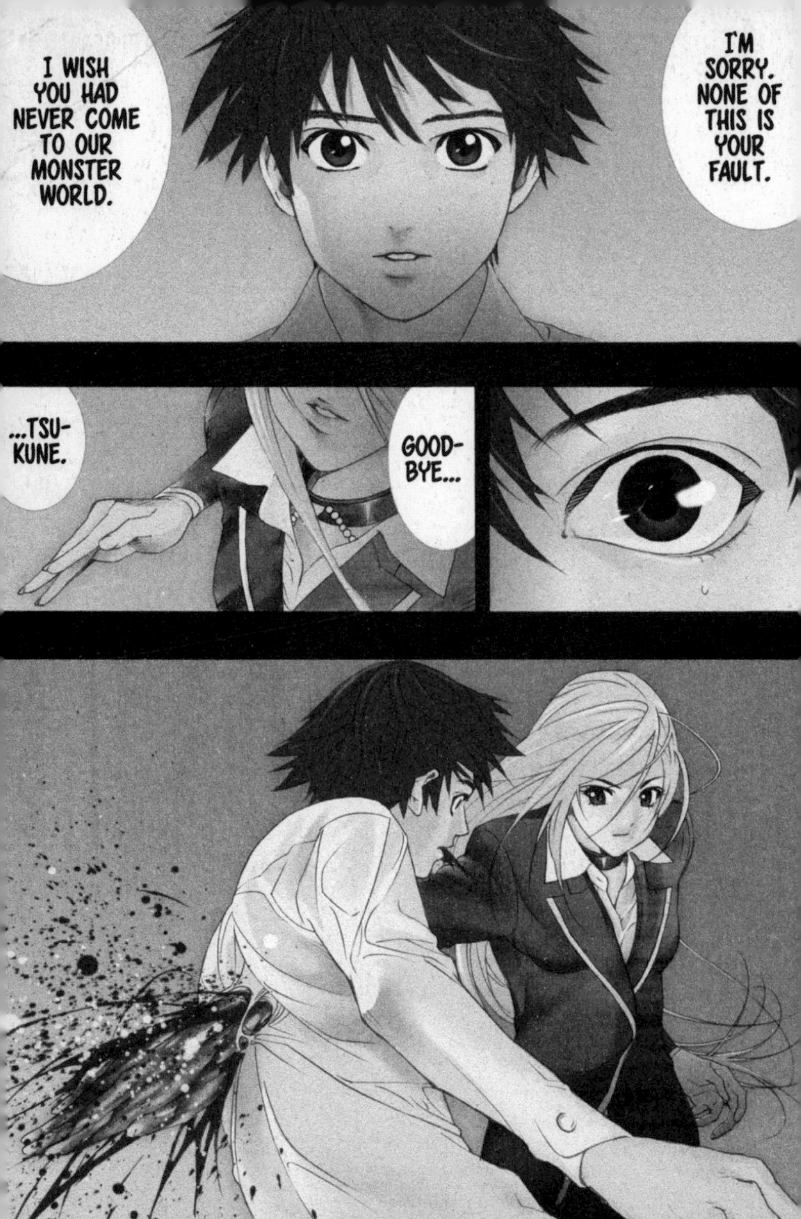
I'M SORRY. NONE OF THIS IS YOUR FAULT.
I WISH YOU HAD NEVER COME TO OUR MONSTER WORLD.
GOOD-BYE...
...TSU-KUNE.

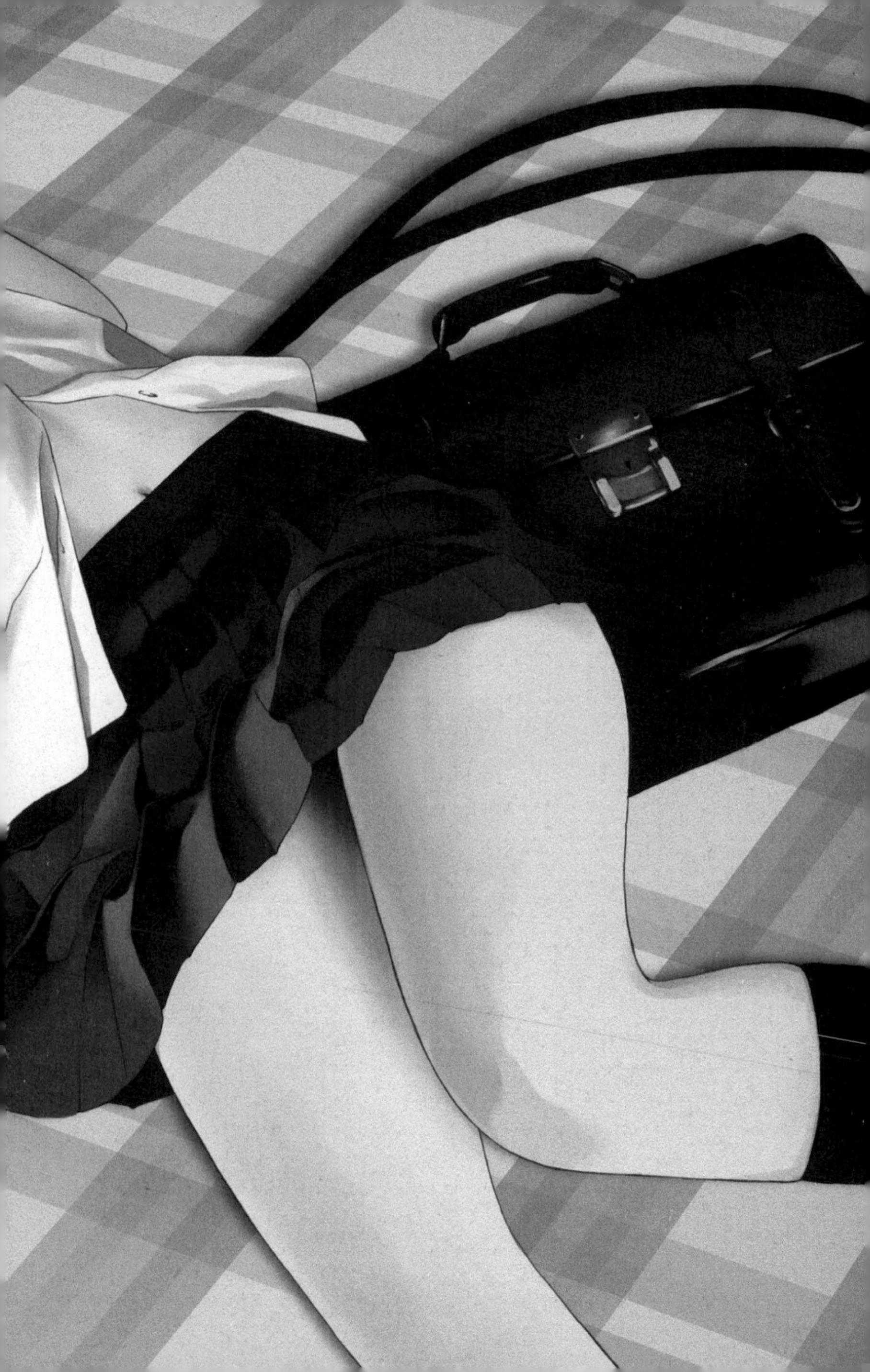

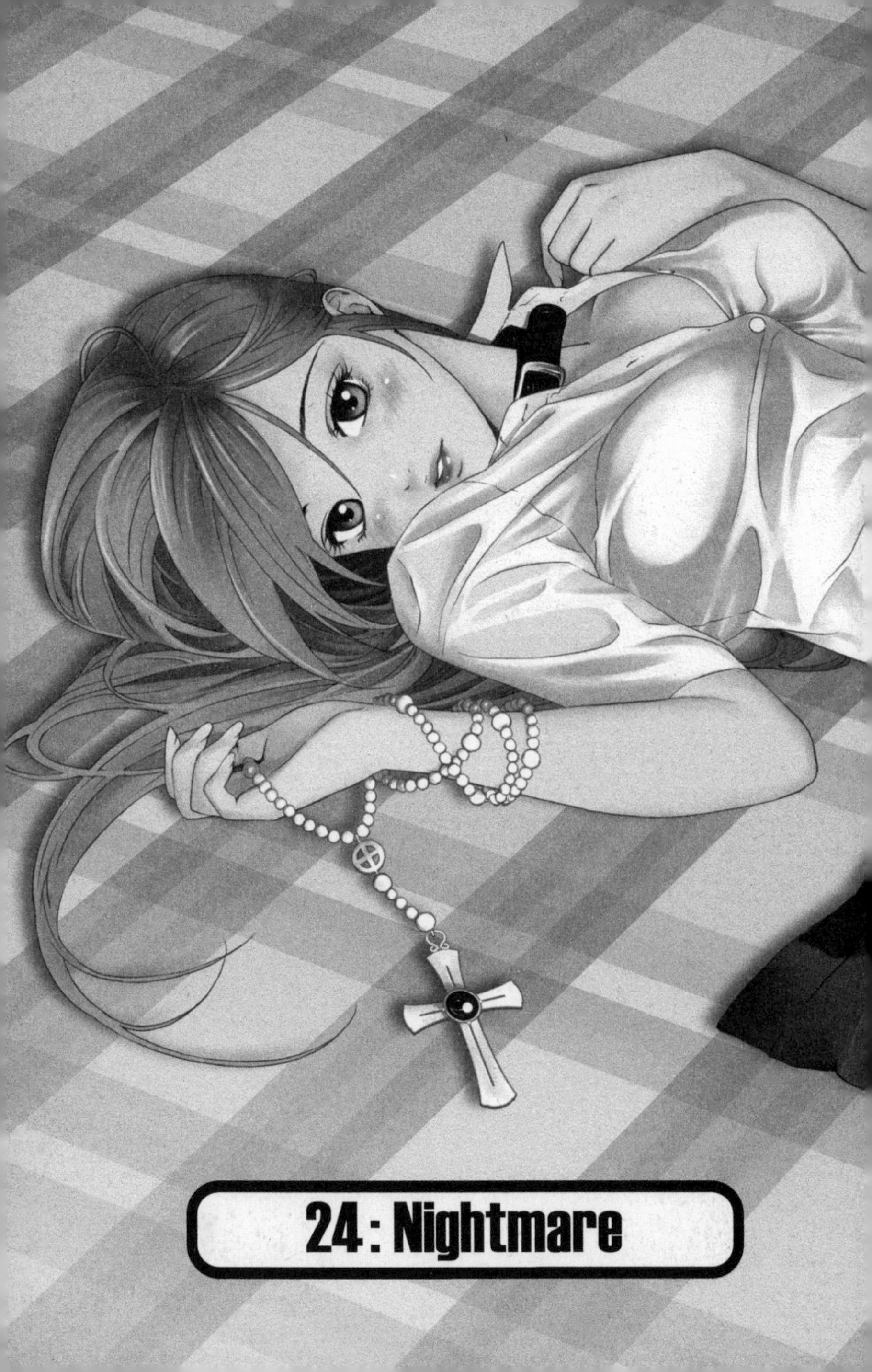

24 : Nightmare

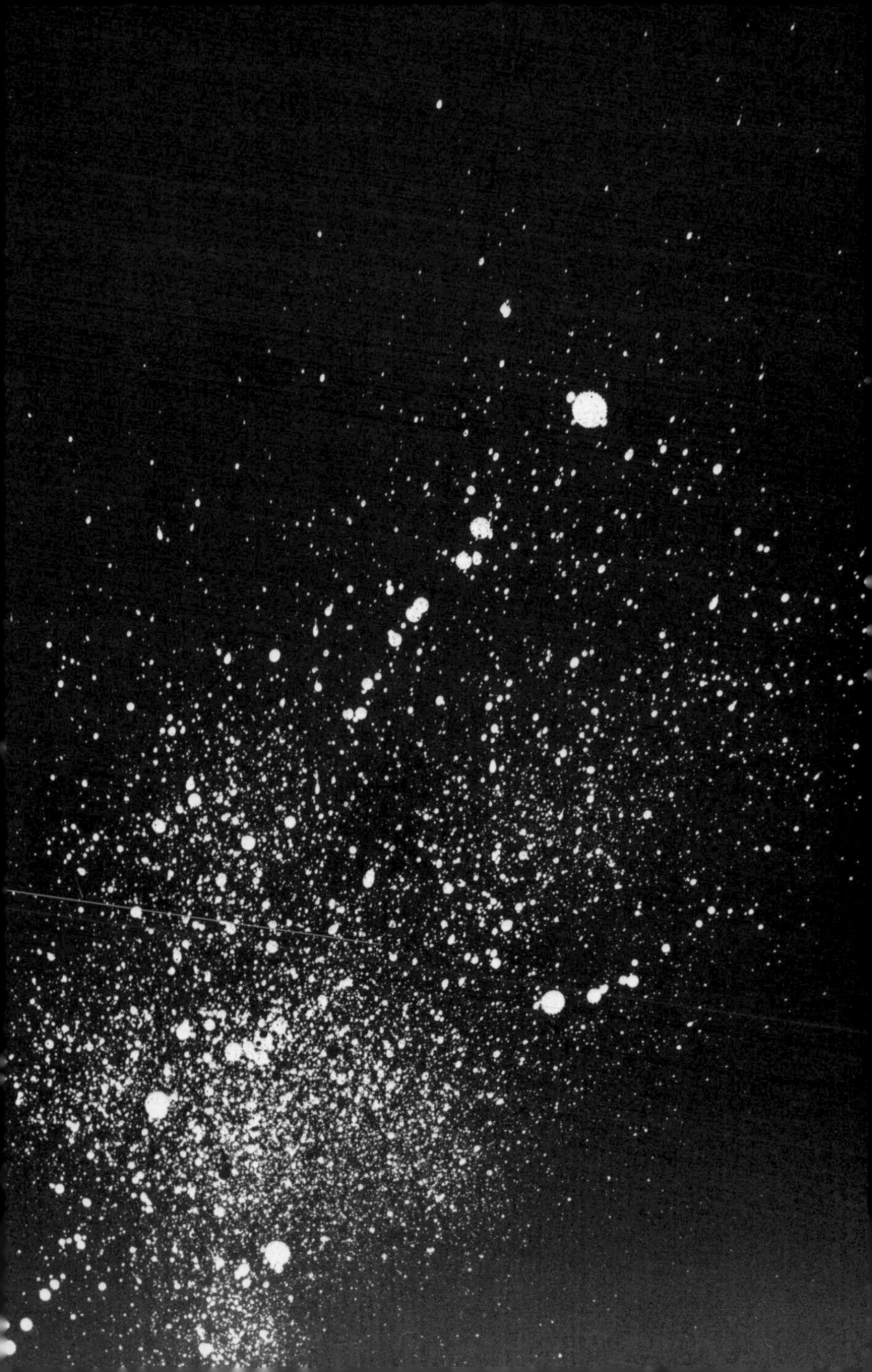

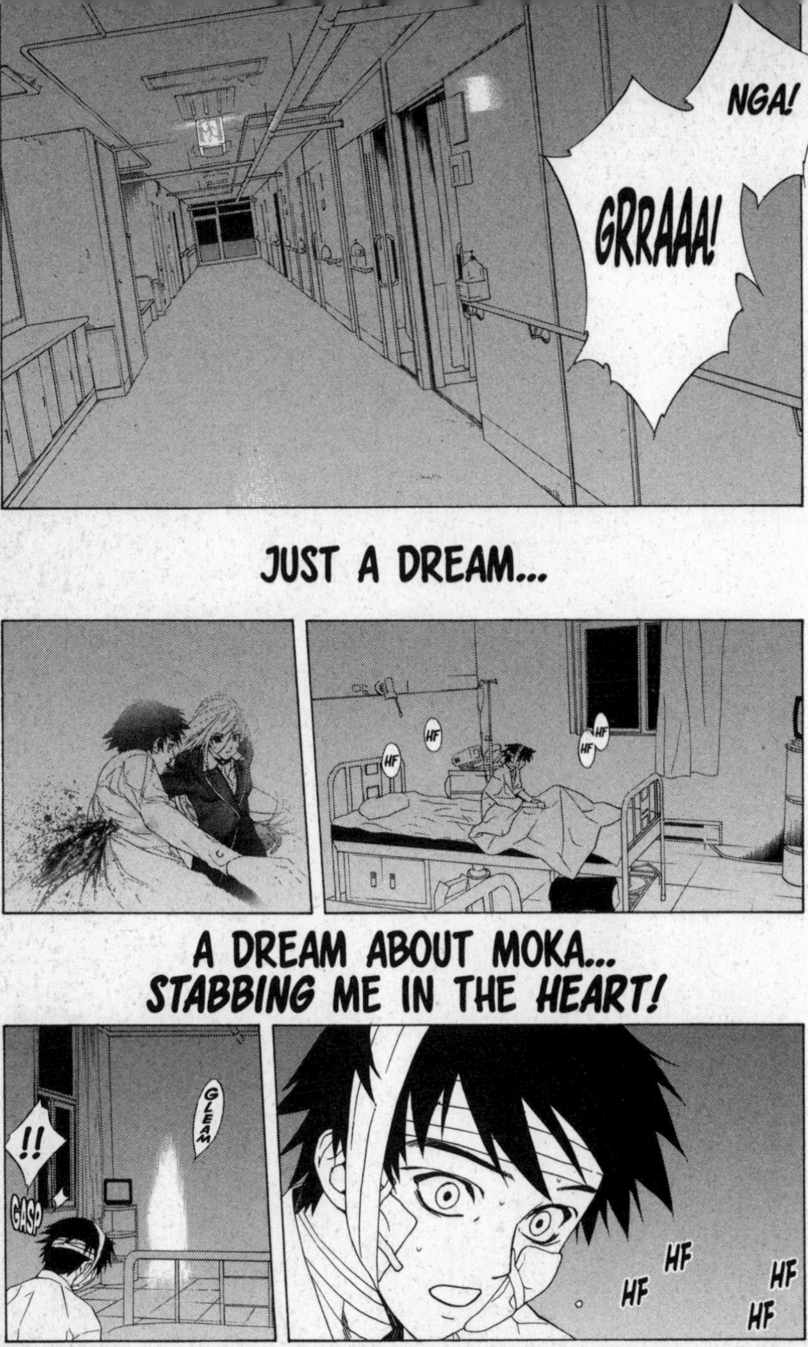
NGA!
GRRAAA!
JUST A DREAM...
HF
HF
HF
HF
A DREAM ABOUT MOKA... STABBING ME IN THE HEART!
HF
HF
HF
HF
GLEAM
!!
GASP

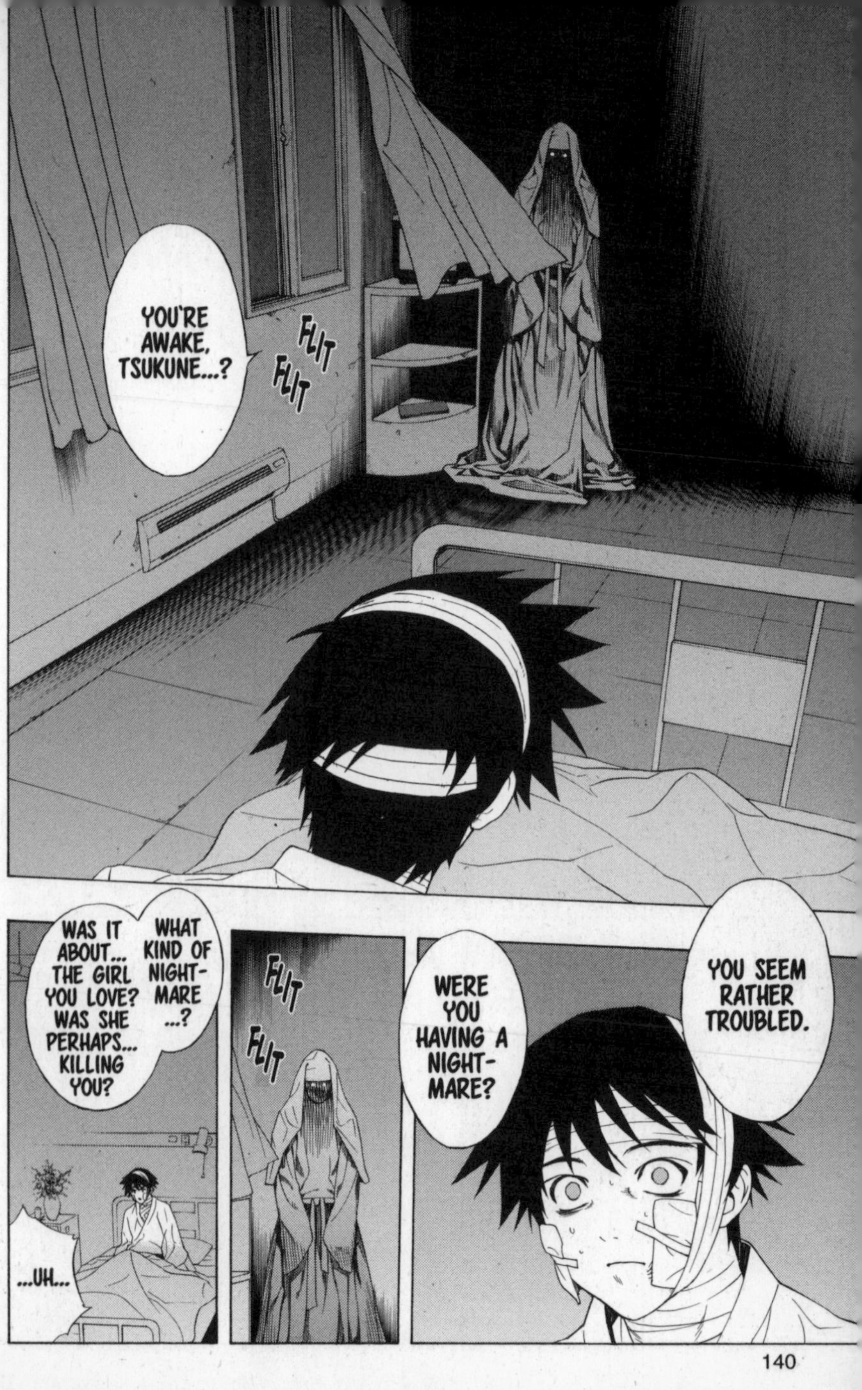
YOU'RE AWAKE, TSUKUNE...?
FLIT
FLIT
YOU SEEM RATHER TROUBLED.
WERE YOU HAVING A NIGHT-MARE?
FLIT
FLIT
WHAT KIND OF NIGHT-MARE ...?
WAS IT ABOUT... THE GIRL YOU LOVE? WAS SHE PERHAPS... KILLING YOU?
...UH...

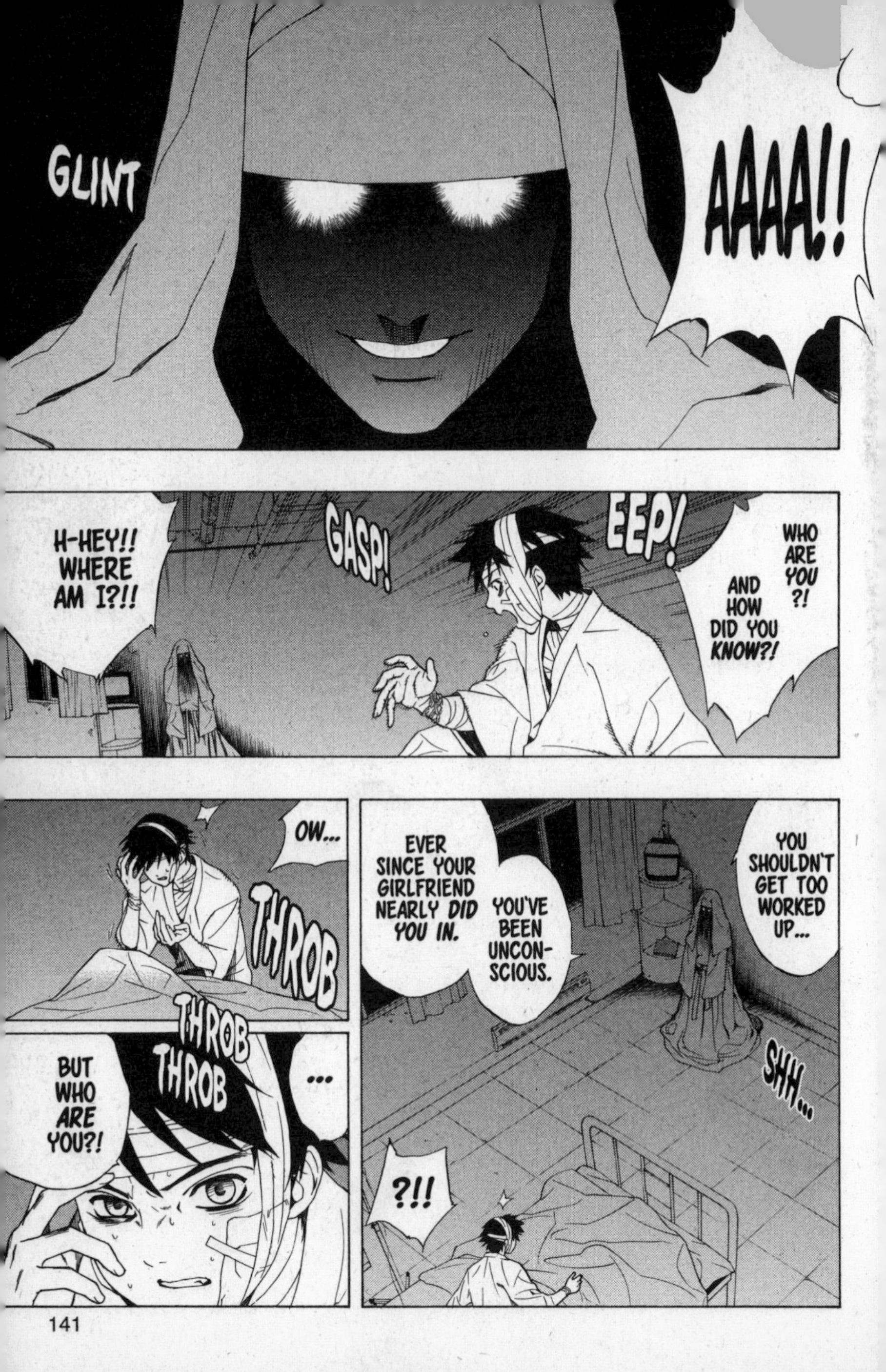
AAAA!!
GLINT
WHO ARE YOU?!
AND HOW DID YOU KNOW?!
EEP!
GASP!
H-HEY!! WHERE AM I?!!
YOU SHOULDN'T GET TOO WORKED UP...
YOU'VE BEEN UNCONSCIOUS.
EVER SINCE YOUR GIRLFRIEND NEARLY DID YOU IN.
OW...
THROB
THROB THROB
SHH...
?!!
...
BUT WHO ARE YOU?!

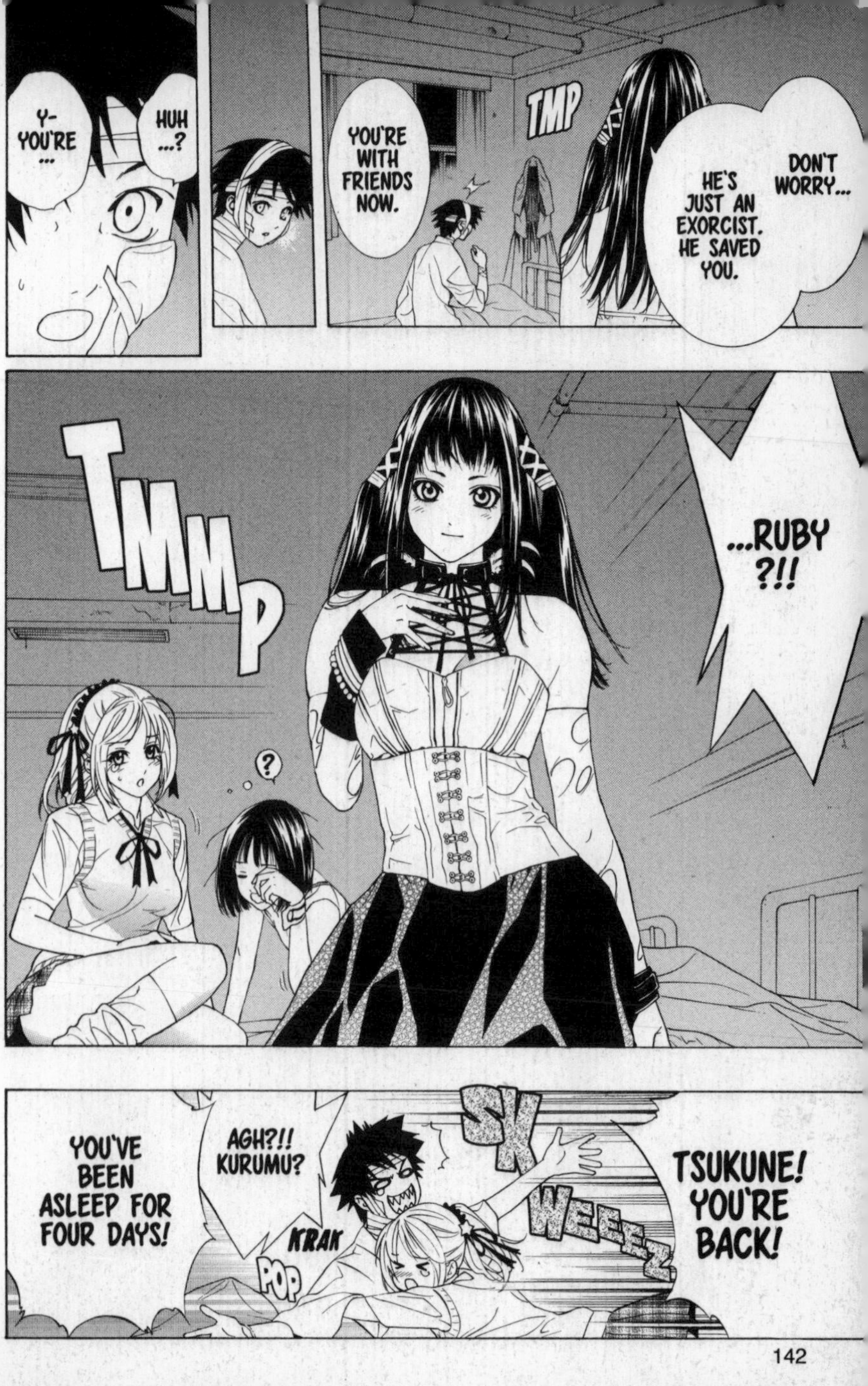
DON'T WORRY...
HE'S JUST AN EXORCIST. HE SAVED YOU.
TMP
YOU'RE WITH FRIENDS NOW.
HUH ...?
Y- YOU'RE ...
...RUBY ?!!
TMMP
TSUKUNE! YOU'RE BACK!
SK
WEEEZ
KRAK
POP
AGH?!! KURUMU?
YOU'VE BEEN ASLEEP FOR FOUR DAYS!

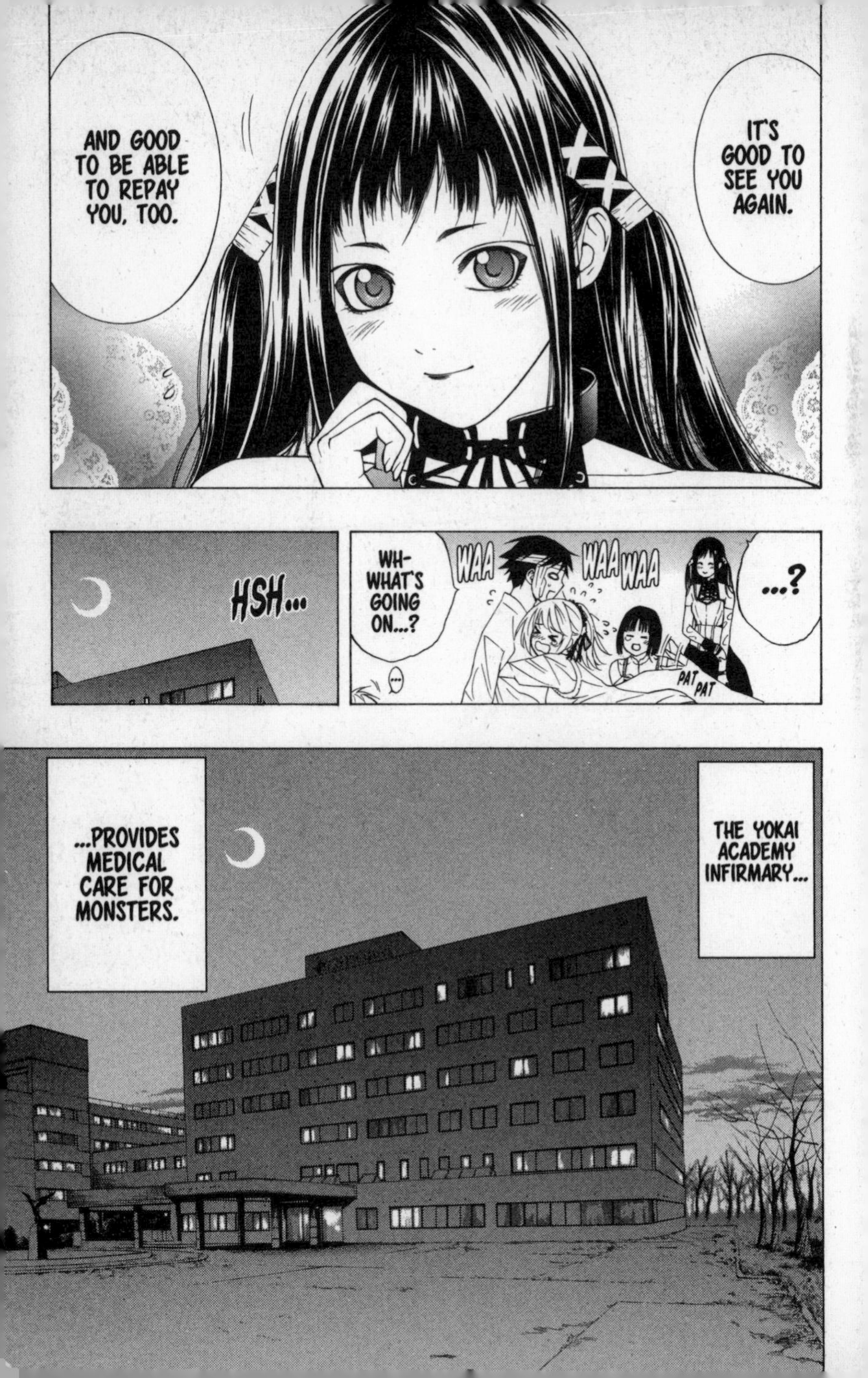
IT'S GOOD TO SEE YOU AGAIN.
AND GOOD TO BE ABLE TO REPAY YOU, TOO.
...?
WAA WAA
PAT PAT
WAA
WH-WHAT'S GOING ON...?
...
HSH...
THE YOKAI ACADEMY INFIRMARY...
...PROVIDES MEDICAL CARE FOR MONSTERS.

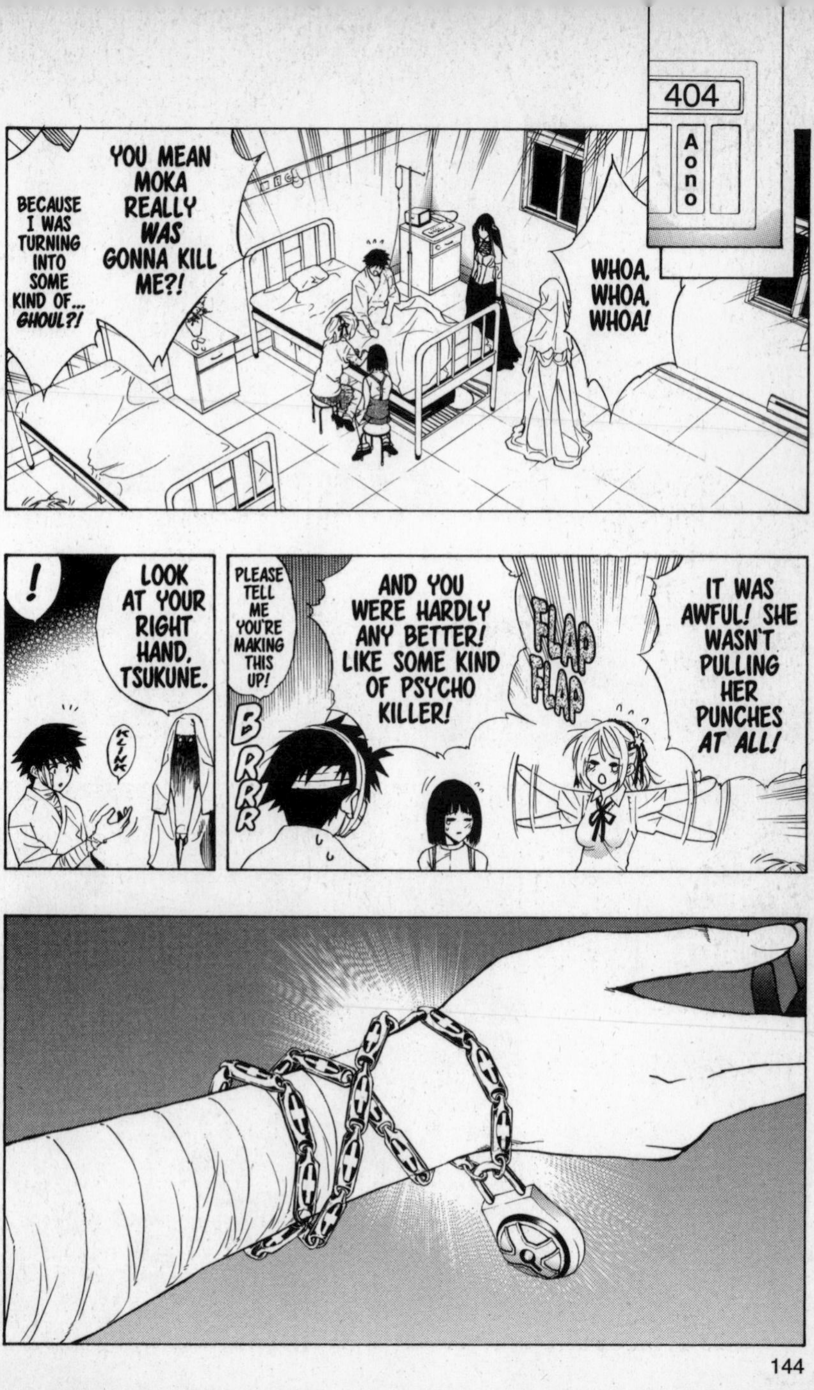
404
Aono
WHOA, WHOA, WHOA!
YOU MEAN MOKA REALLY WAS GONNA KILL ME?!
BECAUSE I WAS TURNING INTO SOME KIND OF... GHOUL?!
IT WAS AWFUL! SHE WASN'T PULLING HER PUNCHES AT ALL!
FLAP FLAP
AND YOU WERE HARDLY ANY BETTER! LIKE SOME KIND OF PSYCHO KILLER!
PLEASE TELL ME YOU'RE MAKING THIS UP!
BRRR
LOOK AT YOUR RIGHT HAND, TSUKUNE.
KLINK
!

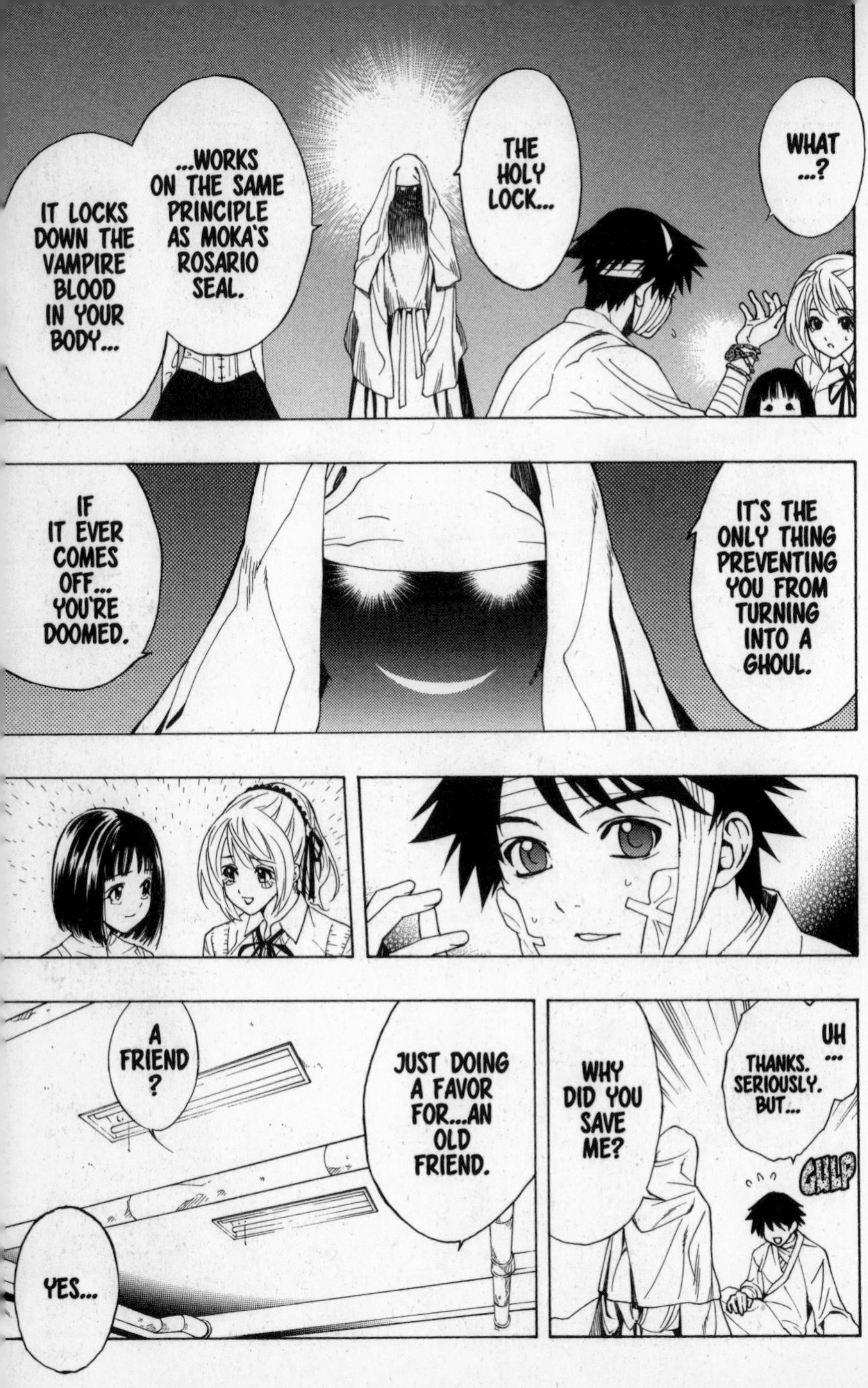
WHAT ...?
THE HOLY LOCK...
...WORKS ON THE SAME PRINCIPLE AS MOKA'S ROSARIO SEAL.
IT LOCKS DOWN THE VAMPIRE BLOOD IN YOUR BODY...
IT'S THE ONLY THING PREVENTING YOU FROM TURNING INTO A GHOUL.
IF IT EVER COMES OFF... YOU'RE DOOMED.
UH ...
THANKS. SERIOUSLY. BUT...
GULP
WHY DID YOU SAVE ME?
JUST DOING A FAVOR FOR...AN OLD FRIEND.
A FRIEND ?
YES...

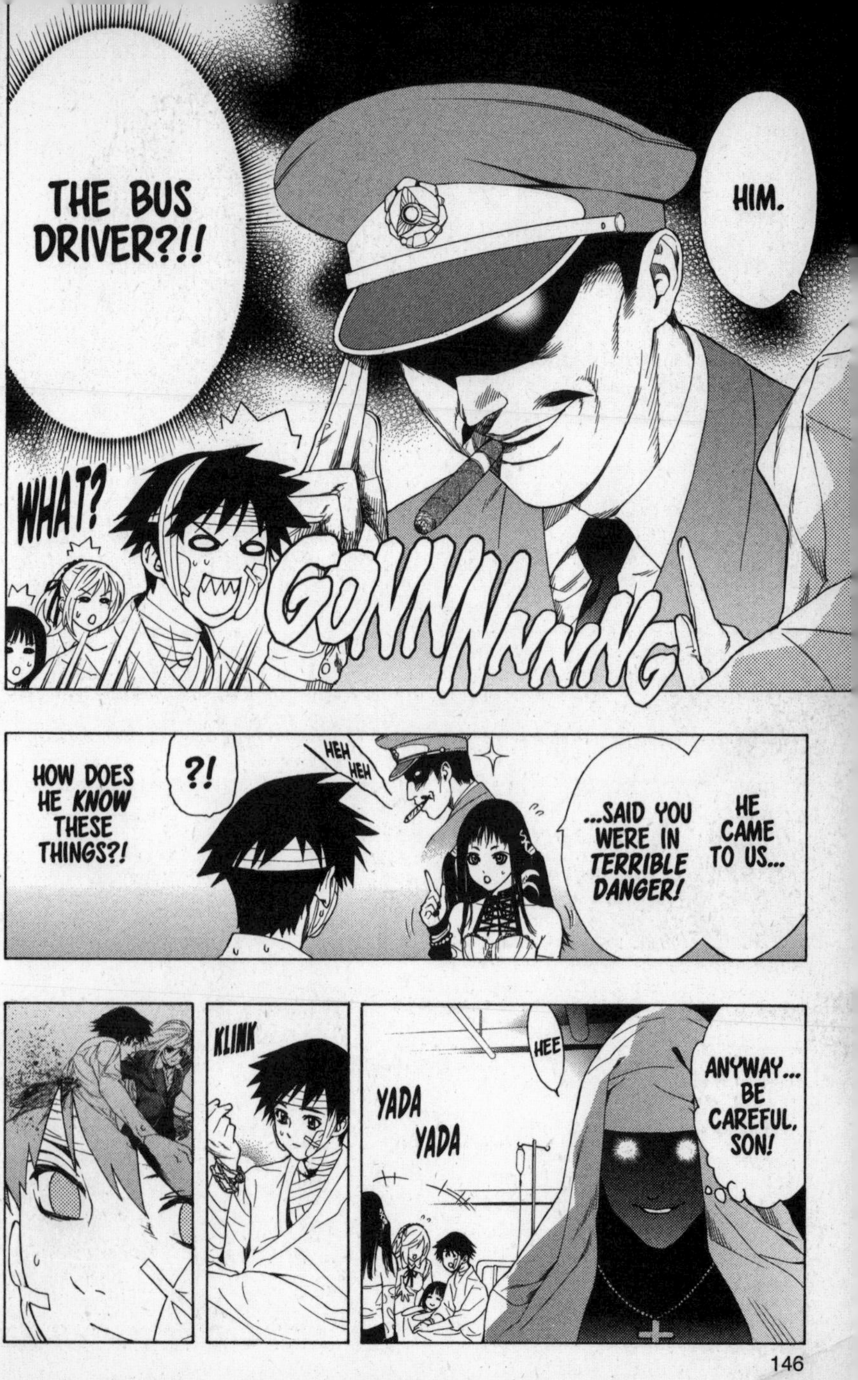

HIM.
THE BUS DRIVER?!!
WHAT?
GONNNNNNNG
HE CAME TO US...
...SAID YOU WERE IN TERRIBLE DANGER!
HEH HEH
?!
HOW DOES HE KNOW THESE THINGS?!
ANYWAY... BE CAREFUL, SON!
HEE
YADA YADA
KLINK

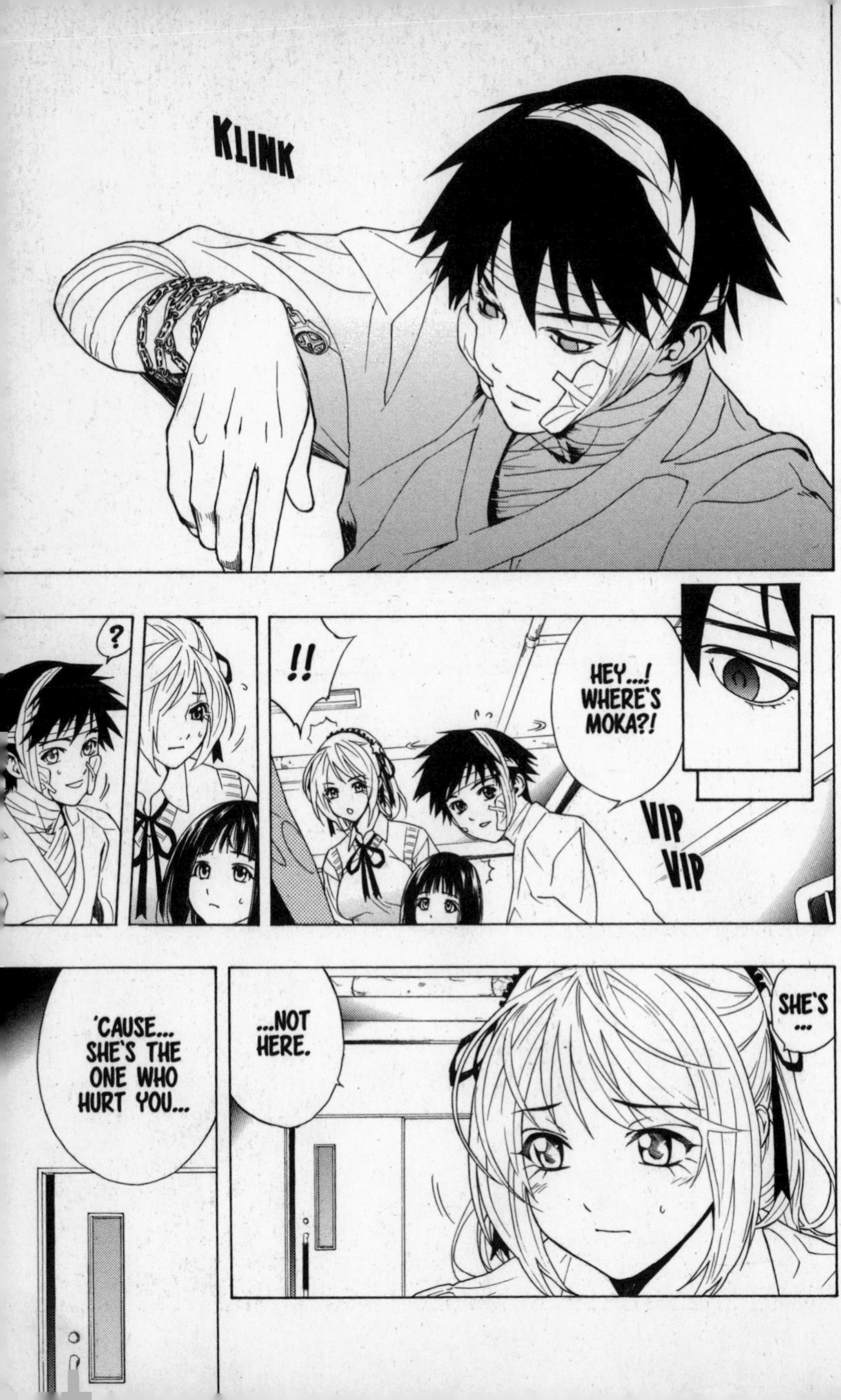
KLINK
HEY...! WHERE'S MOKA?!
VIP VIP
!!
?
SHE'S ...
...NOT HERE.
'CAUSE... SHE'S THE ONE WHO HURT YOU...

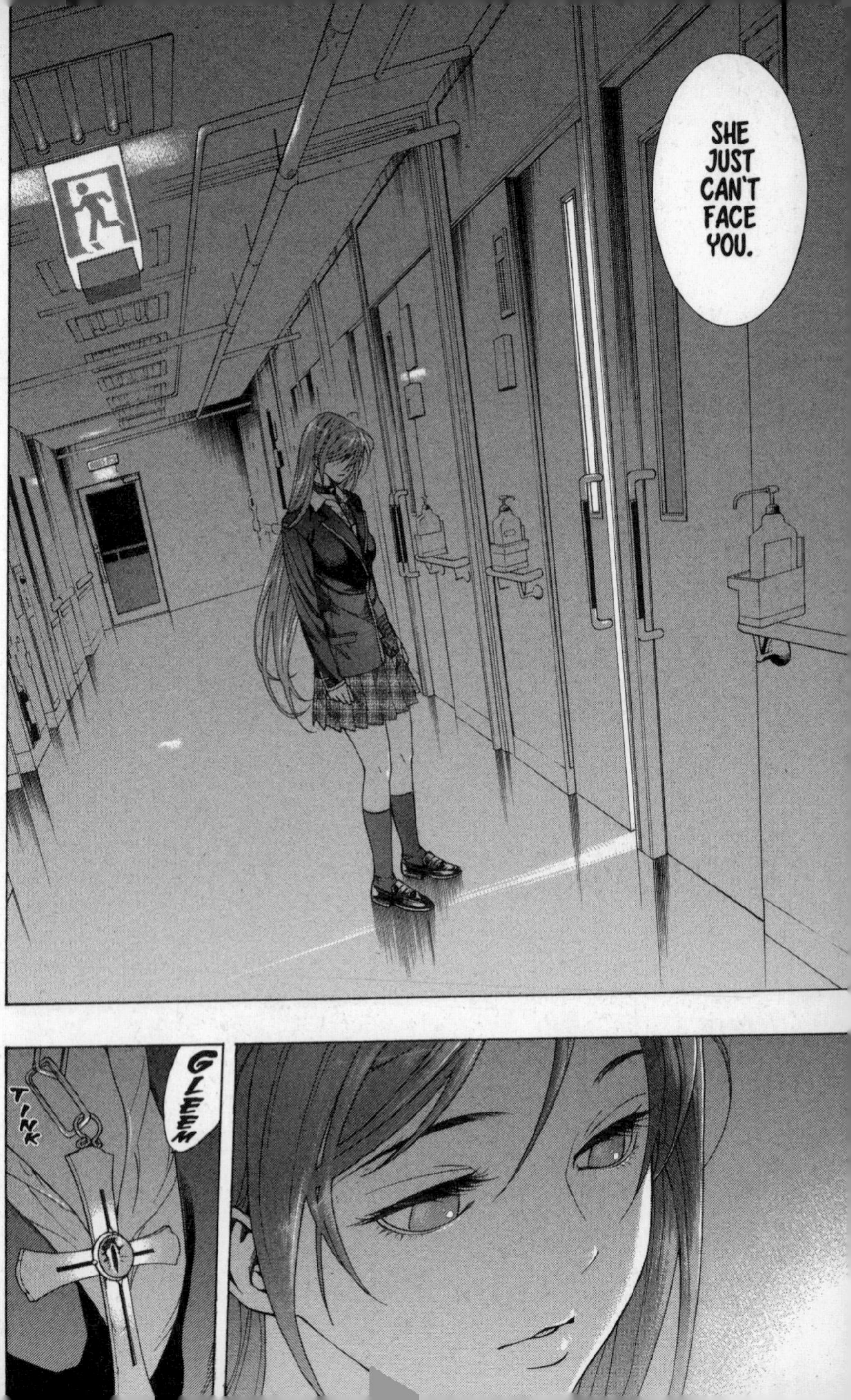
SHE JUST CAN'T FACE YOU.
GLEEM
TINK

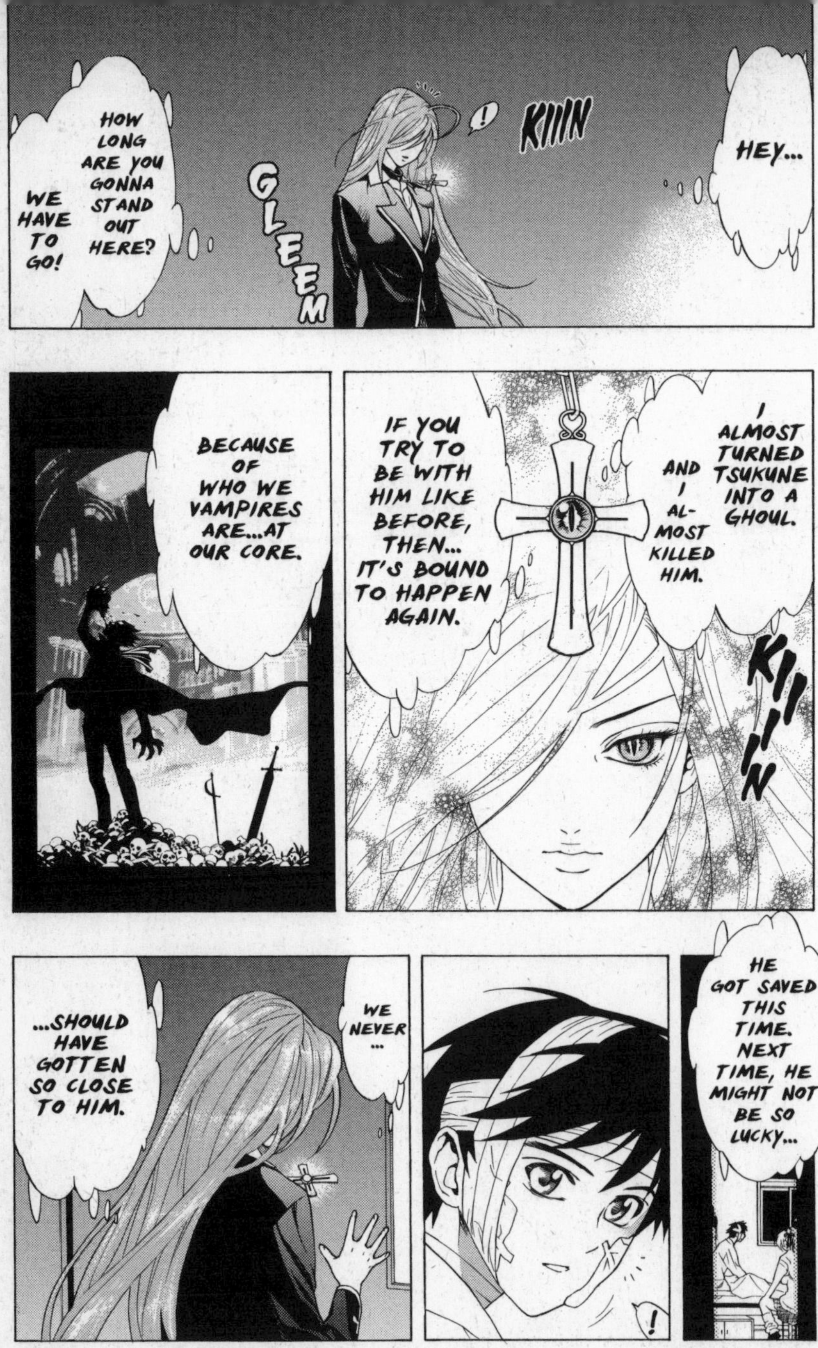
HEY...
!
KIIIN
GLEEM
HOW LONG ARE YOU GONNA STAND OUT HERE?
WE HAVE TO GO!
I ALMOST TURNED TSUKUNE INTO A GHOUL.
AND I AL-MOST KILLED HIM.
IF YOU TRY TO BE WITH HIM LIKE BEFORE, THEN... IT'S BOUND TO HAPPEN AGAIN.
KIIIIN
BECAUSE OF WHO WE VAMPIRES ARE...AT OUR CORE.
HE GOT SAVED THIS TIME. NEXT TIME, HE MIGHT NOT BE SO LUCKY...
!
WE NEVER...
...SHOULD HAVE GOTTEN SO CLOSE TO HIM.

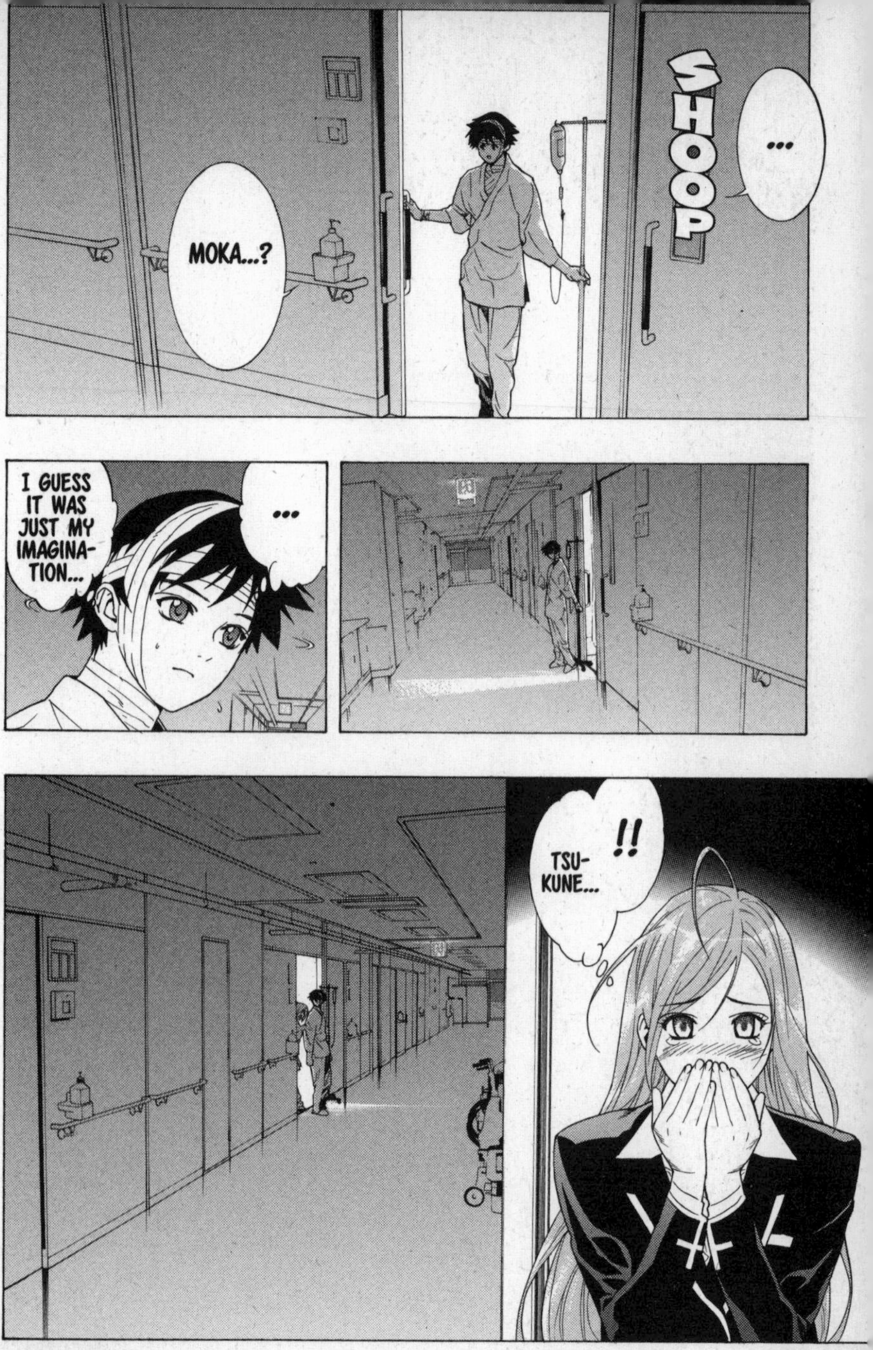
...
SHOOP
MOKA...?
...
I GUESS IT WAS JUST MY IMAGINA-TION...
!!
TSU-KUNE...

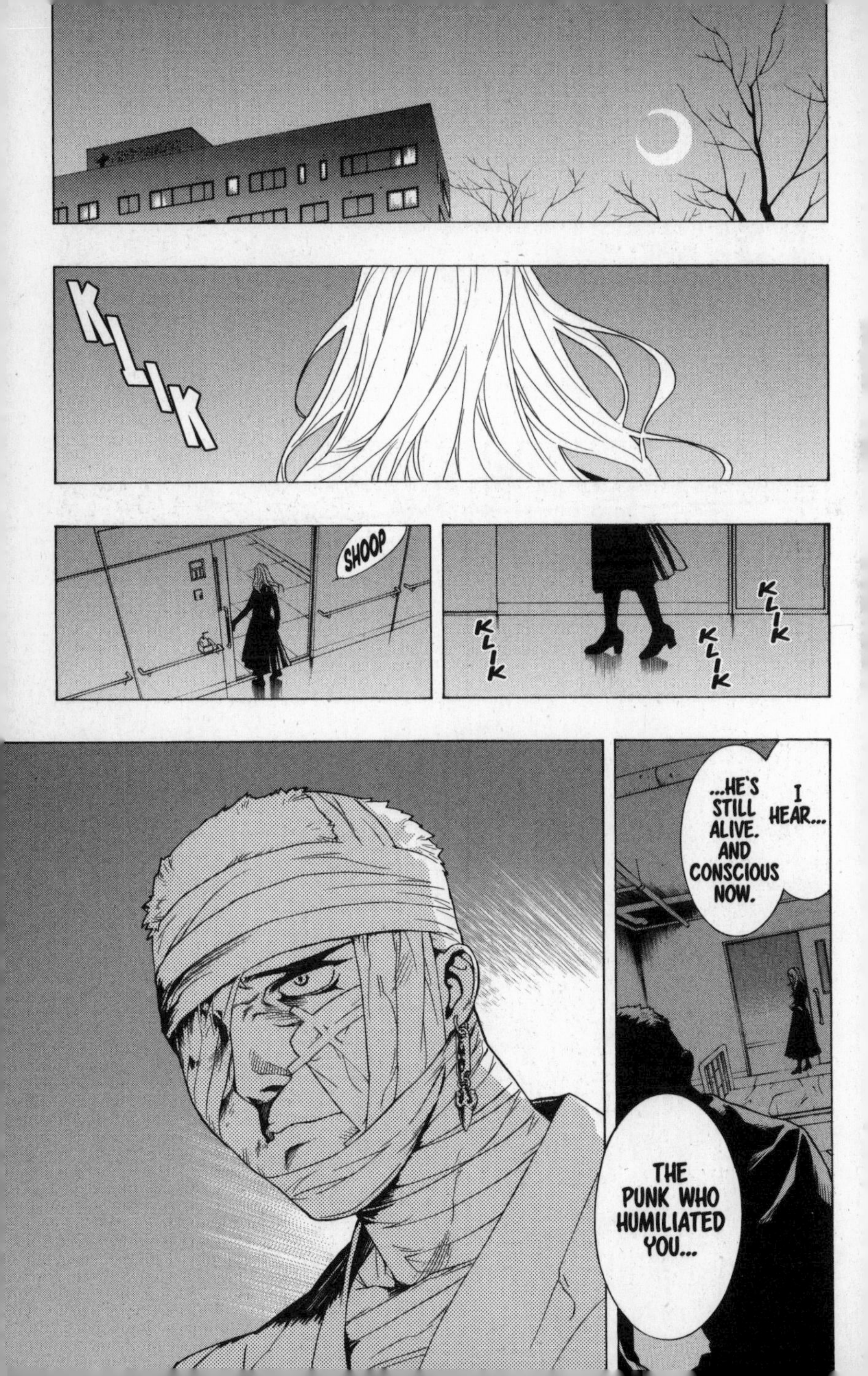

KLIK
SHOOP
KLIK
KLIK
KLIK
I HEAR...
...HE'S STILL ALIVE. AND CONSCIOUS NOW.
THE PUNK WHO HUMILIATED YOU...

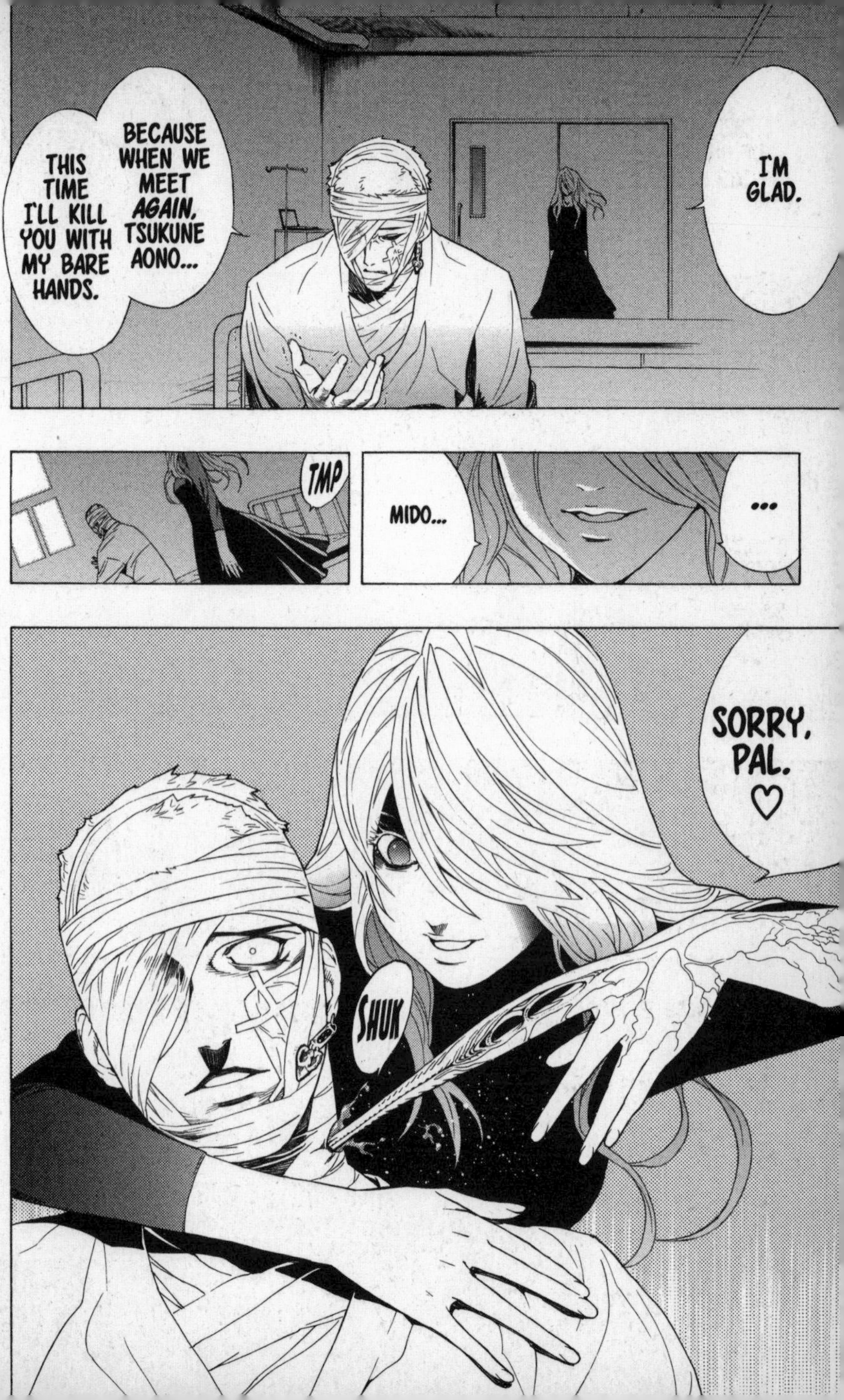
I'M GLAD.
BECAUSE WHEN WE MEET *AGAIN,* TSUKUNE AONO...
THIS TIME I'LL KILL YOU WITH MY BARE HANDS.
...
MIDO...
TMP
SORRY, PAL. ♡
SHUK

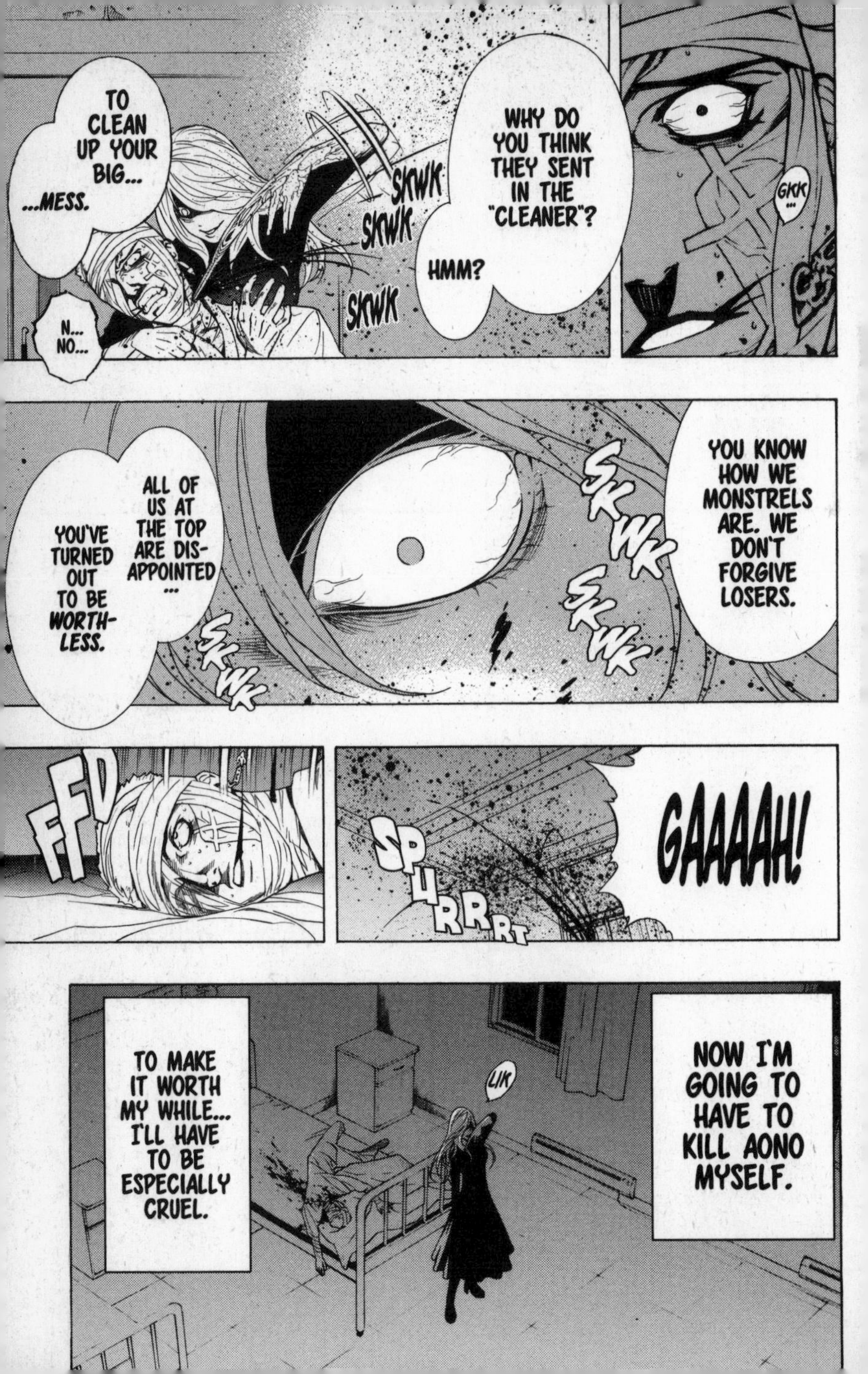
GKK...
WHY DO YOU THINK THEY SENT IN THE "CLEANER"?
HMM?
SKWK SKWK SKWK
TO CLEAN UP YOUR BIG... ...MESS.
N... NO...
YOU KNOW HOW WE MONSTRELS ARE. WE DON'T FORGIVE LOSERS.
SKWK SKWK
ALL OF US AT THE TOP ARE DIS-APPOINTED...
YOU'VE TURNED OUT TO BE WORTH-LESS.
SKWK
GAAAAH!
SPURRRT
FFD
NOW I'M GOING TO HAVE TO KILL AONO MYSELF.
LIK
TO MAKE IT WORTH MY WHILE... I'LL HAVE TO BE ESPECIALLY CRUEL.

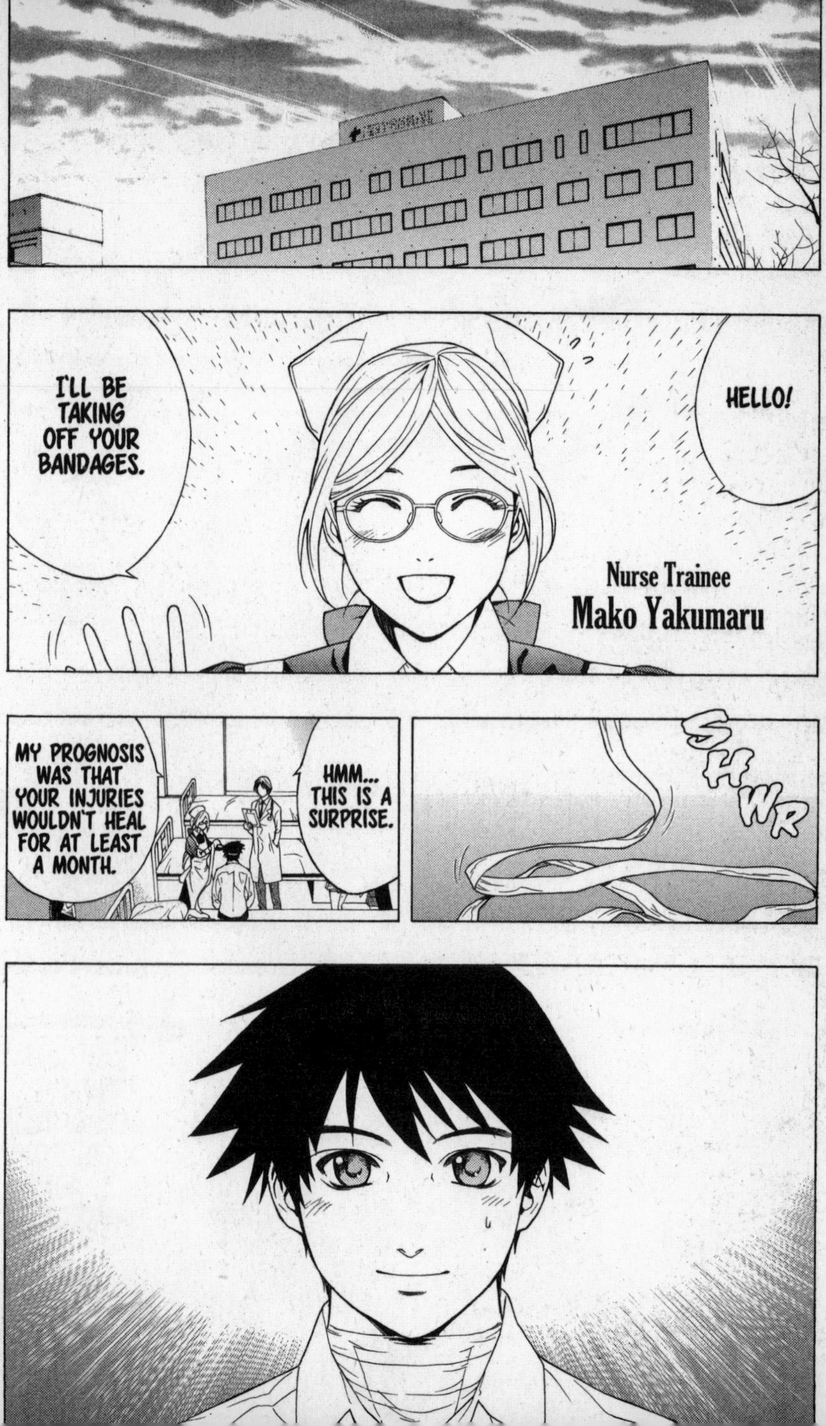
HELLO!
I'LL BE TAKING OFF YOUR BANDAGES.
Nurse Trainee
Mako Yakumaru
SHWR
HMM... THIS IS A SURPRISE.
MY PROGNOSIS WAS THAT YOUR INJURIES WOULDN'T HEAL FOR AT LEAST A MONTH.

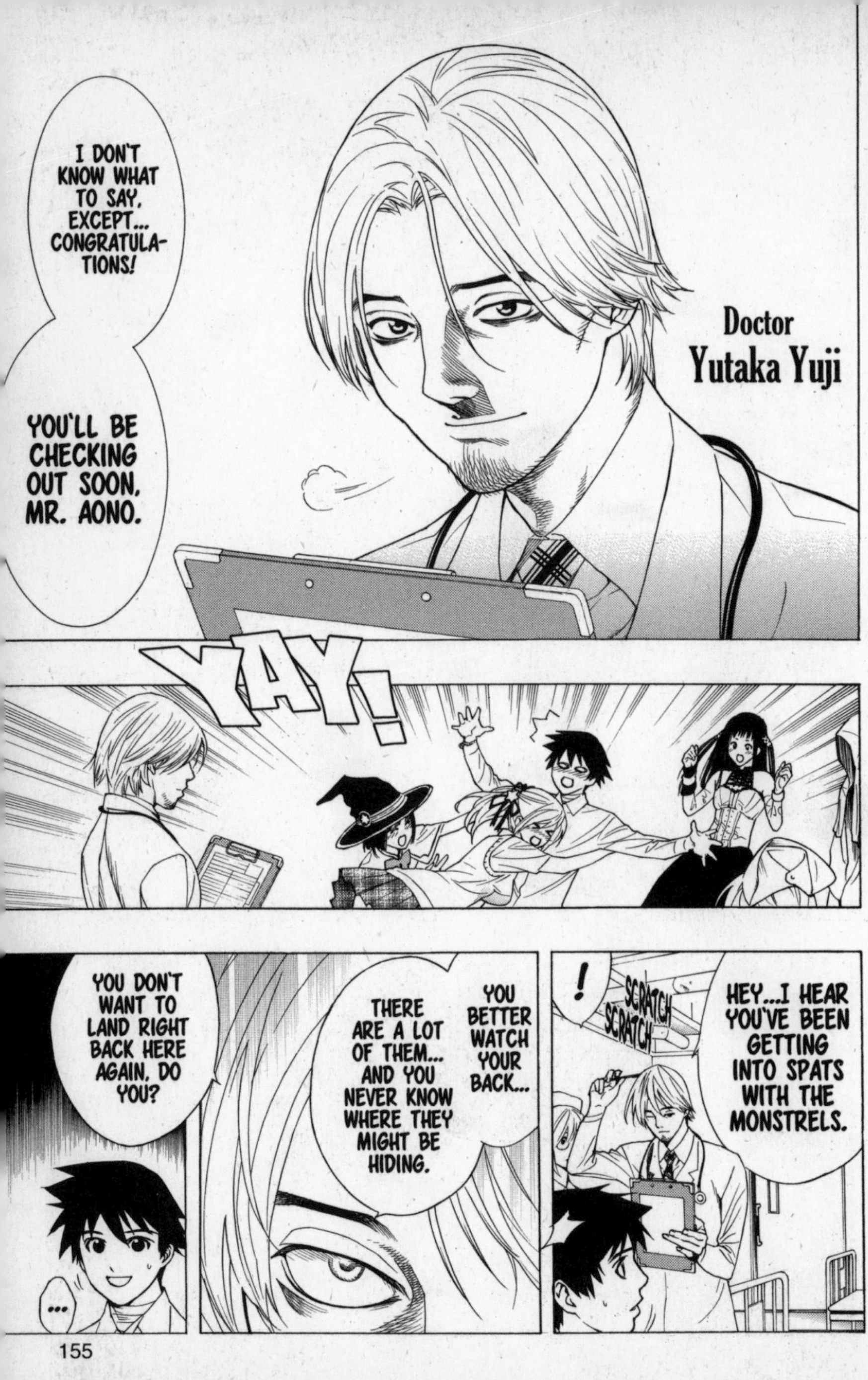
I DON'T KNOW WHAT TO SAY, EXCEPT... CONGRATULATIONS!
YOU'LL BE CHECKING OUT SOON, MR. AONO.
Doctor Yutaka Yuji
YAY!
HEY...I HEAR YOU'VE BEEN GETTING INTO SPATS WITH THE MONSTRELS.
SCRATCH SCRATCH
!
YOU BETTER WATCH YOUR BACK...
THERE ARE A LOT OF THEM... AND YOU NEVER KNOW WHERE THEY MIGHT BE HIDING.
YOU DON'T WANT TO LAND RIGHT BACK HERE AGAIN, DO YOU?
...

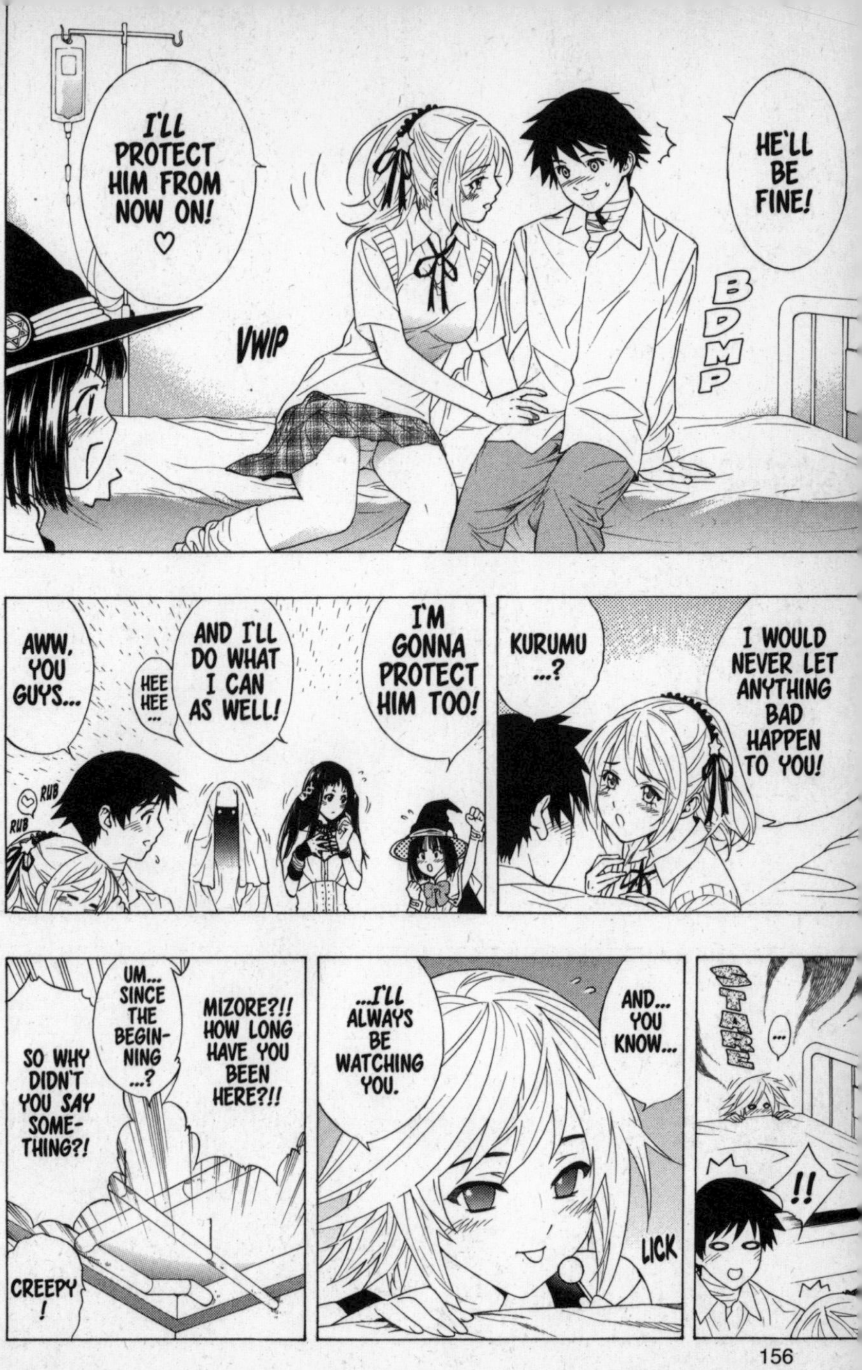
HE'LL BE FINE!
I'LL PROTECT HIM FROM NOW ON! ♡
BDMP
VWIP
I WOULD NEVER LET ANYTHING BAD HAPPEN TO YOU!
KURUMU ...?
I'M GONNA PROTECT HIM TOO!
AND I'LL DO WHAT I CAN AS WELL!
HEE HEE ...
AWW, YOU GUYS...
RUB
RUB
STARE
...
!!
AND... YOU KNOW...
...I'LL ALWAYS BE WATCHING YOU.
LICK
MIZORE?!! HOW LONG HAVE YOU BEEN HERE?!!
UM... SINCE THE BEGIN-NING ...?
SO WHY DIDN'T YOU SAY SOME-THING?!
CREEPY!

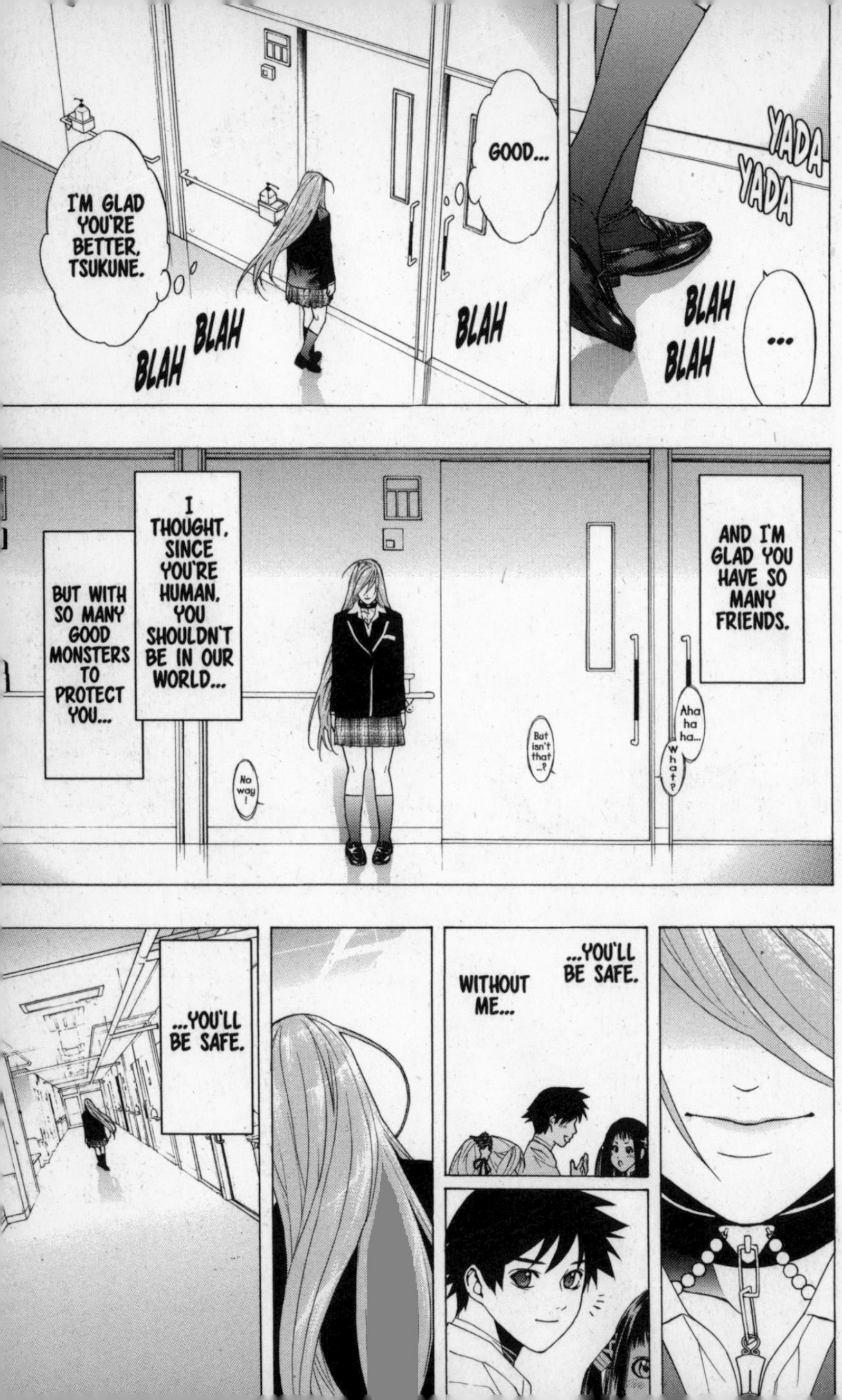
YADA YADA
...
BLAH BLAH
GOOD...
BLAH
I'M GLAD YOU'RE BETTER, TSUKUNE.
BLAH BLAH
AND I'M GLAD YOU HAVE SO MANY FRIENDS.
Aha ha ha...
What?
But isn't that...?
I THOUGHT, SINCE YOU'RE HUMAN, YOU SHOULDN'T BE IN OUR WORLD...
No way!
BUT WITH SO MANY GOOD MONSTERS TO PROTECT YOU...
...YOU'LL BE SAFE.
WITHOUT ME...
...YOU'LL BE SAFE.

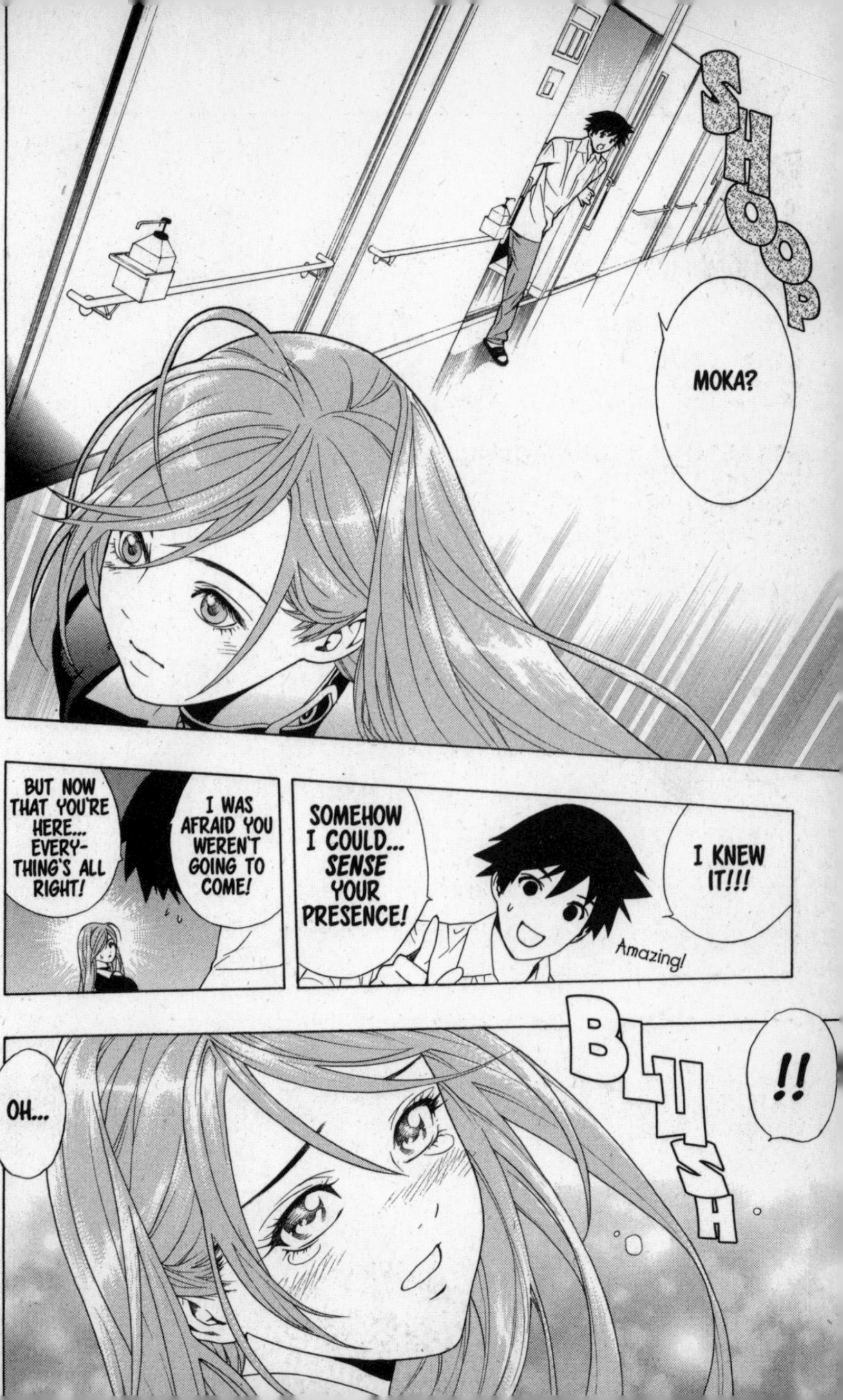
SHOOP
MOKA?
I KNEW IT!!!
Amazing!
SOMEHOW I COULD... *SENSE* YOUR PRESENCE!
I WAS AFRAID YOU WEREN'T GOING TO COME!
BUT NOW THAT YOU'RE HERE... EVERY-THING'S ALL RIGHT!
!!
BLUSH
OH...

READ THIS WAY

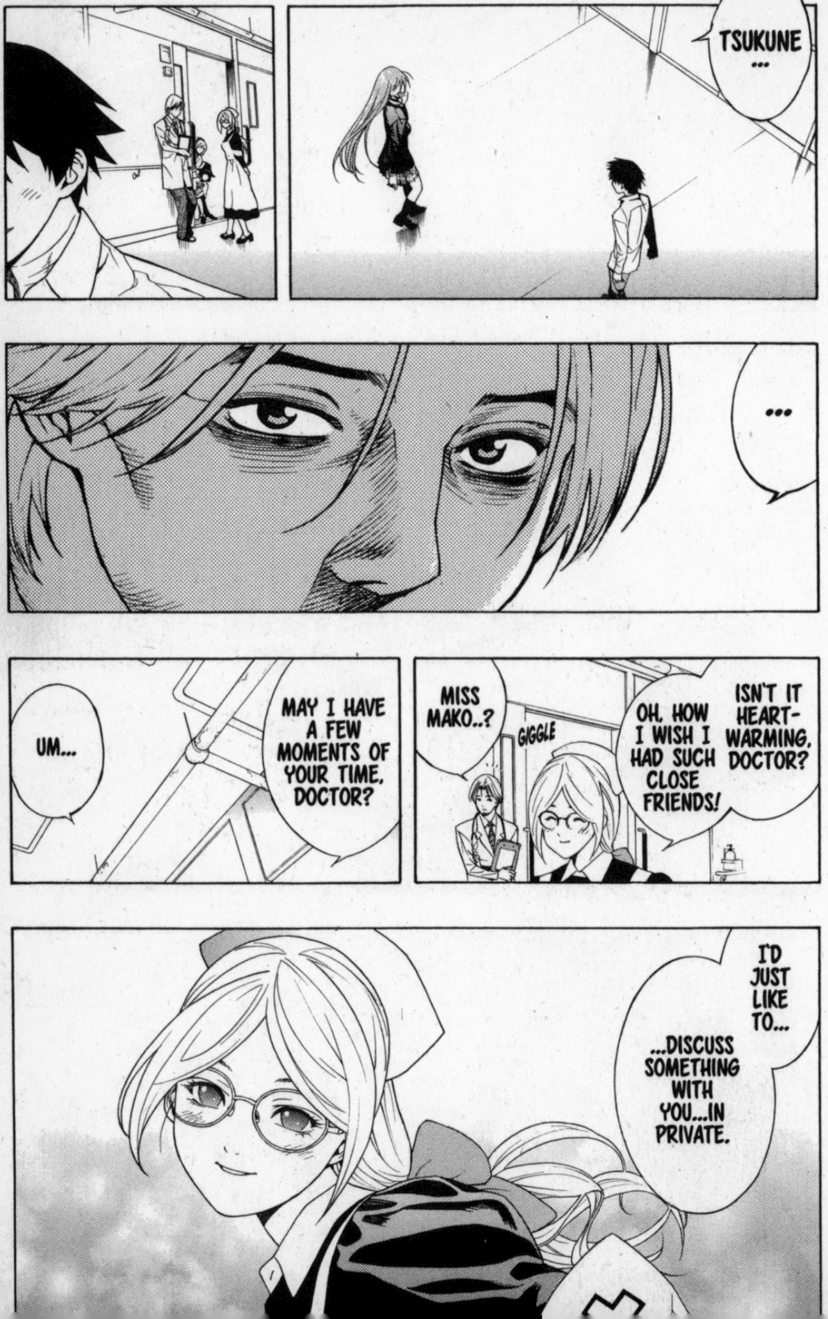
TSUKUNE ...
...
ISN'T IT HEART-WARMING, DOCTOR?
OH, HOW I WISH I HAD SUCH CLOSE FRIENDS!
GIGGLE
MISS MAKO..?
MAY I HAVE A FEW MOMENTS OF YOUR TIME, DOCTOR?
UM...
I'D JUST LIKE TO...
...DISCUSS SOMETHING WITH YOU...IN PRIVATE.

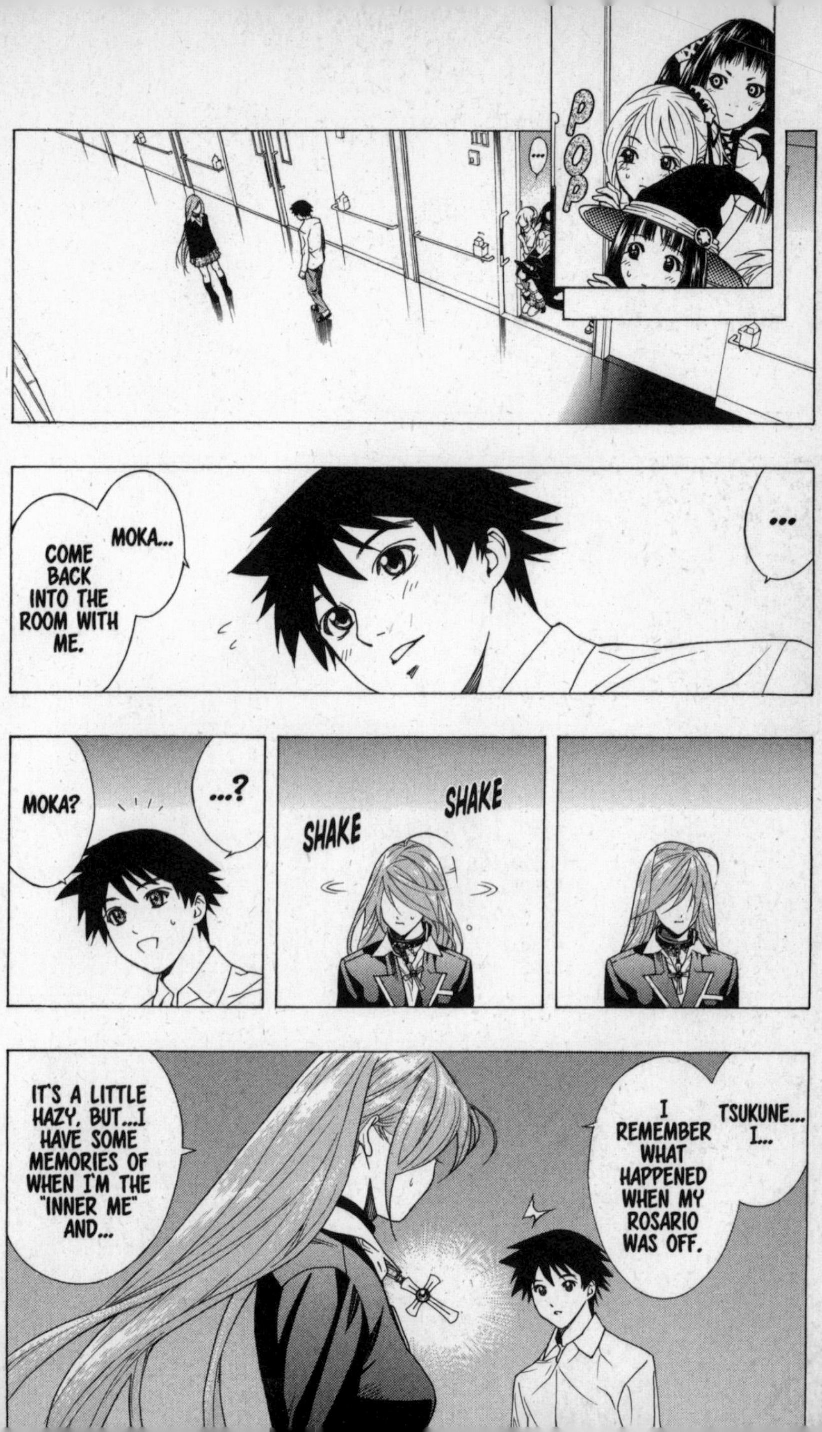
POP
...
...
MOKA... COME BACK INTO THE ROOM WITH ME.
SHAKE
SHAKE
...?
MOKA?
TSUKUNE... I...
I REMEMBER WHAT HAPPENED WHEN MY ROSARIO WAS OFF.
IT'S A LITTLE HAZY, BUT...I HAVE SOME MEMORIES OF WHEN I'M THE "INNER ME" AND...

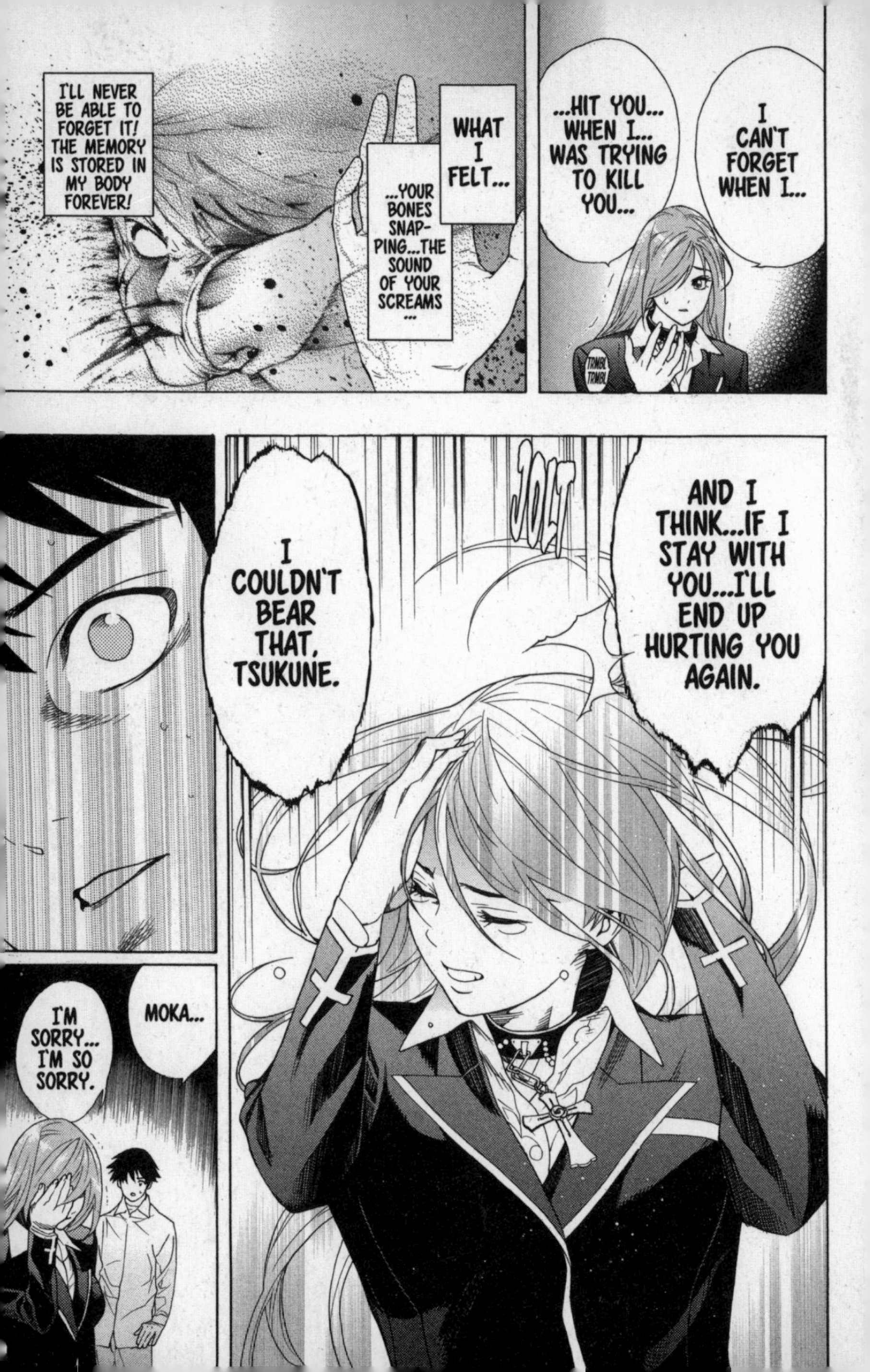
I CAN'T FORGET WHEN I...
...HIT YOU... WHEN I... WAS TRYING TO KILL YOU...
TRMBL TRMBL
WHAT I FELT...
...YOUR BONES SNAP-PING...THE SOUND OF YOUR SCREAMS ...
I'LL NEVER BE ABLE TO FORGET IT! THE MEMORY IS STORED IN MY BODY FOREVER!
JOLT
AND I THINK...IF I STAY WITH YOU...I'LL END UP HURTING YOU AGAIN.
I COULDN'T BEAR THAT, TSUKUNE.
MOKA...
I'M SORRY... I'M SO SORRY.

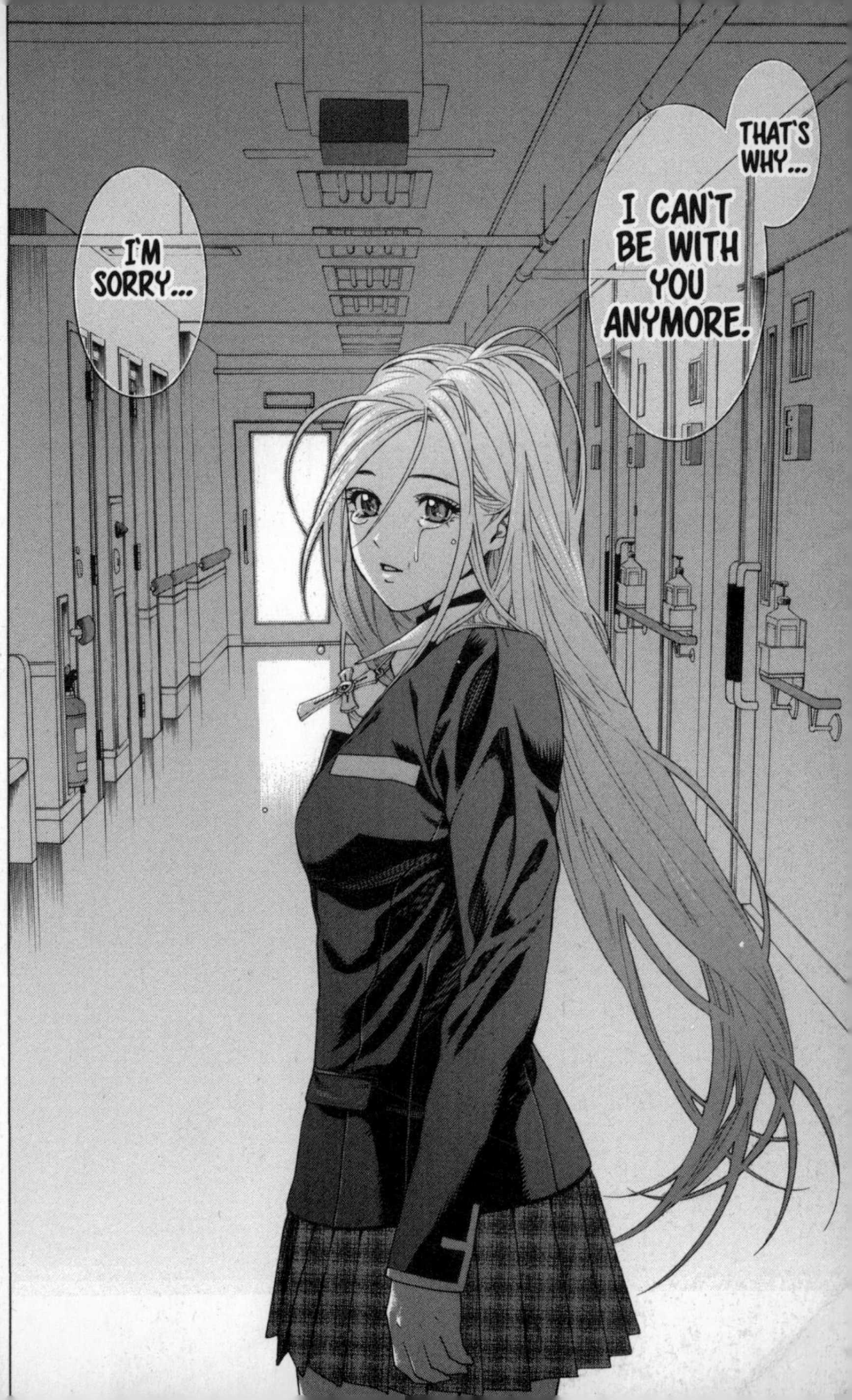
THAT'S WHY...
I CAN'T BE WITH YOU ANYMORE.
I'M SORRY...

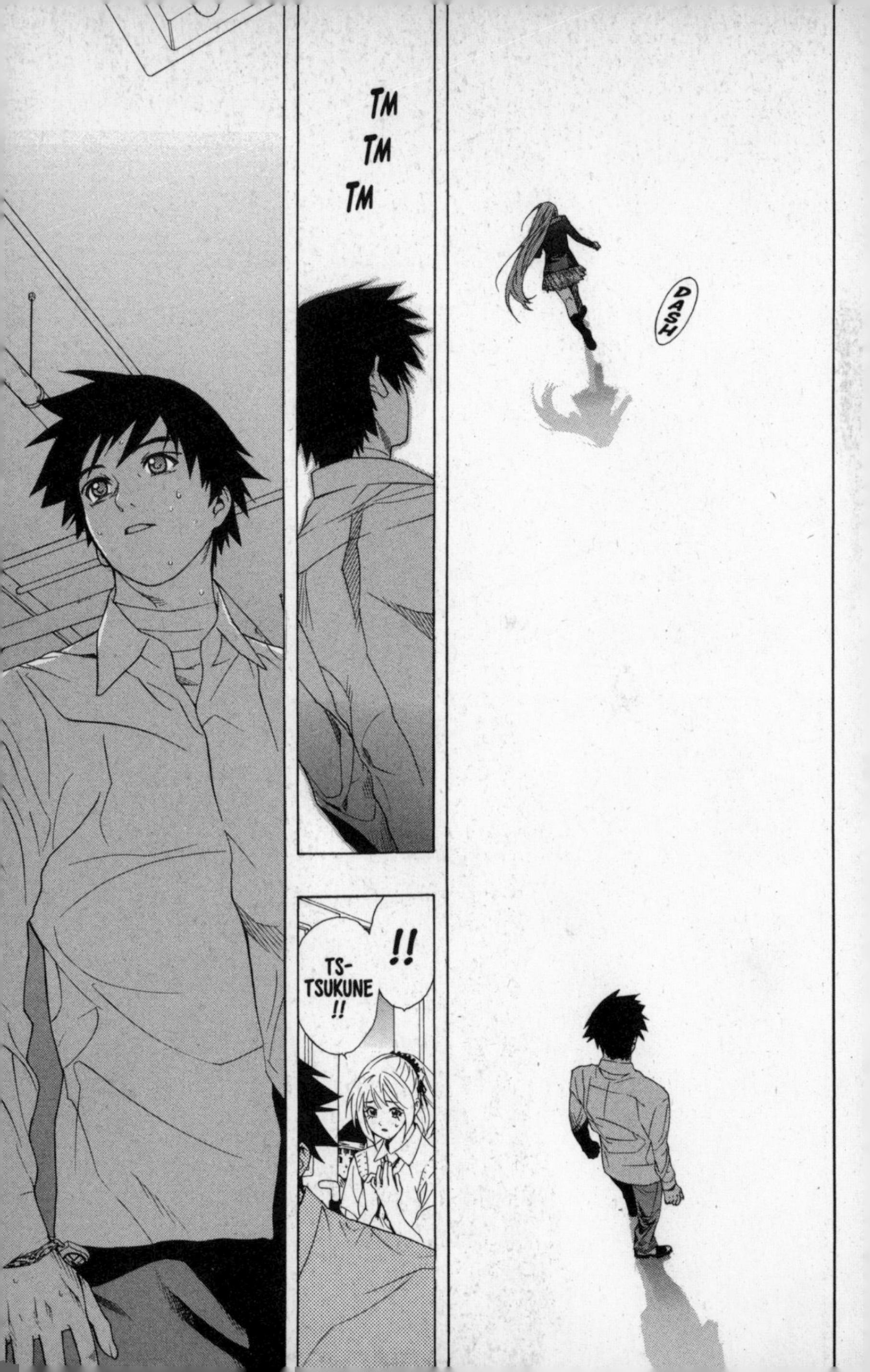
DASH
TM
TM
TM
TS-TSUKUNE!!
!!

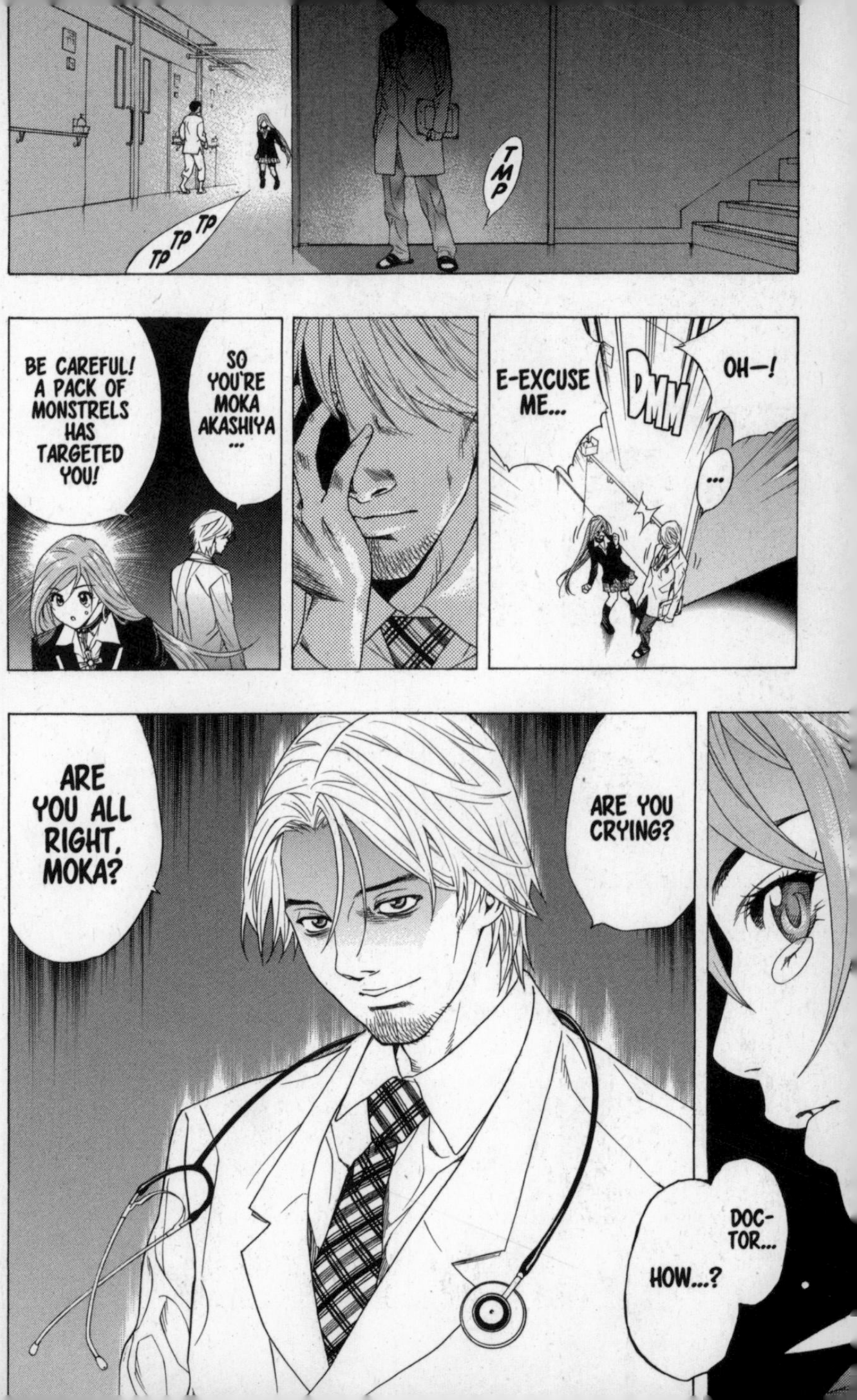
TMP
TP TP TP
OH—!
DMM
E-EXCUSE ME...
...
SO YOU'RE MOKA AKASHIYA ...
BE CAREFUL! A PACK OF MONSTRELS HAS TARGETED YOU!
DOC-TOR...
HOW...?
ARE YOU CRYING?
ARE YOU ALL RIGHT, MOKA?

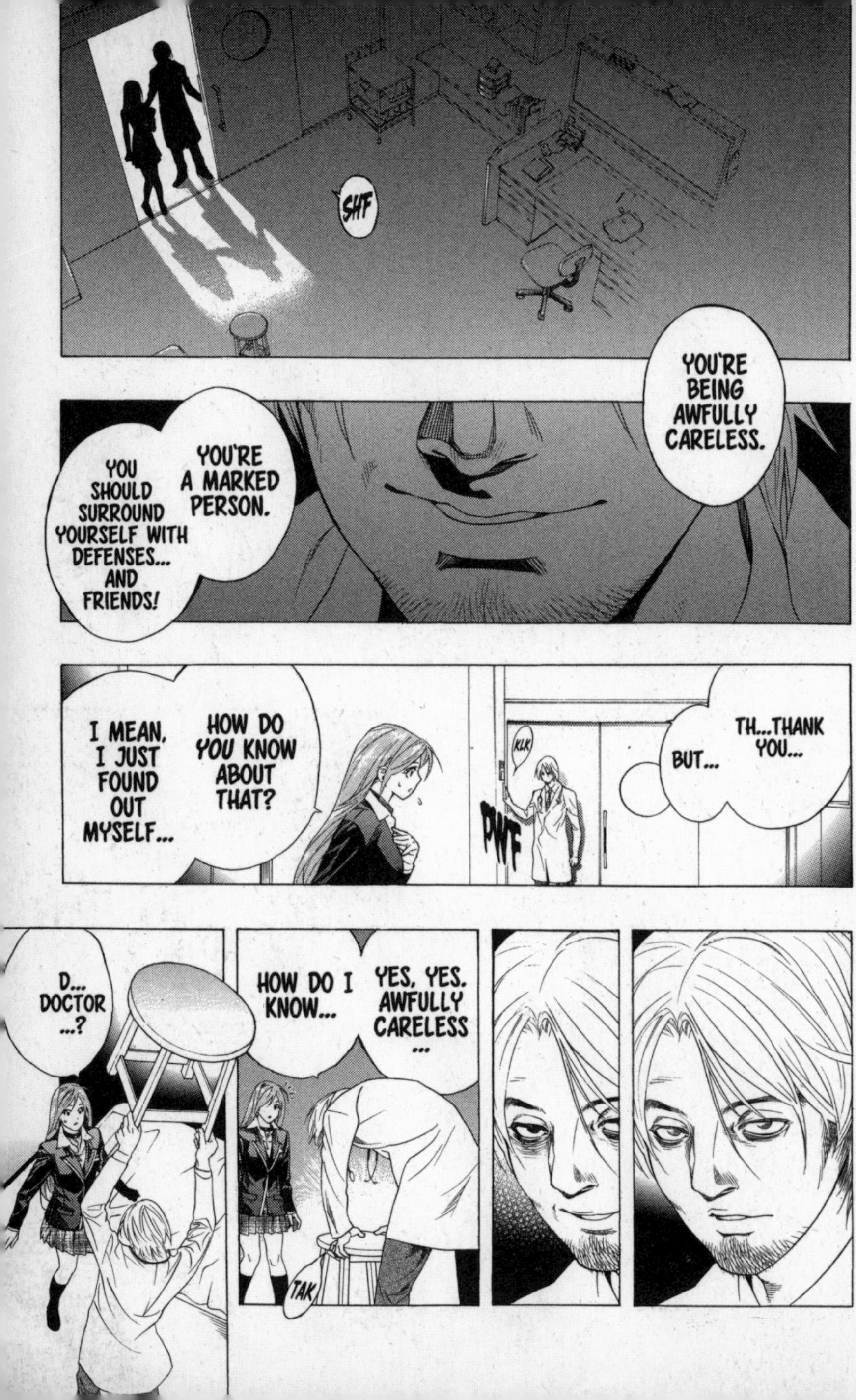
SHF
YOU'RE BEING AWFULLY CARELESS.
YOU'RE A MARKED PERSON.
YOU SHOULD SURROUND YOURSELF WITH DEFENSES... AND FRIENDS!
TH...THANK YOU...
BUT...
KLIK
PWF
HOW DO YOU KNOW ABOUT THAT?
I MEAN, I JUST FOUND OUT MYSELF...
YES, YES. AWFULLY CARELESS ...
HOW DO I KNOW...
TAK
D... DOCTOR ...?

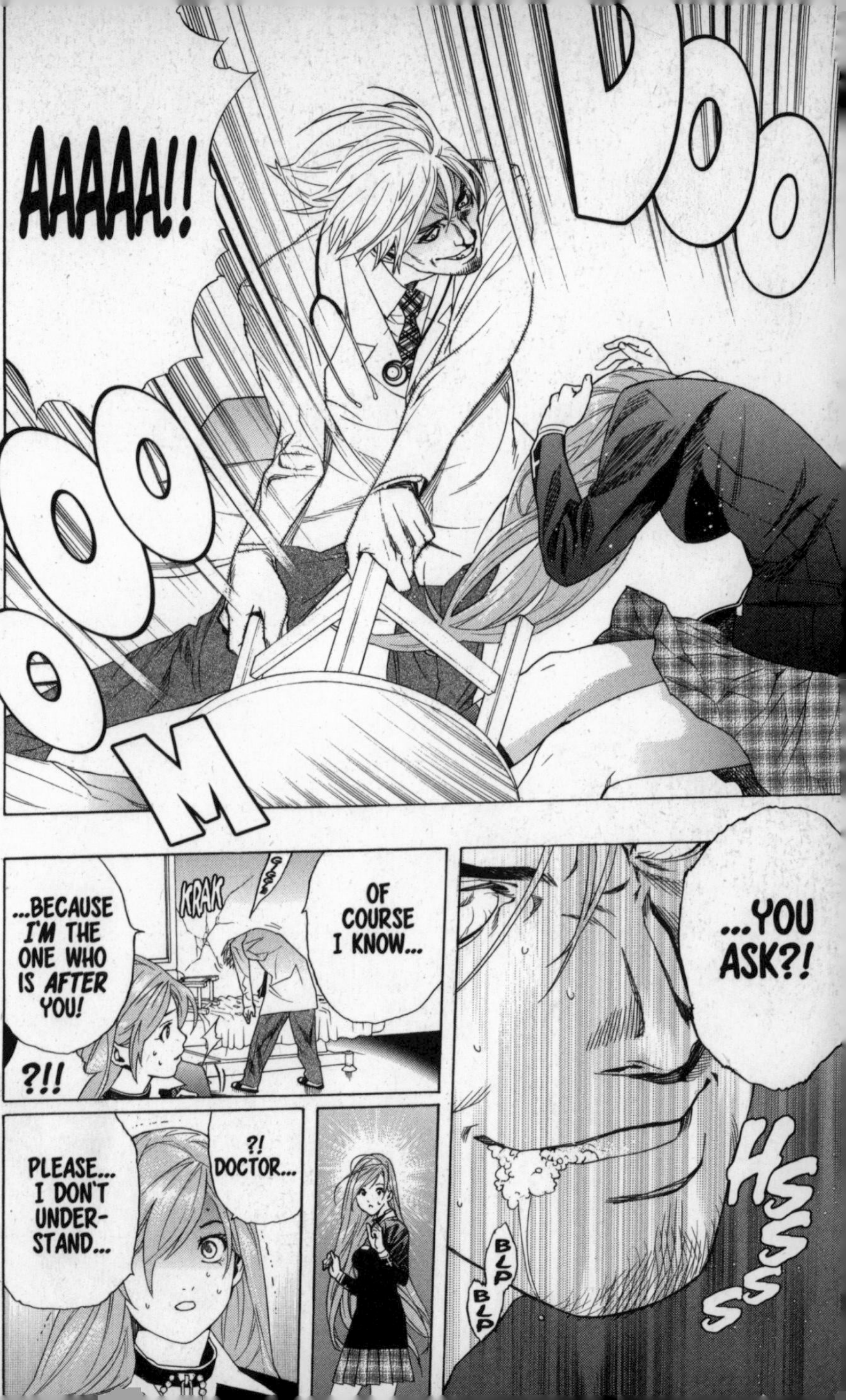
DOOOO
OOOOM
AAAAA!!
...YOU ASK?!
HSSSSS
BLP BLP
OF COURSE I KNOW...
KRAK
...BECAUSE I'M THE ONE WHO IS AFTER YOU!
?!!
?! DOCTOR...
PLEASE... I DON'T UNDER-STAND...

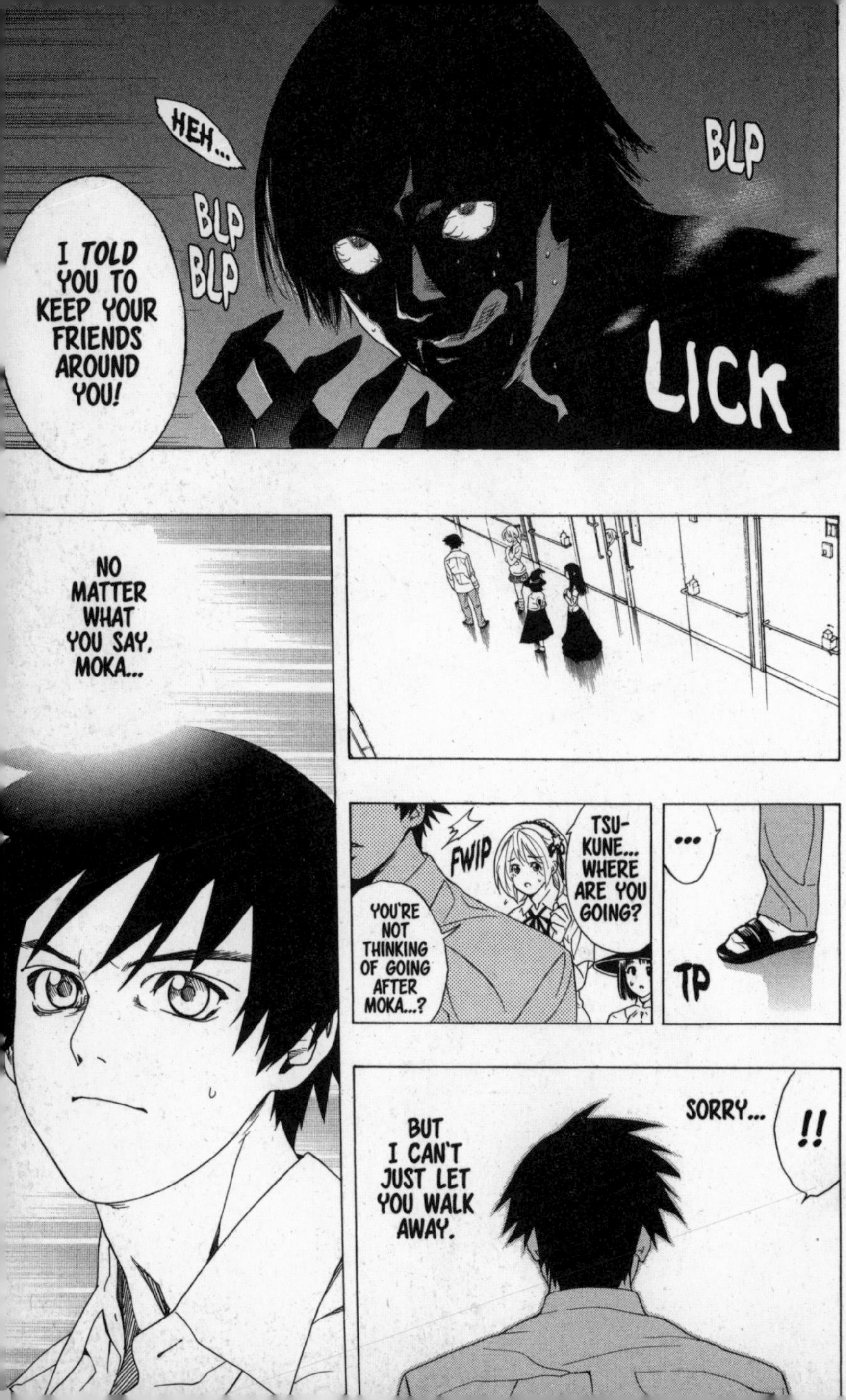
BLP
LICK
HEH...
BLP BLP
I *TOLD* YOU TO KEEP YOUR FRIENDS AROUND YOU!
...
TP
TSU-KUNE... WHERE ARE YOU GOING?
FWIP
YOU'RE NOT THINKING OF GOING AFTER MOKA...?
NO MATTER WHAT YOU SAY, MOKA...
!!
SORRY...
BUT I CAN'T JUST LET YOU WALK AWAY.

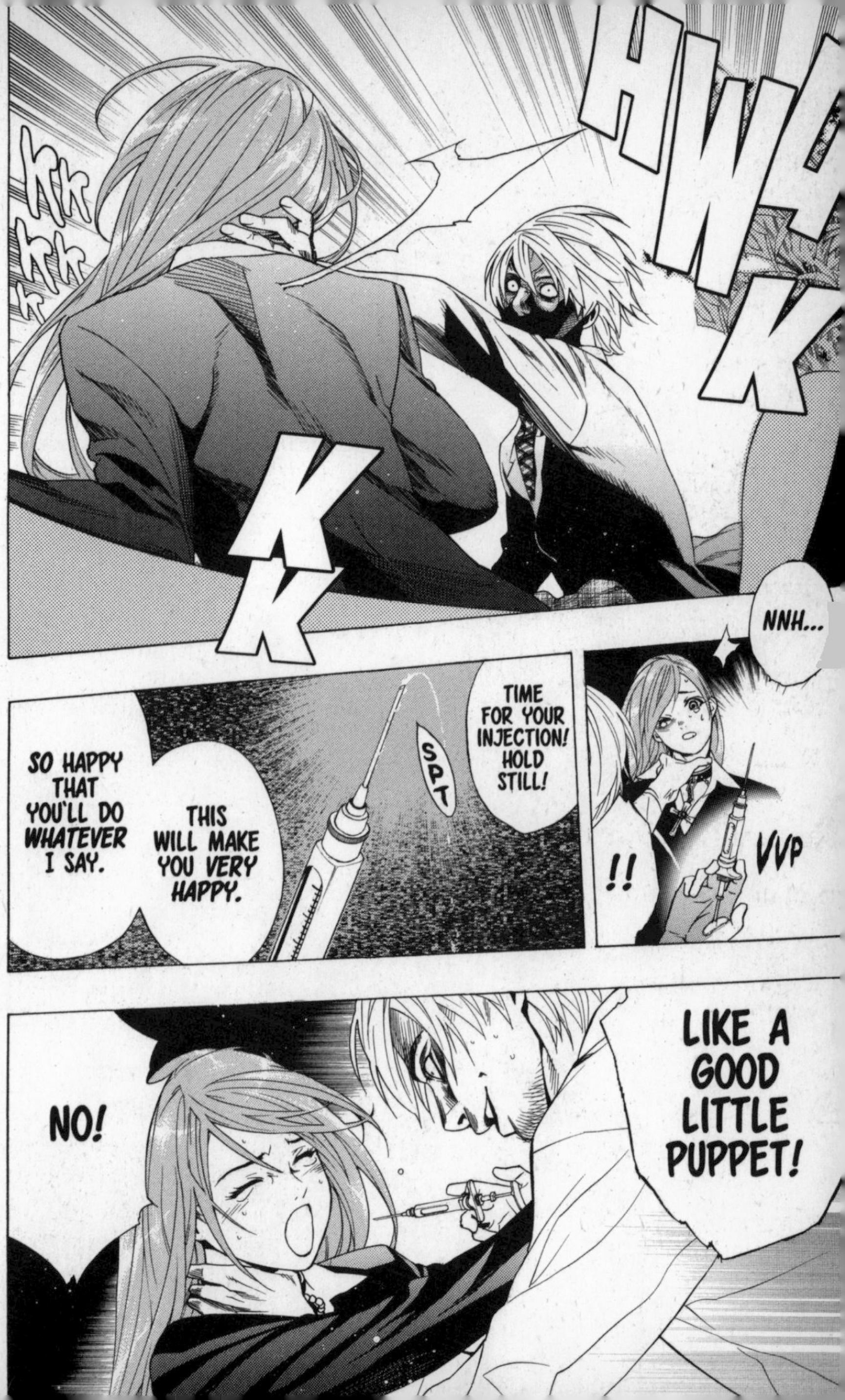
HW
K
Kk kk k
K
K
NNH...
VVP
!!
TIME FOR YOUR INJECTION! HOLD STILL!
SPT
THIS WILL MAKE YOU VERY HAPPY.
SO HAPPY THAT YOU'LL DO WHATEVER I SAY.
LIKE A GOOD LITTLE PUPPET!
NO!

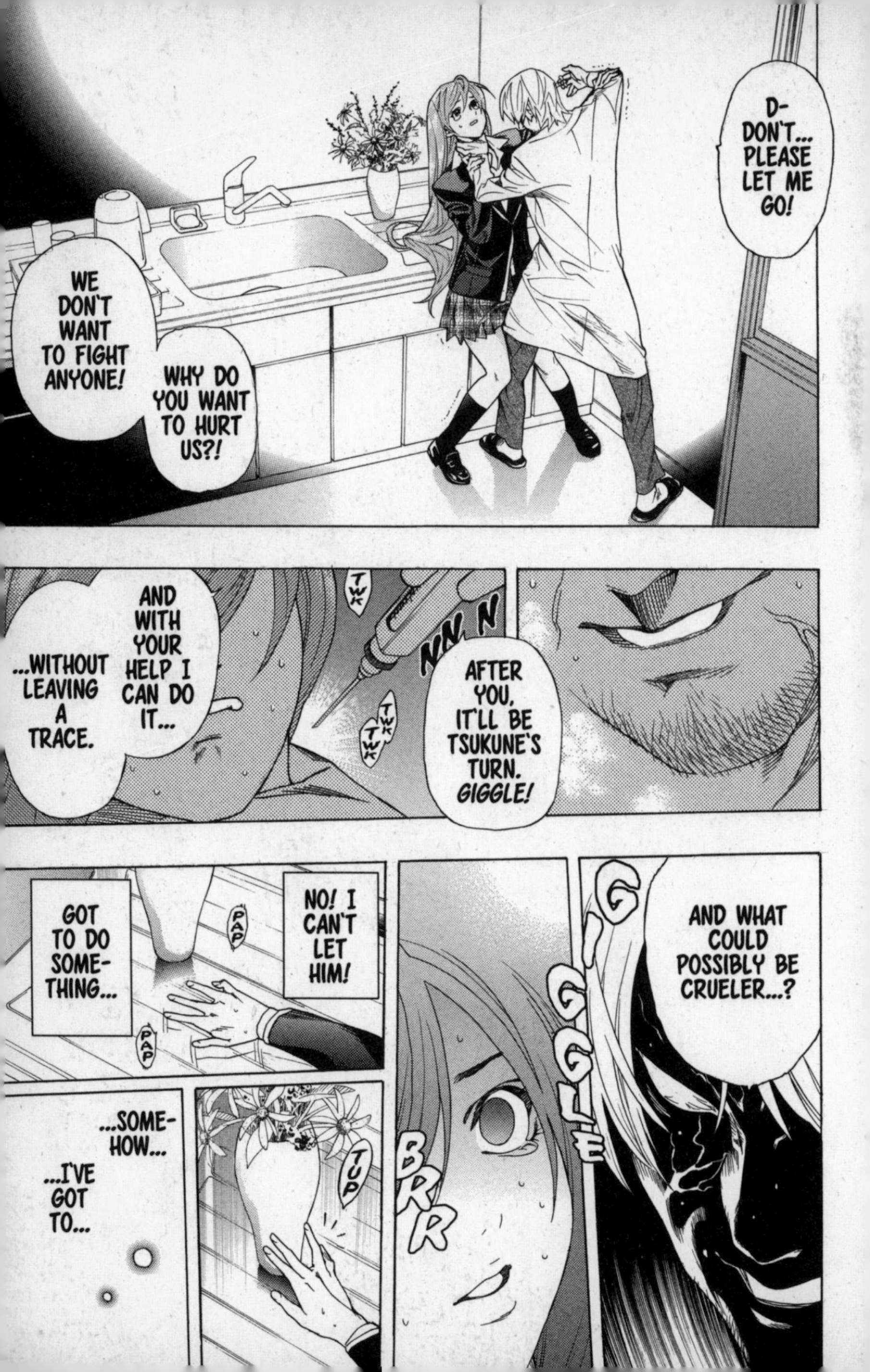
D-DON'T... PLEASE LET ME GO!
WE DON'T WANT TO FIGHT ANYONE!
WHY DO YOU WANT TO HURT US?!
AFTER YOU, IT'LL BE TSUKUNE'S TURN. GIGGLE!
NN N
TWK TWK TWK
AND WITH YOUR HELP I CAN DO IT...
...WITHOUT LEAVING A TRACE.
AND WHAT COULD POSSIBLY BE CRUELER...?
GIGGLE
BRR
NO! I CAN'T LET HIM!
PAP
GOT TO DO SOME-THING...
PAP
TUP
...SOME-HOW...
...I'VE GOT TO...

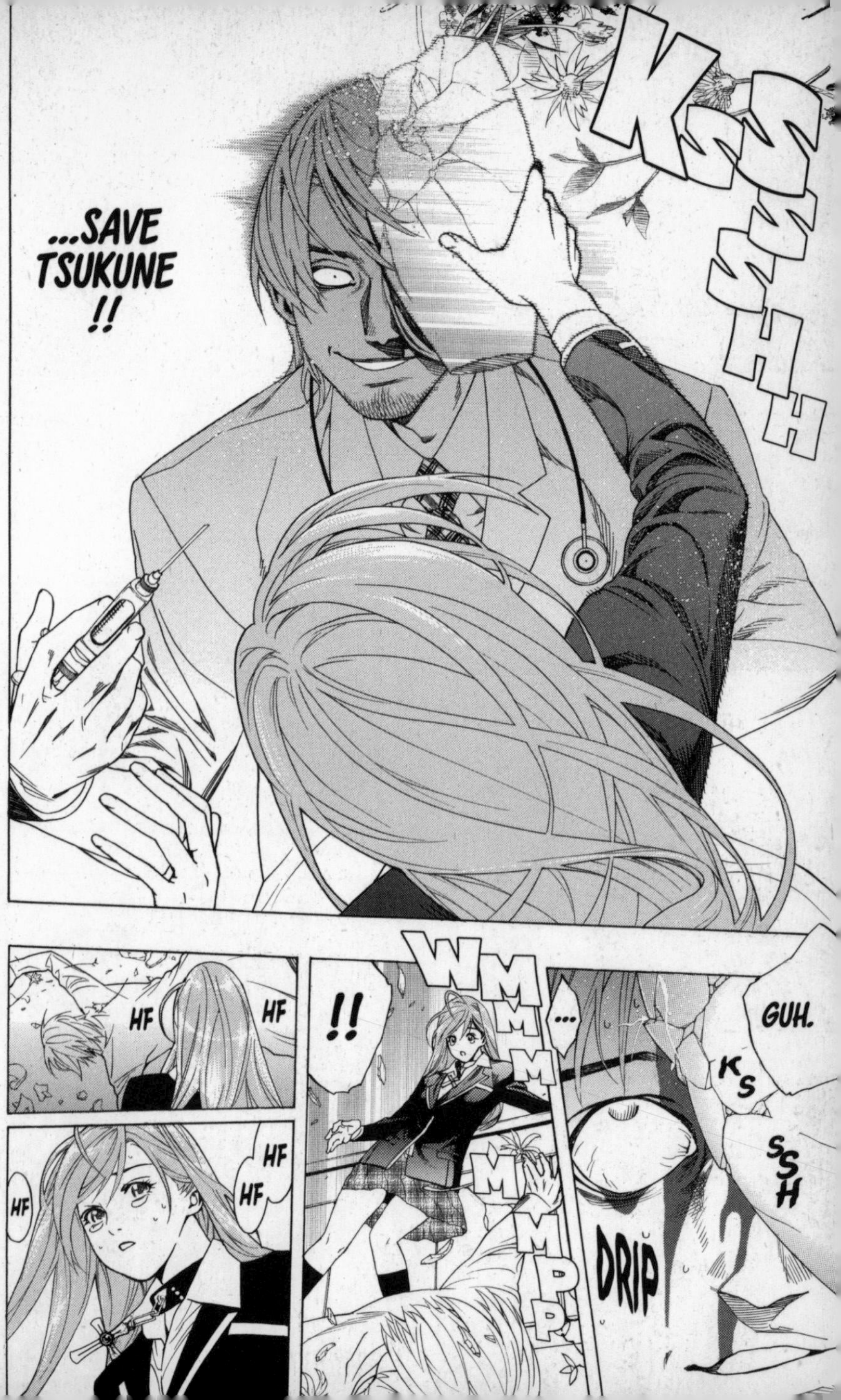
KSSSHHH
...SAVE TSUKUNE !!
GUH.
KS
SSH
DRIP
...
WMMMMMMMP
!!
HF
HF
HF
HF
HF

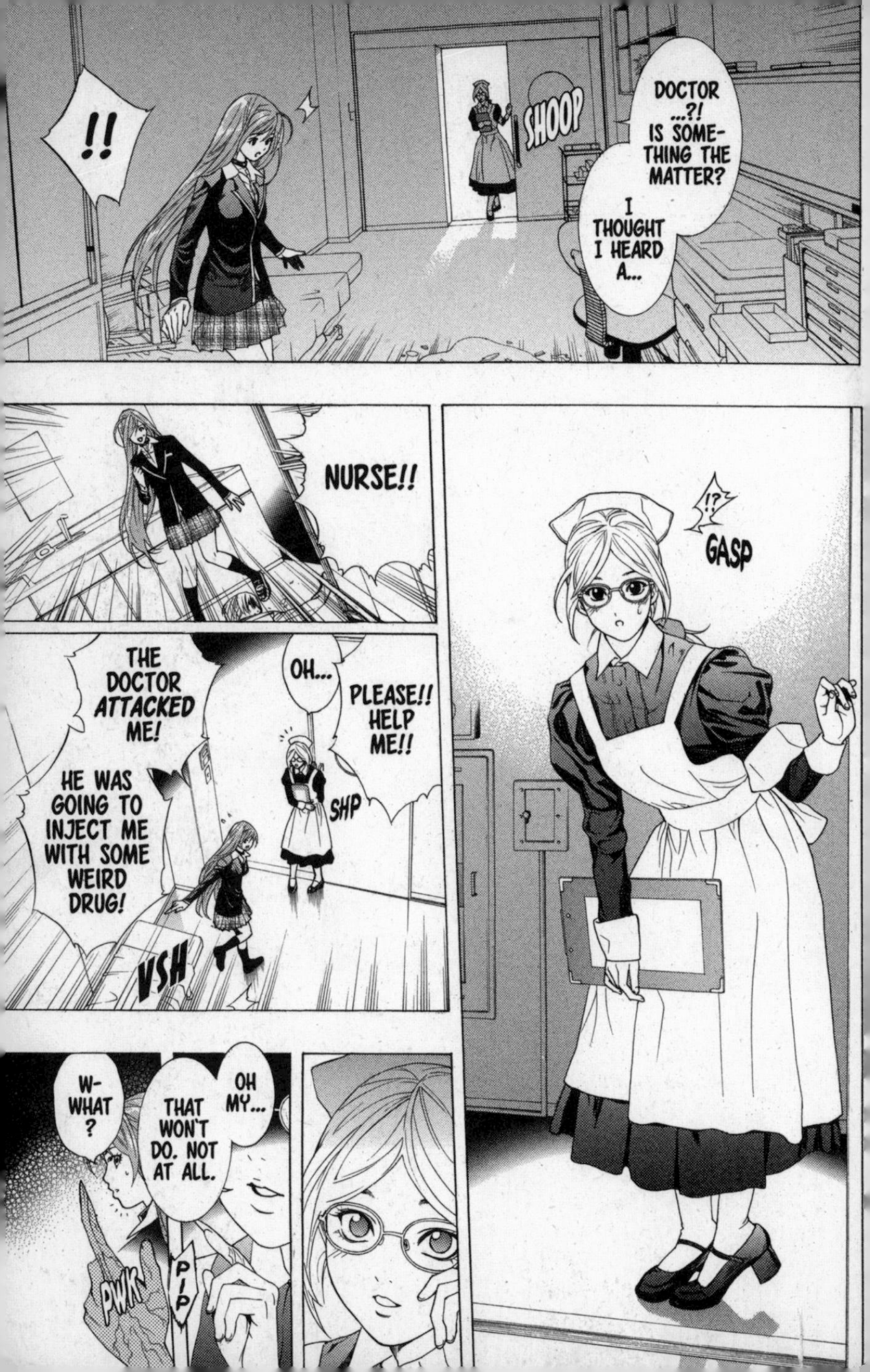

DOCTOR ...?! IS SOMETHING THE MATTER?
I THOUGHT I HEARD A...
SHOOP
!!
!?
GASP
NURSE!!
OH...
PLEASE!! HELP ME!!
SHP
THE DOCTOR ATTACKED ME!
HE WAS GOING TO INJECT ME WITH SOME WEIRD DRUG!
VSH
OH MY...
THAT WON'T DO. NOT AT ALL.
W-WHAT?
PIP
PWK

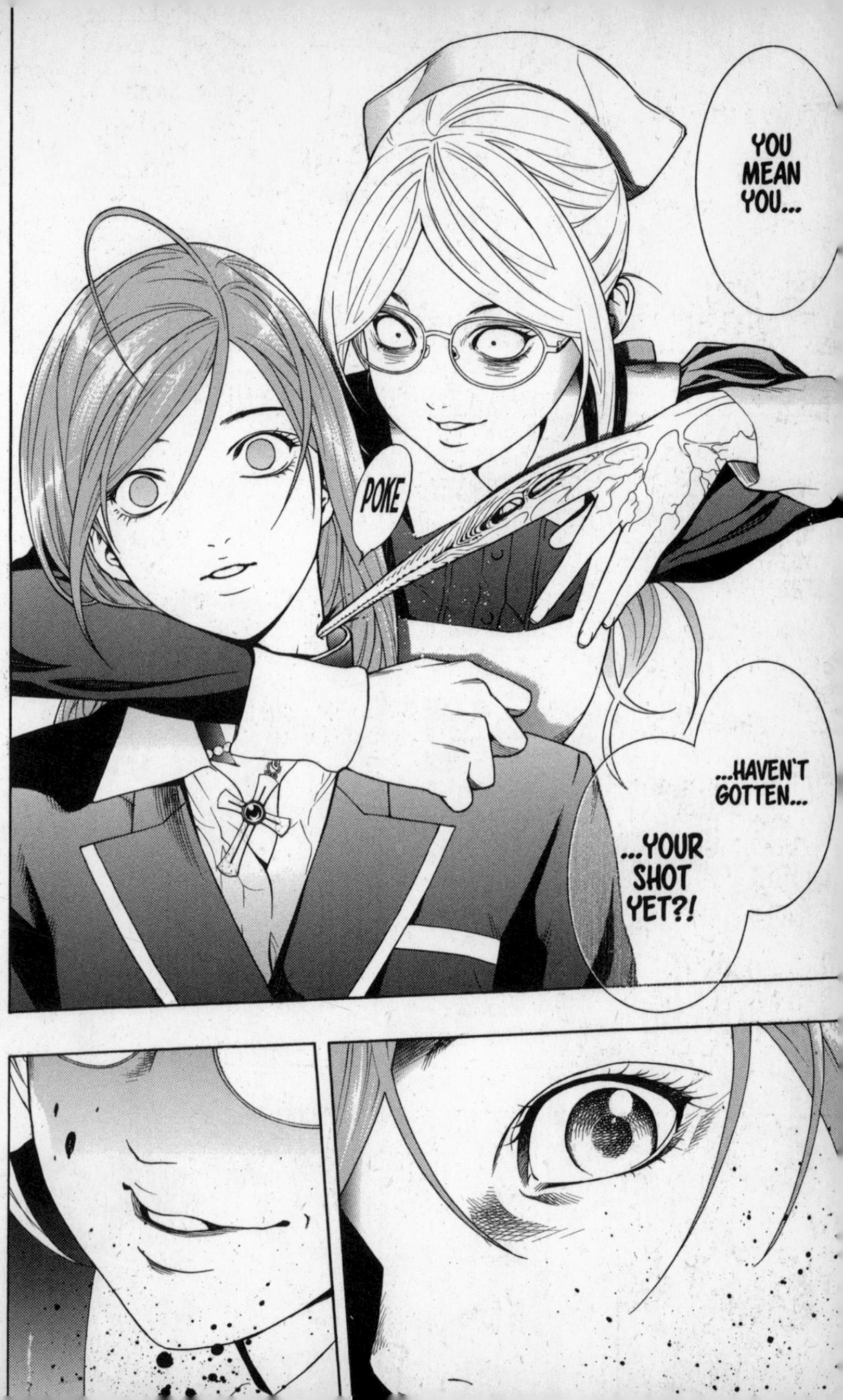
YOU MEAN YOU...
POKE
...HAVEN'T GOTTEN...
...YOUR SHOT YET?!

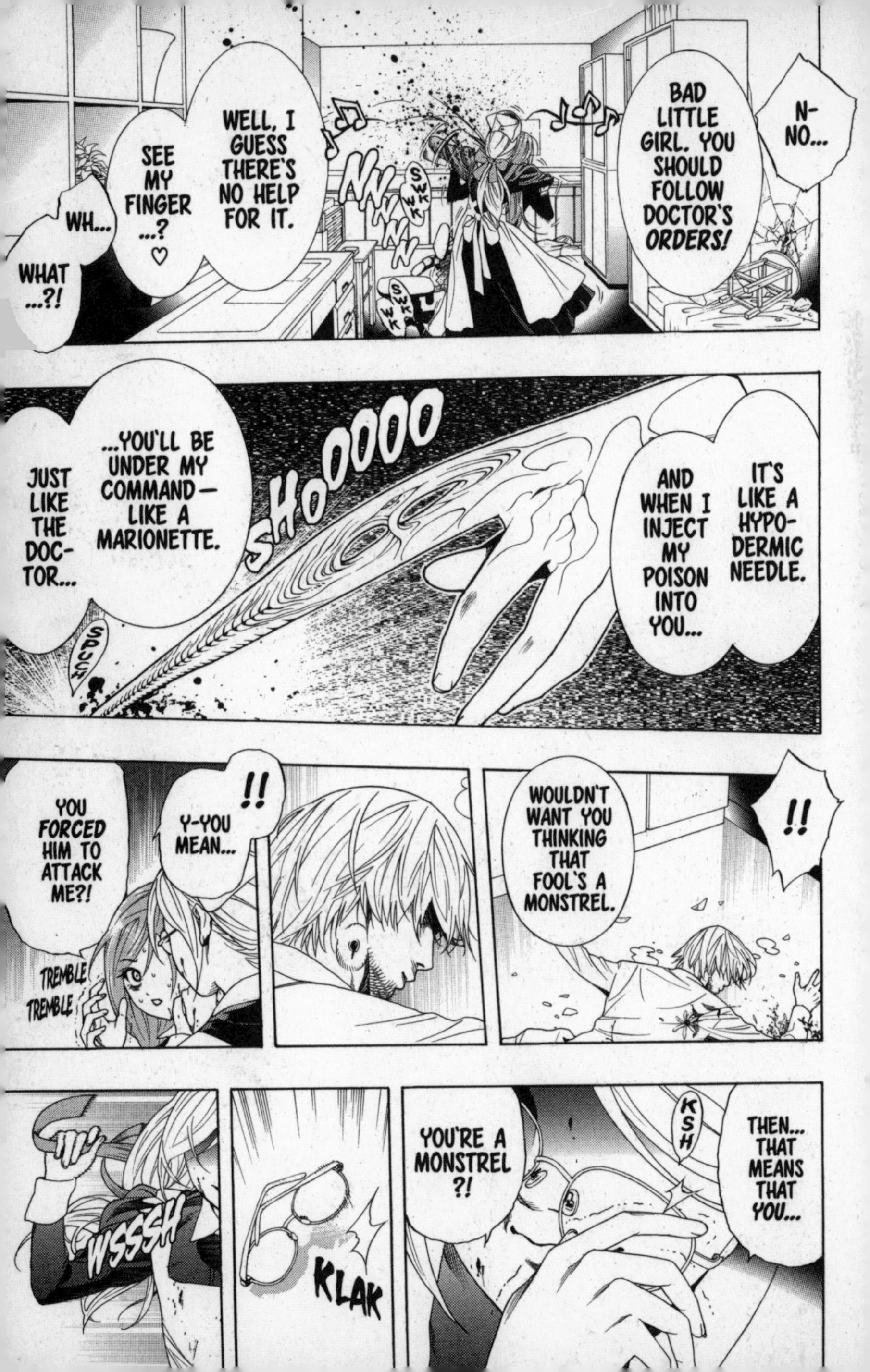
N-NO...
BAD LITTLE GIRL. YOU SHOULD FOLLOW DOCTOR'S ORDERS!
NNNNN
SWK SWK
SWK SWK
WELL, I GUESS THERE'S NO HELP FOR IT.
SEE MY FINGER ...? ♡
WH...
WHAT ...?!
IT'S LIKE A HYPODERMIC NEEDLE.
AND WHEN I INJECT MY POISON INTO YOU...
SHOOOOO
...YOU'LL BE UNDER MY COMMAND—LIKE A MARIONETTE.
JUST LIKE THE DOCTOR...
SPUCH
!!
WOULDN'T WANT YOU THINKING THAT FOOL'S A MONSTREL.
!!
Y-YOU MEAN...
YOU FORCED HIM TO ATTACK ME?!
TREMBLE TREMBLE
THEN... THAT MEANS THAT YOU...
KSH
YOU'RE A MONSTREL ?!
KLAK
WSSSH

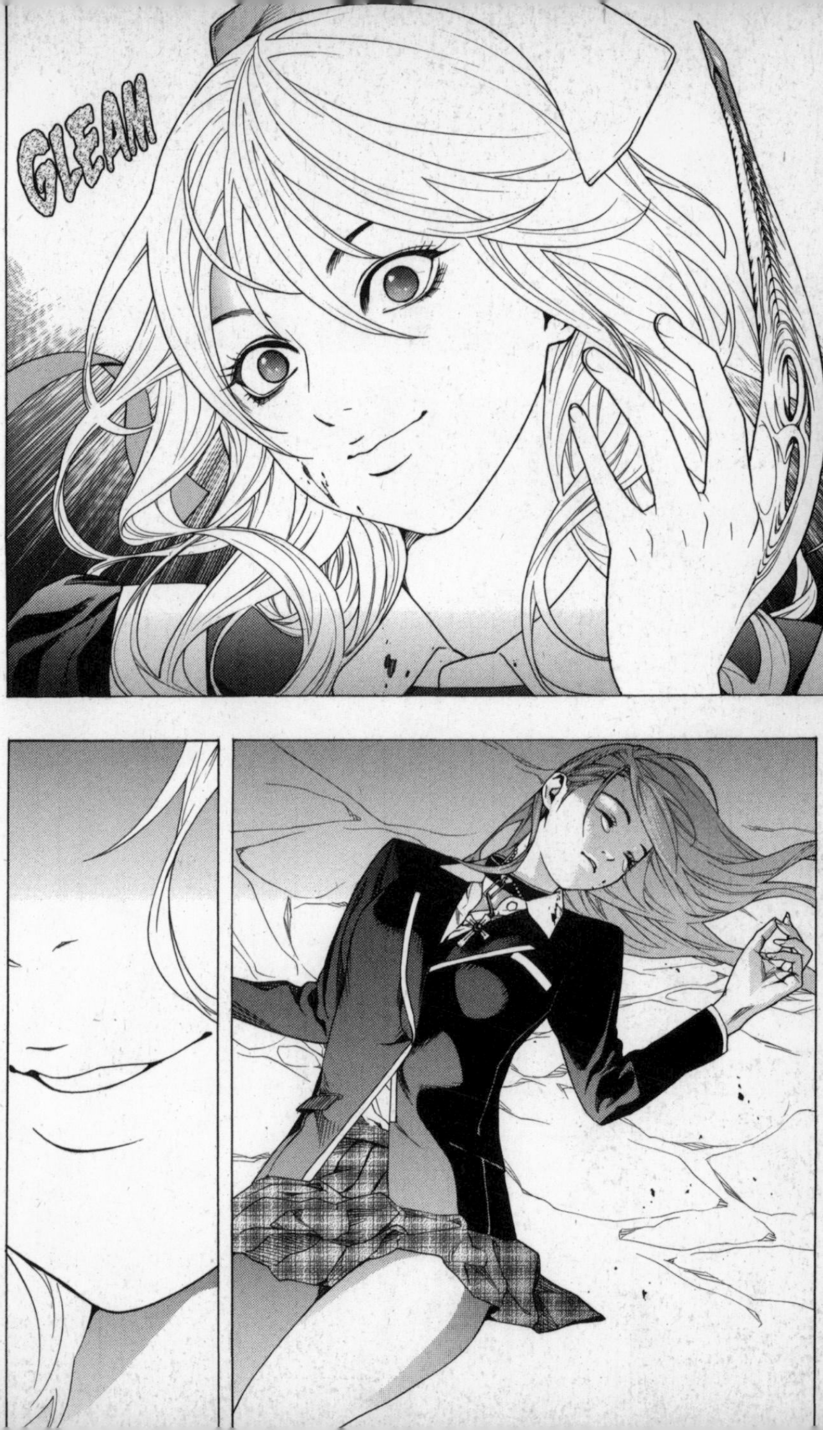
GLEAM

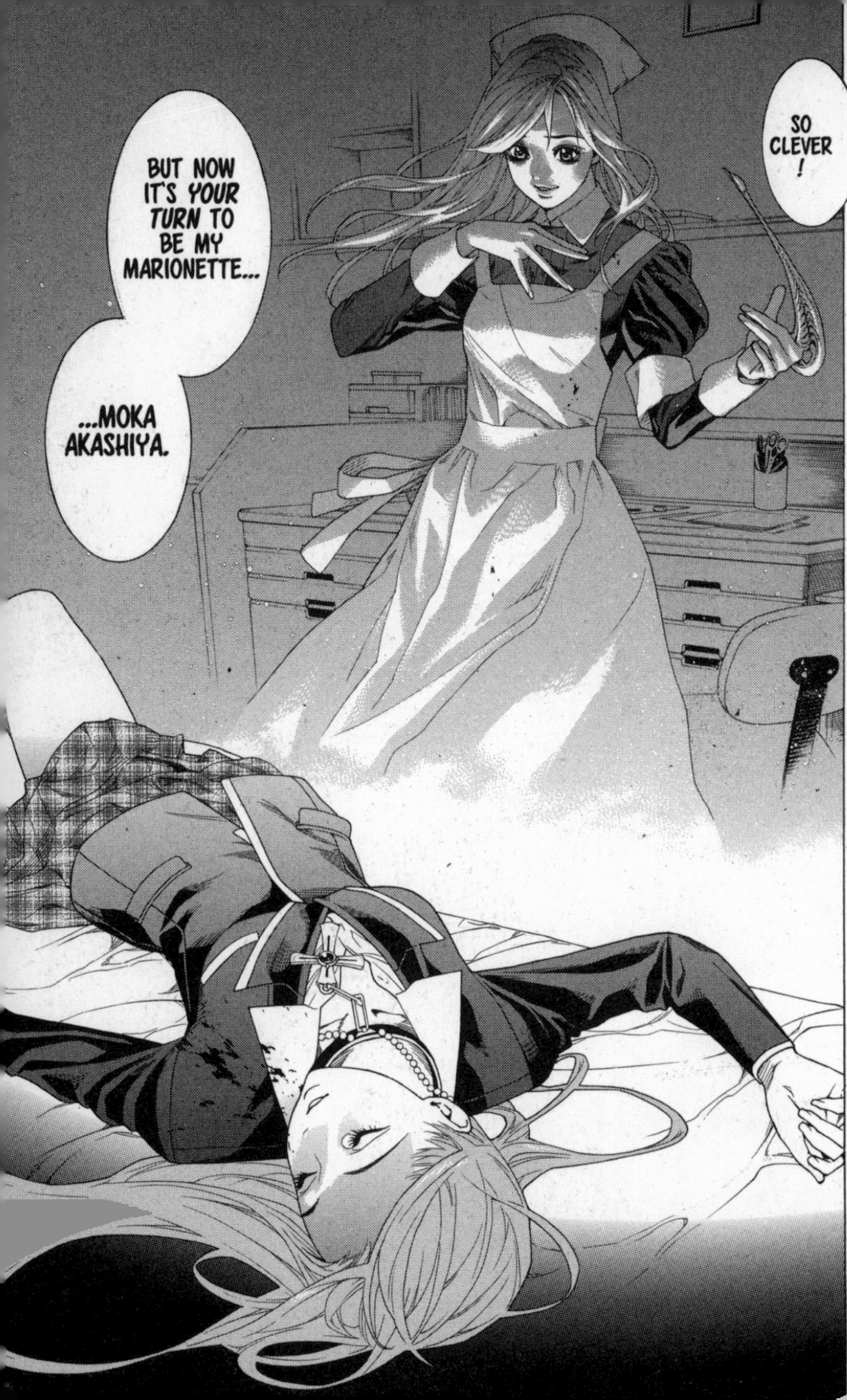
SO CLEVER!
BUT NOW IT'S YOUR TURN TO BE MY MARIONETTE...
...MOKA AKASHIYA.

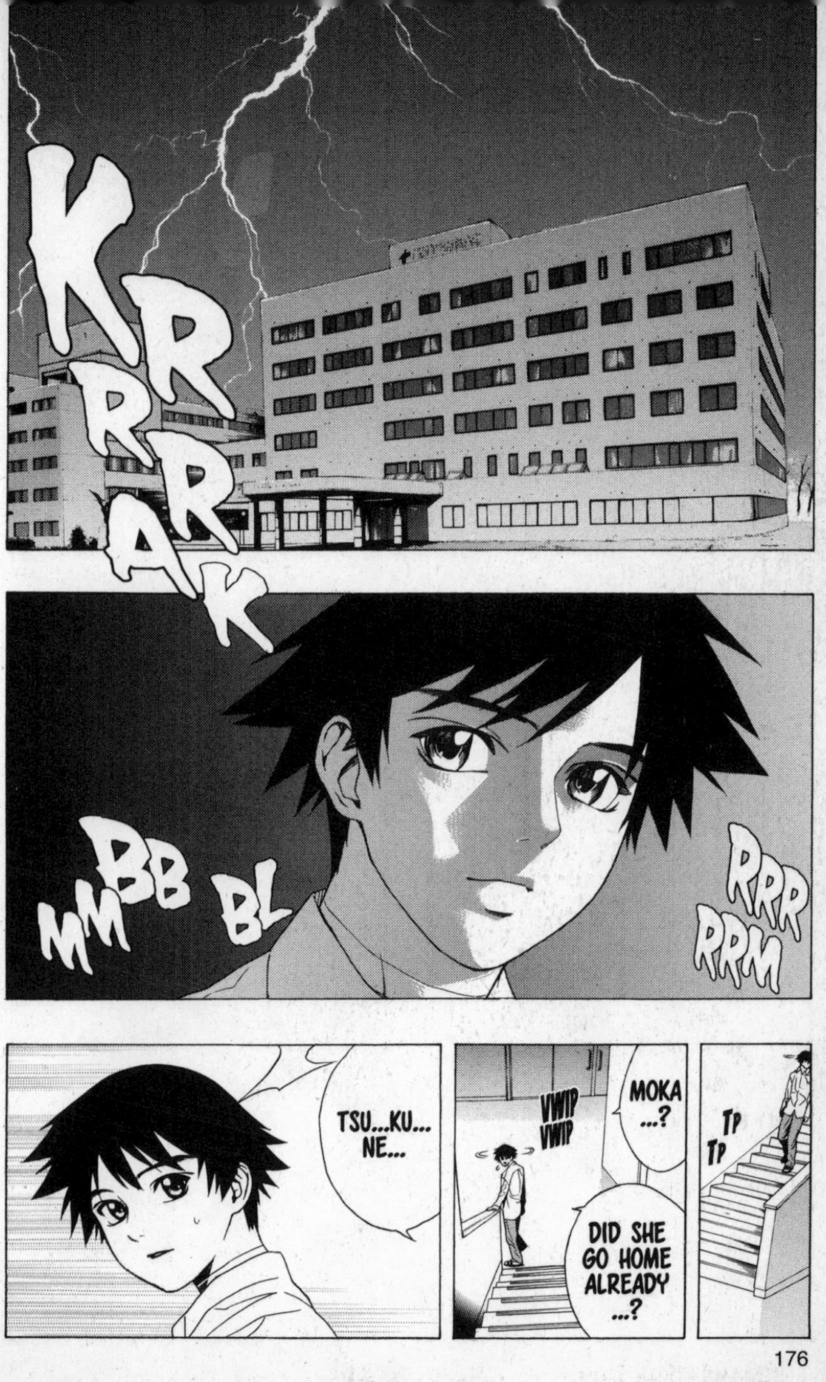
KRRRAK
MMBB BL
RRRRRM
MOKA ...?
VWIP VWIP
DID SHE GO HOME ALREADY ...?
TSU...KU... NE...
TP TP

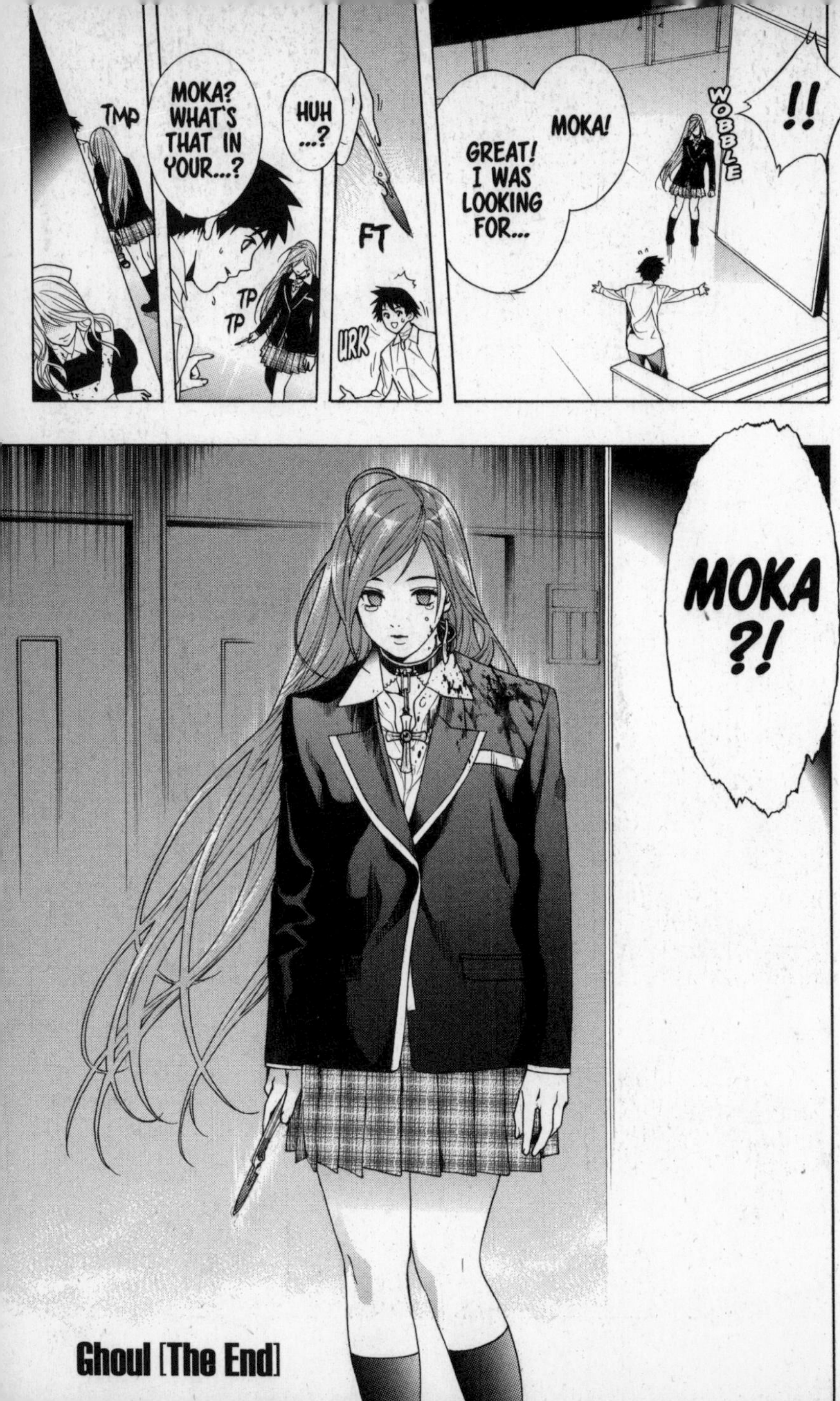
!!
WOBBLE
MOKA!
GREAT! I WAS LOOKING FOR...
FT
URK
HUH ...?
MOKA? WHAT'S THAT IN YOUR...?
TP TP
TMP
MOKA ?!
Ghoul [The End]

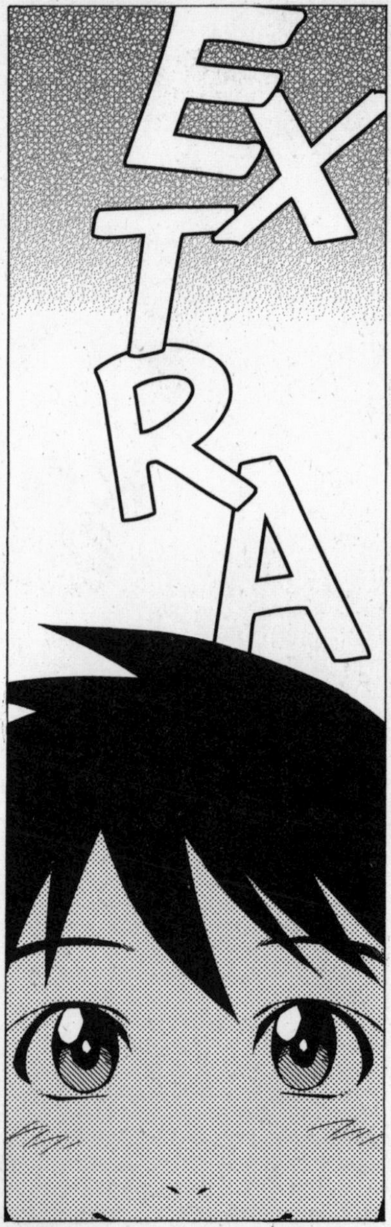
EXTRA

ROSARIO + VAMPIRE

End-of-Volume Theater

VI

Tell Us ♡, Teacher!

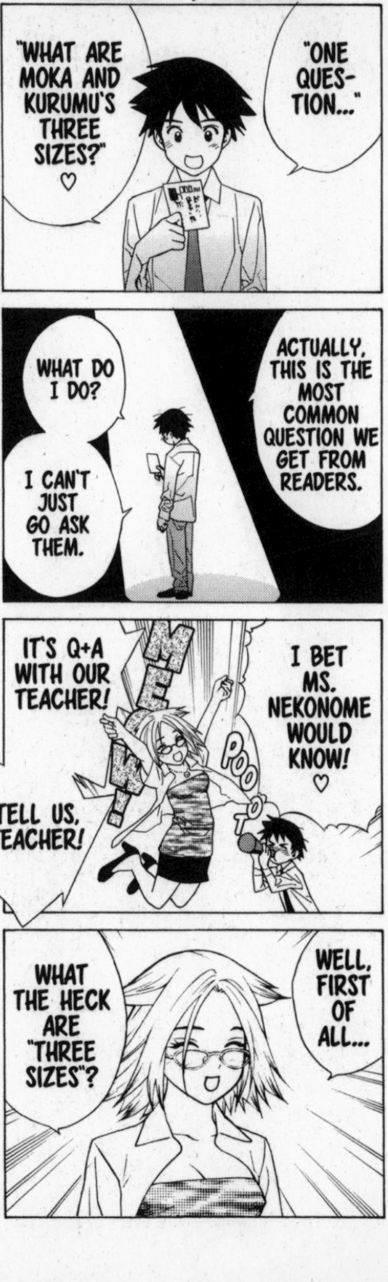
"ONE QUES-TION..."
"WHAT ARE MOKA AND KURUMU'S THREE SIZES?" ♡
ACTUALLY, THIS IS THE MOST COMMON QUESTION WE GET FROM READERS.
WHAT DO I DO?
I CAN'T JUST GO ASK THEM.
I BET MS. NEKONOME WOULD KNOW! ♡
IT'S Q+A WITH OUR TEACHER!
MEOW!
POO TOOT
TELL US, TEACHER!
WELL, FIRST OF ALL...
WHAT THE HECK ARE "THREE SIZES"?

The Answer Is...♡

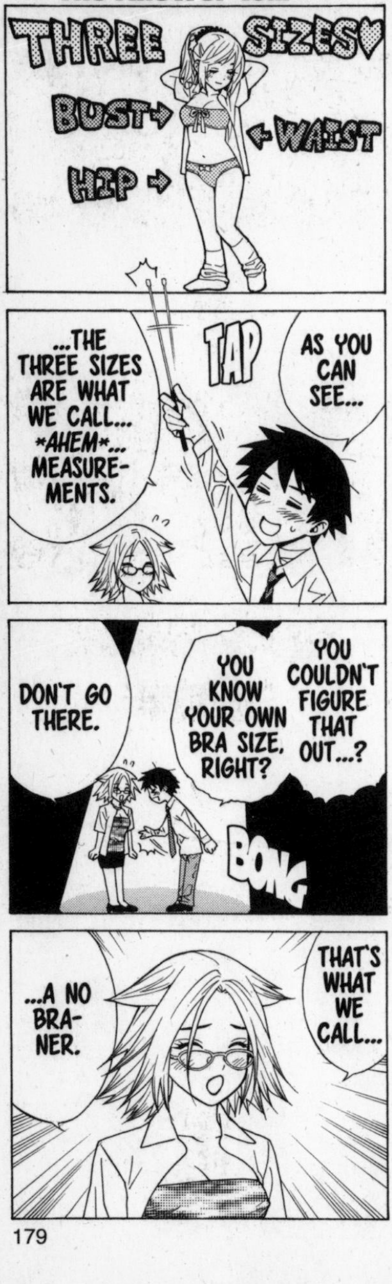
THREE SIZES♡
BUST
WAIST
HIP
AS YOU CAN SEE...
TAP
...THE THREE SIZES ARE WHAT WE CALL... *AHEM*... MEASURE-MENTS.
YOU COULDN'T FIGURE THAT OUT...?
YOU KNOW YOUR OWN BRA SIZE, RIGHT?
DON'T GO THERE.
BONG
THAT'S WHAT WE CALL...
...A NO BRA-NER.

A Girl's Heart

YEAH...

BE GLAD YOU'RE NOT A G LIKE ME!

A BIG BOSOM CAN BE HARD ON YOUR BACK.

Sure...

THAT MEANS YOU'RE LUGGING FOUR EXTRA POUNDS AROUND!

A G-CUP BREAST WEIGHS TWO POUNDS!

YOU SHOULDN'T MAKE LIGHT OF BIG BREASTS!

Hee hee

4 lbs ?!

YOU'RE FIGHTING A LOT OF GRAVITY!

B O O M

TEE HEE

I WOULDN'T MIND A LITTLE MORE...

STILL...

The Truth Behind The Three Sizes

...FROM JUST HER "3 SIZES."

YOU CAN'T REALLY KNOW A WOMAN'S PHYSIQUE...

Please send questions and fan letters to ➡ Rosario+Vampire Fan Mail, VIZ Media, P.O. Box 77064, San Francisco, CA 94107

YOU REALLY KNOW YOUR STUFF!

THAT'S HOW YOU DETERMINE THE BRA SIZE!

FOR INSTANCE, THE BUST HAS A "BREAST" AND A "FRAME"...

Wow...

BREAST/FRAME DIFFERENCE	CUP SIZE
10	A
12.5	B
15	C
17.5	D

BREAST

FRAME

LEAVE ME ALONE!

I DON'T SEE ANY DIFFERENCE AT ALL!

GRR

AHAHA!

Rosario & Vampire

Akihisa Ikeda

• Staff •

Makoto Saito

Takafumi Okubo

• Help •

Kenji Tashiro

Yuichiro Higuchi

• CG •

Takaharu Yoshizawa

Akihisa Ikeda

• Editing •

Satoshi Adachi

• Comic •

Kenju Noro

BOW
Please read Volume 7...

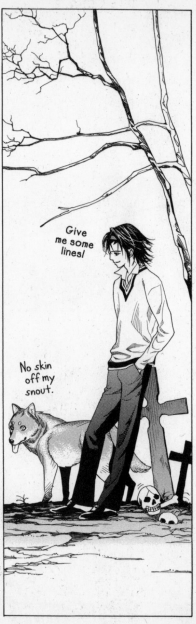

Give me some lines!
No skin off my snout.

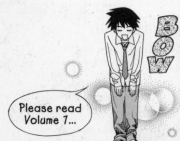

Crypt Sheet for Volume 7: Shikigami

QUIZ 7

AS A HUMAN ATTENDING A SCHOOL FOR MONSTERS, ENCOUNTERING AN EXORCIST MIGHT EXPEL...

a. the demon inside you

b. you from school

c. a big burp

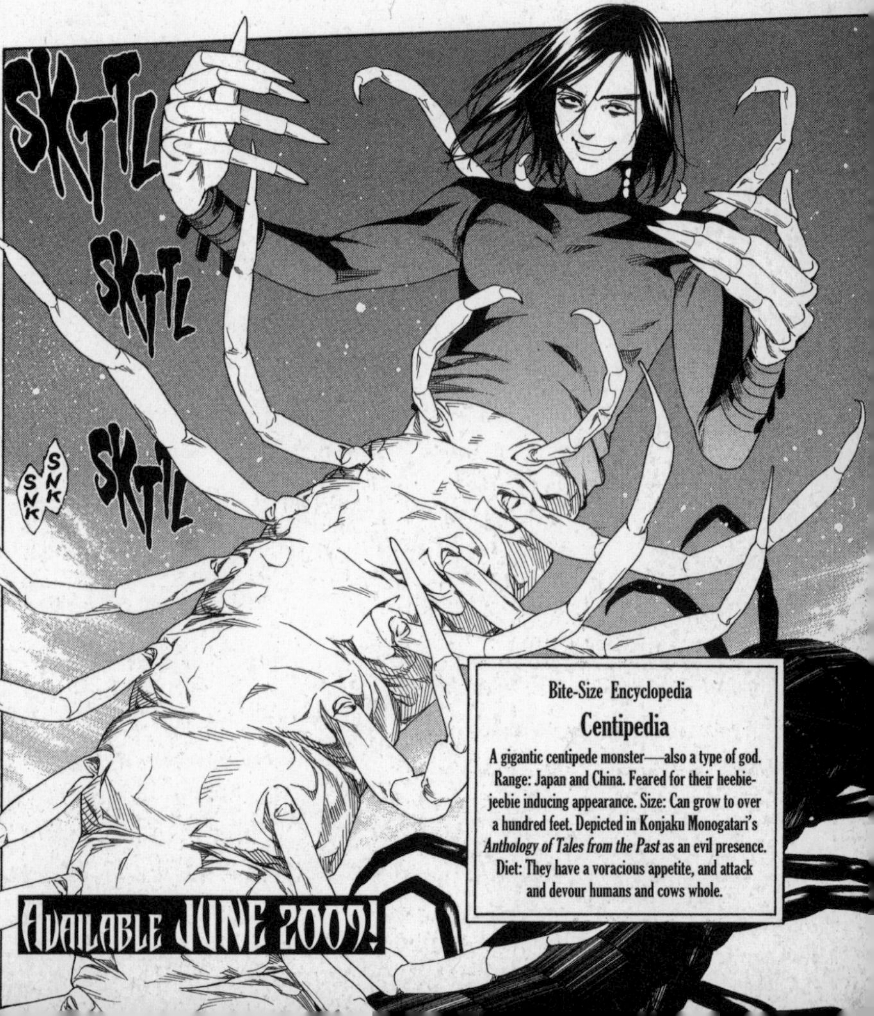
SKTTL
SKTTL
SKTTL
SNK SNK
Available JUNE 2009!

Bite-Size Encyclopedia

Centipedia

A gigantic centipede monster—also a type of god. Range: Japan and China. Feared for their heebie-jeebie inducing appearance. Size: Can grow to over a hundred feet. Depicted in Konjaku Monogatari's *Anthology of Tales from the Past* as an evil presence. Diet: They have a voracious appetite, and attack and devour humans and cows whole.

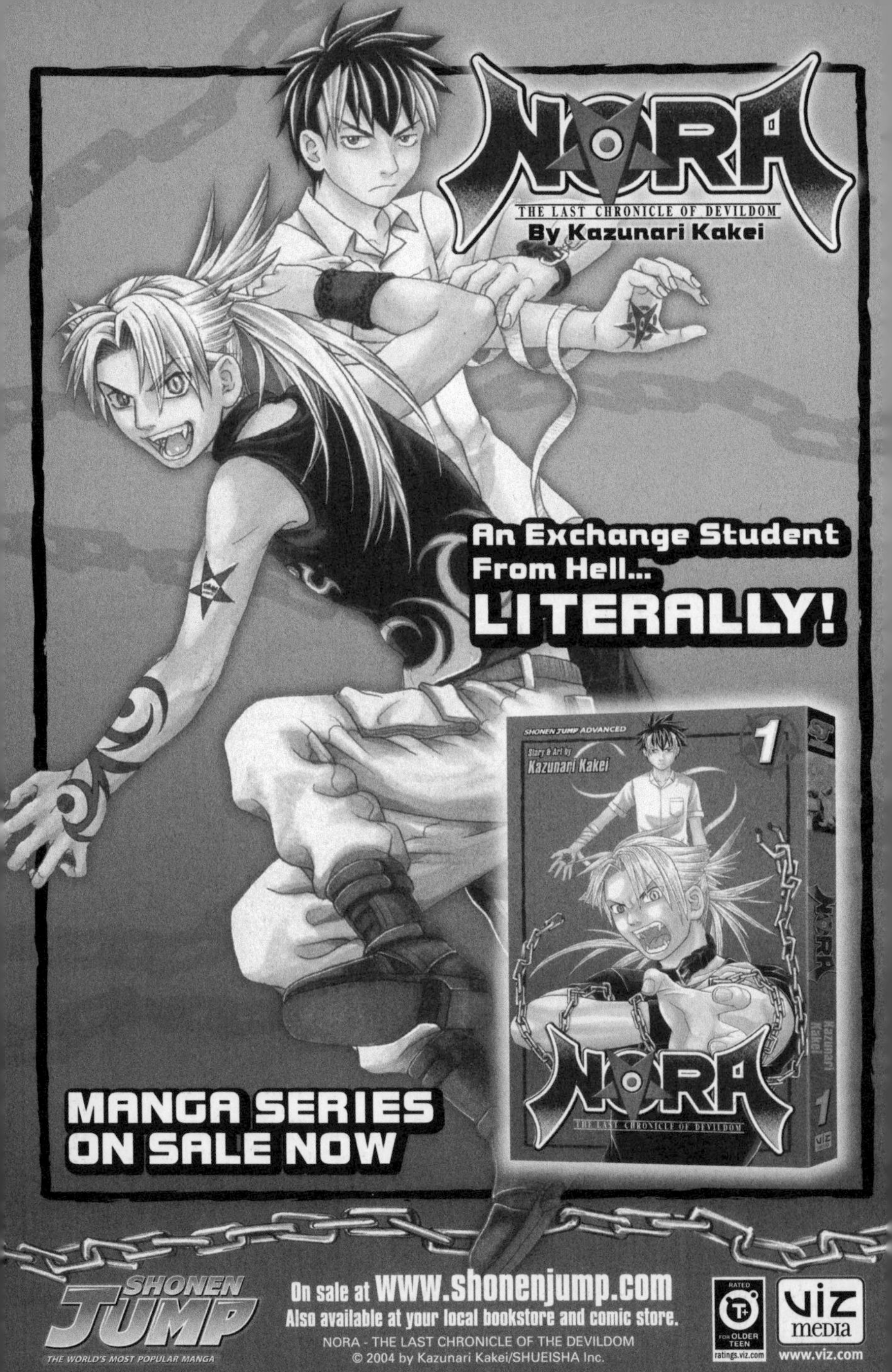
NORA
THE LAST CHRONICLE OF DEVILDOM
By Kazunari Kakei
An Exchange Student From Hell...
LITERALLY!
SHONEN JUMP ADVANCED
Story & Art by
Kazunari Kakei
1
NORA
THE LAST CHRONICLE OF DEVILDOM
MANGA SERIES ON SALE NOW
SHONEN JUMP
THE WORLD'S MOST POPULAR MANGA
On sale at www.shonenjump.com
Also available at your local bookstore and comic store.
NORA - THE LAST CHRONICLE OF THE DEVILDOM
© 2004 by Kazunari Kakei/SHUEISHA Inc.
RATED T+ FOR OLDER TEEN
ratings.viz.com
viz media
www.viz.com

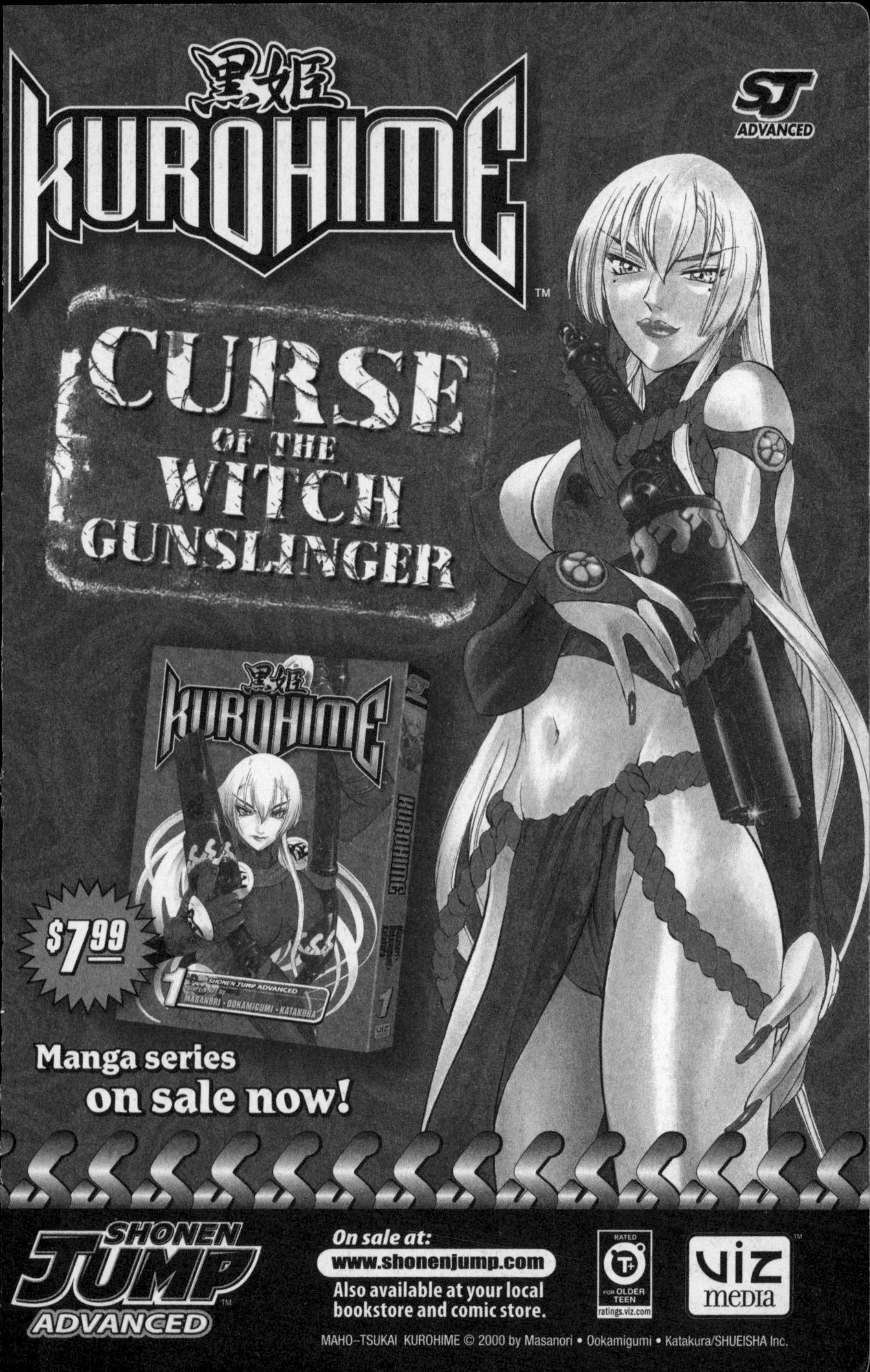
黒姫
KUROHIME
SJ ADVANCED
CURSE OF THE WITCH GUNSLINGER
KUROHIME
$7.99
SHONEN JUMP ADVANCED
MASANORI · OOKAMIGUMI · KATAKURA
Manga series on sale now!
SHONEN JUMP ADVANCED
On sale at:
www.shonenjump.com
Also available at your local bookstore and comic store.
RATED T+ FOR OLDER TEEN ratings.viz.com
viz media
MAHO-TSUKAI KUROHIME © 2000 by Masanori • Ookamigumi • Katakura/SHUEISHA Inc.

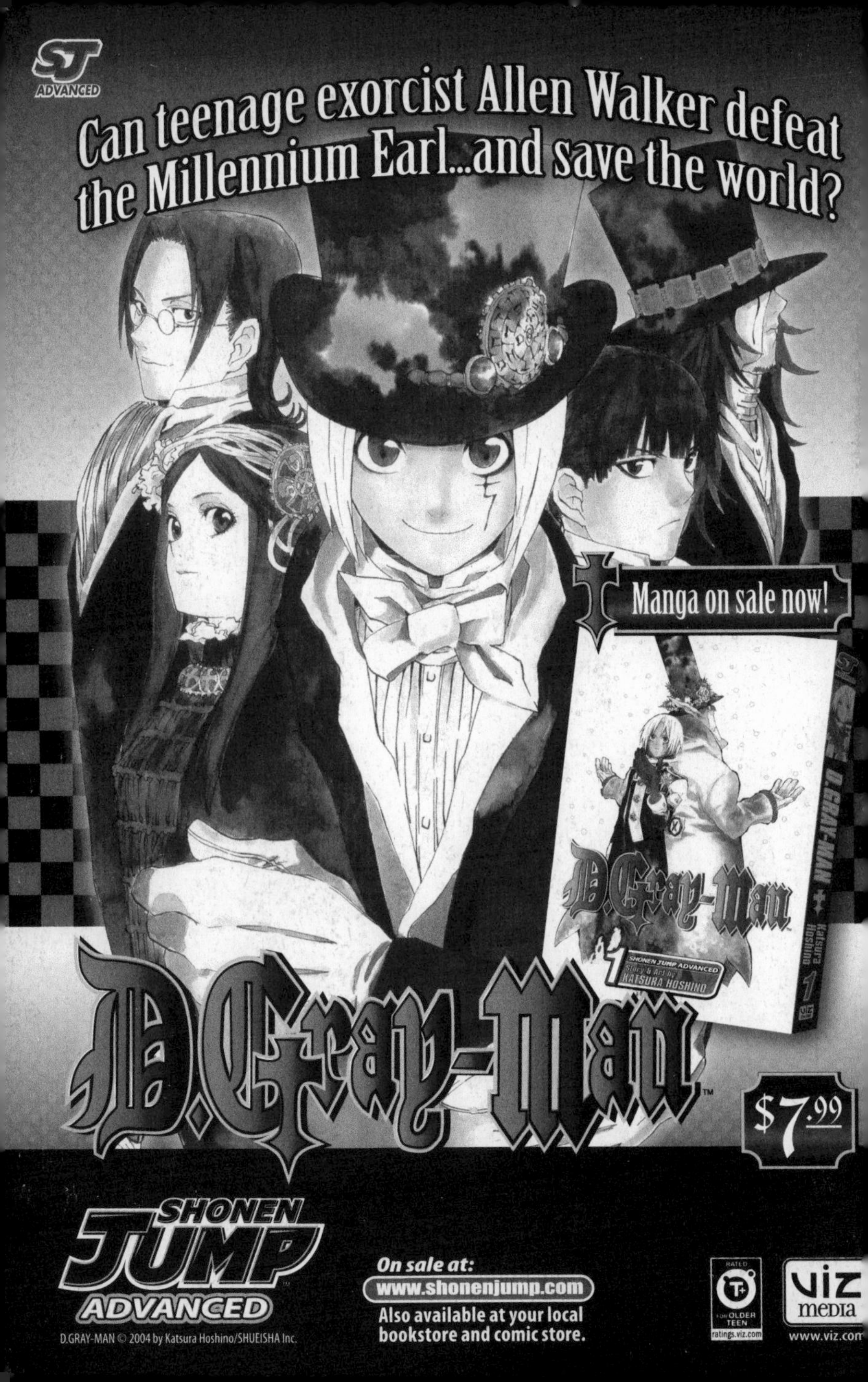
SJ ADVANCED
Can teenage exorcist Allen Walker defeat the Millennium Earl...and save the world?
Manga on sale now!
D.GRAY-MAN
SHONEN JUMP ADVANCED
Story & Art by KATSURA HOSHINO
D.GRAY-MAN™
$7.99
SHONEN JUMP ADVANCED
On sale at:
www.shonenjump.com
Also available at your local bookstore and comic store.
RATED T+ FOR OLDER TEEN
ratings.viz.com
VIZ media
www.viz.com
D.GRAY-MAN © 2004 by Katsura Hoshino/SHUEISHA Inc.

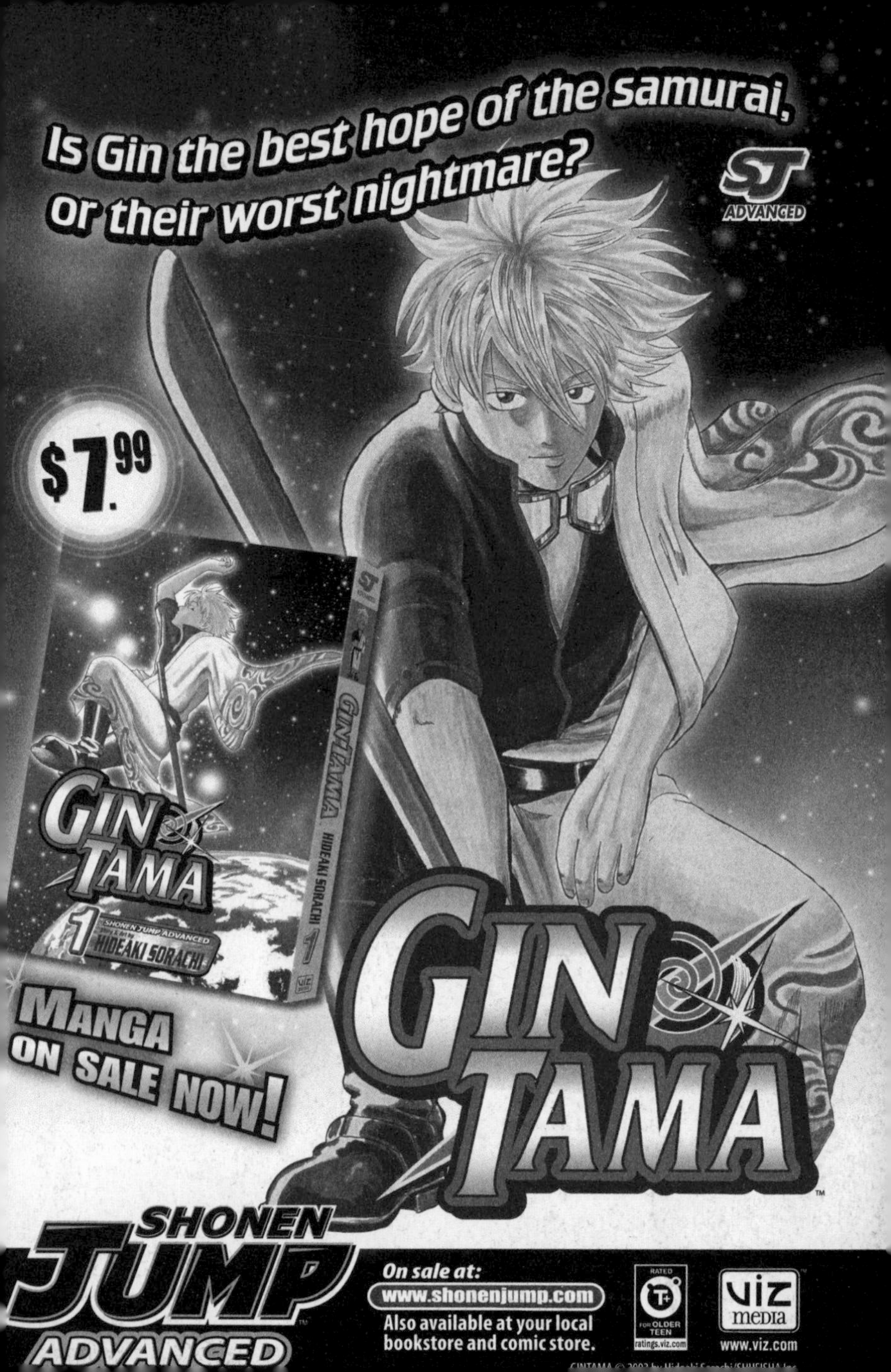

Is Gin the best hope of the samurai, or their worst nightmare?
SJ ADVANCED
$7.99
GIN TAMA
1
SHONEN JUMP ADVANCED
HIDEAKI SORACHI
MANGA ON SALE NOW!
GIN TAMA™
SHONEN JUMP ADVANCED
On sale at:
www.shonenjump.com
Also available at your local bookstore and comic store.
RATED T+ FOR OLDER TEEN
ratings.viz.com
viz media
www.viz.com

BEHIND THE SHADOWS
SJ ADVANCED
RalΩGrad
From the artist of Death Note
Manga series on sale now!
Story by TSUNEO TAKANO
Art by TAKESHI OBATA
SHONEN JUMP
THE WORLD'S MOST POPULAR MANGA
On sale at: www.shonenjump.com
Also available at your local bookstore and comic store.
RATED T+ FOR OLDER TEEN
ratings.viz.com
viz media
www.viz.com
RALΩGRAD © 2006 by Tsuneo Takano, Takeshi Obata/SHUEISHA Inc.

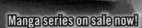

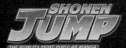

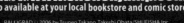

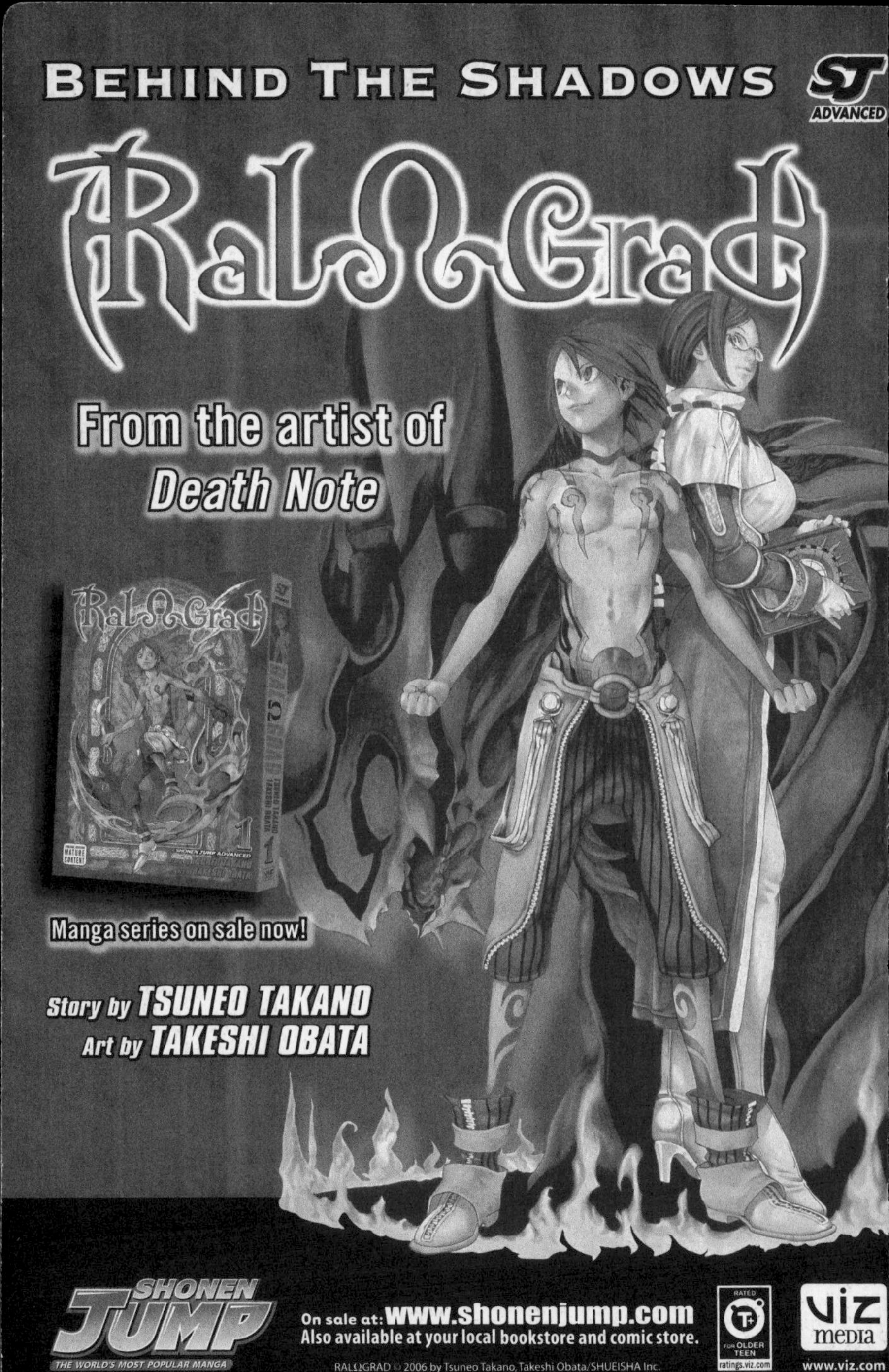

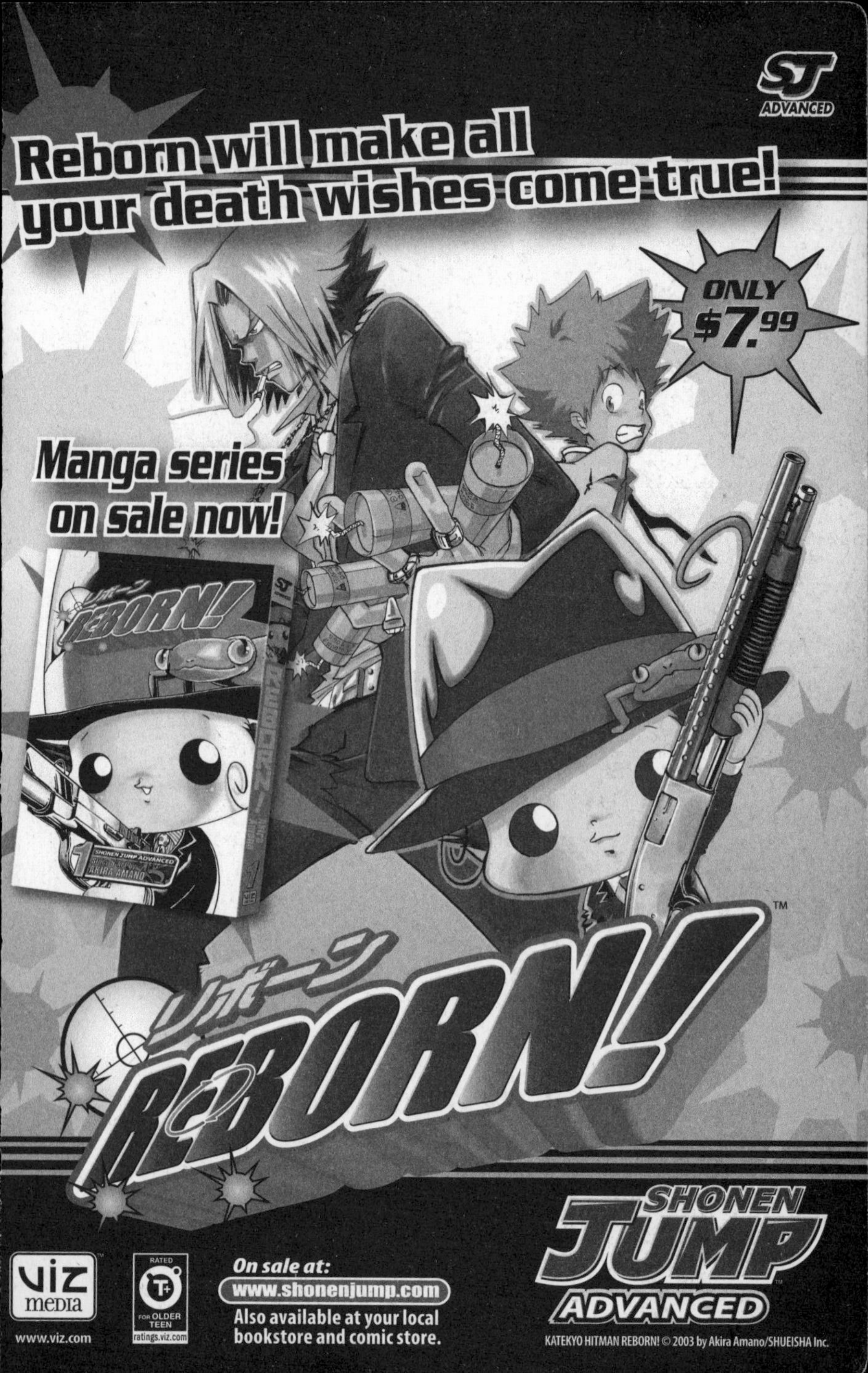
SJ ADVANCED
Reborn will make all your death wishes come true!
ONLY $7.99
Manga series on sale now!
REBORN!
SHONEN JUMP ADVANCED
AKIRA AMANO
リボーン
REBORN!
TM
SHONEN JUMP ADVANCED
viz media
www.viz.com
RATED T+ FOR OLDER TEEN
ratings.viz.com
On sale at:
www.shonenjump.com
Also available at your local bookstore and comic store.
KATEKYO HITMAN REBORN! © 2003 by Akira Amano/SHUEISHA Inc.

Tell us what you think about SHONEN JUMP manga!

Our survey is now available online.
Go to: www.SHONENJUMP.com/mangasurvey

Help us make our product offering better!

THE REAL ACTION
STARTS IN...

SHONEN JUMP
THE WORLD'S MOST POPULAR MANGA
www.shonenjump.com

ST
ADVANCED

ST

viz
media

CH